Realist Perspectives on Management and Organisations

Organisational and managerial regimes directly impact on our everyday lives, which partly explains why they are so widely studied. However, systematic study of organisation and management does not happen by accident. It requires some reflection upon how best to study them: it requires *methodology*. And here we enter into a minefield of theoretical disagreement.

Whilst management science uses a method very similar to that (allegedly) used in the natural sciences, namely *positivism*, there are no shortage of critics prepared to argue that what might be appropriate for the natural sciences is inappropriate for the social sciences. However, the rejection of positivism often appears to engender a reaction that does not so much resolve the problems of positivism as replace them with those associated with *postmodernism*. There is, however, an alternative to both positivism and postmodernism, namely *realism*. And elaborating how this realist perspective has influenced organisation and management studies provides the rationale for this collection.

It brings together two kinds of work that have been informed by realism. One set of papers originate from scholars who have explicitly sought to employ, or in some cases to develop, a realist perspective. The other set of papers are from those who have implicitly employed something like a realist perspective in their work, albeit without conscious reflection on their methodological roots.

The collection goes some way to demonstrating that realism has the capacity to overcome the severe limitations inherent in positivist and postmodern approaches to organisation and management studies.

Stephen Ackroyd is Professor of Organisational Analysis in the Department of Behaviour in Organisations, Lancaster University Management School. **Steve Fleetwood** is a Lecturer in Employment Studies in the Department of Behaviour in Organisations, Lancaster University Management School.

Critical realism: interventions
Edited by Margaret Archer, Roy Bhaskar, Andrew
Collier, Tony Lawson and Alan Norrie

Critical Realism
Essential Readings
Edited by Margaret Archer, Roy Bhaskar, Andrew Collier,
Tony Lawson and Alan Norrie

The Possibility of Naturalism
A Philosophical Critique of the Contemporary Human Sciences
Roy Bhaskar

Being & Worth
Andrew Collier

Quantum Theory and the Flight from Realism
Philosophical Responses to Quantum Mechanics
Christopher Norris

From East to West
Odyssey of a Soul
Roy Bhaskar

Realism and Racism
Concepts of Race in Sociological Research
Bob Carter

Realist Perspectives on Management and Organisations

Edited by Stephen Ackroyd
and Steve Fleetwood

London and New York

First published 2000
by Routledge
11 New Fetter Lane, London EC4P 4EE

Simultaneously published in the USA and Canada
by Routledge
29 West 35th Street, New York, NY 10001

Routledge is an imprint of the Taylor & Francis Group

Typeset in Garamond by Taylor & Francis Books Ltd
Printed and bound in Great Britain by MPG Books Ltd, Bodmin

British Library Cataloguing in Publication Data
A catalogue record for this book is available from the British Library

Library of Congress Cataloging-in-Publication Data
Realist perspectives on management and organizations/edited by
Stephen Ackroyd and Steve Fleetwood.
Includes bibliographical references and index.
1. Management. 2. Organization. 3. Realism. I. Ackroyd, Stephen.
II. Fleetwood, Steve. III. Series.
HD31 .R432   2001
060'.1–dc21   00-056025

ISBN 0–415–24273–8 (hbk)
ISBN 0–415–24274–6 (pbk)

Contents

List of illustrations   vii
Notes on contributors   viii
Preface   xiii
Acknowledgements   xv

PART I
The character of contemporary realism   1

1   Realism in contemporary organisation and management
    studies   3
    STEPHEN ACKROYD AND STEVE FLEETWOOD

2   What is management? An outline of a metatheory   26
    HARIDIMOUS TSOUKAS

3   In praise of duality and dualism: rethinking agency and
    structure in organisational analysis   45
    MICHAEL I. REED

4   Structure, culture and agency: rejecting the current
    orthodoxy of organisation theory   66
    ROBERT WILLMOTT

5   Connecting organisations and societies: a realist analysis
    of structures   87
    STEPHEN ACKROYD

6   Structure, agency and Marx's analysis of the labour process   109
    STEPHEN PRATTEN

PART II
Substantive contributions   139

  7 Critical realist ethnography: the case of racism and
    professionalism in a medical setting   141
    SAM PORTER

  8 Routines, strategy and change in high-technology
    small firms   161
    NEIL COSTELLO

  9 Managers' innovations and the structuration of organisations   181
    JOHN COOPEY, ORLA KEEGAN AND NICK EMLER

 10 Case research as a method for industrial networks:
    a realist apologia   205
    GEOFF EASTON

 11 Structuring the labour market: a segmentation approach   220
    JAMIE PECK

 12 The British production regime: a societal-specific system?   245
    JILL RUBERY

    Index   265

Illustrations

Figures

2.1	A realist redescription of management	36
2.2	Industrial structure and the causal powers of management	38
5.1	The connectedness of organisational constitution and societal structuration	100
9.1	A generic account	185
10.1	The structures of causal explanation	209
12.1	Selected elements of a societal system	250

Tables

1.1	A structured ontology	13
2.1	Ontological assumptions of the realist view of science	29
2.2	Management functions vis-à-vis organisational requirements	32
10.1	Bhaskar's (1978) classification of the real, actual and empirical domains	208

Contributors

Stephen Ackroyd is Professor of Organisational Analysis in Lancaster University Management School. His main academic interest is in the ways organisations (both public and private) mediate social and economic power. He has written and researched widely on many aspects of organisations, including contemporary organisational change. His most consistent subject matter in recent years has been the organisation of the National Health Service and British manufacturing industry. His most recent book, which he wrote with Paul Thompson, is a dissection of the responses of working people to management. It is called *Organisational Misbehaviour* and was published in 1999. Stephen is also actively interested in the question of what is the appropriate theory and method for organisational studies at present, and this volume is a product of that interest.

John Coopey is a currently Visiting Fellow in the Department of Management Learning at Lancaster University. He taught and researched previously in organisational behaviour at Dundee University and, prior to that, Birkbeck College, following an extensive career in personnel management. In 1993 his long-standing interest in creativity and innovation culminated in an ESRC-funded project into managers' innovation from which the paper in this collection emerged. More recently he has linked innovation to issues of organisational learning with a theoretical framework in which power and politics are central elements. Currently John is attempting to bring this perspective to bear on questions of environmental sustainability and management.

Neil Costello is Head of Economics at The Open University. His current research interest is stability and change in small and medium-sized, high-technology firms and, in particular, the importance of rules, habits and routines in understanding their behaviour. The primary research approach is to build rich, detailed case studies based on fieldwork.

Geoff Easton is currently Professor of Marketing and Head of the Department of Marketing at Lancaster University. He has degrees from Bristol University, Manchester and London Business Schools and has been researching industrial markets for over thirty years. His current research interests are industrial network dynamics, competition, case research methodology and managerial work.

Nick Emler is Professor of Social Psychology at Oxford University and has been a Visiting Professor at the Universities of Bologna, Geneva and Tulsa, Johns Hopkins University and the École des Hautes Études en Science Sociales in Paris. His research interests are broadly concerned with the moral dimension in human relations and to this end he has published various studies and reviews on children developing moral insight, on political and economic socialisation in adolescence, on delinquency and more recently on organisational leadership and the significance of moral integrity in effective leadership. He is the author, with Stephen Reicher, of *Adolescence and Delinquency: The Collective Management of Reputation* (1995) and, with M. Banks and others, a co-author of *Careers and Identities* (1991).

Steve Fleetwood left an engineering apprenticeship in Liverpool in the mid 1970s to devote more time to his chosen sport, namely cycle racing. After a career as an amateur, semi-professional and eventually professional, he finally retired from the cycle racing circuit when grey hair and a loss of pace caught up with him. He is now a Lecturer in Employment Studies in Lancaster University Management School. Steve is author of *Hayek's Political Economy: The Socio Economics of Order* (1995), and editor of *Critical Realism in Economics: Development and Debate* (1998). His research reflects his general trans-disciplinary approach to social science, and covers the philosophy of science, social theory, sociology of work, HRM, employment relations and the economics of the labour market. He is currently interested in using critical realism to facilitate the development of a theoretical framework to unifying these diverse approaches to the study of labouring activity.

Orla Keegan has a Masters in Social and Organisational Psychology and currently holds two posts. She is Health Research Board Health Services Research Fellow at the Department of Psychology, Royal College of Surgeons in Ireland, and Director of Bereavement Services (Research and Education) at the Irish Hospice Foundation. She has conducted research on quality of care for dying patients and broader research into patients' views of health services.

Jamie Peck is Professor of Geography at the University of Wisconsin–Madison. His research interests are in political-economic restructuring, urban political economy and theories of economic regulation. Recent work has focused on the political economy of welfare/'workfare' reforms and the reorganisation of contingent labour markets. An editor of *Antipode* and *Environment and Planning A*, his publications include *Work-Place: The Social Regulation of Labor Markets* (1996) and *Workfare States* (2001).

Sam Porter is Professor of Nursing Research in the School of Nursing and Midwifery, Queen's University of Belfast. He has a background in both clinical nursing and academic sociology. His research interests are social theory, methodology and the sociology of nursing and health care. His most recent book, *Social Theory and Nursing Practice*, was published in 1998.

Stephen Pratten is a Lecturer in Economics in the Management Centre, Kings College London. His main research area is the methodology of economics and he has several publications in this area. He is a member of the editorial board of the *Cambridge Journal of Economics*.

Michael I. Reed is Professor of Organisation Theory in the Department of Behaviour in Organisations, Lancaster University Management School. His publications include: *Redirections in Organisational Analysis*, *The Sociology of Management* and *The Sociology of Organisations*. His research interests include theoretical developments in organisational analysis, the restructuring of expert labour, and managerialist control strategies in public sector organisations. He is also part of the editorial team of *Organization*.

Jill Rubery is Professor of Comparative Employment Systems at the Manchester School of Management, UMIST. Her main research interest is in the organisation of labour markets, including both the role of organisations and the role of societal factors in shaping work and employment. Her publications include both UK-based and European comparative analysis of issues such as pay, working time, welfare systems and gender relations. Recent publications include *Women's Employment in Europe* (1999) and *Equal Pay in Europe* (1998).

Haridimous Tsoukas is a Professor of Organization Theory at the Athens Laboratory of Business Administration (ALBA) and at the University of Essex. His publications have appeared in the *Academy of Management Review*, *Strategic Management Journal*, *Organization Studies*, *Journal of Management Studies*, *Organization and Human Relations*. He edited *New Thinking in Organizational Behaviour: From Social Engineering to Reflective Action* (1998). He is currently working (with Christian Knudsen) on editing *The Oxford Handbook of Management Theory: Meta-theoretical Perspectives*. Haridimous is a co-editor of *Organization Studies and Organization*, and sits on the editorial board of *Organisation Science, Emergence, and Human Relations*. His research interests include: social theory and organisation theory; organisational knowledge; the epistemology of management research; the management of organisational change; and new science and organisation theory.

Robert Willmott is Lecturer in Organisational Behaviour in the School of Management, University of Bath. He has research interests in organisation theory, philosophy of social science and education policy. His current research examines the impact of the new managerialism on public sector restructuring. He has published articles in *The Sociological Review*, *British Journal of Sociology of Education*, *Educational Studies* and *Journal of Philosophy of Education*. With Chris Carter, Peter Clark and Damian Hodgson, he is co-editing and contributing to a double issue on American management knowledge, *Journal of Managerial Psychology* (forthcoming in 2001). Future research plans include developing the morphogenetic approach in organisation and management studies and extending ethnographic studies of the impact of the new managerialism.

Preface

This volume presents some of the most fruitful writing in management and organisation studies produced in the last few years, whilst claiming that such writing is fruitful precisely because it is rooted in a philosophically realist approach. From scattered sources, the collection brings together recent work which is either explicitly realist in approach (and which self-consciously attempts to emphasise the value of realism in studies of management and organisation) or implicitly adopts a realist perspective and uses it to promote a penetrating analysis of contemporary institutions. Both philosophically inclined and more substantive realist studies are, therefore, included in the collection.

The editors argue not only that realist-orientated writing in organisation and management has a long history, but also that it has consistently provided a powerful alternative to both 'positivist' and 'postmodernist' orientations. The collection reveals that these traditional emphases are continued in many recent papers, offering an impressive analysis of contemporary organisations, management and related institutions. The substantive work in the collection ranges from studies of the contemporary labour process, via an elaboration of the nature of the firm, to a comparative analysis of socio-economic systems. It constitutes an impressive illustration of the range and power of realist-orientated writing and demonstrates that realist perspectives have much to offer the scholar of organisation and management.

Acknowledgements

Special thanks are due to the editors of the following journals for their efforts in support of this project: Karen Legge (*Journal of Management Studies*); David Wilson (*Organisation Studies*); and John Burgoyne (*British Journal of Management*). Last but not least, we thank Stephen Watson, Dean of Lancaster University School of Management, and Mike Reed, Head of the Department of Behaviour in Organisations, without whose practical help this project would not have been possible.

The editors and publisher also wish to thank the following publishers and journals for their permission to use copyright material and to reprint articles. John Wiley & Sons Ltd and the British Journal of Management for Haridimos Tsoukas, 'What is Management: An Outline of a Metatheory' *British Journal of Management* 5 (2) 1994 pp 289–301; De Gruyter and Organization Studies for Michael I. Reed, 'In Praise of Duality and Dualism: Rethinking Agency and Structure in Organizational Analysis' *Organization Studies* 18 (1) 1997 pp 21–42; Basil Blackwell and Journal for the Theory of Social Behaviour for Robert Willmott, 'Structure, Culture and Agency: Rejecting the Current Orthodoxy in Organisational Theory' *Journal for the Theory of Social Behaviour* 27 (1) 1997 pp 93–123; Routledge and Review of Political Economy for Steve Pratten, 'Structure, Agency and Marx's Analysis of the Labour Process' *Review of Political Economy* 5 (4) 1993 pp 403–426; Cambridge University Press and Sociology for Sam Porter, 'Critical Realist Ethnography: The Case of Racism and Professionalism in Medical Setting' *Sociology* 27 (4) 1993 pp 591–609; Basil Blackwell and Journal of Management Studies for John Coopey, Orla Keegan and Nick Emler, 'Managers' Innovations and the Structuration of Organisations' *Journal of Management Studies* 35 (3) 1997 pp 263–84; Elsevier Science for: Easton, G. 'Case Research as a Methodology for Industrial Networks: A Realist Apologia, in Naude, P. and Turnbull, P.W. (eds) *Network Dynamics in International Marketing*, Oxford: Elsevier Science, 1998; Guilford Publications for Jamie Peck, 'Structuring the Labour Market: A Segmentation Approach', in *Work Place: The Social Regulation of Labour Markets*, New York: Guildford Press, 1996; Routledge and Economy and

Society for Jill Rubery, 'The British Production Regime: A Societal-Specific System?' *Economy and Society* 23 (3) 1994 pp 335–54.

Stephen Ackroyd
Steve Fleetwood

Part I

The character of contemporary realism

1 Realism in contemporary organisation and management studies

Stephen Ackroyd and Steve Fleetwood

It has long been argued that the field of organisation and management studies lacks coherence and, more fundamentally, cannot be unified. The first systematic statements of this point of view occurred around 1980 (Burrell and Morgan 1979) and have continued (Morgan 1986; 1997; Alvesson and Deetz 1996; Jackson and Carter 2000; cf. Ackroyd 1992). Certainly, as it is at present, the field is characterised by a diverse collection of sub-disciplines which have little in common, apart, that is, from an interest in a vaguely similar subject matter. The concerns of research accountants and organisational psychologists, for example, or business strategists, econometricians and industrial sociologists are apparently quite different.

One way of making sense of this apparent incoherence and diversity, and perhaps even pointing in the direction of unification, is to approach the subject matter in terms of *methodology* conceived in general terms. At this level, fundamental and systematic differences and similarities emerge. We will argue here that at least three distinct perspectives are discernible.

There are some approaches to management (e.g. operational research, much of business economics, quantitative marketing and the analysis of finance) which clearly involve the assumption that they are little different from natural science and practice here is rooted firmly in the philosophy that justifies much of natural science – *positivism* (defined below). On the other hand, there are some other areas (e.g. marketing and management education) which have seldom been associated with that kind of view. Few writers in the area of organisation theory, to take another example, have espoused positivism. (For a remarkable exception, however, see Donaldson 1996.) Many writers in this area, indeed, have taken the rejection of positivism as their starting point (Morgan 1986; Cooper and Burrell 1988; Gergen 1992; Alvesson 1987; Chia 1996). Indeed, the rejection of positivism is associated with what is often described as a 'postmodern (and/or a poststructuralist) turn', which involves adopting what appears to be an opposite set of assumptions about the world.

Hence we arrive at the commonly held position that there are two basic perspectives on offer: either the world is objectively and unproblematically available and capable of being known by the systematic application of the empirical techniques common to positivism, or it is not knowable objectively at all; and, in the place of claims to objectivity, we find only the idea that what is known is merely the product of discourses.

Among the writers who have helped to popularise the position that there are only two competing perspectives is Martin Parker (Parker 1992; 1998; cf. Thompson *et al.* 2000). In one place Parker suggests that there is a basic distinction to be drawn between what he labels 'modernism' and 'postmodernism'. He distinguishes them in the following way. On the one hand,

> Modernism is described as having elevated faith in reason ... The world is seen as a system which becomes increasingly under human control as our knowledge of it increases. The common terms for this kind of belief are positivism, empiricism and science.

By complete contrast to this 'the post-modernist suggests that this is a form of intellectual imperialism which ignores the fundamental uncontrollability of meaning'. In this alternative view, what is supposedly

> 'out there' is constructed by our discursive constructions of it and these conceptions are collectively sustained and continually re-negotiated in the process of making sense ... The role of language in constituting reality is therefore central, and our attempts to discover truth should be seen for what they are – forms of discourse.
>
> (Parker 1992: 3)

Reaffirming realism

What makes this polarised account of the field of management and organisation studies really surprising are two things. Firstly, there is much substantive work (e.g. detailed investigations of institutions and how they work, or accounts of labour markets or the organisation of business groups and industries) that is rooted neither in positivism nor postmodernism. The best of such synthetic writing draws on a rich and long-established stream of social science thinking which is characterised by the conviction that social structures (mechanisms, relations, powers, rules, resources, institutions and so on), as well as the meanings that actors and groups attribute to their situation (along with the discourse used to convey these meanings), must be taken into account in any explanation of events.

Moreover, for much of the last century, leading thinkers in the social sciences have sought a way between positivism and the ancient doctrine that infuses postmodernism – which used to be identified with relativism (Tsoukas 1992) and even with varieties of idealism. One thinks, for example, of Max Weber's dictum that explanations in social science have to be 'causally adequate and adequate at the level of meaning', a proposition that was first expressed in the early years of the twentieth century. Whilst we do not want to defend Weber's formulations in methodology in their entirety, clearly there has been a great deal of work which cuts across the boundaries set by the extreme possibilities of positivism and postmodernism. History is replete with leading figures from social science who have rejected both positivism and relativism and accepted something like contemporary realism. We would include the likes of Marx, Weber, Durkheim, Commons, Veblen, Mannheim, Mills, Karl Polanyi, Wallerstein, Bourdieu and Chomsky to name but a few scholars from the list one might nominate. Sometimes there have been whole groups of authors whose work is broadly realist in conception: not only Karl Polanyi but also most of the early institutionalists; not only Braverman but numerous subsequent labour process analysts; not only Granovetter but numerous of the later institutionalists; and so on. Many writers in our own day, as will be demonstrated in this book, continue the realist tradition of research in organisations and management studies (cf. Delbridge 2000: 14–15).

Secondly there are philosophical doctrines that are both rich and sophisticated that offer underpinning and support for non-positivist and non-postmodernist writing in organisation and management. One of the most important of these is realism. This is the third possibility we wish to elaborate upon. It offers, as it always has, the foundations for a clear alternative to both positivism and postmodernism.

Since the 1970s the applicability of realism to social sciences has been formally articulated (Harré 1972; 1986; Keat and Urry 1975; Bhaskar 1975; 1979; 1986; Layder 1990; Collier 1994; Lawson 1997; Sayer 1992; 2000). It is perhaps true that the explicit adoption of realism as a philosophy supporting research practice has been relatively rare amongst scholars in the field of management and organisation studies. However, we suggest nonetheless that philosophical realism has been present, if often in part implicit, in a good deal of writing in management and organisational studies for some time. Indeed, a case can be made that realism has been the orthodoxy in several branches of organisation and management studies for much of its recent history. As we have said, much of the writing associated with institutional theory (in both its sociological and economic varieties), with labour process analysis, and regulationist theory, is basically realist in character.

Definitions

Now, before we proceed any further, and in order to minimise terminological and conceptual confusion, it is necessary to define our terms.

Realism

The term 'realism' is used differently in many contexts such as art, literature, film, politics, philosophy and social science. To prevent possible misunderstandings we begin with a sketch of the way it is used here. To be a realist is, minimally, to assert that many entities exist independently of us and our investigations of them. Clearly, then, most people are realists in this basic sense: we differ over what entities we are realist about. The realist social scientist, however, is likely to claim that social entities (such as markets, class relations, gender relations, social rules, social customs or discourses and so on) exist independently of our investigations of them. (We will elaborate upon realism in a later section.) That many of these entities are disputed and not directly observable (and hence refractory to quantification) does not rule them out of consideration for analysis, a position that distances realist- from empiricist- or positivist-orientated analysis. Furthermore, that these disputed entities exist independently of our investigations of them distances realism from postmodernism.

Ontology and epistemology

The term used to identify a focus on, or study of, what things exist is, of course, 'ontology'. Ontology is the enquiry into the nature of being, of existence. Ontological questions are: what kinds of things exist? And: what is the mode of their existence? Note that this is different from epistemeology which is an enquiry into our knowledge of being. An epistemological question is: how do we know what kinds of things exist? Whilst realism (re)focuses our attention on ontology (which does not mean matters of epistemology are ignored) there are good reasons for insisting that these two forms of enquiry are not conflated. It is easy to slide inadvertently from epistemology to ontology, by following something like the following steps. The (ontological) question 'What exists?' is often translated into the (epistemological) question 'How can we know what exists?' Since our knowledge is bound up with our conceptions or even our discourse, it is easy to end up implicitly and illicitly concluding that all that exists are our concepts or our discourse. This conclusion is false; it is a *non-sequitur*.

Positivism

Whilst there are many versions of positivism, we take positivism to consist in the following claims and moves. The social world can be known by applying the same techniques as the natural world, a position referred to as 'scientism'. To proceed directly to fundamentals: knowledge is obtained via sense experience and is made from discrete, atomistic, observed events. If knowledge is to be systematic and general (as opposed to random and particular), then there must be patterns in these events. More specifically, these patterns to be of use must take the form of regularities or constant conjunctions which can be characterised as follows: 'whenever event type x occurs, then event type y will also occur'. Ideally, such event regularities should have no exceptions and apply invariably; in short, they should be laws.

Positivist social scientists hope to discover laws via a range of statistical and experimental techniques that are applied differently from discipline to discipline. Usually, however, people of this outlook have to be content with empirical generalisations arising from their studies. Once discovered, however, it is suggested by positivists that general propositions can be assembled to allow conclusions to be deduced or predicted from a set of initial conditions plus a law-like general statement.[1] Notice that positivism implicitly suggests an ontology indicating that the world consists of the atomistic events of sense experience.

Postmodernism

There are many versions of postmodernism.[2] For some exponents, the position is held expediently. For many, there must be an alternative to the determinism of positivism. The social world *is* manifestly different from the conception of it implied by positivism: there is a plurality of different perspectives held by groups of people; discourses are central to social life; the social world – and even more so the organisational world – is to a considerable degree socially constructed. It is also true that our knowledge of the world is a lot more precarious and contested than was often claimed for it in the past. It is appropriate to criticise the ease at which many (but by no means all) social scientists have made unwarranted truth claims in the past; and to recognise the fragility of knowledge. In these respects there is considerable agreement between realists and others who tend towards postmodernism. For many, then, disagreement between realists and others is a disagreement about what concepts and procedures are best for opening out questions for research.

On this account, remaining tensions and disagreements between parties are often due to the use of radically different concepts and techniques. Human behaviour and institutions are very complex indeed and, for this reason, are capable of being studied and illuminated in numerous ways. The existence of a diverse range of concepts coupled with the advocacy of different kinds of research procedures can give rise to a kind of 'terminological fog'. This makes it difficult for each side to recognise what the other side is saying. It also inhibits the capacity of different groups of researchers to see how their different insights might fit together. However, realists think that there can be intelligent discussion, which, if it takes place, can open out new areas of agreement concerning the way that the world is ordered. Rather than assume that debate is going to be pointless, it is worth taking the trouble to consider differences of view and to establish what they are. In fact, we would go as far as saying that once many who consider themselves to have a postmodern orientation realise that realists are not actually positivists in disguise, they will realise also that there is actually much common ground between their respective positions.

That said, there are versions of postmodernism that are incompatible with realism.[3] Putting matters straightforwardly and boldly, the root of this incompatibility lies in ontology. What we take to be postmodernism, therefore, is any position that presupposes something like the following ontology: the social world is constituted completely, or determined by the concepts we hold; it is concept *determined*; the social world is constructed entirely by us; it is *merely* a social construct; there is no extra-discursive realm that is not expressed in discourse; the social world is generated in discourse. In sum, there is held to be no objective social world existing independently of its identification by lay agents and/or social scientists.[4] Henceforth, we identify as postmodernism any position rooted in an ontology that presumes that the world is *merely* socially constructed or is *determined* by the concepts people hold about it.

Realism: a new 'turn' for management and organisation studies?

Despite its historical importance and continued practice, the distinctive contribution of realist social science, and in particular its potential for unifying the field of management and organisation studies, is currently being overlooked and devalued. Such is the current popularity of postmodernist conceptions that a whole generation is growing up to intellectual maturity not having had the benefit of explicit exposure to realist conceptions of social science and so is now relatively unaware of the qualities of realist writing and research. Clear hold on the differences (philosophical and other) between realism and other approaches is apparently becoming uncommon. Writers and teachers with a postmodern orientation often treat terms and conceptualisations such as positivism, realism, empiricism, objectivism, science and rationalism interchangeably. There is much unwillingness to be precise in the use of terms and to distinguish positions carefully. Karen Legge, otherwise a consummate analyst of contemporary organisation and management, nonetheless remarks on 'positivism, with its realist ontology' (1995: 308). That such confusions affect intellectual leaders amply illustrates the point.

The misconception that positivism and realism are much the same thing has far-reaching implications for organisation and management studies. If positivism is simultaneously rejected as untenable, and treated as synonymous with realism, then the only available alternative is postmodernism. This misconception, then, not only reinforces the conviction that postmodernism is the 'only game in town', it also discourages those who only reluctantly accept postmodernism, and/or those who might actually hold an implicit realist orientation, from seeking another 'game' to play. Serious consideration of alternatives to positivism and postmodernism is, thereby, foreclosed. Hence, even though realist analysis has been a continuous current in social thought which has underwritten a good deal of valuable research in management and organisation studies, some active attempt must now be made to restate its character and value.

The purpose of this book is in fact to accomplish this: to encourage the clear sight of contemporary realism: to collect together some valuable arguments in favour of it and its further development, to present a range of good examples of the sort of work that realist doctrine promotes. We see our task as having these two aspects. The first is to make a clear statement of what realism is in contemporary organisation and management studies; and the second task is to illustrate what it can, and does, routinely do. As with all serious intellectual movements, realism is a complex body of ideas and practices; it is capable of change and development. Our task is principally, therefore, to discuss the current stage of realism and to illustrate what it is that scholars currently accomplish when they work within a realist set of ideas. The present book is divided into two sections: the first part consists of exploration of the current state of realist thinking as applied to organisation and management studies, the second part gives an illustration of the kind of work accomplished by (explicit or implicit) realist analysts.

In a recent book, Peter Clark also comments on the appearance of realism in contemporary organisation and management studies (Clark 2000). He refers to this as a 'realist turn' in scholarship in this field. In doing so, he implies that realism is something that has developed fairly recently and is having an influence after postmodernism. Hence, he does not emphasise the historical depth of substantive realist academic work and research, and the intellectual continuities connecting the institutional analysis undertaken in the 1950s with the Weberian and Marxist scholarship of the 1970s and the neo-institutional writing of the present day. Clark is following many others in using postmodernist's term, 'turn', to describe a change in intellectual priorities. As a conception of intellectual change, the concept 'turn' is a fairly minimal notion: it denotes mainly a change of direction – and perhaps also a succession of different ideas. By contrast with this, we see contemporary realism as emerging from specific intellectual roots, and following a recognisable trajectory of development.

In Clark's defence, however, it is true that there has been in recent years a notable resurgence of explicit discussion of realism. Partly, no doubt, in response to the intellectual challenge offered to realism by postmodernism, there are some new emphases in recent realist writing in organisation and management studies. What is most obviously different is the self-conscious avowal of realism by writers and, often, in addition, their adoption (or recognition) of the highly sophisticated variant of it formulated by Bhaskar, usually known as critical realism (Bhaskar 1986; see also Archer 1995; Fleetwood 1999; Sayer 2000). Hence, the majority of the contributors to this book explicitly tie what they have to say about theory and/or practice in the field of management and organisation studies to a realist philosophical position which draws directly or indirectly on the work of Bhaskar. For example, the next chapter contributed to this collection, by Hari Tsoukas, was one of the first important statements applying the approach of Bhaskar. Tsoukas draws on Bhaskar in order to develop a new synthetic view of management which he refers to as 'a metatheoretical account'. This is correct in the sense that Tsoukas draws on ideas which are, strictly speaking, realist philosophical rather than theoretical concepts. In view of this it is remarkable how much existing research and writing on management, both conceptually informed and empirical, Tsoukas is able to relate to his account. This indicates that there is much to be contributed in ordering existing research by the adoption of critical realism.

Several other contributors to this collection draw on the ideas of Bhaskar either directly or as they are embodied in Tsoukas. But before elaborating on the precise character of the papers included in this book, and indicating how far they exemplify new as opposed to old realism, let us set out more clearly the ideas that inform the doctrines in which we are interested, and how they differ from other doctrines.

Realism elaborated

Realism refocuses our attention on ontology. Ontology is not an optional extra: everyone has an ontology. As social scientists, we make ontological commitments or have ontological presuppositions although these presuppositions remain, typically, implicit and unexamined. But this can be problematic because the way we (implicitly or explicitly) presume the social world is, has a strong influence not only on our ways of studying it (our epistemology), but on the way the whole analytical framework we adopt is conceptualised. For example, if we presume that the social world is completely constituted by discourse, that the social world is merely discourse, then we have an ontology consisting solely of discursive entities. Given this ontology, our analytical attention is focused upon discursive practices: non-discursive practices cannot be investigated or elaborated because they have been ruled out of contention.

Towards a critical realist social ontology

Up to now, we have merely used the term 'realism' without further elaboration. Recent work by realists, as we have seen, draws on the work of Bhaskar. Many researchers in the area of organisation and management studies, then, have been drawing on the philosophy of critical realism and have attempted to make claims about the general nature of the social world; that is, about social ontology. Let us elaborate a little.

What does it mean to write of the *social* world? The natural world is natural because it does not require action on behalf of human beings for its existence.[5] The social world is social because, by contrast, it does require action on behalf of human beings for its existence.

Whilst the social world is a product of human action, it is not necessarily the product of human design, conceptualisation or discourse. That is, whilst phenomena such as class relations exist only in and through human (practical and discursive) activity, there is no necessity that the human beings involved are conscious of the part they play in reproducing these relations. These social phenomena can exist without the human actors involved having knowledge of them, conceptualising them, or constructing them in discourse. Yet they still go on. Hence we can say that some social phenomena exist independently of their identification. Many things exist, in fact most things exist, independently of our identification of them.

That said, the human actors who reproduce social phenomena have some conception of what they are doing – even if it is a misconception. Agents who enter into relations of production in order to earn a living, and who might be entirely ignorant of these relations, clearly have a conception about what they are doing. That is, they have a complex set of conceptions of the nature of employment, and it is partly in virtue of these conceptions that these relations are reproduced. Hence we can say that social phenomena are concept *dependent* or socially constructed. In the field of organisation and management studies, a key point of interest is the extent to which institutions are produced by actors and yet still exist externally to them and shape their behaviour.

In addition to the lay agents who are the subject of social research, we need to consider the part played by social scientists. 'Although social phenomena cannot exist independently of actors or subjects, they usually exist independently of the particular individual who is studying them' (Sayer 1992: 49). For example, although the routines that constitute the firm (discussed by Costello in Chapter 8), industrial networks (discussed by Easton in Chapter 10), segmented labour markets (discussed by Peck in Chapter 11) or the society-wide 'production system' (discussed by Rubery in Chapter 12) cannot and do not exist entirely independently of the agents who reproduce them, they do exist independently of the researchers who study them. It is a mistake therefore to reduce reality to accounts of reality.

This is true whoever the accounts are produced by – social scientists or, for that matter, powerful economic or political institutions. Social scientists, like any other group, do not begin their study without any ideas or concepts of their own: they cannot. They bring their own concepts with them into the study of a concept-dependent world. We might say sociologists have concepts which they use to investigate concepts. This is sometimes referred to as the 'double hermeneutic' (Giddens 1979; cf. Ackroyd 1994). Yet realists do want to hold that better and worse forms of knowledge do exist and that there are reliable procedures for producing better knowledge of things and events. For realists the methods used for investigation are broadly conceived and of critical importance to the development of knowledge (Sayer 1992).

It is, partly, in recognition of the concept dependency of the world that many social scientists mistakenly slide from a belief that the world is socially constructed or concept dependent to a belief that it is merely socially constructed or concept determined. Part of what prevents critical realists from making this mistake is a commitment to materialism. Underlying the concept-dependent nature of social reality is an irreducible material substrate. 'Social beings live neither on bread alone nor on ideas alone' as Sayer (1992: 35) puts it. The unemployed cannot simply become employed by believing and/or declaring themselves to be employed. This depends (minimally) upon the availability of the means of production. Tsoukas (1992) uses the more familiar example of a person's relations with his or her bank manager: no amount of friendly relations will induce the latter to extend credit. Organisations like individuals are 'resource dependent'.

All this gives the critical realist social ontology a sophistication lacking in the two other competing perspectives. It overcomes the weaknesses associated with positivism in the sense that it rejects, as a most unlikely state of affairs, the existence of constant conjunctions of events or 'laws' in the social world. To be more accurate, critical realists argue that event regularities mostly occur in special situations, namely in sets of relations or systems that are artificially isolated from interference, labelled 'closed systems'. Without a great deal of contrivance, these do not exist in the social world. Moreover, critical realists ground their objection to positivism in the claim that search is itself driven by the atomistic ontology that positivism presupposes (Fleetwood 2000).

The critical realist social ontology also overcomes the weaknesses associated with postmodernism, in the sense that while it retains a commitment to the socially constructed nature of the social world, it refuses to take the next, unwarranted step and conclude that the social world is *merely* socially constructed. Let us elaborate a little using the example of gender relations.

Class or gender relations, for example, are social in the sense that (practical and discursive) activity on the part of human agents is necessary to reproduce them. A realist might, variously, claim that these relations are: socially constructed; dependent upon the concepts agents have about their action; mediated in discourse. But, significantly, these relations can be reproduced by agents who have no knowledge of them whatsoever. In fact, they could conceivably be reproduced by agents who even explicitly deny the existence of such relations. Hence, gender relations have a degree of objectivity about them in the sense that they can be reproduced independently of their identification by the males and females who constitute them. In this case, whilst gender relations are socially constructed, they are not *simply* socially constructed; they depend on (at least some of the) agents' concepts about their actions, but they are not determined by agents' concepts; they are, therefore, concept dependent but not concept determined; they are reproduced, in part, via discourse, but are irreducible to, or are not, *only* discourse; gender retains an objective element to its existence which is independent of its identification by human agents. If this were not the case, then discriminatory gender relations could be eradicated simply by altering the concepts or discourse surrounding such activity; we could, literally, conceptualise, or talk discrimination out of existence – a socially and politically naïve, if not dangerous, proposition especially for those who use social science to pursue an emancipatory agenda.

Now, with a rejection of the postmodernists' ontology, coupled with a rejection of the positivists' constant conjunctions of events as unlikely features of social reality and, thereby, abandoning the notion of causality as mere regularity, the critical realist is free to seek the cause of an event elsewhere in the ontological spectrum. Attention turns away from the flux of events and towards the causal mechanisms, social structures, powers and relations that govern them. Rather than the ontology being restricted to the fused domains of the actual and empirical, the critical realist adds another domain, namely the (metaphoric) 'deep'. Table 1.1 illustrates this stratified ontology. The task of explanation in social science is to penetrate behind the surface of experiences and perceptions and to account for what occurs in terms of an understanding of connections at the level of structures.

Table 1.1   A structured ontology

Domain	Entity
Empirical	Experiences, perceptions
Actual	Events and actions
'Deep'	Structures, mechanisms, powers, relations

In an open system, these domains are, typically, out of phase with one another, meaning one cannot connect (say) a power or a causal mechanism to its manifestation at the level of events and perceptions easily or securely by simple inspection. This is because powers and causal mechanisms act transfactually: once set in motion, they continue to have an influence, even if other countervailing powers and mechanisms prevent this influence manifesting itself. An aircraft, for example, has the power to fly even when it remains locked in a hangar. A manager has the power to exercise control over the subordinate even if this power is seldom overtly exercised. Such powers are said to act transfactually.

Now, not only is the ontology adopted by realism stratified, it is also transformational. Bhaskar establishes the possibility of a transformational ontology from an investigation into the nature of society. Whilst traditionally most commentators recognise that society consists (in some sense) of agents and structures, the debate centres upon the way they interact. With the transformational model of social action (TMSA) Bhaskar points out a new area of debate.

Nothing happens out of nothing. Agents do not create or produce structures *ab initio*, rather they recreate, reproduce and/or transform a set of pre-existing structures. Society and institutions continue to exist only because agents reproduce and/or transform those structures they encounter in their social actions. Every action performed requires the pre-existence of some social structures which agents draw upon in order to initiate action, and in doing so they reproduce and/or transform them. For example, communicating requires a medium (e.g. language), and the operation of the market requires the rules of private property. This ensemble of social structures, according to Bhaskar, simply is society. As Bhaskar observes:

> [P]eople do not create society. For it always pre-exists them and is a necessary condition for their activity. Rather society must be regarded as an ensemble of structures, practices and conventions which individuals reproduce and transform, but which would not exist unless they did so. Society does not exist independently of human activity (the error of reification). But it is not the product of it (the error of voluntarism).
>
> (1989: 36; see also 1986: 129)

The transformational principle, then, centres upon the causal mechanisms, structures, powers and relations that are the ever-present condition, and the continually reproduced and/or transformed outcome, of human agency. Agents, acting purposefully or consciously, unconsciously draw upon, and thereby reproduce, the mechanisms, structures, powers and relations that govern their actions in daily life.

From social ontology to the mode of theorisation

Operating with a stratified and transformational ontology, the emphasis of investigation necessarily switches from the domains of the empirical and actual and the ensuing event patterns observed to the domain of the deep and the mechanisms that govern these events. Investigation switches from the consequences, that is from the outcomes or results (in the form of events and their patterns) of some particular human action, to the conditions that make that action possible. As Bhaskar puts matters:

> Looked at in this way with [the transformational model of social action] TMSA ... the task of the various social sciences [is] to lay out the structural conditions for various conscious human actions, for example, what economic processes must take place for Christmas shopping to be possible – but they do not describe the latter.
>
> (1989: 36)

Because of the openness of socio-economic systems and the transfactual nature of the causal mechanisms, consequences or outcomes cannot be deduced or predicted. But the causal mechanisms that govern this human action can be illuminated and explained. Explanation supplants deduction, prediction, solution, determination, calculation and logical consistency as the goals of theorisation.

Moreover, because realists accept that there are multiple perspectives or competing claims about the nature of the social world (epistemic relativism), but reject the possibility that there are multiple realities, they are in a position to accept that the truth is possible. Put another way, because, ontologically speaking, realism retains a place for an objective social world, we do not have to suspend judgement, or claim to be unable to judge between competing statements (judgemental relativism) when faced with competing explanatory accounts. For the realist, a statement is true (or false) in virtue of the way the world is. This does not, of course, imply that the realist knows the truth: it merely implies the truth can be known – irrespective of how difficult this may be. Given this, however, realism licenses an intense interest in finding out what is true, and of finding out how truth can be secured.

As we have argued, realism encourages us to take ontology seriously: it asks us to tease out, reflect upon and elaborate our ontological presuppositions. It encourages us to ask: do we really think the world is like this? Clearly this involves avoiding the epistemic fallacy so that we do not confuse reality with our knowledge of reality and end up asserting that things are so because we perceive them to be so. And, of course, if we subsequently discover that our presuppositions fail to express the way the world is, then we are motivated to revise our ontological presuppositions. In its recognition of the recurrent need to revise and develop, realism displays one of its most valuable attributes.

In sum, then, realism provides a valid social ontology with which the field of organisation and management studies, or indeed, any field, can be addressed. This ontology informs an approach to developing theory that seeks explanation as its goal. Explanation is conceived in terms of revealing the mechanisms which connect things and events in causal sequences and requires the elaboration of structures, mechanisms, powers and relations that are the condition and the continually reproduced and/or transformed outcome of human agency to be achieved. In this account, the criteria for evaluating theory are not concerned with deduction or prediction, but with explanatory power.

The rationale for the collection of papers

The main justification for this collection is to demonstrate the coherency and vitality of the realist tradition in organisation and management studies. Unusually for a collection of readings of this kind, all the papers have been published previously in some sort of way. However, even where these papers have been published in well-respected scholarly journals (see acknowledgements), the likelihood is they will have been read by a small number of professional readers only. All of the papers in the collection, we suggest, deserve to find a wider readership. But it is only when these papers are seen together, and the continuities between them are underlined, that these writings are to be seen in their full importance. Taken together, as they are in this book, these papers display an impressive consistency; and so indicate that the realist tradition in management and organisation studies is vigorous and developing.

The collection of work which follows in the remainder of the text is organised into two sections. The papers which make up the first part set out to state explicitly what a realist approach to organisation and management studies should be like and entail. This sort of self-conscious discussion of realism and how precisely it should be used and applied in the field of organisation and management studies is largely new. These papers make an important contribution by setting out the characteristics of a realist approach and developing the implications of this conception for the field. The papers which make up the second part of the book provide a number of illustrations of what contemporary realism, as employed by social scientists in the field of organisation and management studies, can achieve. Let us give an account of the contents of the two parts of the book in turn.

Part I: the character of contemporary realism

There are three tasks undertaken by the papers in this part: the first is that of setting out and developing a realist approach to organisation and management studies; the second is dealing with the ontological and other implications of adopting such an approach; and the third is taking seriously the theoretical implications of a realist position. The papers included in the initial section of the book do not contain themselves neatly within the boundaries of one of these three objectives, but they do make one of them the most important objective to reach.

Viewed in this way, the paper by Tsoukas, which follows this introduction (Chapter 2), does most to set out in general terms what a realist account of management studies might be. Tsoukas's contribution sets out a synoptic 'metatheory of management', using critical realist philosophical categories. Following this are two chapters (Chapter 3 by Mike Reed and Chapter 4 by Robert Willmott) that are much concerned with the question of the ontology that is appropriate for realist organisation and management studies and the theoretical implications of this. Finally, there are two chapters (Chapter 5 by Stephen Ackroyd and Chapter 6 by Steve Pratten) that deal with some of the explicitly theoretical issues arising from developing realism as an approach to organisation and management studies. In both cases what these authors do is undertake an exercise in theoretical retrieval: going back and reformulating existing theories to make them conform more adequately to realist prescriptions.

Given what we have said in the preceding sections of this chapter, it should perhaps hardly surprise anyone that much of the writing which discusses the features of realism in management and organisation studies is much concerned with ontology and ontological issues. The papers by Reed and Willmott have much to say on these questions, and the implications for what they say, especially for positivist and postmodernist assumptions, deserve special attention.

It is often assumed that an ontology must conceive of the world as a unitary phenomenon, as something made up in a particular way. The ontological assumption of postmodernists is often that the social world is completely constituted by discourses, for example. Realists do not accept this: that is, they deny that the world is entirely constituted by the discursive activities of people. Indeed, this has led realists to dispute the idea that the social world is unitary. In the third chapter of this volume, for example, Mike Reed argues that it is necessary to envisage and adopt a dualistic ontology. One of the things Reed does in his paper is to identify and criticise the ontological assumptions of the ethnomethodological analyst of organisation, Dede Boden, along these lines. He writes:

> Boden's (1994) recent investigations into the 'business of talk' in a range of administrative, commercial and communication organisations continues to insist that 'organisation' is only brought into existence as a temporary and negotiable institutional reality through the conversational practices and linguistic conventions it instantiates. For her, 'there really is no objective environment for organisations, all of whom are dependent on the perceptions of their members, and more centrally, on the ways local perceptions actually constitute the conditions of next actions and thereby outcomes' (Boden 1994: 38). As institutions, that is as that highly transient and mobile historical practice we call 'structure', organisations are literally 'talked into being' (Boden 1994: 215).

Hence one of the key issues which realists in organisation and management studies are currently debating concerns the extent to which it is necessary to adopt a dualistic ontology, and what such adoption will imply. Both Reed and Willmott (in Chapters 3 and 4 of this volume respectively) propose and discuss the need for dualistic ontology, arguing against what they denote the 'depthless' ontological assumptions of other approaches. In his extended defence and exposition of realism, Willmott argues trenchantly for what he labels 'analytical dualism' in organisation studies, and, following Margaret Archer, goes much further than many in asserting the reality of belief systems and cultures as elements that should feature in realist explanations.

The ontology of the realist theorist recognises the simultaneous existence (and causal importance) of ideas and social structures. Indeed, one of the things that contemporary realists are actively debating is the relative importance of these aspects of social reality in producing outcomes both in particular examples of social organisation and in general. There is much evidence from the readings in this book and elsewhere that realists attribute causal weight to the independent action of individuals and groups (which is usually referred to as their 'agency') in producing and reproducing structures. The issue of the way in which belief systems feature in such processes is also being actively discussed. In insisting on the need to recognise the reality of beliefs, Willmott moves a long way towards accepting the influence of belief in the explanation of group behaviour and general social outcomes.

The other pair of papers that make up this part concentrate on reformulating or rereading theory so it gives sufficient weight to factors which realism would lead us to regard as important. The chapter by Ackroyd focuses primarily on the need to give an account of the relationships between structures of different kinds. Ackroyd argues that the agency of groups produces and reproduces work groups, organisational structures and whole societies; but the effects of agency are much less obvious as the scale of structures increases. He also argues that social scientists, even those working within the field of organisation and management studies, have given insufficient emphasis to the organisational level in understanding the outcome of general social processes. Ackroyd's argument shows continuity with earlier kinds of realism, in which agency is firmly subordinated to structures. Nonetheless, even in this account, the beliefs of groups and their agency are implicated in the explanation of the production and reproduction of both organisations and societies. This argument implies going back and drawing selectively on the classic contributions to social science theory.

Steve Pratten's paper (Chapter 6) is also an exercise in theoretical retrieval. Pratten goes back to Marx to argue that there is a different (and arguably much more subtle and non-deterministic) account of the labour process to be found in Marx's original work. There has, of course, been a huge amount of discussion and debate in organisational and management studies over the last three decades concerning the labour process. This began with the seminal work of Braverman (1974) which then stimulated a range of theoretical and research activity in the field (Friedman 1977; Thompson 1979; Littler 1982). It has been suggested already in this chapter that much of this writing is basically realist in character. However, this has not prevented the question of agency or, more precisely, the subjectivity of agents, becoming the matter of sustained debate and controversy within this area of thought and research (cf. Knights and Willmott 1989; 1990). Indeed, disagreement over this and related questions opened the way for some to suggest the need fundamentally to revise labour process analysis, taking it in a postmodernist direction and provoking fundamental schisms between researchers in this field. Pratten, wisely perhaps, does not comment directly on this controversy other than to acknowledge it is there, opting instead to go 'back to basics', and interpret Marx through the prism of critical realism. The implications of his reworking of the analysis of the labour process (in a way that enlarges the importance of agency) indicates that the perceived need to revise labour process analysis in the direction of postmodernism may be misplaced. Again, the argument is that reworking of theory in realist ways is helpful in advancing understanding.

Part II: illustrating contemporary realist practice

The above discussion reveals that a central issue for contemporary realist research in organisation and management studies is how social groups and organisations are produced and reproduced. The extent to which social relations are simply reproduced and the extent to which outcomes can be changed by agents are matters of central concern. All of the papers which are included in the second part of this collection contribute findings concerning the way social relationships are produced and reproduced.

Of the six chapters which comprise Part II of this book, half the authors make some reference to this 'new' realism, though they differ greatly in the extent to which they are explicit about this and the extent to which they identify with it. Indeed, three of the chapters here do not make any explicit reference to realism. These are: Chapter 9 by John Coopey and colleagues, Chapter 11 by Jamie Peck, and Chapter 12 by Jill Rubery. But we make no apology for designating these writings as being realist analyses of their chosen subjects, and obviously have the approval of their authors for inclusion in this collection. Clearly, there are many more papers that might have been included on this sort of basis. Indeed, we think that much ongoing research in organisation and management studies contributes to and develops realist kinds of analysis of organisations and management, whether or not the authors explicitly endorse such views. That this is so gives support to our view that realism is actually endemic to this area of study. We claim, in fact, there is much more work that is implicitly realist in the field of organisation and management studies than that which is implicitly or explicitly postmodernist.

As we shall show in the following pages, contemporary realism in organisation and management studies is strongly into conceptualising the attitudes, values and cultures of the groups of people whose behaviour is discussed. The meanings attributed to situations by people are thus central to the realist project; they figure strongly in the following chapters. Several of the papers included here utilise ethnographic research methods extensively – Porter (in Chapter 7), Costello (in Chapter 8) and Coopey et al. (in Chapter 9) are all examples of this. Such an emphasis, of course, makes nonsense of any claim that a willingness to take the attitudes and values of groups seriously is necessarily subjective and therefore inimical to and incompatible with the search for objectivity. What is different is, of course, that realists are not simply interested in the capacity for individuals and groups to produce and sustain particular views; but also to understand the way that these ideas relate to other features of their situation which they are also (re)producing. In the terms used by both the substantive and more theoretical writing included in this collection, there is an equal interest in the capacities of groups (their agency) and the enduring relationships in which they are also located (their structural location). Because Anthony Giddens is the theorist whose work is centrally concerned with the relationship between agency and structure, many of the chapters here refer to the work of Giddens (1979; 1984; 1993) and several of them make the analysis and criticism of his work central to their arguments. (See in particular: Reed in Chapter 3, Willmott and Ackroyd in Chapters 4 and 5, Coopey *et al*. in Chapter 9). Most commentators are unwilling to see Giddens as a realist, but many of the realist works in this book do take Giddens' ideas about structuration as a critical reference point.

It is characteristic of the papers included in this collection that they vary greatly in their range and scope, whilst the basic conception of the subject matter of organisation and management studies remains the same. At one end of the scale is the sort of analysis of the detailed behaviour of groups within companies and other organisations, in which the question being dealt with is the extent to which and the ways in which individuals and groups are related to each other and how their activity contributes to the production and reproduction of the larger structures in which they are implicated. The first three chapters of the second part of the book all have this in common.

Porter (in Chapter 7) and Costello (in Chapter 8) offer accounts of behaviour that are not centrally concerned with productive activity in the workplace as such, but focus on analysing behaviour that is peripheral in this sense. Although the behaviour they are concerned with is strikingly different (racism on the one hand and new procedures and activities on the other) they both raise similar questions. They consider the question of the way in which behaviour other than work activity is implicated in the performance of work and the reproduction of the context in which it takes place. Porter shows how racist attitudes are deeply woven into the work attitudes of groups of nurses working in the NHS hospital he studied, but he also shows that these attitudes are overridden by the need for conformity to the professional relationships that are treated as fundamental to the organisation of work in such institutions. Costello shows how, despite the lack of anything approximating tradition, or other forms of reliable guide to appropriate behaviour, employees in high-technology firms successfully innovate new practices in the workplace and routinise them, so that out of turbulence and change comes a degree of routine predictability and stability.

The theme of innovation is continued by Coopey *et al*. in Chapter 9. Here the focus of analysis is managers, who are expected to be able to be effective in bringing about changes in the organisations for which they work. Coopey *et al*. show that the capacity of managers to produce change in their organisations is not straightforward, and cannot be accurately described in terms of the routine exercise of power to produce predictable outcomes. These authors demonstrate that contingent events, the outcome of negotiations in related areas, the particular availability of resources at the time they were required are the sorts of contingent events which bore on the outcome of the managerial innovations they considered.

What these papers show is the complexity of the processes that give rise to outcomes within organisations; but that this does not invalidate the notion that there is overall patterning and continuity in organisations. Similar points are made by realist analysts when they shift their focus to consider the relationships and structures that lie beyond the organisation. There are two papers included in this collection that deal with the analysis of meso-level structures – the entities that exist between the organisation and the society as a whole. There are several ways of trying to conceptualise this area, of course. In the papers we have included in this collection, however, there are some new ideas about how to think about entities at this level, and some distinctive reworking of older concepts. Easton (in Chapter 10) argues that it is helpful to analyse interfirm relations in terms of what he calls 'industrial networks'. The conceptualisation here (as that at the level of the firm) implicates the role of human agents in shaping social reality at this level.

In contrast to the work of Easton, Peck (in Chapter 11) argues for the explanatory value of the idea of segmented labour markets. Here the concepts in use have recognisable continuity with traditional ideas of markets, but the ideas are given a radical twist by the notion that markets do not work wholly impersonally, and are not beyond the formative reach of the behaviour of agents. For Peck, labour markets and the way that they are structured constitute a system of social regulation that is all the more formative for the involvement of groups in constituting and replicating them. This area of interfirm and meso-level relations is one of many areas in which there is scope for a great deal of debate about the way that causal sequences in the economy actually work, to which realists are actively contributing. Although here, as elsewhere, realist writing implicates agency in the formation of general patterns of relationship, it is quite difficult to see how postmodernists, relying as they do on the determinant capacity of discourses and/or conceptions, can understand the properties of such entities at all. Within realist discussions, of course, there is scope for a great deal of debate about the way to develop existing knowledge.

Finally we have concluded the collection with the paper by Jill Rubery (in Chapter 12) in which she offers a general account of some of the characteristics of the British economy. Rubery suggests that there is something that can be described as 'the British production regime', which is helpful in describing a large segment of the British economy. The production regime characterises much more than the characteristic management system found in British factories. It also extends to consider the relationships between institutional forms in labour markets, and character and role of other institutions and the traditional form of regulatory agencies including the government. The argument here is that this is a distinctive set of institutions and relationships which exhibit recognisable similarities and continuity over time. By reference to this production regime we can, amongst other things, begin to understand why the manufacturing sectors of the economy perform (or fail to perform) in particular ways.

By way of conclusion

As is hopefully now evident, we have provided a collection of papers that reflect and capture the range of work that is being done in contemporary realist analysis in organisation and management studies. However, it is only considerations of space that have prevented us from including several more papers, so demonstrating even more effectively the scope of realist analysis and its relevance to the development of synthetic and inclusive knowledge in the field of organisation and management studies. We would very much have liked to include at least one good general depiction of a particular kind of managerial regime. These days analyses of factories, for example, have allowed general accounts of different kinds of factory regimes to be clarified. Sayer's brilliant analysis of the just-in-time system of production is a case in point (Sayer and Walker 1997). We might well have included also studies that have an even broader scope than Rubery's. There are examples of the utilisation of realist kinds of analysis which take on the comparative consideration of whole societies. An impressive recent example of work on this scale is Barry Wilkinson's analysis of business organisation in East Asia (Wilkinson 1996). There are many directions in which realist analysis can be employed in the field of organisation and management studies.

We conclude by making three general claims about the realism in organisation and management studies, each of which suggests its value.

The first is that there is a predilection to connect things in realist research and writing, which is not found with such frequency or extent in other types of approach to the field. The impulse of realist analysis is very much to develop concepts and theories that connect ideas and propositions from different areas of substantive work and indeed levels of generality. Realist analysis habitually shows how things are (or indicates how they may be) connected. Examples are connections between such things as: dissenting behaviour and the reproduction of factory structures; the interfirm network and the structure of corporate groups; the particular factory regime and the characteristics of the economic system. It is characteristic of this kind of work to connect the particular with the general, to suggest that despite the particularities of a given case study, it nonetheless exhibits properties that are exemplary for understanding the general case.

The second claim is that realist analysis engenders debate about the nature of the world that research has uncovered or partly uncovered that may contribute to the growth of knowledge. Realism starts with the assumption that what exists can be discovered (though, typically, not without difficulty) and then can be further developed through the consideration of what has been found. Reformulated concepts and the collection of more evidence may, again, reveal more about the world. Recognition that knowledge can only be obtained when the methods used are appropriate to the way the world is, constitutes the essence of good practice in this model.

The third and final claim is that realism has emancipatory potential. By revealing how, despite our failure to acknowledge it, our own acts are implicated in the reproduction of social structures and relations that stand in the way of emancipation, we are, potentially at least, in a position to consider alternative structures and relations that might overturn this state of affairs, and promote genuine human flourishing.

Notes

1   This *modus operandi* is referred to variously as the covering law model or the deductive–nomological (D–N) model. The latter also manifests itself as the inductive–probabilistic (I–P) model where the 'laws' are statistical in nature. Note, however, that whether laws are deterministic or statistical, the ontology presupposed consists of the atomistic events of sense experience.
2   Alvesson and Deetz (1996), recognising the amorphous nature of postmodernism, offer a nice collection of positions that would, if most of them were held, define the holder as postmodern.
3   The editors' position on the similarities and differences between realism and postmodernism is similar to that of Stones (1996).
4   This scepticism appears to stem from something like the following positions: an exaggerated belief in the creative or generative capacity of discourse; the ontological misuse of the recognition of multiple voices (i.e. the assumption that multiple voices equal multiple realities); an exaggeration of the recognition that language can be a poor reflection of reality; the fetishisation of change, volatility and transience; an illicit step from the claim that powerful groups have the ability to have their version of the 'truth' accepted – to the view that 'truth' is a function of power; acceptance of the victory of hyperreality over reality; and a shift from the (welcomed) rejection of the rationality and predictability of positivism to a conflation of the latter with realism (cf. Alvesson and Deetz 1996).
5   We reject as mere word-games arguments to the effect that natural phenomena such as oceans cannot exist independently of human beings, because the word 'ocean' requires human action; or that oceans only exist 'for us' in discourse. We also reject hard versions of social constructivism such as those offered by Grint and Woolgar (1997: chapter six) who effectively commit the epistemic fallacy – that is, they collapse questions of ontology into questions of epistemology (cf. Bhaskar 1989: 133).

Bibliography

Ackroyd, S. (1992) 'Paradigms lost: paradise regained?', in M. Reed and M. Hughes (eds) *Rethinking Organisation*, London: Sage.
——(1994) 'Re-creating common ground: elements for post-paradigmatic organisation studies', in J. Hassard and M. Parker (eds) *Towards a New Theory of Organisations*, London: Routledge, 270–97.
Alvesson, M. (1987) *Organisation Theory and Technocratic Consciousness*, Berlin: De Gruyter.

Alvesson, M. and Deetz, S. (1996) 'Critical theory and postmodernism approaches to organisational studies', in S. Clegg *et al.* (eds) *Handbook of Organization Studies*, London: Sage.

Archer, M. (1995) *Realist Social Theory: The Morphogenetic Approach*, Cambridge: Cambridge University Press.

Bhaskar, R. (1975) *A Realist Theory of Science*, Leeds: Leeds Books (second edition, 1979, Brighton: Harvester).

——(1979) *The Possibility of Naturalism*, Brighton: Harvester.

——(1986) *Scientific Realism and Human Emancipation*, London: Verso.

——(1989) *Reclaiming Reality*, London: Verso.

Boden, D. (1994) *The Business of Talk: Organisations in Action*, Cambridge: Polity Press.

Braverman, H. (1974) *Labour and Monopoly Capital*, New York: Monthly Review Press.

Burrell, G. and Morgan, G. (1979) *Sociological Paradigms and Organisational Analysis*, London: Heinemann.

Chia, R. (1996) *Organisational Analysis and Deconstructive Practice*, Berlin: De Gruyter.

Clark, P. (2000) *Organisations in Action: Competition Between Contexts*, London: Routledge.

Collier, A. (1994) *Critical Realism*, London: Verso.

Cooper, R. and Burrell, G. (1988) 'Modernism, post-modernism and organisational analysis', *Organisation Studies*, 9, 1: 91–122.

Delbridge, R. (1998) *Life on the Line in Contemporary Manufacturing*, Oxford: Oxford University Press.

Donaldson, L. (1996) *For Positivist Organisation Theory*, London: Sage.

Fleetwood, S. (1999) *Critical Realism in Economics: Development and Debate*, London: Routledge.

——(2000) 'Functional relations, laws and tendencies: a realist approach', *Review of Political Economy*, forthcoming.

Friedman, A. (1997) *Industry and Labour: Class Struggle at Work and Monopoly Capitalism*, London: Macmillan.

Gergen, K. (1992) 'Organisation theory in the postmodern era', in M. Reed and M. Hughes (eds) *Rethinking Organisation*, London: Sage.

Giddens, A. (1979) *Central Problems in Social Theory: Action, Structure and Contradiction in Social Analysis*, London: Hutchinson.

——(1984) *The Constitution of Society: Outline of a Theory of Structuration*, Cambridge: Polity Press.

——(1993) *New Rules of Sociological Method*, Oxford: Polity Press.

Grint, K. and Woolgar, S. (1997) *The Machine at Work: Technology, Work and Society*, Cambridge: Polity Press.

Harré, R. (1972) *The Philosophies of Science*, Oxford: Oxford University Press.

——(1986) *Varieties of Realism*, Oxford: Blackwell.

Jackson, N. and Carter, P. (2000) *Rethinking Organisational Behaviour*, London: Pearson Education.

Keat, R. and Urry, J. (1975) *Social Theory as Science*, London: Routledge.

Knights, D. and Willmott, H. (1989) 'Power and subjectivity at work', *Sociology* 23, 4: 535–58.

——(1990) *Labour Process Theory*, Basingstoke: Macmillan.

Lawson, T. (1997) *Economics and Reality*, London: Routledge.

Layder, D. (1990) *The Realist Image in Social Science*, Basingstoke: Macmillan.

Legge, K. (1995) *Human Resource Management: Rhetorics and Realities*, Basingstoke: Macmillan.

Littler, C. (1982) *The Development of the Labour Process in Capitalist Societies*, London: Heinemann.

Morgan, G. (1986) *Images of Organisation*, London: Sage.

——(1997) *Images of Organisation*, second edition, London: Sage

Parker, M. (1992) 'Post-modern organisations or postmodern organisation theory?', *Organization Studies*, 13, 1: 1–17.

——(1998) 'Capitalism, subjectivity and ethics: debating labour process analysis', *Organization Studies*, 20, 1: 21–45.

Sayer, A. (1992) *Method in Social Science: A Realist Approach*, London: Routledge.

——(2000) *Realism and Social Science*, London: Sage.

Sayer, A. and Walker, R. (1997) *The New Social Economy: Reworking the Division of Labour*, Oxford: Blackwell.

Stones, R. (1996) *Sociological Reasoning*, Basingstoke: Macmillan.

Thompson, P. (1979) *The Nature of Work: An Introduction to Debates on the Labour Process*, London: Macmillan.

Thompson, P., Smith, C. and Ackroyd, S. (2000) 'If ethics is the answer, you are asking the wrong questions', *Organisation Studies*, forthcoming.

Tsoukas, H. (1992) 'Postmodernism, reflexive rationalism and organisation studies', *Organisation Studies*, 13, 4: 643–49.

Wilkinson, B. (1996) 'Culture, institutions and business in East Asia', *Organisation Studies*, 17, 3: 420–47.

2 What is management?

An outline of a metatheory

Haridimous Tsoukas

Introduction

The emergence of managerial hierarchies for the co-ordination and control of economic activities is one of the most distinguishing features of late capitalism (Chandler 1977; Williamson 1975). The importance of managers, therefore, as a distinctive occupational category for organisational decision making has long been recognised (Taylor 1911; Fayol 1949; Barnard 1966). However, despite the increasing centrality of managers in the co-ordination of complex organisational activities, and the enhanced visibility of their tasks and functions, it has not been easy to answer the question: 'What is management?'

Part of the difficulty lies in the ambiguity inherent in the term 'management'. For example, does 'management' designate a collective institutional process or simply a set of individuals distinguished by the activities they carry out? If management is conceived as a collective process then management is an institutional necessity, abstract and anonymous, much like the concepts of 'class', 'bureaucracy' or 'market'. From such a perspective, what management is cannot be decided by looking into the micro-actions of individuals, but into the logic of management (derived from its embedding into a particular socio-economic system) which is empirically manifested in its trajectory of development in particular societal contexts (cf. Heilbroner 1985 for similar remarks on the logic of capitalism). Understood this way, management (and any other concept indicating an abstract collectivity) can be theorised via the construction of models seeking to explain, on a macro-scale, the context-depended rise and demise of particular forms of management. Neo-Marxists, for example, are particularly inclined to such a mode of analysis. Braverman (1974), Burawoy (1979) and Littler (1982), to mention only a few, have attempted to conceptualise management in terms of its efforts to control labour, along different periods in the development of particular market economies or industrial sectors (cf. also Friedman 1977; Thompson 1983).

If, on the other hand, management is seen as a particular set of individuals then management is conceptualised in terms of what these individuals regularly do. Consequently, one tends to theorise, at a micro-level of analysis, on the circumstances that give rise to particular managerial tasks and roles (Hales 1986; Kotter 1982; Mintzberg 1973; Stewart 1982). Management textbooks have found it particularly difficult to integrate these two perspectives and the result has been a rather fragmented literature on management and managerial work (Carroll and Gillen 1987; Reed 1989).

It will be suggested in this paper that the chief source for the polarisation between macro- and micro-perspectives on management, and the concomitant fragmentation of the relevant literature, stems from the manner in which management has been conceptualised. More specifically, it will be argued that the ontological and epistemological assumptions that have been implicit in past conceptualisations account for a great deal of the confusion surrounding management. It will be argued here that a realist ontology and epistemology provide a useful set of concepts which allow us to construct a metatheory of management.

A question that may be asked at this point is this: 'Given that there is not a generally acceptable theory of management, why should one bother with a metatheory?' My answer would turn such a hypothetical question on its head: it is precisely because there is not an acceptable theory of management that a metatheory is necessary. We need to sort out the logical inconsistencies and conceptual ambiguities before theoretical progress can be made. Management is a highly complex phenomenon and to hope that a unifying grand theory will explain all its aspects is futile (cf. Morgan 1986; Poole and Van der Ven 1989). What, however, can be done is to outline a theory of theories of management, namely a *metatheory*. The latter can do two things. Firstly, it will articulate a set of ontological and epistemological principles that will help clarify the nature of management and our possible knowledge of it (cf. Turner 1987). Secondly, it will help bring together, in a logically consistent manner, a number of perspectives on management by specifying their individual domains of application (cf. Poole and Van der Ven 1989 for a similar attempt to outline a metatheory of innovation). In this way, the relationships between various perspectives will be clarified and, ideally, the scope of application of these perspectives will be specified.

The paper is organised as follows. Firstly, a brief description of the realist paradigm is sketched highlighting the latter's ontological assumptions and epistemological principles. This epistemological excursion is necessary for it will equip us with a conceptual vocabulary which will be put to use in the rest of the paper. Secondly, a brief review of the literature is undertaken in order to identify the claims and assumptions made by the main perspectives on management. Thirdly, drawing on the concepts derived from a realist epistemology, the nature of management as an object of study is redescribed. Management is shown to consist of four layers with each exhibiting its own distinctive characteristics and dynamics. A deeper layer is argued to be a necessary (but not sufficient) condition for the existence of the layer above it. Different perspectives on management are shown to apply at different layers.

The realist paradigm

Causal powers

Realist philosophers of science, such as Bhaskar (1978), Harré and Madden (1975), Harré and Secord (1972) and Outhwaite (1987), assume that the natural and social worlds alike do not consist of discrete atomistic events whose regular co-occurrences are the task of scientists to record, but of complex structures existing independently of scientists' knowledge of them. For realists, patterns of events are explained in terms of certain generative mechanisms (or causal powers) which are independent of the events they generate. Generative mechanisms reside in structures and endow them with particular causal capabilities. Generative mechanisms endure even when they are not acting, and act in their normal way even when the consequents of the law-like statements they give rise to are not realised, because of countervailing forces or the operation of other intervening mechanisms. For example, the HIV virus in a patient acts in its normal way (i.e. the generative mechanism of the virus is active) but whether or not it will produce results consistent with the AIDS symptoms depends on a variety of circumstances which may or may not be conducive to the development of the virus. A one-to-one relationship between a causal power and the pattern of events it prescribes obtains only under conditions of closure in which all interfering variables are under control (e.g. in experiments) (Bhaskar 1978; Harré 1989; Harré and Madden 1975; Sayer 1984; Tsoukas 1989). The significance of causal powers for management will be demonstrated in the next section.

Three domains of reality

According to the realist paradigm, reality consists of three domains: the real, the actual and the empirical. *Causal powers* are located in the real domain and their activation may give rise to patterns of *events* in the actual domain, which in turn, when identified, become *experiences* in the empirical domain. The distinction between causal powers and patterns of events implies that the former may be out of phase with the latter. It is up to human agency (typically manifested in experiments) to construct the conditions of closure so that the domains of *real* and *actual* can be fitted together, and thus for the causal powers to give rise to patterns of events. Similarly, when events have not yet been detected, and thus the transition from the actual to the *empirical* domain has not yet been made, human agency is required to identify correctly and transform events into experiences (Bhaskar 1978). Schematically, the domains of the real, the actual and the empirical are distinct (see Table 2.1), and the move from the real domain to the actual domain and then to the empirical domain is a *contingent* accomplishment (Outhwaite 1983; 1987).

Table 2.1   Ontological assumptions of the realist view of science

	Domain of real	Domain of actual	Domain of empirical
Mechanisms	✓		
Events	✓	✓	
Experiences	✓	✓	✓

Notes: Checkmarks (✓) indicate the domain of reality in which mechanisms, events and experiences respectively 'reside', as well as the domains involved for such a 'residence' to be possible. Thus, for instance, experiences are events which have been identified in the empirical domain. Experiences presuppose the occurrence of events in the actual domain independently of our observation of them. In turn, events presuppose the existence of mechanisms in the real domain which have been responsible for the generation of events.
Source: Based on Bhaskar (1978: 13).

Generative mechanisms may lie dormant for a while or they may be counteracted by opposing mechanisms, thus cancelling each other out and leading to no events. For instance, efficiency gains expected to be realised with the introduction of new technology may be neutralised because of managerial obsession with control (cf. Buchanan and Boddy 1983). In turn, events, when generated, may fail to be identified and thus turn into experiences. For example, as the analysis of industrial accidents reveals (cf. Mitroff 1988; Shrivastava *et al.* 1988), there have almost always been certain signals (events) presaging a forthcoming industrial accident, without, however, management having taken proper notice of them (i.e. without events having been transformed into experiences). It is partly because of the contingent nature of the link between the three domains of reality that human action is both necessary and possible.

The nature of explanation

From the realist viewpoint, causal explanation is not about recording the deterministic or stochastic association of patterns of events, but the ascription of causal powers to objects. To ascribe a power or potentiality to an object is to specify its necessary ways of acting or, to put it differently, what it is *capable* of doing in the appropriate set of circumstances (Harré and Madden 1975; Harré and Secord 1972). For instance, dynamite has the power to explode, birds have the power to fly, or people have the power to work, learn, to speak, etc. Whether a particular causal power is activated, and whether it manifests itself in the actual and/or empirical domains, depends on the ambient *contingent* conditions. For instance, the right conditions must be created for a bomb to explode or, by contrast, to avoid breaking a fragile vase while moving house. In other words, causal powers operate as tendencies whose activation, as well as the effect(s) of their activation, are not given but contingent. In the next section, management will be redescribed in terms of a set of causal powers.

Necessary and contingent relationships

Within the realist paradigm the world is not only differentiated between the real, the actual and the empirical domains, but also *stratified*. That is to say, natural and social structures have *emergent* powers which are irreducible to those of their constituent parts. For instance, the managerial causal powers of control and co-operation cannot be explained by reducing them to the powers of specific individuals, but by conceptualising the latter in a way that connects them to the wider structure of relations of production from which they derive their existence (more about this later).

Emergent powers are created when some entities are *necessarily* (or *intrinsically*) related to each other to form a structure (e.g. the relationship between a manager and a worker, or the relationship between a parent and a child). Entities are necessarily linked when their identity depends on their being in a relationship with the rest of the components of the structure (Berger 1987; Sayer 1984). A structure is a set of simultaneously constraining and enabling rules and resources which are implemented in human interaction. These rules shape interaction while at the same time being reproduced in this very process of interaction (Giddens 1976; 1984; Manicas 1980). For example, my renting a flat is possible via my drawing upon a wider enabling structure, comprising (in addition to myself as a tenant) the landlord, the existence of rent, owners and non-owners of property, as well as the existence of private property (cf. Sayer 1984). The terms of my tenancy, however, are not determined, though they are constrained, by this structure. I have to pay rent to my landlord – hence I feel constrained – although the amount is contingent upon several factors (e.g. housing market conditions, legal provisions, personal relations, etc.). In addition, my role as a tenant simultaneously and unintentionally contributes to the perpetuation of the above structure, independently of my liking or disliking it.

By contrast, when two entities are *contingently* related (e.g. a person's transactions with his or her bank) their powers are not modified. Consequently, an explanation of the aggregate pattern can be done by reducing it to its constituent parts (e.g. the end-of-month current account figure can be explained by reference to the withdrawals and deposits during the month).

Four perspectives on management: a brief overview

Management functions

There have been three schools of thought that have made use of the concept of management functions: the classical school, the systems approach and the historical approach. The classical school of management has sought to define the essence of management in the form of universal fundamental functions. These, it was hoped, would form the cognitive basis for a set of relevant skills to be acquired, by all would-be managers through formal education (Fayol 1949; Koontz and O'Donnell 1955; Mintzberg 1973; Simon 1957; Whitley 1989).

Management functions were rarely derived from theoretical reflection or empirical research but were very often based on a codification of work experiences of the individuals concerned or on commonsense descriptions of management practices. Traditionally, it has been accepted, and found its way into virtually all relevant textbooks, that the essence of management can be summarised in terms of the following four functions: planning, organising, leading and controlling. Extending this list, new functions were added later (e.g. representing) in order to reflect contemporary organisational realities (Mahoney *et al.* 1965). The classical school has not sought to relate explicitly these functions to particular purposes, requirements or functions of organisational subsystems; personal experience or experience of others was the basis for delineating the necessary management functions.

Building on the classical school, writers in the systems approach have developed the experience-based descriptions of management functions by grounding the latter on certain objective organisational requirements. Organisations have been thought of as consisting of subsystems having their own requirements for survival and effectiveness (Carroll and Gillen 1987). The systems approach comprises several authors whose contributions range from offering neat and simple frameworks which are essentially based on commonsense categories (cf. Daft 1988; Robbins 1991) to putting forward highly abstract models usually derived from organismic analogies (Beer 1981; 1985; Miller 1978). As the latter authors are the most theoretically sophisticated, I will briefly illustrate the nature of their arguments with a description of the work of Beer (1981; 1985).

Beer's modelling of the firm on the human nervous system has yielded an elaborate conception of organisations. For him, organisations need to develop management systems for carrying out the functions of co-ordination, the internal and now, the external and future, and securing the organisational identity and legitimacy. These organisational functions are carried out by separate management systems labelled systems 2, 3, 4 and 5, respectively. In other words, for Beer and other systems theorists (cf. Miller 1978), organisational survival entails that certain systemic functions need to be carried out in all organisations, which give rise to certain distinctive management functions.

The historical approach traces back the development of management in the context of the evolution of firms in market economies and, thus, seeks to derive the functions of management from such a historical development (Chandler 1977). Teulings' (1986) analysis will help illustrate this approach. Teulings has argued that following the development of capitalist economies, management has undergone a process of increasing differentiation. Historical analyses show that management has progressively developed from a state marked by an identity of entrepreneurial and labour control functions, through the emergence of an organisational apparatus concerned with the allocation of investments and an active interest in product markets, to the institutional interest in providing a clear course of action in the face of competition and preserving organisational legitimacy. Thus, in modern large-scale corporations, Teulings argues that four functions of management can be identified: the ownership function concerned with the accumulation of capital and the preservation of legitimacy; the administrative function dealing with the allocation of investments; the innovative function concerned with the development of new product markets; and finally the production function exercising control of the direct labour process.

Thus, the classical, the systems and the historical approaches to management share the assumption that the essence of management can be distilled to a number of functions which need to be carried out in all formal organisations (see Table 2.2), although how they are carried out may differ. The functions of management can be empirically verified by recording observable management practices and sorting them out in terms of superordinate organisational functions which they theoretically fulfil.

Table 2.2   Management functions *vis-à-vis* organisational requirements

Management functions, organisational requirements	Co-ordination	Internal and now	External and future	Identity and legitimacy
Planning			System 4, Innovative function; Administrative function	
Organising	System 2, Production function	Production function		
Leading				System 5, Institutional function
Controlling		System 3, Production function		

Management task characteristics

The functions of management are carried out in organisations whose distinctive nature as semi-autonomous loci of resource allocation and transformation entails certain requirements for what managers have to do. Following a sociological line of enquiry, Whitley (1987; 1989) has sought to delineate the distinguishing characteristics of the tasks that managers have to do as well as the management skills these tasks imply. The nature of management tasks, he argued, stems from two fundamental premises: firstly, the organisational nature of management activities, and secondly, the discretionary nature of management in the allocation, control and use of animate and inanimate resources.

The organisational nature of management arises from the inseparability of management functions from systems of coordinated resource allocation and transformation. For organisations to exist at all, human and material resources must be combined in such a way that their integration generates more value than their individual utilisation (Whitley 1987; 1989). This implies, in turn, that managers must have delegated authority and discretionary rights over the integration of resources so that they can make a difference to the resources being combined and transformed. It is the process of 'authoritative communication' (Barnard 1966) which imparts a distinct, cohesive and relatively continuous character to business organisations.

Based on the above analysis, Whitley (1989) suggested the following five characteristics of managerial tasks:

1   managerial tasks are highly interdependent and context dependent;
2   they are relatively unstandardised;
3   they are developing and fluid;
4   they are oriented towards both the maintenance and innovation of administrative structures, and;
5   they are characterised by the lack of visible outputs which can be directly linked to individual inputs.

In such an account of the characteristics of management tasks, there is no reference to *what* these tasks are *in concreto*. Instead, Whitley's analysis is mainly concerned with outlining the nature of these tasks, not their content.

Management roles

In his well-known study of managerial work, Mintzberg (1973) criticised the classical school of management for offering universal prescriptions of what managers ought to do, but bearing little relationship to what managers actually do. His empirical study sought to redress this imbalance. Mintzberg concluded that managers' jobs can be analysed in terms of ten interrelated roles, namely in terms of ten different sets of behaviours that are attributed to managerial positions. These ten roles were further grouped into three major categories: interpersonal, informational and decisional roles. Similar studies by Stewart (1982) and Kotter (1982) have described various types of roles – not too different from those of Mintzberg – that managers perform in the execution of their tasks.

Mintzberg's study generated some controversy with regard to both the rationale behind his study and the alleged lack of linkage between observable management practices and broader organisational requirements, as well as for the particular conceptualisation of management roles he recommended (Lau *et al.* 1980; Carroll and Gillen 1987). Both Mintzberg and his critics, however, have pointed out that more research is needed in clarifying the links between management roles on the one hand and types of jobs, hierarchical position, organisational effectiveness, industry characteristics; national features, etc., on the other. Mintzberg's assumption seems to have been that management is whatever managers do. This has also been criticised not only on the grounds that inductive generalisations are inherently dubious, but also because of the lack of a priori theoretical criteria to justify the selection of the individuals who have been studied as 'managers' (Hales 1986; Willmott 1984; Whitley 1988; 1989).

Management control

The neo-Marxist approach to management has criticised the preceding perspectives for concentrating excessively on the surface of managerial behaviour at the expense of elucidating the structural basis of managers' power in organisations (Armstrong 1989; Hales 1986; 1989; Willmott 1984; Knights and Willmott 1986; Reed 1989). Proponents of this approach have argued that traditional approaches do not take into account the institutional context by virtue of which management is made possible. An individualist, asocial and contextual view of management remains oblivious to the *raison d'être* of management, which is the maintenance of control over employees in the pursuit of capital accumulation.

Arising from the nature of the relations of production in capitalist economies, management is institutionally compelled to create structures of control over labour in order to transform labour power to actual labour (Thompson 1983). By reducing the study of managers to the study of individual actors on the stage, the script and the setting which enable actors to perform in the first instance are neglected. In short, according to the proponents of the neo-Marxist perspective, the structurally embedded need for managers to be the agents of capital, as well as the processes through which this agency relationship is sustained and reproduced, is what requires theoretical elucidation (Armstrong 1989).

The neo-Marxist approach has in turn been criticised for making too great a conceptual leap from concrete managerial activities to abstract relations of production. In a more sophisticated version, Hales (1989) has attempted to make up for this weakness by suggesting that managers' work be linked to management divisions of labour which depend, in turn, on broad management strategies. The latter emanate from the structural position of management in the process of capital accumulation and reproduction. His analysis seeks to reconcile a labour process analysis of organisations with the management functions of the classical school.

A neo-Marxist perspective on management oscillates between a deterministic conception of managers as the bearers of class relations and a contingency view of managerial work that is tied to the specific circumstances facing organisations. If one, however, relaxes the link between the logic of capitalist relations of production and the characteristics of managerial work by introducing a number of mediating contingencies, the question arises as to whether the influences on managerial work are the result of the nature of capitalism, or simply the tentative effects of specific sets of contingencies. In other words, is there a direct link between capitalist production relations and managerial work?

Outline of a metatheory of management

The preceding cursory review of the literature has served to highlight a tension in the field of management studies: to conceive of managers either in abstract and universal terms, or as simply those individuals who just happened to be wearing the managerial badge. Clearly, the more abstract a conceptualisation of management is, the less empirically refutable it becomes (at least directly). Conversely, the more one observes changes in the roles of managers, the more one is inclined to disagree with an abstract conception of management.

The danger with focusing exclusively on what individual managers *do*, without having some a priori theoretical conception of the basis on which management roles are founded, is that it neglects the crucial question as to what managers are *capable* of doing. An answer to the latter would presuppose that, ontologically, management is endowed with certain powers or capabilities which are not exhausted in their empirical manifestations. An empiricist view of management is, of necessity, confined to the empirical domain (see Table 2.2), namely it cannot see beyond observed managerial practices. An empiricist view is informed by an ontology that collapses the domains of real and actual into the domain of empirical and, consequently, it is unable to define an object of study in terms of its causal capabilities. As Hales (1986: 110) has aptly remarked, an empiricist approach '[is reluctant] to treat managers' *observable* behaviour as problematic and to ask — or keep asking the question: why these behaviours and activities?'

Conversely, while a highly abstract conception of management may sketch the latter's causal capabilities (located in the domain of real — see Table 2.2), it does not make direct links with the empirical manifestations of management at the micro-level of managerial practices. This happens because such an ontology collapses the actual and empirical domains into the real domain. A metatheory of management would have to provide answers to the following questions. When management changes, what is it that changes? What are those who are invested with managerial authority capable of doing, and why? How are the empirical manifestations of managerial practices linked to the capabilities of management? Or to put it in another way, by virtue of what necessary conditions are management practices what they are?

In Figure 2.1 an attempt is made to illustrate how these questions might be answered. TD1, TD2, TD3 and TD4 represent the previously reviewed four theoretical descriptions of management found in the literature. They have been arranged in a sedimented manner to make the point that they refer to four distinct ontological layers of management (i.e. OL1, OL2, OL3 and OL4). Different layers exhibit different dynamics (i.e. rate of temporal change): the closer to the surface, the more likely it is that changes occur (depending on changes of various contingencies); hence the different shape of lines in Figure 2.1. Deeper theoretical descriptions penetrate further down into the object of study and capture new layers. Moving from a phenomenon located at a particular layer to the layer immediately below it reveals the conditions by virtue of which the phenomenon under study is 'made' possible. The ontological core of management is a conceptualisation of its nature and is intrinsically related to the causal powers management possesses. Ultimately, changes in the empirical forms manifested in the other layers are traceable to the causally powerful ontological core (Maki 1985). These claims are now explained in a bit more detail.

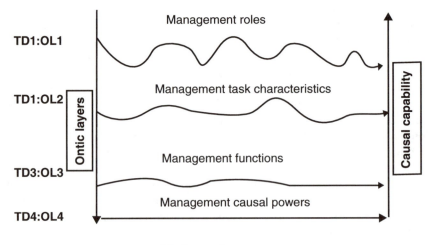

Figure 2.1   A realist redescription of management

1   The study of management roles (TDl, OL1), namely the study of organ-
    ised sets of behaviour identified with managerial positions (Mintzberg
    1973; 1975), has attempted to deal with the directly observable prac-
    tices of managers in carrying out their tasks within specific
    organisations. This type of study is certainly valuable in offering us a
    picture of what managers do, and any further research at this layer will
    have to deal with essentially contingency questions: what are the contin-
    gencies (e.g. type of job, hierarchical position, management strategy,
    type of industry, national features, etc.) which are systematically associ-
    ated with how particular managerial roles emerge, demise or gain
    importance? It seems plausible to assume that it is at this layer that
    management will be most fluid and context dependent. However, 'if our
    descriptions are restricted to the surface level, we are forced to refute or
    modify them every time a substantial change on that level occurs' (Maki
    1985: 128) – hence the need for deeper theoretical descriptions.

2   Why are management roles what they are? Or, to put it differently,
    what must the necessary conditions be for management roles to be what
    they are? To answer this question one needs to look for an explanation at
    a yet deeper layer of management. The perspective on the nature of
    management tasks (TD2, OL2) is in a position to yield some answers.
    For instance, the high interdependence of managerial tasks noted by
    Whitley (1989) gives rise to certain interpersonal and informational
    roles observed by Mintzberg (1973) and others. Similarly, the manage-
    rial concern with both continuity and innovation that has been
    emphasised by Whitley implies the existence of roles such as resource
    allocating, disturbance handling and entrepreneurship – all of them
    subsumed by Mintzberg under the rubric of decisional roles. As it will
    have, hopefully, become clear by now, the reasoning behind this analysis
    is that for particular management roles to be possible a certain configu-
    ration of management task characteristics must be in place.

3   By virtue of what features of management is a configuration of manage-
    ment task characteristics what it is? Again, to answer this question one
    needs to move into a deeper layer of management. The existence of
    specific management functions is a necessary condition for the existence
    of a configuration of management task characteristics. Indeed, a study of
    management functions (TD3, OL3) helps explain the derivation of the
    task characteristics of management. According to Whitley (1989), the
    particular nature of management tasks emanates from the organisational
    and discretionary nature of management. Following Penrose's (1959)
    analysis of the nature of the firm, Whitley (1989: 212) argues that since
    managerial activities are constitutive of firms as administrative systems
    controlling economic resources, they are clearly organisational in nature.
    It is by establishing, maintaining and improving some system for co-
    ordinating and controlling resources that they fulfil their economic

function, and so managerial work is inherently collective and interdependent.

4   In other words, it is by virtue of the fact that managers are organisationally compelled to make a difference to the resources they combine via performing the functions of planning, organising, leading, controlling, etc., that certain characteristics of management tasks are possible.

5   Finally, in the same vein of questioning, by virtue of what conditions are management functions possible? An answer to this question 'closes' the argument about the nature of management and its empirical manifestations, by locating management into its wider socio-economic context and conceptualising the manner in which this context endows management with a set of causal powers (namely, it imparts to management a necessary way of acting). The causal powers attributed to management 'reside' in the domain of real and are not directly observable in the empirical domain (TD4, OL4).

The neo-Marxist perspective on management has emphasised the centrality of management control in securing the transformation of labour power to actual labour in the context of capitalist relations of production. The excessive preoccupation, however, with the substantive issue of control, as well as an ontologically undifferentiated view of reality and our knowledge of it, renders this perspective incapable of focusing on causal powers of management *other* than control, and gives it a deterministic character (cf. Littler and Salaman 1982; Kelly 1985; Storey 1985). Later, a conceptualisation of the causal powers of management will be suggested which makes the existence of certain management functions possible.

Management, understood as a collective institutional process, is rendered possible by virtue of the industrial structure that underlies the empirically

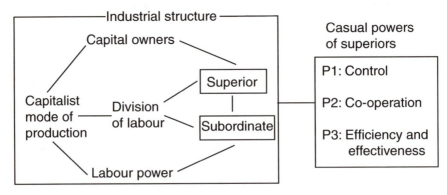

Key: — Necessary relation

Figure 2.2   Industrial structure and the causal powers of management

accessible surface of modern business organisations (Heilbroner 1985). This industrial structure consists of superiors (i.e. management), subordinates, the division of labour, the existence of capital owners, the existence of labour power and the capitalist mode of production (see Figure 2.2). Within this structure there are particular positions that endow their holders with a theoretically necessary way of acting. By virtue of being part of the industrial structure, management is vested with a set of causal powers that defines its nature.

It is suggested here that the causal powers of management are the following:

1   The ability to *control* the transformation of labour power of subordinates to actual labour (Braverman 1974; Burawoy 1979; Thompson 1983). In contrast to the inanimate nature of other production factors, the indeterminacy of labour potential compels management to construct suitable regulatory mechanisms for the translation of labour power to actual labour. The problem for management here is twofold: how, on the one hand, to avail itself of the 'open' nature of labour (i.e. human capacity for self-development and learning, as well as for innovative responses to unanticipated stimuli) by increasing its potential; and on the other hand, how to channel this potential into wider organisational targets which are not necessarily of the subordinates' choosing.

2   The ability to elicit active *co-operation* from subordinate members through the provision of material and symbolic rewards. This again stems from the need to transform labour power to actual labour, and from the 'open' nature of labour. The nature of rewards varies with the superordinate sets of values that are legitimate in different organisations, industries and societies, as well as depending on the individuals involved. As we know from cybernetics (cf. Ashby 1956; Beer 1985; Clemson 1984) no system of regulation is comprehensive enough to achieve complete control over the system to be regulated. This means that labour power must always be, at least in part, self-regulating. Consequently, the active co-operation of subordinates is a *conditio sine qua non* for the operation of an organisation (Castoriadis 1987).

3   The drive towards *efficiency and effectiveness* (cf. Lupton 1986). In the context of competitive product markets and scarcity of resources, managers are organisationally compelled to 'make a difference' to the resources they manage, so that their integrated utilisation generates more value than their separate use (Watson 1986; Whitley 1989). Also organisational outputs must be at least minimally valued and legitimated in the context of specific societies, if the organisation is to have a relatively continuous existence.

The preceding set of causal powers is related intrinsically to the nature of management in market economies; it is also a contradictory set. The effects generated through the exercise of these contradictory powers are contingent upon prevailing conditions at the organisational, sectoral and societal levels. Furthermore, causal powers are not immutable: they can be augmented or diminished depending on wider shifts in societal power relations, and/ or on contingent organisational or sectoral factors. For instance, labour resistance, or labour market and product market conditions, may favour an emphasis on co-operation rather than on control, or vice versa (Lupton *et al.* 1981; Friedman 1977; Kelly 1985). Additionally, management preferences and value systems may influence the manner in which causal powers are exercised (Watson 1986).

The exercise of causal powers raises inevitably the issue of *choice*: as causal powers are only tendencies 'residing' in the domain of real and they may or may not produce a desirable set of effects in the domain of empirical, it follows that it is incumbent upon management to construct those mechanisms which will render the appearance of certain sets of effects possible. In other words, management must create conditions of organisational *quasi-closure* so that certain activities of interest are controlled (e.g. the translation of labour power to actual labour, the smooth function of technology, etc.) and particular results are obtained. Thus although the causal powers of management operate in open systems it is only when quasi-closed systems are *constructed* that a set of desirable regularities accrues.

Thus, to summarise the argument, the nature of management stems from the incorporation of superiors into the industrial structure. The latter endows management with a set of causal powers which are related intrinsically to its nature. Causal powers reside in the domain of real and the effects of their contradictory composition are contingent upon prevailing contingencies. It is by virtue of management's causal powers of control, co-operation, and efficiency and effectiveness that the carrying out of the previously outlined management functions is possible. Management causal powers *and* their contingent exercise compel managers to plan, organise, lead and regulate. Research at this layer of management ought to outline the crucial contingencies facing organisations or populations of organisations in particular societal contexts (e.g. labour and product markets, technological developments, etc.) and the relevant management strategies in response to those contingencies, and link management strategies with the empirical exercise of management causal powers (cf. Friedman 1977). For example, as Friedman (1977), Kelly (1985) and Littler (1982), among others, have shown, particular shifts in product and labour markets may give rise to distinctive management strategies regarding the management of the employment relationship, which emphasise either co-operation or control. Thus the activation of the causal power of control or co-operation depends on the particular circumstances an organisation finds itself in, and this is an empirical matter.

Conclusions

In this paper, it has been argued that a metatheory of management is necessary in order (a) to elucidate the nature of management, and (b) to delineate the scope of applicability of various perspectives on management. By adopting the ontological assumptions and the epistemological principles of the realist paradigm, the initial steps towards constructing such a metatheory have been taken in this paper. Four distinctive perspectives on management have been presented briefly. Each one of them refers to only certain aspects of management. The management roles perspective focuses on the observable practices of managers and attempts to offer a typology of the various management roles, as well as to link the latter to various job, organisational and environmental contingencies. The management task characteristics perspective outlines the dominant features of management tasks, while the management functions perspective delineates the functions managers need to carry out in response to given organisational requirements. Finally, the neo-Marxist perspective locates management in its wider socio-economic context, and argues that management control is the most salient characteristic of management in market economies.

All the preceding perspectives deal with different aspects of management in a manner that may appear too heterogeneous to synthesise. However, drawing on the realist paradigm, it has been suggested here that these perspectives can be conceived as dealing with four different, yet logically connected, ontological layers of management. Each layer constitutes a relatively autonomous area of study, and the transition from one layer to the one below it denotes an interest in penetrating deeper into the object of study and investigating the conditions that render the preceding layer possible. Different layers exhibit different rates of change depending on how various contingencies influence a particular layer.

The rationale behind the conceptualisation of management as a sedimented structure has been the following. For a particular set of management *roles* (i.e. what managers actually do) to be possible, management *tasks* (i.e. what managers have to do given the organisational nature of their activities) must possess certain characteristics. Similarly, for management tasks to have the features that they do, certain management functions (i.e. what has to happen for an organisation to be managed) need to be carried out. Finally, for management functions to be what they are, management must have a certain nature (described here as a set of *causal powers*) which endows management with a theoretically necessary way of acting. The causal powers of management derive their existence from management's incorporation into the industrial structure. They 'reside' in the real domain and, taken together, their logics are contradictory. The concrete effects of the exercise of management causal powers are dependent on prevailing contingencies at the organisational or interorganisational levels.

This metatheoretical conceptualisation of management presents three advantages. Firstly, it gets away from the atheoretical, empiricist view of management which confines itself to the observable management practices only. Empiricists are unable to offer explanations of the *possibility* of these practices as well as outlining what managers are *capable* of doing, instead of merely noting what they are doing.

Secondly, the various perspectives on management have been logically related to each other, thus defining their individual scope of reference. At the same time, while the analysis presented here is avowedly structuralist in orientation it is not deterministic: the existence of particular features of management at a particular layer is only a *necessary* (but not sufficient) condition for the existence of features at the preceding layer. It is worth noting that the conceptualisation adopted here leaves room for other causal influences on management (e.g. ethnicity, gender, etc.) to be analogously conceptualised (cf. Whittington 1992).

Finally, the metatheoretical outline proposed here moves beyond the 'either/or' polarisation that management literature has hitherto exhibited, namely conceiving of management either as a collective institutional necessity or as a set of individual practices. Indeed, as argued above, management is both of these things plus a few more; hence its inherent ambiguity in being conceived in impersonal institutional terms *and* as personalised practices. As one moves from the ontological core to the empirically observable layers (see Table 2.1), management increasingly becomes more personalised – that is, 'management' is identified with managers. Conversely, in moving from the empirically observable management roles to the causal powers that have been imputed to management (see Table 2.1), the latter acquires the features of abstract institutional necessity, removed from the concrete practices of managers. Thus, depending on the level of analysis chosen, legitimately management can be approached differently, and in that respect I hope to have shown the scope of application of otherwise diverse theoretical perspectives.

Bibliography

Armstrong, P. (1989) 'Management, labour process and agency', *Work, Employment and Society*, 3, 3: 307–22.

Ashby, R. W. (1956) *An Introduction to Cybernetics*, London: Chapman and Hall.

Barnard, C. (1966) *The Functions of the Executive*, Cambridge, MA: Harvard University Press.

Beer, S. (1981) *Brain of the Firm*, Chichester: Wiley.

——(1985) *Diagnosing the System for Organizations*, Chichester: Wiley.

Berger, P. (1987) *The Capitalist Revolution*, Aldershot: Gower.

Bhaskar, R. (1978) *A Realist Theory of Science*, New York: Harvester Press.

Braverman, H. (1974) *Labour and Monopoly Capital*, New York: Monthly Review Press.

Buchanan, D. and Boddy, D. (1983) *Organizations in the Computer Age: Technologist Imperatives and Strategic Choice*, Aldershot: Gower.

Burawoy, M. (1979) *Manufacturing Consent: Changes in the Labour Process under Monopoly Capitalism*, Chicago: University of Chicago Press.

Carroll, S. I. and Gillen, D. J. (1987) 'Are the classical management functions useful in describing managerial work?', *Academy of Management Review*, 12, 1: 38–51.

Castoriadis, C. (1987) *The Imaginary Institution of Society*, Cambridge: Polity Press.

Chandler, A. (1977) *The Visible Hand*, Cambridge, MA: Harvard University Press.

Clemson, B. (1984) *Cybernetics: A New Management Tool*, Tunbridge Wells: Abacus Press.

Daft, R. (1988) *Organisation Theory and Design*, St Paul, MN: West.

Fayol, H. (1949) *General and Industrial Management*, London: Pitman.

Friedman, A. L. (1977) *Industry and Labour*, London: Macmillan.

Giddens, A. (1976) *New Rules of Sociological Method*, London: Hutchinson.

——(1984) *The Constitution of Society*, Cambridge: Polity Press.

Hales, C. P. (1986) 'What do managers do? A critical review of the evidence', *Journal of Management Studies*, 23, 1: 88–115.

——(1989) 'Management processes, management divisions of labour and managerial work: towards a synthesis', *International Journal of Sociology and Social Policy*, 9, 5/6: 9–38.

Harré, R. (1989) 'Modes of explanation', in D. Hilton (ed.) *Contemporary Science and Natural Explanation: Commonsense Conceptions of Causality*, Brighton: Harvester, 129–44.

Harré, R. and Madden, E. H. (1975) *Causal Powers*, Oxford: Blackwell.

Harré, R. and Secord, P. F. (1972) *The Explanation of Social Behaviour*, Oxford: Blackwell.

Heilbroner, R. (1985) *The Nature and Logic of Capitalism*, New York: Norton.

Kelly, J. (1985) 'Management's redesign of work: labour process, labour markets and product markets', in D. Knights, H. Willmott and D. Collinson (eds) *Job Redesign*, Aldershot: Gower, 30–51.

Knights, D. and Willmott, H. (eds.) (1986) *Managing the Labour Process*, Aldershot: Gower.

Koontz, H. and O'Donnell, C. (1955) *Principles of Management: An Analysis of Managerial Functions*, New York: McGraw-Hill.

Kotter, J. P. (1982) *The General Managers*, New York: Free Press.

Lau, A. W., Newman, A. R. and Broedling, L. A. (1980) 'The Nature of Managerial Work in the Public Sector', *Public Management Forum*, 19: 513–21.

Littler, C. R. (1982) *The Development of the Labour Process in Capitalist Societies*, Aldershot: Gower.

Littler, C. R. and Salaman, G. (1982) 'Bravermania and beyond: recent theories of the labour process', *Sociology*, 16, 2: 252–69.

Lupton, T. (1986) 'The management of change to advanced manufacturing systems', in T. Lupton (ed.) *Human Factors: Man, Machine and New Technology*, Bedford: IFS Publications, 85–200.

Lupton, T., Tanner, I. and Schnelle, T. (1981) 'Humanistic design of manufacturing systems in western Europe', *Design Studies*, 2, 2: 83–96.

Mahoney, T. A., Jerdee, T. H. and Carroll, S. J. (1965) 'The jobs of management', *Industrial Relations*, 4: 97–110.

Maki, U. (1985) 'Issues in redescribing business firms', in K. Lilja, K. Rasanen and R. Tainio (eds) *Proceedings of the First Summer Seminar of the Group on the Theory of the Firm, 7–8 August 1984*, Espoo, Finland, Helsinki School of Economics, Studies B-73.

Manicas, P. (1980) 'The concept of social structure', *Journal for the Theory of Social Behaviour*, 10, 2: 65–82.

Miller, J. G. (1978) *Living Systems*, New York: McGraw-Hill.

Mintzberg, H. (1973) *The Nature of Managerial Work*, New York: Harper & Row.

——(1975) 'The manager's job: folklore and fact', *Harvard Business Review*, 53, 4: 49–61.

Mitroff, I. (1988) 'Crisis management: cutting through the confusion', *Sloan Management Review*, 29, 2: 15–20.

Morgan, G. (1986) *Images of Organisation*, Beverly Hills, CA: Sage.

Outhwaite, W. (1983) 'Toward a realist perspective', in G. Morgan (ed.) *Beyond Method: Strategies for Social Research*, Beverly Hills, CA: Sage, 321–30.

——(1987) *New Philosophies of Social Science: Realism, Hermeneutics and Critical Theory*, London: Macmillan.

Penrose, E. (1959) *The Theory of the Growth of the Firm*, Oxford: Blackwell.

Poole, M. S. and Van der Ven, A. (1989) 'Toward a general theory of innovation processes', in A. Van de Yen, H. Angle and M. S. Poole (eds) *Research on the Management of Innovation*, New York: Harper & Row, 637–62.

Reed, M. (1989) *The Sociology of Management*, Brighton: Harvester Wheatsheaf.

Robbins, S. (1991) *Management*, third edition, Englewood Cliffs, NJ: Prentice Hall International.

Sayer, A. (1984) *Method in Social Science: A Realist Approach*, London: Hutchinson.

Shrivastava, P., Mitroff, I., Miller, D. and Miglani, A. (1988) 'Understanding industrial crises', *Journal of Management Studies*, 25: 285–303.

Simon, H. (1957) *Administrative Behavior*, New York: Macmillan.

Stewart, R. (1982) 'A model for understanding managerial jobs and behavior', *Academy of Management Review*, 7: 7–14.

Storey, J. (1985) 'Management control as a bridging concept', *Journal of Management Studies*, 22: 269–91.

Taylor, F. W. (1911) *The Principles of Scientific Management*, New York: Harper.

Teulings, A. W. M. (1986) 'Managerial labour processes in organised capitalism: the power of corporate management and the powerlessness of the manager', in D. Knights and H. Willmott (eds) *Managing the Labour Process*, Aldershot, Gower, 142–65.

Thompson, P. (1983) *The Nature of Work: An Introduction to Debates on the Labour Process*, Basingstoke: Macmillan.

Tsoukas, H. (1989) 'The validity of idiographic research explanations', *Academy of Management Review*, 14: 551–61.

Turner, J. (1987) 'Analytical theorising', in A. Giddens and J. Turner (eds) *Social Theory Today*, Cambridge: Polity Press.

Watson, T. J. (1986) *Management, Organisation and Employment Strategy: New Directions in Theory and Practice*, London: Routledge.

Whitley, R. (1987) 'Taking firms seriously as economic actors: towards a sociology of firm behaviour', *Organisation Studies*, 8: 125–47.

——(1988) 'The management sciences and managerial skills', *Organisational Studies*, 9, 1: 47–68.

——(1989) 'On the nature of managerial tasks and skills: their distinguishing characteristics and organisation', *Journal of Management Studies*, 26: 209–24.

Whittington, R. (1992) 'Putting Giddens into action: social systems and managerial agency', *Journal of Management Studies*, 29, 6: 693–712.

Williamson, O. E. (1975) *Markets and Hierarchies*, New York: Free Press.

Willmott, H. (1984) 'Images and ideals of managerial work: a critical examination of conceptual and empirical accounts', *Journal of Management Studies*, 21, 3: 349–68.

3 In praise of duality and dualism

Rethinking agency and structure in organisational analysis

Michael I. Reed

Introduction

The 'agency/structure debate' refuses to lie down or quietly fade into obscurity. It raises fundamental questions about the nature of social reality, the manner in which it is conceptualised and the theoretical means most appropriate in explaining the relationship between its constituent elements. In raising unavoidable, and difficult, questions about the nature of and link between 'human activity and its social contexts' (Layder 1994: 5), the 'agency/structure debate' forces students of organisation to confront a set of issues that defines irrevocably the constitution of their subject matter and the analytical and methodological terms on which it is to be researched and explained (Reed 1988).

If, as Archer (1995: 22) suggests, 'ontology ... acts as both gatekeeper and bouncer for methodology', then the ways in which we define the nature of and relationship between social action and structural constraint will tightly regulate the terms on which we understand and account for 'organisation'. It will also have major implications for the ways in which we, as students of organisation, evaluate the state of affairs to which the latter concept refers and the strategies through which they are preserved and/or transformed – in short, for ethics and politics. In these respects, then, the 'agency/ structure' debate continues to haunt organisation studies with ontological, analytical and methodological dilemmas that cannot be simply 'wished away' or contained within a form of philosophical quarantine so that empirical social scientists can be set free to get on with the business of research and analysis unencumbered by epistemological angst. The ways in which we engage with these dilemmas – and avoidance is inevitably a form of (dis)engagement – frames what we, as students of organisation, do, how we do it and why it matters. This relatively tight coupling between ontology, methodology and theory entails that decisions about the constitution of our subject matter and the precise links between its constituent analytical components will have ramifying effects throughout the social practice in which we are engaged and the social structures it reproduces. A retreat back into a golden age of philosophical innocence and/or empirical pragmatism is unlikely to be an attractive or viable option when the 'genie' of ontological and epistemological reflection has been let out of the bottle and there is no chance of forcing or coaxing it back in.

In this paper, a number of claims are advanced about the current 'state of play' in the 'agency/structure' debate in organisation studies. Overall, they suggest that a number of highly influential theoretical interventions in contemporary organisational analysis have encouraged the widespread acceptance of a 'flat' or 'compacted' social ontology that has debilitating explanatory and political consequences. These claims establish a wider intellectual context in which a critical realist position is developed as providing a 'layered' or 'stratified' social ontology on which more structurally robust and inclusive theoretical approaches and explanations can be constructed. While a number of substantive theoretical approaches are seen to be consistent with a critical realist position (Outhwaite 1987), the paper concludes with the argument that the approaches reviewed in the first section of the paper cannot be reconciled with the latter. As such, they are seen to reduce the explanatory power of organisational analysis and to weaken the wider ethical and political significance that it entails.

Against dualism

The underlying trajectory of theoretical development in organisation analysis over the last two decades or so has been to reject the binary or dualistic mode of thinking enshrined in the 'agency/structure' debate as a precondition for transcending its outmoded and redundant terms of reference. Participation within the latter necessarily entailed the formulation of a crucial analytical distinction between actors' abilities to engage in forms of social conduct that 'make a difference to the world' (Giddens 1984), as opposed to the objective structural conditions or constraints which limit and regulate the innate transformative capacity of social action. It also required the, however crude, assignment of relative explanatory weights or priorities to one or other of the binary elements within this analytical divide. Once these analytical elements were conceptually separated, they had to be linked or realigned through an explanatory logic accounting for their interplay and the emergent outcomes that it generated. In both these respects, involvement within the 'agency/structure' debate necessitated a confrontation with social ontology and a recognition of the significance of that engagement for theory construction and development. Out of this confrontation, some form of analytical dualism usually emerged that highlighted the simultaneous interaction and separation of 'agency' and 'structure' over time.

It is exactly this 'confrontation with social ontology' and its ramifying analytical implications that has been refused by a growing body of theoretical opinion within organisational studies as represented in approaches such as ethnomethodology, actor–network theory and poststructuralism (Cooper 1992; Knights 1992; Law 1994; Clegg 1994; Chia 1994; 1996). These approaches articulate a shared commitment to a social ontology that dispenses with the need to distinguish analytically between different levels or forms of social reality as represented in the 'agency/structure' distinction. They also set out to eradicate the putative explanatory deformities which result from this dualistic mode of thinking. Thus, for rather different reasons and in different ways, ethnomethodology, actor–network theory and Foucauldian-inspired poststructural theory offer distinctive theoretical approaches to the study of organisation that break with the endemic dualism and determinism they perceive in alternative frameworks which continue to take their ontological and analytical cue from the 'agency/structure' debate such as institutional theory (Powell and Dimaggio 1991; Scott 1995) and structuration theory (Giddens 1979; 1984; 1990).

All three of the previously mentioned theoretical approaches also share in and contribute to what, somewhat loosely, might be referred to as the post-modernist 'turn' or 'sensibility' (Reed 1993; Layder 1994; Morrow and Brown 1994; Sayer 1995) in which the search for ontological order and explanatory coherence is rejected as a fallacy perpetrated by 'representationalist' methodologies (Gergen 1992; Chia 1996; Knights 1997). Representationalism is an epistemological doctrine which suggests that scientific research and analysis can produce an objective, exact and unmediated copy or simulacrum of the reality to which it pertains. Various analytical, methodological and theoretical manipulations are then legitimated, and privileged, on the basis of this quest to 'represent accurately in our minds using linguistic or visual forms what the world "out there" is really like' (Chia 1996: 36). Those sympathetic to a postmodernist ethos reject representationalism and realism as perpetrating a myth of moral and political neutrality and a 'subject/object' ontological dualism that cannot be sustained in the light of recent findings in the sociology and philosophy of science (Knights 1992). For them, social analysis focuses on a highly fragmented, disordered and contingent reality. The latter can only be understood on the basis of the linguistic, analytical and cultural resources that researchers must rely on in constructing a highly partial and selective account of its constituents and their interrelationships.

Relocated within this critique of representationalism, the 'agency/structure' debate is seen as a fundamental obstacle to recognising that '*reality* is in perpetual flux and transformation and hence unrepresentable through any *static* conceptual framework or paradigm of thought' (Chia 1996: 46, italics in original). By rejecting the highly static, mechanistic and deterministic ontology on which the various positions taken up within the 'agency/structure' debate have traded, theoretical approaches that are sympathetic to the postmodernist turn in social and organisational analysis – particularly in regard of its one-level, process-dominated social ontology and its inherent analytical tendency to collapse agency and structure into localised or micro-level social practices – offer a very different explanatory agenda and dynamic to that proffered by more structurally inclined perspectives. Thus, substantive theoretical approaches in contemporary organisational analysis such as ethnomethodology, actor–network theory and Foucauldian poststructuralism converge around a shared hostility to stratified social ontologies, analytical dualisms and representational methodologies. In their place, they work with 'flat' or 'horizontal' social ontologies, in which the processual character of social reality totally occupies the analytical and explanatory space available for a form of organisation analysis, in which the socially constructed and mediated nature of scientific knowledge counteracts the naïve objectivism and determinism of representational methodologies. These approaches occupy a shared epistemological niche in which the study of 'the local, the decentered, the marginal and the excluded is superior to examining what is at the centre' (Rosenau 1992: 136).

Ethnomethodological research has always been preoccupied with the localised and contextualised accounting practices through which 'organisation' achieves a highly precarious and temporary stabilisation of an ever-shifting and fragmented interactional order (Silverman 1975; Heritage 1984; Hassard 1990). Empirical research carried out within an ethnomethodological frame in the 1960s and 1970s, such as Bittner's (1967) classic study of the police on skid row and Zimmerman's (1971) investigation into case workers in a social security organisation, exemplified a radically subjective/micro-level approach that rejected a focus on structural phenomena as legitimate research interests in their own right. Studies such as these maintained that if social structures were not instantiated in talk, discourse or interaction, then they had no ontological status or legitimate explanatory role in organisational analysis. Boden's (1994) recent investigations into the 'business of talk' in a range of administrative, commercial and communication organisations continue to insist that 'organisation' is only brought into existence as a temporary and negotiable institutional reality through the conversational practices and linguistic conventions it instantiates. For her, 'there really is no objective environment for organisations, *all* of whom are dependent on the perceptions of their members, and more centrally, on the ways local perceptions actually *constitute* the conditions of next actions and thereby outcomes' (Boden 1994: 38, italics in original). As institutions, that is as that highly transient and mobile historical practice we call 'structure', organisations are literally 'talked into being' (Boden 1994: 215). This provides a classic restatement of a single-level social ontology that conflates 'agency' and 'structure' in such a way that they are analytically rendered down to localised social practices bereft of any institutional underpinnings or contextualisation. The ontological status and explanatory power of 'structure' – that is, as a concept referring to relatively enduring institutionalised relationships between social positions and practices located at different levels of analysis that constrain actors' capacities to 'make a difference' – is completely lost in a myopic analytical focus on situated social interaction and the local conversational routines through which it is reproduced.

Actor–network theory (Law 1992; 1994) shares a common analytical focus with ethnomethodology on the local and heterogeneous 'orderings' that make organisation possible as a highly contingent and essentially unstable patterning of the constant ebb and flow of social interaction. Institutions, organisations and actors are viewed as the temporary products or effects of micro-level processes of ordering and patterning that fashion the interactional chains through which social structuring is practically realised. Thus, the latter are regarded as inherently precarious and fragile attempts to contain and sculpt social interaction so that it, at least partially, conforms to certain representational and technological expectations. Once again, micro-level practices and patterns are to be regarded as the 'ontological bedrock' on which organisational analysis is to be conducted (Chia 1994). This position simply reinforces the trend towards a de-institutionalised or 'miniaturised' conception of organisation in which any form of sustained structural analysis is conspicuous by its absence.

Law's (1994) specification of actor–network theory articulates an approach to the study of organisation in which 'agents' and 'organisations' are treated as the effects of a process of temporarily integrating heterogeneous materials and local narratives through which questions of 'degree, of quantities, of gradients, as well as qualities' (Law 1994: 33–4) are settled. He makes passing reference to the 'political economy of representation in enterprise' and to the role that it plays in shaping social interaction (Law 1994: 27). Yet, this faint, and some-what muffled, analytical and explanatory gesture towards relatively enduring institutional or structural phenomena and their constraining influence is not developed to any significant degree. The world of the actor–network theorist, as that of the ethnomethodologist, seems to consist almost totally of verbs and hardly any nouns; there is only process, and structure is regarded as its passing effect. Structure is denied any kind of ontological status or explanatory power as a relatively enduring entity that takes on stable institutional and organisa-tional forms generating scarce resources that actors, both individual and collective, have to draw on in a selective and constrained manner before they can 'move on' and 'make a difference'. We are left with an entirely process-driven conception of organisation in which any, even residual, sense of social structures 'possessing properties which can be understood to be relatively independent of the agents whose behaviour is subject to their influence' (Layder 1990: 23) dissolves away in the analytical fascination with the local, contingent and indeterminate. Schumpeter's (1974: 12–130) warning that

> social structures, types and attitudes are coins that do not readily melt. Once they are formed, they persist, possibly for centuries … things economic and social move by their own momentum and the ensuing situ-ations compel individuals and groups to behave in certain ways whatever they may wish to do – not indeed by destroying their freedom of choice but by shaping the choosing mentalities and by narrowing the possibili-ties from which to choose

is conveniently forgotten in a cacophony of celebrations to the essential flux, fragmentation and indeterminacy of social reality.

It is Foucauldian-inspired poststructuralist analysis that has advocated most strongly a form of analysis in which micro-level concerns, localised interactional orders and cultural/representational practices predominate to the virtual exclusion of enduring structures of material, social and political power. Certain aspects of Foucault's work (1979; 1981; 1991) have been appropriated to formulate and defend a structural interpretation and analysis of long-term shifts in control regimes where punishment-centred and coercive systems gradually give way to therapeutic modes of self-surveillance and discipline (Reed 1996a). Nevertheless, his writings have largely been exploited and appropriated to legitimate repeated deconstruction of the concept of organisation into a miniaturised, decentred and localised discursive or representational practice. In turn, this results in a radical ontological and theoretical self-denial of any form of realist or structuralist analysis which flirts with hierarchical or stratified conceptions of social reality and the analytical distinctions between agency and structure on which they necessarily trade.

Foucault's abiding distrust of the universalising and totalising impulse that he perceives in all forms of realist and/or structuralist analyses that consort with notions of 'sovereign power' (Wolin 1988; Burrell 1988; Garland 1990; McNay 1994) has received a very warm welcome in a number of intellectual quarters within organisation studies that are sympathetic to the irreverent, subversive and tactical thrust of his detailed and meticulous examination of the operation of 'bio-power' (Alvesson and Willmott 1992; Gane and Johnson 1993; Jermier *et al.* 1994; Barry *et al.* 1996). The latter, Foucault argues, refers to a control regime in which increasing areas of individual and collective life are subjected to a continuum of political technologies and administrative mechanisms directed to the subjugation of bodies and large-scale population management (Foucault 1981: 141–2). It signifies

> nothing less than the entry of life into history, that is, the entry of the phenomena peculiar to the life of the human species into the order of knowledge and power, into the sphere of political techniques ... a relative control over life averted some of the imminent risks of death. In the space for movement thus conquered, and broadening and ordering that space, methods of power and knowledge assumed responsibility for the life processes and undertook to control and modify them.
>
> (Foucault 1981: 141–2)

It is these methods of power and knowledge, intimately connected to the development and diffusion of bio-power, that provide the substantive focus for Foucault's organisational analysis (Cooper and Burrell 1988; Burrell 1988). Such an analysis rests on a view of the social world as consisting only in and through an endless, and ultimately meaningless, series of power games bereft of any enduring institutional rationale or structural embodiment (Mouzelis 1995: 43–5). This conception of socio-organisational reality as an amorphous, fragmented and indeterminate process is analytically aligned with a deconstructivist methodology that simultaneously manages to efface the contribution that agency makes to structural reproduction and elaboration (Best and Kellner 1991; Archer 1995). It also denies the latter any constraining influence on subsequent phases of social interaction.

By analytically rendering down agency and structure to discursive practice, Foucault and his followers within organisation analysis disconnect the latter from the social actors and the action that initially generated them, while simultaneously obscuring, if not obliterating, the constraining or regulating role that social structures play in the process of institution building. As in the case of ethnomethodology and actor–network theory, we are offered a one-level, unstructured and highly compressed social ontology in which there are no enduring and stratified institutional landscapes within which social actors and action can be located and explained. Agency and structure are analytically conflated in such a way that the interplay between the two and its vital role in reproducing and/or transforming social structures is denied by an ontological vision and explanatory logic that can only 'see' flat social services without the stratified structural relations and mechanisms that give them shape, consistency and continuity over time. Institutional and organisational forms can only be described and interpreted within their local interactional settings or contexts if we are to gain any appreciation of their inherent 'complexity, contingency and fragility ... as transitory manifestations of relations of dominance-subordination and as mere embodiments of an underlying relationship of forces' (Burrell 1988: 232).

Within Foucauldian organisation analysis, this approach has been applied primarily to explore the processes through which organisational subjectivities and identities are formulated repeatedly and reformulated out of the perennial micro-level power struggles and emerging control regimes characteristic of organisational life (Sewell and Wilkinson 1992; Barker 1993; Knights and Vurdubakis 1994; Grey 1994; Star 1995; Liggett and Perry 1995). The overall effect of this empirically-based work on organisational identities and control technologies has been to lose human agency in the constitution of the subject solely through discourse (Newton 1995) and to regard surveillance practices and mechanisms as beyond the influence, much less power, of social actors (Thompson and Ackroyd 1995). By treating analytical dualism as such an unforgivable transgression of ontological rectitude and theoretical respectability, the 'Foucauldians' are unable to see the reciprocity between agency and structure and, perhaps unintentionally, deny both sides of this divide any independent explanatory status or wider socio-political significance. Consequently, there is an analytical retreat into a form of micro-contextual reductionism in which institutionalised power and control are always derived from below, rather than from the social structural mechanisms and locations that generate such practices and through which such structures are elaborated and/or transformed (Porter 1996).

This is entirely consistent with a general Foucauldian/postmodernist ontology and methodology that totally deconstructs socio-historical processes and structural forms into localised discourses and practices that are *sui generis* in terms of their self-reinforcing and self-renewing capacities (Wolin 1988). The recurring matrices of social structures in which social interaction is embedded and the forms of social action through which they become institutionalised are denied any ontological standing or explanatory relevance. Yet, rather than setting agency free as a capacity to shape and change relational structures, this analytical conflation of interactional processes and institutional constraints robs social action of its innate capacity to transform existing arrangements. At most, the latter simply reconfirms the power of pre-existing surveillance and control technologies to determine the micro-level practices through which they are operationalised. This removes the explanatory need for intermediate concepts, such as 'position' (Collier 1994; Archer 1995), to account for the reality of 'the complex and often contradictory relations that exist between different forms of institutionalised power' (McNay 1994: 106). These, middle-range, concepts sensitise us to the recurring interpenetration of agency and structure as it shapes our social reality and to the analytical imperative of separating heuristically these two different aspects of the latter if we are to stand any chance of understanding and explaining the interplay between them and the institutional outcomes it produces.

Taken together – as a family of theoretical approaches with overlapping ontological and analytical resemblances as well as differences – the three perspectives reviewed in this section of the paper, ethnomethodology, actor–network theory and poststructuralist theory, exhibit a shared commitment to a form of organisation analysis that denies the meaning and relevance of the agency/structure duality/dualism. As a result, they attach – both in their theoretical protocols and empirical practice – overwhelming importance to the localised interactional contexts and discursive, representational and technical practices through which 'organisation' is instantiated as a temporary ordering or patterning of the continuous flow of social life. They feel no need to look beyond these micro-level processes and practices because, as far as their advocates are concerned, there is nothing, ontologically or analytically, 'there'; flat ontologies and miniaturised local orderings construct a seductive vision of our social world in which everything and everybody is constantly in a 'state of becoming' and never in a 'condition of being'. This socio-organisational world is disassembled into some of its elemental constituents, but these are never reassembled with a view to gaining a broader understanding of and explanatory purchase on the structural mechanisms through which they were originally generated and are subsequently elaborated. At its most despairing, this vision can degenerate into a Hobbesian nightmare of 'all against all' (Porter 1996) which requires the discipline of some sovereign Leviathan – such as the party, or the market or the nation – to regulate and mitigate its atomising and alienating effects. Nevertheless, it is only by rejecting this vision and putting some, better, alternative in its place that we can equip organisation analysis to engage with a social world in which the duality and dualism of agency and structure receive their just deserts.

Beyond flat ontologies and local orderings

In this section of the paper, critical realism will be proposed as providing the ontological and analytical foundations of that better alternative. It will also be contended that a range of substantive theoretical approaches are consistent with the conceptual foundations that critical realism lays down. However, it will also be argued that the theoretical approaches reviewed in the previous section of the paper cannot, by their very nature, be made compatible with the latter.

Critical realism is based on a philosophy of science most closely associated with the work of Roy Bhaskar (1978a; 1978b; 1979; 1986). Bhaskar develops an ontology and epistemology of science which has major implications for social thought and analysis (Collier 1994). This is true to the extent that the former specifies a general theory of natural necessity in which nature is presumed to exhibit real structures generating real necessities which can be transposed to the social realm. This conception of nature rejects the 'flatlands of the Humean succession of impressions' (Collier 1994: 61) and necessitates a model of scientific practice in which explanation consists of identifying underlying 'generative mechanisms' designating the 'causal powers' of structures as they work themselves through as interacting tendencies to produce complexly codetermined outcomes. Thus, Bhaskar is arguing for an essential unity of method between the natural and social sciences such that both entail the identification and explanation of 'real structures which exist and operate independently of the pattern of events they generate' (Bhaskar 1978a: 3). Consequently, the logic and practice of scientific research and explanation consists of identifying the underlying generative mechanisms that produce manifest phenomena as observable contingent tendencies or patterns.

This realist ontology and epistemology leads Bhaskar to make a *categorical* distinction between human action and social structure; the properties possessed by the latter are fundamentally different from the former to the extent that they pre-exist the social activities through which they are reproduced or transformed. Social structures are not given in, but are presupposed, by social interactions; they are

> *existentially interdependent* but *essentially distinct*. For while society only exists by virtue of human agency, and human agency (or being) always

> presupposes (and expresses) some or other definite social form, they
> cannot be reduced or reconstructed from one another ... The *social
> sciences* abstract from human agency to study the structure of reproduced
> outcomes, the enduring practices and their relations.
>
> (Bhaskar 1986: 123–4, italics in original)

In these terms, Bhaskar rejects the atomistic reductionism of individualistic
theory and the abstracted reificationism of methodological collectivism.
Insofar as the former reduces knowledge of and explanations to society for
people and the latter to groups, they both fail to grasp the 'persistent *relations* between individuals (and groups), and with the relations between these
relations (and between such relations and the nature and the products of
such relations)' (Bhaskar 1979: 28–9). While agency and structure are ontologically interdependent, they refer to two distinct *strata* located within and
reproducing or transforming that network of social relations we call society.
Only by recognising fully the constraining aspects of both social structure
and practice can we begin to understand the complex, and *non-reductive*, relationship between them. This leads Bhaskar to conclude that sociology
requires

> a system of mediating concepts, encompassing both aspects of the
> duality of praxis, designating the 'slots', as it were, in the social struc-
> ture into which active subjects must slip in order to reproduce it; that
> is, a system of concepts designating the 'point of contact' between
> human agency and social structures. Such a point, linking action to
> structure, must *both* endure and be immediately occupied by individ-
> uals. It is clear that the mediating system we need is that of the *positions*
> (places, functions, rules, tasks, duties, rights, etc.) occupied (filled,
> assumed, enacted, etc.) by individuals, and of the *practices* (activities,
> etc.) in which, by virtue of their occupancy of these positions (and visa
> versa), they engage ... positions and practices, if they are to be individu-
> ated at all, can only be done so *relationally*.
>
> (Bhaskar 1979: 40–1, italics in original)

What we have here is a 'nested' social ontology (McLennan 1989: 192–7) in
which social mechanisms and processes operate at different levels of abstraction that tie into each other within a stratified, multilevel and relational
model of society. Enduring social structures are of strategic ontological and
analytical significance to the latter because they consist of multilayered
'positions–practices' through which social relations are reproduced and
transformed. In this respect, 'organisation' can be conceptualised as an
enduring structural form or entity produced, reproduced and transformed
through the engagement of people in 'positions–practices' at different levels
of social organisation that designate the 'points of contact' between human
agency and social structure. Agency and structure are interrelated, but they

possess emergent properties distinct from the level of social reality to which they refer, i.e. social interaction between individuals and groups, as opposed to enduring social relations that 'exist and are reproduced over time, independently of the activities and conceptions of specific groups of individuals who are subject to them' (Layder 1990: 61; see also Archer 1995: 132–4).

Analytical dualism is a methodology required for examining the interplay between these interdependent, but emergent, strata of social reality. Social structures necessarily pre-date the social actions which reproduce and transform them; the former establish the extant limits or constraints within which contemporaneous social situations and sequences of interaction occur. Social actors draw on the, unequally distributed, assets that such pre-existing structures make available as a basis for their engagement in forms of social activity which will reproduce and transform the institutionalised positions–practices in which they are located. This 'conditioning effect' of structure on agency is not one of mechanical determination; rather, it is that the former supplies the 'reasons for different courses of action to those who are differentially positioned' (Archer 1995: 154). Thus, the prior emergence of the relational properties and principles that inhere in social structures necessarily impinge on current actors and their situations as unavoidably they find themselves operating in pre-structured contexts and interests that shape the social struggles in which they are implicated.

It is clear from the previous, and extremely schematic, exposition of Bhaskar's critical realism that a realist position substantially 'raises the stakes in the opposition between structure and agency. In insisting on a realistic interpretation, it may increase the temptation to reduce one to the other' (Outhwaite 1987: 111; see also Urry 1982). However, Outhwaite is confident that this temptation can be resisted if the sociological description and explanation of social structures in realist terms strenuously avoids the reification and determinism of non-realist structuralism (such as Althusserian Marxism), where agents are reduced to 'bearers' of structures and agency to the predetermined outcome of structural imperatives. While the latter approach explains 'action' as the programmed outcome of immutable structural forces and relations, critical realism insists that agency possesses its own 'causal powers' which are revealed in its mediated interplay with structure. The constraining influence of social structure is not, critical realists insist, to be interpreted in terms of impersonal, reified forces that compel people to act in certain ways without them being able to exercise any element of choice. Instead, structural constraints are seen as operating only through the intentional motives and actions of agents, and are thus inherently tied to their capacity to act and 'make a difference'.

On these grounds, 'the realist model of explanation involves three basic steps, the postulation of a possible mechanism, the attempt to collect evidence for or against its existence, and the elimination of possible alternatives' (Outhwaite 1987: 58). Within this general model of explanation, 'structure' takes on a particular explanatory value to the extent that analytically it focuses our attention on the underlying generative mechanisms that reproduce specific structures and the relations between the 'positions–practices' through which social interaction is ordered. By rejecting the action-reductionism consistently exhibited by each of the three theoretical approaches previously reviewed, critical realism provides a general conceptual framework in which the interplay between them, and its implications for the reproduction and transformation of organisations as interrelated networks of 'positions–practices' occupied and engaged in by individuals and groups, can be recognised adequately and explained. This requires that the relative independence or autonomy of social structures and their vital role in contextualising and constraining social interaction between individuals and groups is given the analytical and explanatory significance it is due. This stands in marked contrast to the approaches previously discussed, given their refusal to give either 'structure' or 'agency' their appropriate ontological status and analytical standing as separable but interrelated aspects of social reality. By granting both agency and structure their just ontological and analytical deserts, organisation analysis will be much better placed to describe and explain the complex interplay between structural conditioning and social action as it reproduces or transforms the social forms through which struggles over material and symbolic resources are organised.

Realism and organisational analysis

The realist position outlined in the previous section is entirely consistent with a logic of explanatory pluralism which says that

> there can be no objective 'primacy' of one factor over others within a structural constellation, or of one structural logic over others. Primacy is rather a matter of the local, internal weightings of variables relative to a specific set of concerns.
>
> (McLennan 1989: 263)

However, realism does commit its proponents to a form of 'structural contextualisation' in which macro-level theories identify the structural and developmental parameters within which lower, meso- and micro-level analyses are to be located. In this sense, realism not only rejects the conflation of agency and structure characteristic of theoretical approaches sympathetic to the postmodern turn in organisational analysis, but also rediscovers and revivifies a focus on the more inclusive, extensive and enduring structures in which local orderings and knowledges are necessarily situated (Layder 1993: 231–4). Consequently, the explanatory pluralism entailed within a realist position has definite limits; it cannot admit substantive theoretical approaches to the study of organisation that dissolve structure into agency and consequently remain blind to the structural contextualisation and conditioning of social interaction.

A number of broad theoretical principles can be drawn from the earlier exposition of critical realism to establish a general framework for organisation analysis. First, the study of organisation must rely on a range of substantive theoretical approaches that give due analytical and explanatory weight to agency and structure and to the complex interplay between them. Second, it must recognise the fact that 'agency derives from the simultaneously enabling and constraining nature of the structural principles by which people act' (Whittington 1994: 72). Organisational forms consist of relational structures into which people enter and pre-exist the people who enter into them, and whose activity reproduces or transforms them. They are structures by virtue of the fact that they have spatially, temporally and socially enduring institutional properties that are irreducible to the activities of contemporary agents. Yet, these same structures derive from the historical actions which generated them and which establish a structured context for current action. Such structures are identified through a process of analytical abstraction and are composed of those 'sets of internally related objects or social practices' (Sayer 1992: 92) required to form coherent institutional systems. Thus, the institution of slavery presupposes the relation of master/servant and the structure of private housing rental presupposes relations between landlords and tenants in which the appropriation of an economic surplus by the former from the latter sets the terms on which that relationship is organised. These structures possess certain 'causal powers' or capabilities that explain their 'ways of acting' on social practices. In Layder's (1993: 57–8) view,

> structures have an external dimension and are rather impersonal in nature ... However, institutions are not just an 'external' resource for people to draw on in formulating their behaviour; they also enter into activity in the form of actors' reasons and motivations.

As Tsoukas (1989) has argued, generative mechanism structures reside in objects of study, such as organisation, and cause the latter to act in certain ways. These structures have causal powers which operate 'as tendencies whose activation, as well as the effects of their activation, are not given but contingent' (Tsoukas 1989: 552).

Third, these relational structures necessarily contain contradictory and competing principles of structuration such as class, gender, ethnicity and race (Ferguson 1994) that have to be counterposed against each other in the analytically structured narratives through which we attempt to explain their operation as underlying generative mechanisms and the contingent empirical tendencies which they produce. Fourth, as a mediative concept that identifies analytically the point of contact between relational structures and social conduct, 'organisation' refers to configurations of positions–practices that are struggled over by social actors in their attempts to defend or enhance their assets within enduring hierarchies of economic, political and social power (Savage *et al.* 1992). If we fail to recognise these realities and to incorporate them within our analyses, then we will severely limit our capacity to acknowledge, much less explain, the nature of the phenomena that constitute the subject matter of our field or to provide well-informed critiques of their restrictive influence and emancipatory potential.

Finally, realist explanation and critique in organisation analysis is likely to be advanced most positively through the in-depth analysis of the multiple mechanisms and tendencies that reproduce or transform particular organisational forms – such as bureaucratic control (Reed 1996a; 1996b) – and the outcomes they produce for social actors. This will require students of organisation to construct and assess different, often competing, analytical narratives (Barley and Tolbert 1995) – based on contrasting principles of structuration – of structural reproduction and elaboration (Archer 1995) that allow us to move analytically back and forth between localised situations of co-presence and globalised contexts of absence. As Layder (1990: 124–5) puts it,

> reproduced social relations [such as organisation] stretch forward and backward in time and space in relation to specific instances of social activity ... Analytically, we can say there is a constant 'switching' between these two levels of reality as situated activity unfolds over time.

Critical realism facilitates this switching between different levels of social reality to the extent that it is committed to an explanatory framework which identifies and incorporates

> (a) pre-existent structures as generative mechanisms, (b) their interplay with other objects possessing causal powers and liabilities proper to them in what is a stratified social world, and (c) non-predictable but none-the-less explicable outcomes arising from interactions between the above, which take place in the open system that is society.
>
> (Archer 1995: 159, italics in original)

Whittington (1989: 81) has argued that any form of organisational analysis that bases itself on a realist ontology and explanatory framework must recognise that 'the extent to which actors are also agents depends on the powers society affords them ... institutionalised systems afford actors, by their structural properties, certain definite powers which they deploy, expend and transmit in their interactions'. It is these underlying structures or generative mechanisms and their complex interplay with human agency, as it reproduces or transforms existing organisational forms, that provide the explanatory focus and agenda for a realist organisation theory. While the three approaches reviewed in the first section of this paper – ethnomethodology, actor–network theory and poststructuralist theory – analytically oscillate between the extremes of action reductionism and structural determinism, a realist organisation theory offers a social ontology and explanatory framework in which both the generative capacity and constraining limitations of social structures are accorded due analytical respect. Social structures do not 'take to the streets', but they do constitute the key underlying mechanisms by which enduring organisational forms – such as capitalist corporations and bureaucratic control regimes – are generated, reproduced and transformed. They are of fundamental ontological importance and strategic explanatory significance to any theory of organisation analytically and ideologically anchored in a realist social science.

Selected elements of the latter are evident in a number of recent contributions to the analysis of structural elaboration in capitalist forms of political economy and work organisation. Technological, economic and cultural change within Western capitalist societies is said to undermine established social structures and the distribution of assets and powers that traditionally they made available to collective social actors such as corporations, professions, trade unions and consumers. In turn, this process of global and corporate restructuring is seen to have major consequences for existing organisational control regimes and the shifting pattern of localised distributional outcomes which this produces within specific organisational sites or locales. Thus, recent research by Castells (1989), Zukin (1991) and Casey (1995) provides broad-ranging explorations of the 'interrelations of social structure, especially institutions of power and class, and social reproduction, or of the forms that represent, transmit and transform institutionally embedded power relations' (Zukin 1991: 21).

Castells' research (1989) focuses on the structural crises (rampant inflation, escalating industrial and social conflict, the pervasive effects on energy costs and supplies of the oil stocks, etc.) which were experienced by most Western capitalist political economies in the 1970s and their subsequent restructuring during the 1980s in response to the destabilising effects of the former. In particular, he concentrates on the manifold ways in which the design, development and implementation of new technologies were largely conditioned by the characteristics and logic of the capitalist restructuring process. He shows how information technology was deployed within capitalist restructuring processes to generate a new form of capitalist organisation in which a 'space of flows', rather than a 'place of hierarchies', now constitutes the logic of dominant organisations in the economy, the state and the city. Consistently, analytically he contextualises these transformations in organisational forms within the wider structural configurations in which necessarily they take shape to effect certain substantive outcomes rather than others. For him, the 'fundamental impacts of information technologies are taking place in the organisation of production and management, and in the sphere of the exercise of power by state institutions' (Castells 1989: 5).

The process and outcome of technological change is analysed in relation to the underlying generative mechanisms (capitalist restructuring in the economy and state) that produced it and the substantive organisational outcomes that it facilitates. Three major generative mechanisms are identified as bringing about this shift to a new model of capitalism and its organisational correlates: a higher share of surplus from the production process going to capital and a correspondingly lower share to labour; a substantial shift in the pattern of state intervention from political legitimation and social redistribution to political domination and capital accumulation; and, finally, the accelerated internationalisation of all economic processes to increase profitability and open up new markets for transnational corporations. Taken together, these underlying mechanisms constitute a collective response to the structural challenges faced by Western capitalist political economies from the 1970s onwards. As a complex conjuncture of structural mechanisms, unintendedly they generate a new mode of capitalist production and development in which information processing is the primary source of profitability and 'centralisation/decentralisation' its primary regime of organisational control (Reed 1996a; 1996b).

Zukin (1991) is interested in the link between global economic transformation and local socio-spatial restructuring in a number of North American cities. For her, the localised urban political and cultural structures that mediate global economic change play a

> vital role in revealing the ways in which the 'structural rules of order of the capitalist economy' are translated into forms of social action that transform regional conurbations. As the processes that make and remake the city become more abstract, more dependent on international capital flows, and more responsive to the organisation of consumption than the organisation of production
>
> (Zukin 1991: 54)

so the need to understand the complex interplay between structures of centralised economic and political power and strategies of localised intervention becomes more urgent and relevant. Once again, the model of social reality as a 'nested' hierarchy of structures, reproduced and transformed through social struggle between collective actors differentially positioned within this multilayered and stratified world, emerges as a vital analytical framework for explaining the remaking of the 'landscapes of power' through which North American cities are being transformed.

Finally, Casey's (1995) study of the transformation of work in advanced capitalist societies and its impact on corporate control systems reveals a similar concern with developing the concept of organisation as a mediating mechanism connecting macro-level restructuring with local reordering. She is particularly interested in the ways in which new technologies of surveillance and control are reshaping occupational structures and ideologies established under earlier phases of capitalist industrialisation. The latter provide the pre-existing structures within which current collective actors, such as employers, managers, professions and unions, struggle to control the agenda for technological and organisational change within a global economy that destroys the modes of political and social regulation established under previous phases of capitalist development. Traditional conceptions of occupation, Casey argues, are in terminal decline under the extreme pressures exerted by global restructuring and new systems of corporate surveillance and control that undermine the social status, economic power and cultural capital previously associated with occupationally based divisions of labour. However, the new corporate cultures and structures through which 'pan-occupational' forms of work organisation are socially constructed have to be contextualised and accounted for within the changing global power structures in which they are embedded.

Each of these studies illustrates the kind of organisation analysis that critical realism encourages and legitimates; i.e., a form of organisation analysis that is consistently attuned to the interplay between structure and agency at various levels of analytical abstraction as it shapes the organisational forms through which social reproduction and transformation are realised. By rejecting the one-level, flat ontologies of postmodernist relativism–constructivism and its restricted focus on local orderings, realism provides the analytical means by which a more resourceful and inclusive organisation analysis can be developed. While the latter is consistent with a range of substantive organisation theories that deal with specific problems or issues, it cannot be made consistent with forms of theorising that deny the ontological duality of social practice and the analytical dualism of agency and structure. This necessarily results in the analytical collapsing of structure into agency and its debilitating effect on the explanatory power of any theory of organisation which remains sensitive to the stratified nature of social reality and its implications for social action.

Conclusion

This paper has advanced the view that more recent theoretical interventions in organisational analysis, inspired to a considerable extent by the general ideas and sensibilities associated with postmodernism, have weakened seriously the intellectual capacity and sapped the political will of contemporary researchers to explain 'the forces that lie outside the control and often the comprehension of place-bound actors' (Kumar 1995: 188). Indeed, as Kumar (1995: 188) contends, the various ways in which a more advanced regime of capital accumulation 'typically exploits a wide range of seemingly contingent geographical circumstances, and reconstitutes them as structured elements of its own encompassing logic' simply are lost in a postmodernist celebration of local knowledges and identities. Consequently, postmodernist social and organisation analysis 'sees and applauds diversity as expressions of local autonomy. It misses the hidden forces behind the apparently free play of local self-assertion' (Kumar 1995: 188).

The 'forces' that Kumar refers to can only adequately be theorised and explained by a general analytical framework that facilitates the 'in-depth interpretation of action by situating agents within a context of conditions of which they are ignorant' (Thompson 1989: 177). It has been suggested that critical realism establishes the most promising analytical and explanatory framework for conducting the in-depth analysis of the interplay between structure and agency as it shapes the reproduction and transformation of organisational forms. The study of organisation cannot be confined to what is close to us in time and space and familiar in our everyday lives; it must engage with 'the frame breaking experiences that only come from examining and comprehending organisations operating in other places and other times' (Scott 1995: 151). Those 'frame breaking' experiences are unlikely to be recognised, much less explained, if students of organisation remain wedded to social ontologies and theoretical approaches that are ill-equipped to move beyond immediate social situations and everyday interactional orders. This need to contextualise and explain social interaction by locating it within the broader social structures of which it is a part is vital to rekindling the persistent exercise of a sociological imagination that always connects the 'personal troubles of milieu' with the 'public issues of social structure' (Mills 1959: 6–8). It is only by rediscovering the interplay between agency and structure that the intellectual and political resources required by organisational analysts to keep that vision alive and make it prosper can be sustained. In this way, the development of organisational analysis as 'a social science which, whilst involving both interpretive and explanatory understanding, unifies these in the analysis of structural relations, and the ways in which these affect, and are affected by, the subjective meanings of human beings' (Keat and Urry 1982: 174) becomes a real possibility.

Bibliography

Alvesson, M. and Willmott, H. (1992) *Critical Management Studies*, London: Sage.

Archer, M. (1995) *Realist Social Theory: The Morphogenetic Approach*, Cambridge: Cambridge University Press.

Barker, J. R. (1993) 'Tightening the iron cage: concertive control in self-managing teams', *Administrative Science Quarterly*, 38: 408–437.

Barley, S. R. and Tolbert, P. S. (1995) 'Institutionalisation as structuration: methods and analytical strategies for studying links between action and structure', unpublished manuscript presented at the 'Action, Structure and Organisations' Workshop, 1–12 May, Essec-IMD, Paris.

Barry, A., Osborne, T. and Rose, N. (1996) *Foucault and Political Reason*, London: UCL Press.

Best, S. and Kellner, D. (1991) *Postmodern Theory: Critical Interrogations*, London: Macmillan.

Bhaskar, R. (1978a) 'On the possibility of social scientific knowledge and the limits of naturalism', *Journal for the Theory of Social Behaviour*, 8: 1–28.

——(1978b) *A Realist Theory of Science*, Brighton: Harvester Press.

——(1979) *The Possibility of Naturalism*, Hemel Hempstead: Harvester Wheatsheaf.

——(1986) *Scientific Realism and Human Emancipation*, London: Verso.

Bittner, E. (1967) 'The police on skid row: a study of peacekeeping', *American Sociological Review*, 32: 669–715.

Boden, D. (1994) *The Business of Talk*, Oxford: Polity Press.

Burrell, G. (1988) 'Modernism, postmodernism and organisational analysis 2: the contribution of Michel Foucault', *Organisation Studies*, 9, 2: 221–35.

Casey, C. (1995) *Work, Self and Society after Industrialism*, London: Routledge.

Castells, M. (1989) *The Informational City*, London: Blackwell.

Chia, R. (1994) 'The concept of decision: a deconstructive analysis', *Journal of Management Studies*, 31: 781–806.

——(1996) 'The problem of reflexivity in organisational research: towards a postmodern science of organisation', *Organisation*, 3: 31–60.

Clegg, S. (1994) 'Social theory for the study of organisation', *Organisation*, 1: 149–78.

Collier, A. (1994) *Critical Realism: An Introduction to Roy Bhaskar's Philosophy*, London: Verso.

Cooper, R. (1992) 'Formal organisation as representation: remote control, displacement and abbreviation', in M. Reed and M. Hughes (eds) *Rethinking Organisation: New Directions in Organisation Theory and Analysis*, London: Sage, 254–72.

Cooper, R. and Burrell, G. (1988) 'Modernism, postmodernism and organisational analysis: an introduction', *Organisation Studies*, 9, 1: 91–112.

Ferguson, K. E. (1994) 'On bringing more theory, more voices and more politics to the study of organisation', *Organisation*, 1: 81–100.

Foucault, M. (1979) *Discipline and Punish: the Birth of the Prison*, Harmondsworth: Penguin.

——(1980) *Power/Knowledge: Selected Interviews and Other Writings, 1972–1977*, ed. C. Gordon, Brighton: Harvester Press.

——(1981) *The History of Sexuality. Volume 1, An Introduction*, Harmondsworth: Penguin.

——(1991) 'Governmentality', in G. Burchell, C. Gordon and P. Miller (eds) *The Foucault Effect: Studies in Governmentality*, London: Harvester Wheatsheaf, 87–104.

Gane, M. and Johnson, T. (eds) (1993) *Foucault's New Domains*, London: Routledge.

Garland, D. (1990) *Punishment and Modern Society: A Study in Social Theory*, Oxford: Oxford University Press.

Gergen, K. (1992) 'Organisation theory in the post-modern era', in M. Reed and M. Hughes (eds) *Rethinking Organisation: New Directions in Organisation Theory and Analysis*, London: Sage, 207–26.

Giddens, A. (1979) *Central Problems in Social Theory: Action, Structure and Contradiction in Social Analysis*, London: Macmillan.

——(1984) *The Nation State and Violence*, Oxford: Polity Press.

——(1990) *The Consequences of Modernity*, Oxford: Polity Press.

Grey, C. (1994) 'Career as a project of the self and labour process discipline', *Sociology*, 30: 479–98.

Hassard, J. (1990) 'Ethnomethodology and organisational research: an introduction', in J. Hassard and D. Pym (eds) *The Theory and Philosophy of Organisations*, London: Routledge, 97–108.

Heritage, J. (1984) *Garfinkel and Ethnomethodology*, Oxford: Polity Press.

Jermier, J., Knights, D. and Nord, W. R. (1994) *Resistance and Power in Organisations*, London: Routledge.

Keat, R. and Urry, J. (1982) *Social Theory as Science*, London: Routledge & Kegan Paul.

Knights, D. (1992) 'Changing spaces: the disruptive power of epistemological location for the management and organisational sciences', *Academy of Management Review*, 17: 514–36.

——(1997) 'Organisation theory in the age of deconstruction: dualism, gender and postmodernism revisited', *Organisation Studies*, 18, 1: 1–19.

Knights, D. and Vurdubakis, T. (1994) 'Foucault, power, resistance and all that', in J. Jermier, D. Knights and Walter. N. (eds) *Resistance and Power in Organisations*, London: Routledge, 167–98.

Kumar, K. (1995) *From Post-industrial to Post-modern Society: New Theories of the Contemporary World*, Oxford: Blackwell.

Law, J. (ed.) (1992) *A Sociology of Monsters? Essays on Power, Technology and Domination*, London: Routledge.

——(1994) *Organizing Modernity*, Oxford: Blackwell.

Layder, D. (1990) *The Realist Image in Science*, London: Macmillan.

——(1993) *New Strategies in Social Research*, Oxford: Polity Press.

——(1994) *Understanding Social Theory*, London: Sage.

Liggett, H. and Perry, D. C. (1995) *Spatial Practices*, Thousand Oaks, CA: Sage.

McLennan, G. (1989) *Marxism, Pluralism and Beyond*, Oxford: Polity Press and Blackwell.

McNay, L. (1994) *Foucault: A Critical Introduction*, Oxford: Polity Press.

Mills, C. Wright (1959) *The Sociological Imagination*, New York: Oxford University Press.

Morrow, R. A. and Brown, D. D. (1994) *Critical Theory and Methodology*, London: Sage.

Mouzelis, N. (1995) *Sociological Theory: What Went Wrong? Diagnosis and Remedies*, London: Routledge.

Newton, T. (1995) *Managing Stress: Emotion and Power at Work*, London: Sage.

Outhwaite, W. (1987) *New Philosophies of Social Science: Realism, Hermeneutics and Critical Theory*, London: Macmillan.

Porter, S. (1996) 'Contra-Foucault: soldiers, nurses and power', *Sociology*, 30: 59–78.

Powell, W. W. and DiMaggio, P. J. (1991) *The New Institutionalism in Organisational Analysis*, Chicago: University of Chicago Press.

Reed, M. I. (1988) 'The problem of human agency in organisational analysis', *Organisation Studies*, 9, 1: 33–6.

——(1993) 'Organisations and modernity: continuity and discontinuity in organisation theory', in J. Hassard and M. Parker (eds) *Postmodernism and Organisations*, London: Sage, 163–82.

——(1996a) 'From the cage to the gaze? The dynamics of organisational control in high modernity', unpublished manuscript presented at 'European Management and Organisations in Transition' workshop, Manchester Business School, Manchester, 16–18 May.

——(1996b) 'Expert power in late modernity', *Organisation Studies*, 17, 4: 573–97.

Rosenau, P. (1992) *Postmodernism and the Social Sciences*, Princeton, NJ: Princeton University Press.

Savage, M., Barlow, J., Dickens, P. and Fielding, T. (1992) *Property, Bureaucracy and Culture: Middle Class Formation in Contemporary Britain*, London: Routledge.

Sayer, A. (1992) *Method in Social Science*, second edition, London: Routledge.

——(1995) *Radical Political Economy: A Critique*, Oxford: Blackwell.

Schumpeter, J. A. (1974) *Capitalism, Socialism and Democracy*, London: Allen and Unwin.

Scott, R. W. (1995) *Institutions and Organisations*, Thousand Oaks, CA: Sage.

Sewell, G. and Wilkinson, B. (1992) 'Someone to watch over me: surveillance, discipline and just-in-time labour process', *Sociology*, 26: 271–89.

Silverman, D. (1975) 'Accounts of organisations: organisational structure and the accounting process', in J. B. McKinlay (ed.) *Processing People: Cases in Organisational Behaviour*, New York: Holt, Rinehart and Winston, pp, 269–302.

Star, S. L. (1995) *Ecologies of Knowledge: Work and Politics in Science and Technology*, New York: State University of New York Press.

Thompson, J. B. (1989) 'The theory of structuration', in D. Held and J. B. Thompson (eds) *Social Theory and Modern Societies: Anthony Giddens and his Critics*, Cambridge: Cambridge University Press, 56–76.

Thompson, P. and Ackroyd, S. (1995) 'All quiet on the workplace front? A critique of present trends in British industrial sociology', *Sociology*, 29: 615–34.

Tsoukas, H. (1989) 'The validity of ideographic research explanations', *Academy of Management Review*, 14: 551–61.

Urry, J. (1982) 'Science, realism and the social', *Philosophy of Social Science*, 12: 311–18.

Whittington, R. (1989) *Corporate Strategies in Recovery and Recession: Social Structure and Strategic Choice*, London: Unwin Hyman.

——(1994) 'Sociological pluralism, institutions and managerial agency', in J. Hassard and M. Parker (eds) *Towards a New Theory of Organisation*, London: Routledge, 53–74.

Wolin, S. (1988) 'On the theory and practice of power', in J. Arac (ed.) *After Foucault: Humanistic Knowledge, Postmodern Challenges*, New Brunswick, NJ: Rutgers University Press, 179–201.

Zimmerman, D. (1971) 'The practicalities of rule use', in J. Douglas (ed.) *Understanding Everyday Life*, London: Routledge & Kegan Paul, 285–95.

Zukin, S. (1991) *Landscapes of Power: From Detroit to Disney World*, Berkeley, CA: University of California Press.

4 Structure, culture and agency

Rejecting the current orthodoxy of organisation theory

Robert Willmott

Introduction

All theory makes assumptions about the nature of reality (either implicitly or explicitly) and such ontological assumptions necessarily regulate how one studies the things and events under investigation. Successful study is inextricably dependent upon an adequate ontology. As Bryant neatly puts it, 'Effective application, in turn, is connected with adequate working assumptions about the constitution of society. Argument about the constitution of society is thus not a recondite activity which most sociologists [and organisation theorists] can safely ignore' (1995: 58, interpolation added). The central concern in this paper is with the ontological underpinnings of much of the current literature in organisation studies in respect of structure and culture. It will be argued that conflation of irreducible and causally-efficacious strata of social reality in the shape of social structure and culture permeates much of the current literature, thus rendering analysis of the interplay between them and their relationship with human agency difficult to elucidate. The ontological underpinnings of organisational analysis have arguably turned full circle from the depth of social reality acknowledged by functionalism, structural Marxism and systems theory to the generic endorsement of Giddens' structuration theory. As will be argued, Giddens' theory entails a depthless ontology, which necessarily precludes methodological prescription.

Conceptualising structure and culture: emergence and stratification

This paper argues that much contemporary writing in organisation studies and sociology involves the conflation of different strata of social reality. In order to do this, an alternative view of both structure and culture from those widely accepted in the literature will be proffered, defending the essential irreducibility of each. Hence, the springboard for theorising the interplay of culture, structure and agency is *analytical* dualism (Archer, 1982; 1988; 1995; 1996: ch. 6; Willmott, 1996). Analytical dualism is possible in virtue of the intrinsically *stratified* nature of reality. What is at issue here is not the (undeniable) profitability of cultural (and structural) analysis *per se*, but *how* it should be approached methodologically.

Structure: an emergent stratum of reality

As Hays emphasises, the concept 'social structure' is ubiquitous in sociological literature, and its meaning is foundational for the work of social theorists (1994: 57). It is generally taken as axiomatic that structure refers to resilient *patterns* that order social life. However, the exact ontological status that one accords structure is contested. The organisational literature seems to support the view that structure is not ontologically distinct from agency. The two are held to be so intimately intertwined and mutually influential that to accord each an ontological status of their own would be to reify them. This renders a temporal examination of their interplay difficult, if not impossible. The fact that the two *are* mutually influential does not mean that they are analytically inseparable. Social structure is conceptualised as being composed of rules and resources *à la* Giddens. Indeed, many organisation theorists (as well as sociologists for that matter) were quick to join the structurationist bandwagon. Quintessentially, social theory is concerned with the now-familiar dualisms of individual versus society; determinism versus voluntarism; micro- versus macroscopic; that is, the perennial 'problem of structure and agency'. Resolution in terms of linking the latter does not lie in some ostensibly possible transcendence, especially Giddens' structuration theory.

It will be argued that both structure and culture can be approached via the *same* methodological device, viz. analytical dualism, since both are held to be irreducibly-efficacious strata of reality. Analytical dualism is fundamentally not the same as Cartesian dualism. Although Cartesian dualism is appropriate for conceptualising culture, in that as product it does not depend upon continuous human activity, structure cannot be conceptualised in terms of such dualism *vis-à-vis* agency. Instead, *analytical* dualism is appropriate for theorising the relative interplay of structure and agency; analytical because the two are interdependent and dualist because each is held to possess its *own* emergent causal powers. To transcend the Cartesian mind/body dualism *and* to eschew the concomitant temptation of reductionism, one must conceptualise the mind as *emergent* from the body – dependent upon, but not reducible to, that from which it emerged. Thus, conceptualising human agency as a causally and taxonomically irreducible mode of matter is *not* to posit a distinct substance, 'mind', endowed with reasons for acting *apart* from the causal network, 'but to credit intentional embodied agency with distinct (emergent) causal powers from the *biological matter out of which* agents *were formed, on which they are capable of reacting back*' (Bhaskar 1993: 51).

Bhaskar's approach is materialist only in the sense that, while it does not rule out mind as an immaterial substance, it would insist that any such substance ontologically presupposes material substances, because the criteria for the existence of any imperceptible entity must be the causal criteria – the capacity to produce effects on matter (Collier 1994: 156). Bhaskar's approach is clearly a theory of synchronic emergence. He is bracketing off questions about temporal priority and the causes of emergence. Collier argues that while all the strata of reality that we know about *do* seem to have emerged at some particular time, there are instances where it is arguable 'that two or more strata, one of which is rooted in and emergent from the other, *must* have emerged simultaneously, since they ontologically presuppose each other ... society, mind and language are related in this way' (ibid.: 157).

However, in eschewing reductionism, one does not by theoretical *fiat* have to ground one's approach in synchrony, for specific strata *do* emerge over time, but nonetheless are relatively efficacious and irreducible to the entities from which they emerged.

Contra Descartes, then, we are not dealing with an absolute division between mind and body – between two distinct substances – but with an emergent property *sui generis*, which itself generates further emergent, irreducible properties (society); hence my endorsement of a stratified conception of reality. Structure, like mind, is an emergent property, whose causal powers/liabilities are irreducible to, though emergent from, *sustained* human agency. Hence the possibility of *analytical* dualism, not Cartesian dualism, to examine their relative interplay over time, for the two are mutually dependent but distinct because of their emergent causal powers and the crucial fact that they operate over different tracts of time (Archer 1995; Porpora 1989). Society is peopled, and people have their own emergent powers of reflection and creativity. As the section on culture will argue, however, beliefs are not ontologically dependent upon believers. Although they clearly would not exist without the agents from which they emerge, what Bhaskar and other social realists mean by a stratified ontology is that, while beliefs are emergent from agency, such beliefs are separable and capable of consideration as an emergent system.

To develop this analysis I now turn to the prevailing orthodoxy in organisation theory, namely the generic endorsement of structuration theory. In view of Weick and Sandeland's (1990) contribution to the *Journal for the Theory of Social Behaviour*, in which they delineate the influence of structurationists on organisation theory, this paper is of substantive import. Indeed, as Reed points out, 'the most influential development ... has been Giddens' attempt to construct a theory of Structuration ... Thus, the theory of Structuration is invoked and deployed by a growing number of organisational theorists (1992: 187).

Meek (1992), among others, confidently endorses the structurationist conception of social structure. His principal concern is to demolish the myth of cultural integration, thus correctly arguing that 'organisational culture' is rarely, if at all, shared, and open to manipulation by management. He approvingly refers to Patricia Riley, who maintains that

> [Structures] are both the medium and the outcome of interaction. They are the medium, because structures provide the rules and resources individuals must draw on to interact meaningfully. They are its outcome, because rules and resources exist only through being applied and acknowledged in interaction – they have *no reality independent of the social reality they constitute.*
>
> (Riley 1983: 415)

The denial of independent ontological status for structure is evident in Meek's assertion that 'Culture and structure are not concrete entities; rather they are abstract concepts that are to be used to interpret behaviour'; it therefore follows to Meek that the principal task of the social theorist 'is to observe and describe the actions of human beings and *their* characterizations of social reality: social science is the researcher's constructions of the layman's constructions of what he and his compatriots are up to' (Meek 1992: 204). Yet the very possibility of social theory is predicated on the autonomous existence of real social structures and systems *qua* emergent entities that operate *independently* of our conception of them, though are nonetheless dependent upon agential activity while they endure. Mere observation, description and dependence upon agential characterisation, *contra* Meek, are hardly firm grounds for theorising socio-cultural change.

Meek's position, along with many others in his field, is in diametric opposition to the transcendental realist's assertion that it is precisely in virtue of a stratified reality that social science is possible (Bhaskar 1979: 25). To Mills, for instance, organisations are viewed as key sites of 'rule enactment, mediation and resistance' (1988: 366); and for Greenwood and Hinings, organisational structures should be conceptualised as 'embodiments of ideas, beliefs and values ... Structures are reflexive expressions of intentions, aspirations and meanings, or "interpretative schemes"' (1988: 295). Hence, what can be identified as ontological depthlessness is widespread. There is no sense in which structure is accorded an ontological status of its own, i.e. distinct from, and irreducible to, human agency, whereby rules, meanings, etc., are held to be temporally posterior. Intrinsic to a stratified or 'depth' ontology is the subject/object dichotomy.

A standard riposte is to maintain that communication proceeds *solely* on the basis of intersubjective agreement, thereby obviating the logical necessity of *common* access to an objective world: in other words, to reduce issues of truth and falsity to local groups. But then, of course, the problem of disagreement arises. Here, the classic response is to adopt the Wittgensteinian fallacy of rendering specific conceptual schemes incommensurable. Indeed, attacks on realism almost invariably enjoin the incommensurability of conceptual schemes. Thus, those who disagree are held a priori to be part of a hermetically-sealed conceptual scheme, possessing its own, *internal* criteria for truth. But if no conceptual scheme can be wrong, then none can be right either. Truth must be grounded in the way things are, *independently* of *truth-believers*, for otherwise communication *per se* becomes an impossibility. The invocation of incommensurability is clearly untenable, for how can its advocates logically *know* that specific schemes are incommensurable in the first place? What needs to be recognised is that objective reality (natural and social) *constrains*: it predisposes, not determines, cultural emergent properties; hence the latitude for human error. We must recognise our fallibility (which is not the same as epistemic relativism, for we are indeed right about many matters) and recognise also that to ignore the wholesale importance of objective reality which humankind confronts ineluctably removes the motive for expending intellectual energy in the search for truth.

Many writers in the organisational field (Willmott 1990; Meek 1992; Riley 1983; Pettigrew 1985; Whittington 1989) derive support from Giddens' structuration theory. Hugh Willmott, for example, wrongly maintains that Giddens has successfully transcended the age-old dualisms of objectivity/subjectivity and structure/agency. Giddens' *oeuvre* represents part of a trajectory which started with Berger and Luckmann's social constructionism (1966). All who subscribe to it effectively disclaim an independent ontological status for social structure (and culture), thereby rendering impossible methodological examination of the conditions maintaining for stability or change.

Structuration versus emergence: providing the basis for analytical dualism

Willmott summarises thus:

> In the theory of structuration, attention is focused upon the way in which actors accomplish their practices by drawing upon a knowledge of rules ... and a command of resources ... and thereby reconstitute the considerations that provide for the very possibility of such accomplishments. In this formulation, 'structure' or 'objective facticity' *does not* exist *independently of the* actor.
>
> (1990: 53; emphasis added)

This is congruent with Giddens' assertion that 'structure has no existence independent of the knowledge that agents have about what they do in their day-to-day activity' (Giddens 1984: 26). At first glance it seems that Giddens is simply asserting that social structure could not exist without some conception on the part of the actors concerned. However, this is not the same as asserting the real, relative independent existence of emergent structures, whose causal powers/liabilities are not dependent upon, or reducible to, agential awareness. Giddens wrongly believes that talk of emergent (structural) properties is to be culpable of committing the crime of reification (Giddens 1984: 171; Archer 1996: 695). To argue for activity-dependence and simultaneously to dismiss Giddens' a priori over-accentuation of concept-dependence is not to reify structure, for the structural causes of poverty entail activity-dependence in terms of its continued reproduction, yet full or even partial 'discursive penetration' is not an ineluctable concomitant or precondition. How else can Giddens explicate the acceptance among sections of the middle and working classes that the poverty-stricken are so because of their putative indolent or scrounging nature? As will be argued shortly, an emergent ontology of social reality does not entail reification. Far from it: social theory presupposes it.

To Giddens,

> The constitution of agents and structures are not two independently given sets of phenomena, a dualism, but represent a duality ... Structure is not 'external' to individuals: as memory traces, and as instantiated in social practices ... Structure is not to be equated with constraint but is always both constraining and enabling.
>
> (ibid.: 25)

The key word here is *dualism*. Giddens' dismissal of Cartesian dualism accounts for his conflation of structure and agency, as conceptually compacted in his 'duality of structure'. Arguably, Giddens conceptualises dualism as Descartes does, which explains his assertion that to talk of structure as independent is inevitably to engage in reification. He writes in a rejoinder to Archer that 'Structure and action *cannot* form a dualism, save from the point of view of situated actors, because each is constituted by and in a single 'realm' – human activity' (Giddens 1990: 299). This is where Giddens ultimately enters the wrong theoretical door, for as argued above, Cartesian dualism *can* be transcended via the idea of emergence. It is also by virtue of an emergentist ontology that social theory is possible. To deny a stratified world is to deny the very possibility of social theory.

It is the relative autonomy of structure, as an emergent irreducible entity, that provides social theory with its object of study. Conceptualising structure as rules and resources is ultimately to render methodological analysis of their interplay intractable, for, *inter alia*, which rules are the most important, for whom and, moreover, why? The basic problem with Giddens' emphasis upon the simultaneity of constraint and enablement is that it really amounts to an unhelpful and misleading truism. All organisations constrain and enable their occupants, but do so differentially. Some are more enabled than constrained and vice versa. But Giddens would no doubt resist this, since to acknowledge the stringency of constraints is to follow the treacherous path of externality, something which actors *confront*. But to confront structure (and culture) is *not* perforce to confront a reified entity.

Rendering rules constitutive of structure is to rule out an adequate explanation of constraint/enablement, and more fundamentally, *why* actors engage in patterned reproduction. When I enter a university as a student, am I merely entering an admixture of rules and resources? Am I not entering a set of *relations*, which are *independent* of such rules and resources? Rules are not enough to account for the differential distribution of life-chances and resources in society. Indeed, in what conceivable sense are there rules attaching to unemployment and poverty? As Craib (1992) and Thompson (1989) have rightly pointed out, to account for the importance of specific rules, one has to make reference to relatively enduring and independent structures. To assent to the latter is to accord structure an ontological status of its own, something which Giddens and others are at pains to repudiate. Indeed, Giddens fails to realise that whilst rules are constitutive of social positions, such positions acquire relative autonomy from their incumbents. As Porpora puts it, social relations 'do have independent causal properties and, moreover, such relationships, once established, are analytically prior to the subsequent rule following behaviour of actors' (1989: 206).

Yet, Giddens cannot completely distance himself from structure as pre-existent, durable and causally efficacious (1984: 212). His concept of system is more or less coterminous with the traditional conception of structure. Here Giddens is admitting the necessity of pre-existence through the back-door. Indeed, Giddens writes that 'the constraining elements themselves have to be seen as expressing the "givenness" of the social environment of actors to particular agents' (Giddens 1989: 258). To accede 'givenness' is immediately to embroil oneself in the ontology of emergence, because here we have an acknowledgement of pre-existence and relative durability: actors confront organisational structures which continue to exist even when such actors have either died or moved on elsewhere. This is in contradiction of his dictum that 'structure is both the medium and the outcome of interaction', since the latter denies pre-existence, entailing a vicious circularity, for structure is *ever* the medium *and* outcome, never a pre-existent given with which agency starts and either elaborates upon or merely replicates.

The other, equally untenable way in which Giddens endeavours to disclaim an ontological status for structure is to render it 'virtual' until instantiated by agency. But his implicit acknowledgement of pre-existence entails that structure is *real* – not 'virtual' – by virtue of its independent causal efficacy, its 'givenness' which we necessarily confront either as enablement or constraint but are not determined by. Giddens cannot avoid the non-Cartesian dualism of structure and agency. This is precisely his problem. He cannot but avoid ontologically distinguishing between the two, but he wrongly believes that to do so is to be culpable of invoking Cartesian dualism; hence his attribution of a 'virtual' status to structure. But this is not so: to accord structure an ontological status of its own is not to indulge in gratuitous reification, for emergent structural properties are irreducible to agency but have to be *mediated* by them to have any efficacy (Archer 1995: 195).

To recognise that specific, relatively independent, social forms do not necessarily lead all to acquire full 'discursive penetration', as Giddens puts it, is not to adopt Cartesian dualism; rather the job here is one of theorising separable, rather than separate, entities, which is transcendentally possible by virtue of a stratified social reality. There are occasions when agency *cannot* do otherwise, because of stringent socio-cultural constraints (e.g. the poverty-stricken). This is not to deny human creativity and reflexivity, but to show that for some in society emergent socio-cultural properties are not enabling. As I have already suggested, the constraint/enablement dichotomy is unhelpful. This issue is not one of simultaneity but one of theorising the *degrees* of constraint and enablement which structurationists are keen to eschew. And in assessing the relative degrees of freedom that some agents may have, analytical dualism is indispensable. The advocacy of inseparability necessarily precludes this methodological procedure – hence Archer's onto-logical arraignment of Giddens on the charge of 'central conflation', for structure and agency are held to be inseparable by him.

In defending the explanatory indispensability of emergence and stratifica-tion, I am not in any way invoking a Cartesian 'substance', utterly divorced from human agency. On the contrary, emergent structural properties onto-logically presuppose agency for their efficacy. Structural emergent properties are only possible because of human activity, but once they have emerged by virtue of their internal necessity they possess irreducible causal powers/liabilities. Fundamentally reification is not entailed, for emergent properties only have efficacy *through* people: they have to be mediated and thus compel no-one. Thus a student may decide not to attend lectures, complete coursework, and sit examinations, but to do so would invoke a hefty, structured price, namely possible expulsion. As Archer rightly argues, structural and cultural emergent properties *condition* interaction by supplying actors with reasons for pursuing maintenance or change which work on a priori prior distribution of vested interests (Archer 1995, ch. 7).

Importantly, emergent social structures are such by virtue of internally-related positions or roles that actors *occupy*. What we have to accept is that whilst social relations are constituted by rules, such relations possess an ontological status of their own by virtue of their irreducible emergent causal powers. This is not to say that such causal powers are wholly independent of agency or that such powers have effects analogous to that of a magnetic field (cf. Manicas 1993). Rather, it is in virtue of their *internal necessity* that they come to possess relative autonomy and causal efficacy from role incumbents. This is how one can conceptualise social relations apart from rules. That structure is activity-dependent does not entail that roles do not have autonomy and causal efficacy. As Archer succinctly argues,

> Roles ... are more important for understanding what is going on between landlords and tenants ... than their relations as persons. Moreover the role has to be granted some autonomy from its occupant or how else do we explain the similar actions of a succession of incumbents ... ? Once again the fact that roles are necessarily activity dependent is insufficient to deny the independent capacity to structure individuals' activities.
>
> (Archer 1996: 682)

Thus, the role of teacher necessarily presupposes a student. On the other hand, a more general notion of organisational structure is required before a system of related roles – a hierarchy of staff including a head teacher, administrators, staff, cleaning personnel, etc., all of which positions are relatively independent of the actors who occupy them.

Sayer defines emergence in terms of

> the distinction between internal and external relations. Where objects are externally or contingently related they do not affect one another in their essentials and do not modify their causal powers, although they may interfere with the effects of these powers ... Even though social structures exist only where people reproduce them, they have powers irreducible to those of individuals (you can't pay rent to yourself).
>
> (1992: 119)

Porpora nonetheless recognises that structure is an emergent stratum with *sui generis* causal properties. According to this author, we have to distinguish three things: 'the original constitutive rules that establish relationships of domination, *those relationships themselves*, and the tacit, informal rules that emerge when people enter those relationships and begin interaction' (Popora 1989: 208, emphasis added). The middle part is what social realists hold to be structure – irreducible and causally efficacious. The final part is what I hold to be cultural. And as Porpora rightly points out, Giddens conflates parts one and two of his three-part schema, thereby obscuring the 'causal role of relationships in his treatment of domination' (ibid.). Thus, *pace* Juckes and Barresi (1993: 204), marriage *qua* structural relationship is such by virtue of internally-related roles, viz. those of husband and wife, and is not constituted by the marriage certificate! Certainly, other emergent structural entities, such as the state and the Church, can combine to confront married couples with objective penalties in times of divorce (e.g. two-year cooling-off period before divorce is legally granted). But certificates, ceremonies and 'stag nights' are *cultural* phenomena, which serve to buttress marriage, they are contingent and thus external (cf. Porpora 1989). However, Juckes and Barresi are right to insist upon the *pre-existence* of structural forms. Social relations *do* pre-exist their incumbents; hence the possibility of analytical dualism to examine the interplay of 'the parts' and 'the people' because of the temporal elements involved. The real sin of methodological individualism is not, as Manicas maintains, its failure to 'see that the materials with which people work enable and constrain them in profoundly different ways', *but its denial of pre-existence* (Manicas 1993: 223). Such an a priori denial necessarily results in voluntarism. Agents must have reasons for pursuing maintenance or change and such reasons must be grounded in something *anterior*, some antecedently-existing state of affairs.

To reiterate, emergent properties denote a *stratified* social world which is composed of non-observable entities which are real by virtue of their internal necessity. *Contra* Giddens, then, the social system constitutes a further stratum of social reality, which arises through a combination of internally-related emergent structures and relations between organisations. Because society is an open system, emergent structures possess *tendential* powers/liabilities, for other contingent factors may (and indeed do) intervene. Water boils at 100°C. However, this is a *tendential* emergent power, because other factors may intervene, such as impurities deposited as a result of pollution. This applies equally to societies and organisations. It is in virtue of the irreducible relations which constitute a university, for example, that one can claim that students will, tendentially, arrive at lectures, complete coursework and sit examinations. The effects of the structural mechanism (university relations) produced by them at the empirical level depend upon contingently related conditions.

To recapitulate, it is precisely on the basis of the reality of a stratified social world that analytical dualism gains its methodological foothold, thus providing social theory with its object of study. There is an important onto-logical distinction, then, between 'the parts' and 'the people' of society: or between system and social integration, where varying conjunctions between the two account for socio-cultural transformation or replication (Archer 1995: ch. 6). The parts refer to the emergent properties that arise from the relations between (emergent) structures and the people, to embodied agents, whose emergent properties are those of modification *vis-à-vis* other agents or group-ings *idem*. It is indeed profitable to distinguish between orderly or conflictual relations maintaining between groups of actors from orderly or con-flictual relations prevailing between the parts of society. Moreover, one can in turn theorise about the various conjunctions between the social and the systemic on a *multi-level* basis, for instance, at the level of roles, i.e. with the difference between roles and their occupants. Thus, high social malintegra-tion within a particular organisation may be endemic but does not issue in structural change if the organisation's roles are complementary, and *qua* structured whole is not incongruent with its external systemic environment.

Structuration theory disavows the fact that people enter into pre-existing organisational structures, which specific actors may subsequently endeavour to change or maintain: social interaction leads either to transformation or replication. Structuration inherently disclaims the temporal elements involved in the structuring and restructuring of organisations (and society itself). It should be clear from the foregoing that current organisation theory, in its endorsement of structuration, conflates irreducible strata of reality – viz. structure and agency, *inter alia*, thus precluding examination of their relative interplay over time. However, such conflationism permeates analysis of culture.

Culture: establishing its 'World Three' status

As Crane points out, contemporary sociological and anthropological theory on the whole continues to adhere to a conception of culture as consistent and coherent which is 'more an ideal or an ideology than a reality' (Crane 1994: 4). Organisation theory has not been immune from such a conception. In fact, culture is almost invariably held to be embedded in structure rather than ontologically distinct from it. Meek also argues that 'a conceptual distinction be made between "culture" and "structure"' but immediately adds that 'it must be kept in mind, though, that both culture and structure are abstractions, and have use only in relation to the interpretation of observed concrete behaviour' (Meek 1992: 209). By suggesting this, Meek conflates culture and agency, rather than reducing one to the other. Meek, like many of his colleagues, does not conceptualise culture as an emergent, irreducible stratum of objective reality. It will be argued here that culture, like structure, constitutes an irreducible stratum of reality, but whose existence, unlike structure, is not dependent upon the continued reproductive actions of human agency: we are dealing with two separate, rather than separable, entities.

While some tentatively grant culture autonomy from structure (e.g. Mills 1988), others grant it autonomy but hold it to be part of structure (e.g. Hays 1994). Hays argues that 'social structure consists of two central, inter-connected elements: systems of social relations and systems of meaning. Such systems ... remain analytically distinct, as two aspects of social structure' (Hays 1994: 65–6). They are *ontologically distinct*, with *culture irreducible* to *both structure and* agency. Moreover, she also maintains that culture is '*both external* and *internal, objective and subjective*, material and ideal ... it confronts us ready-made' (ibid.: 70, emphasis added). Hays here is confusing culture and its social reception, i.e. what agency *makes* of it. Culture as product cannot be both objective and subjective. This is not to deny that culture is produced by agency or that it is material in origin, but *qua* product it possesses an ontological status of its own. Essentially, one needs to make an ontological distinction between culture *per se* or the cultural system (henceforth, the CS) and what agency makes of it, namely socio-cultural interaction (henceforth, S-C).

Culture, like structure, is an emergent stratum of reality that may be used to start the motor of social theory. Cultural emergent properties, like structural ones, are intransitive, i.e. once registered they automatically belong to what Bhaskar terms the 'intransitive dimension'. As Bhaskar argues the transfactuality of laws and socialisation into science implies the distinction between the intransitive or ontological and the transitive or epistemological dimensions of science. This latter must logically be extended to include the whole *material and cultural* infrastructure of society.

(Bhaskar 1994: 255)

The intransitive dimension is concerned with objects, processes and events that are held to exist or occur independently of human conception; the transitive dimension is concerned with (fallible) knowledge of the latter. Culture constitutes a distinct stratum of reality since it is *about* facts *vis-à-vis* objective reality, which obtain independently of our claims. Again, this is not to disclaim that culture is a human product. Rather, as a product it immediately establishes its existential intransivity, i.e. it acquires an ontological status *apart* from the human activity that created it. If this were not so, then we would not be able to distinguish what it entails in holding certain beliefs and what it is for such beliefs to be true or false.

However, Bhaskar's intransitive dimension does not capture the important ways in which the CS has relational causal properties of its own when actualised or activated by agency – powers that do not depend upon agential cognisance for their efficacy. In fact, cultural emergent properties do not depend upon agency at all *once* produced (written down, spoken, etc.): we thus have *knowledge without a knowing subject*. The defining feature of *cultural* emergence is not internal necessity (although at the S-C level the CS has relational causal properties which exert an influence) but its 'World Three' status, as Popper would put it (Popper 1979). Popper distinguishes three worlds: World One refers to *physical* states and processes; World Two refers to *mental* states and process; and World Three refers to *products* of human minds. Such products include such objects as sculptures and paintings, even Shakespeare's plays. More important, however, is Popper's emphasis upon *objective knowledge*, namely, hypotheses, theories, arguments, ideologies, unsolved problems. Given the heterogeneous nature of World Three, Popper points out that one should distinguish more than three worlds, for example make objective knowledge a separate world from that of the arts. This is precisely what Archer (1988; 1995) does. Archer's equation of the CS with objective knowledge, specifically with that which is propositional, is neither illegitimate nor arbitrary.

As Popper argues, the CS is objective in the sense that it is 'totally independent of anybody's claim to know; it is also independent of anybody's belief, or disposition to assent, or to act. Knowledge in the objective sense is *knowledge without a knower*: it is *knowledge without a knowing subject*' (Popper 1979: 109). Here, then, we have near full-blooded Cartesian dualism in the sense that if the human race were to be obliterated overnight by a killer virus, books, journals, etc., would remain in libraries across the world, paintings in galleries, and so on. Social structure, on the other hand, would clearly cease to exist. Thus, the CS is not largely autonomous, since although we act upon the CS and it acts upon us, were we no longer to exist, it would not die with us. This in no way negates the fact that the CS originates as a product of human activity. 'Full-blooded' dualism, however, would, of course, disavow the latter.

What is being resisted is the (ontological) assumption that culture is not objective, that is, not merely analytically separable from, but actually *separate* from, its social production and actualisation. Such a disclaimer of objectivity has led many down the path of central conflation. In other words, such writers withdraw autonomy from agency and culture, rendering them so mutually constitutive that analysis of their interplay becomes impossible.

Following Archer: 'However, the differences between the exact nature of culture and structure vis-à-vis agency are not of major importance. The issue is one of activity-dependence'. The CS can be analysed in terms of its *logical consistency*, that is the degree of consistency between the component parts of culture which exist independently of knowing subjects. Cultural *effects*, on the other hand, are properties of people (the S-C level), and can thus be analysed in terms of *causal consensus*, that is the degree of cultural uniformity produced by the imposition of ideas by one set of people on another. It is worth quoting Archer at length here:

> it is the pre-existence, autonomy and durability of the constituents of the Cultural System which enables their identification as entities distinct from the meanings held by agents at any given time. The distinction is made by virtue of the fact that there are causal relations prevailing between items [of the CS], whereas it is *causal* relations which maintain between cultural agents. The logical consistency or inconsistency which characterizes relationships within the Cultural System is a property of the world of ideas ... we utilise this concept everyday when we say that the ideas of X are consistent with those of Y ... These are quite different from the other kind of everyday statement, to the effect that the ideas of X were influenced by those of Y, in which case we are talking about causal effects which are properties of people.
>
> (Archer 1995: 179)

Hence, it is not being denied that culture and agency mutually influence each other; but rather, because of the quasi-Cartesian status accorded to the CS as an emergent product, one can indeed examine their interplay over time. For many this entails an unacceptable reification. But does it? Culture *qua* product is a concrete system which is completely divorced from agency. Thus, I wish to defend philosophical dualism *vis-à-vis* culture, but not structure. As Archer herself would concur, a manual that is left to gather dust for hundreds of years still retains the *dispositional capacity to be understood and used*. Structure, on the other hand, is never divorced from agency. However, the differences between the exact nature of culture and structure *vis-à-vis* agency are not of major importance. The issue is one of activity-dependence.

The essential problem with many who deny objectivity to culture is reliance on the idea that cultural artifacts are context-dependent to be found meaningful. Joanne Martin (1992), like Meek, ultimately makes culture dependent upon social reception for its validity. In order to understand people's meanings constant reference has to be made to the S-C level. Yet are not people's 'meanings' independent of the CS? Martin's methodological injunction can be refuted with one of her own examples. She maintains that 'culture is not reified out there – to be *accurately* observed' (Martin 1992: 13). But in what sense can ideologies be observed? Here Martin is conflating the S-C and the CS. She focuses solely on the S-C level, i.e. agential actualisation. In fact, Martin rightly argues that there is nothing intrinsically natural about categorising people in terms of discrete, homogeneous 'races' on the basis of phenotypical characteristics. Yet this is to adopt dualism, for racism is quintessentially ideological (CS level) and is manipulated by certain groups to exclude others (S-C level).

Indeed, to put forward the proposition that all black people are intrinsically inferior to white people is to make a truth-claim – a claim about objective reality. If the latter were not objective in the sense of being true or false independently of our claims to either, then we would (i) not be able to put forward such a proposition, and (ii) be able subsequently to refute it. The CS is, as Archer puts it, society's 'propositional register'. It is analysable without reference to agency via the universal law of non-contradiction. Therefore, racism *qua* ideology may either stand in a complementary relationship or an incompatible one in relation to other CS components, independently of agential awareness. Essentially, those who do not assent to the CS/S-C distinction maintain that in practice the CS cannot be examined separately via analytical dualism.

Stanley and Wise object to Popper's ontological schema of 'Three Worlds' on this basis:

> In our approach these three 'worlds' overlap and are inextricably interwoven; and even *for analytic purposes we feel that there is little justification for so separating them*. We believe that what are material things, what is subjectivity, what is knowledge all overlap.
>
> (Stanley and Wise 1993: 130, emphasis added)

Yet if the two cannot be separated analytically, how can one examine, for example, the relative interplay of sexist ideology and capitalism? This is precluded by Stanley and Wise. Instructively, they maintain that

> 'Social facts' embody people's understandings of what is factual and, because factual, what constrains them ... We treat a whole range of

things as 'facts', as 'scientifically proven', as 'what everyone knows to be true', and these become constraining upon us.

(1993: 131–2)

Against Stanley and Wise, *truth is independent of our claims to it*. If this were not so, then we could never be right or wrong. The two are culpable of committing the epistemic fallacy, reducing ontology to epistemology.

It is difficult to understand why 'facts' and 'scientifically proven' are wrapped with inverted commas. Water has the (tendential) emergent power to boil at 100°C, a state of affairs that is independent of us. There *are* scientifically-proven facts, without which daily life would be impossible. What Stanley and Wise do not accept is that scientific theories, hypotheses, etc., belong to the CS as autonomous components. Naturally, as Popper points out, somehow or other the thing has to be started by us (World Two processes), but once it gets going it produces its own problems which are independent of us. Popper gives the example of a mathematical problem which is placed into a computer: assume that the problem has been solved by the computer, and that the computer is so made that it can print the solution, and that the paper which it produces is at once put into the library and forgotten there. Nobody ever looks at it! Of course the human mind was involved in devising the computer. But nobody knows that this particular problem has been solved. It is just there to be found in the library for those who wish to find it (Popper 1994: 37).

However, it may be argued that sexist ideology, beliefs, etc., are not so neatly lodged in the library or the CS, for there exists no equivalent of a mathematics manual, for checking the correctness of a formal proof. Whilst there is no sexist manual *per se* (although historically one can easily dig up numerous pamphlets, books, etc., regarding women's 'natural' role in the home and so on), *propositions can be passed on orally*. As Popper argues, as far as objective knowledge is concerned (World Three), 'it may be said to be the world of libraries, of books and journals, but also of oral reports and traditions' (Popper 1994: 32). My rejoinder here is quite simply: *what* is being passed on? For something to be passed on, it has to be *outside* of people's heads. Moreover, even if sexist ideology is not written down, it can contradict or be consistent with other propositions independently of us. This of course is not to say that we always live logically; but rather a proposition stands in a *logical relationship* (of complementarity or contradiction) to other propositions.

Dualism: the parts and the people revisited

As with structure, culture is methodologically analysable by virtue of its emergent status. Indeed, like structure, culture has relational, causal properties of its own, which confront actualising agency in the form of situational logics (see Archer 1995: ch. 7). Cultural analysis is also a multi-level affair, from the doctrinal level, where, for instance, religious doctrine may contradict welfare policy, down to the micro-level. Just as any role within an organisation can have contradictory requirements, so can cultural values. However, the problem currently vitiating the literature on 'organisational culture' is precisely how one can examine the relative interplay between society's 'propositional register' and agency when culture is reduced to, or defined solely in terms of, what goes on at the level of causality. The realist assertion that culture as an emergent product has properties of its own is thrown out of the analytical window; or, following Archer, the S-C level is conflated with the CS level.

The parallel with structuration theory is palpable. Indeed, given the generic nod in the direction of structuration theory, it is hardly surprising to find that at best some will only accord culture an 'analytical' status. It would not be accepted that actors within organisations confront emergent relational causal properties of the CS as stringent obstructions or welcome opportunities, yet for which they are not responsible. Is it not the case that both the Commission for Racial Equality and the Equal Opportunities Commission were set up in response to the social manipulation of racism and sexism (*qua* CS components) which excluded many women and black people from positions for which they were suitably qualified? According such pernicious ideologies an analytical status is simply not enough, since they are irreducible to their producers. If they were not then we could not examine their relative interplay with structure and agency.

Given that both racism and sexism have social efficacy they must therefore be accorded an ontological status of their own. They pre-exist extant actors and would continue to exist if all were unaware of their existence. People enter into organisations and are consequently differentially able to respond. What is of interest to the practical social theorist is how, for instance, men in organisations respond to the situational logic of a constraining contradiction when they uphold sexist ideology in justifying their exclusion of women from certain positions or turning a blind eye to sexual harassment. As Mills rightly points out, the processes of gender differentiation do not operate 'as a one-way street. Women can and do reflect upon their existence, observing the contradictions in the way men and women are treated in organisational practices. They can and do resist those contradictions' (Mills 1988: 365). Mills correctly argues that gender is a cultural phenomenon. However, he does not accord gender ideology the ontological status it deserves. I would certainly not want to deny that gender ideology is the (revisable) product of ideational development, which is located within a material context. Rather, *qua* product such ideology immediately remains an inhabitant of World Three and stands in a logical relationship to other World Three denizens.

Against Anthony, then, 'cultures' are not 'owned' by members of organisations (Anthony 1994). Members may indeed internalise specific cultural components or uphold others to further their interests, but they internalise or uphold something which is an irreducible denizen of the CS. Furthermore, given the intransitive nature of the CS, it is untenable to assert, as many currently do, that each and every 'organisational culture' is somehow unique (cf. Martin *et al.* 1983). To Taylor Cox, for instance, 'organisations may be thought of as having their own distinctive cultures' (Taylor Cox 1993: 21). Although one can talk of structures in the plural, this is not permissible for culture, since all cultural components belong to the CS. In fact, my main concern is that to permit talk of discrete or unique cultures is to provide relativists with much-needed ammunition, since the next step has been to disclaim the invariant nature of the law of non-contradiction which is employed to study culture anywhere in the world (e.g. Bloor 1976). The salient point, however, is that it is untenable both to assert uniqueness and to talk of 'organisational culture' itself. Asserting the latter is to elide structure and culture. Indeed, *pace* Newman (1995: 23), culture is something apart from human identity and agency: methodological examination would otherwise be impossible.

The ideational elements of culture (CS) are intimately anchored in language. Language presupposes the objective reality of objects, processes and events. As Bhaskar argues, language presupposes referential detachment, which 'establishes at once its existential intransitivity and the possibility of another reference to it, a condition of any intelligible discourse at all. Referential detachment is implicit in all language-use' (Bhaskar 1994: 257). By existential intransitivity Bhaskar is referring to ontology, specifically to the independent existence of events, objects, etc. Cultural emergent properties must logically be about something in order to have any sense. In other words, they have to be grounded in the way things are. Indeed, as Trigg nicely puts it, 'Any account of human activity is liable to lapse into incoherence without such notions as reason, truth and reality. Certainly without them all human belief would lose its point' (Trigg 1994: 34).

Furthermore, the current orthodoxy regarding culture does not accord it the relational causal powers to direct agency. Instead, the tendency is to confuse culture with structure or downplay dissensus at the S-C level. Indeed, both Hampden-Turner (1990) and Handy (1993) confuse culture with structure. Handy proffers a typology of four cultures: power, role, task and person. In contradistinction, power is an emergent relational property; roles are constitutive of structure, with tasks being an integral aspect; and finally, personhood is the metaphysical anchorage for the agent and actor. All four are irreducible strata of reality (cf. Archer 1995).

I make no apologies for my brief, critical rejoinder to current orthodox views on culture, since each is ontologically depthless *vis-à-vis* culture, structure and agency. Conflationary theorising is amethodological, for analytical dualism is possible only on the basis of real objects of study. If ideologies and structures are efficacious then they are real and thus ontologically distinguishable from their progenitors. The ghost of empiricism still haunts many of the texts on 'organisational culture'. Contrary to Pheysey (1993), social structure may not be visible, but its effects are. One can employ the causal criterion to establish its reality. This is equally applicable to culture. Culture is quintessentially not something an organisation is. Contra Anthony, ideologies are not immune from counter-criticism, though their implications may not be realised for structural reasons. 'Impenetrability' is a myth: 'corporate culture is not bereft of logical protection' (Anthony 1994: 36). It can only be 'protected' via S-C containment strategies. And when these fail, structural power is employed often with impunity.

The practical implications of analytical dualism

My reason for reconceptualising structure is not simply to elucidate how conflationary theorising effectively is transported to the cultural scene in the literature, but to insist that the two cannot be analysed in isolation. Focusing on culture alone is to vitiate the enterprise of theorising change versus stability in organisations. Any approach which accentuates one or the other will prove to be inadequate in the long run. The practical theorist's task is to examine the relative interplay of culture, structure and agency: each interpenetrates the other, but each is nonetheless ontologically (and thus methodologically) distinguishable from the other. The purpose of this paper has been threefold: (i) to reconceptualise structure and culture as emergent strata; (ii) to maintain their equal necessity for adequate theorising; and (iii) to argue for the necessity of viewing any organisation from both a social- and a system-integration perspective, i.e. as a set of interacting actors and as a configuration of parts or complexes that both differentially enable and constrain actors. Analytical dualism disengages the emergent powers of people from those of the parts of society (structural and cultural), for the emergent properties and powers of the parts and the people are *sui generis*. S-C dynamics are interrelated in determinate ways, but without one determining the other. Obviously analysis of the S-C level will involve reference to material interests, to power, alliances, and so on, but this merely means that the practical theorist's life is not an easy one!

Agents resist – some more than others – and the overriding question for the practical analyst is how this results in a lack of change. For example, the issue of equal opportunities for women in organisations remains firmly on the agenda. Women still lag behind their male counterparts in terms of pay and promotion. Sexism (the CS level) is often employed to justify exclusionary practices (the S-C level). How do culture and structure interpenetrate here? In large part, the key to explication lies in disengaging the emergent powers of people from those of the parts. The job of the practical analyst is to find out whether the emergent structural powers remain unexercised, or exercised but unperceived. For instance, a male senior manager may have the power (by virtue of his structural location) to promote a female colleague, but because of his adherence to sexist ideology, such powers remain unexercised. Of course, it may indeed be that the male manager disagrees fundamentally with sexism, but feels that he cannot promote the woman because of a perceived antagonism among male clerical staff.

The task, therefore, is to pinpoint objective opportunities for the enhancement of women, which can be derived from the emergent structure of the organisation concerned. The scenario is indeed brief and certainly not exhaustive of the causal factors that may be involved, but it does nonetheless transcend subjectivism and evince the indispensability of analytical dualism. 'Organisational culture' is thus not merely about increasing productivity or designing company logos! Cultural items do not remain at the gates of all organisations. Again, it is only in virtue of a stratified reality that analytical dualism is possible. *Pace* Bryant (1995), theorising the relative interplay of generative structures (which may remain unexercised or exercised but unperceived) is not to embroil oneself in an ineluctable regression. Rather, it provides a much more robust analytical grip on S-C dynamics, eschewing the twin nightmares of empiricism and positivism.

The main impetus behind this paper has been to redirect attention away from the elisionist preoccupation with 'organisational culture'. Whether one wants to analyse generic economic failure or gender relations within organisations, then attention must be paid to both culture and structure: both constitute irreducible, causally-efficacious strata of reality and can thus be approached via the same methodological device of analytical dualism – from the macro- to the microscopic level. Both culture and structure are presently being denied an ontological status of their own in the organisation literature. Indeed, it has been argued that the current literature has been influenced by the conflationism of Giddens' structuration theory. This has been explicitly adopted by many and implicitly transferred to the cultural realm. Any form of conflation precludes analysis of the interplay of culture, structure and agency. Undoubtedly analytical dualism and its anchorage in a stratified reality will still be dismissed by many. My final riposte to such dissenters is that a stratified ontology is presupposed by social theory. All human beings enter involuntaristically into S-C relations which are not of their making. Hence, there is the very possibility of methodological analysis and subsequent practical intervention.

Bibliography

Anthony, P. (1994) *Managing Culture*, Buckingham: Open University Press.

Archer, M. S. (1982) 'Morphogenesis versus structuration', *British Journal of Sociology* 33: 455–83.

——(1988) *Culture and Agency: The Place of Culture in Social Theory*, Cambridge: Cambridge University Press.

——(1995) *Realist Social Theory: The Morphogenetic Approach*, Cambridge: Cambridge University Press.

——(1996) 'Social integration and system integration', *Sociology*, 30: 679–99.

Berger, P. L. and Luckman, N. T. (1966) *The Construction of Social Reality*, New York: Doubleday.

Bhaskar, R. (1979) *The Possibility of Naturalism*, Brighton: Harvester.

——(1993) *Dialectic: The Pulse of Freedom*, London: Verso.

——(1994) *Plato Etc.: The Problems of Philosophy and Their Resolution*, London: Verso.

Bloor, D. (1976) *Knowledge and Social Imagery*, London: Routledge & Kegan Paul.

Bryant, C. G. A. (1995) *Practical Sociology: Post-Empiricism and the Reconstruction of Theory and Application*, Oxford: Polity.

Collier, A. (1994) *Critical Realism: An Introduction to Roy Bhaskar's Philosophy*, London: Verso.

Cox, T. (1993) *Cultural Dimensions in Organizations: Theory, Research and Practice*, San Francisco: Berrett-Koehler.

Craib, I. (1992) *Anthony Giddens*, London: Routledge.

Crane, D. (ed.) (1994) *The Sociology of Culture*, Oxford: Blackwell.

Frost, P. J., Moore, L. F., Louis, M. R., Lundberg, C. C. and Lundberg, N. J. (eds) (1991) *Re-framing Organizational Culture*, London: Sage.

Giddens, A. (1979) *Central Problems in Social Theory: Action, Structure and Contradiction in Social Analysis*, London: Hutchinson.

——(1984) *The Constitution of Society: Outline of a Theory of Structuration*, Berkeley, CA: University of California Press.

——(1989) 'A reply to my critics', in D. Held and J. B. Thompson (eds) *Social Theory of Modern Societies*, Cambridge: Cambridge University Press, 249–301.

——(1990) 'Structuration theory and sociological analysis', in J. Clark, C. Modgil and S. Modgil (eds) *Anthony Giddens: Consensus and Controversy*, Brighton: Falmer Press, 297–315.

——(1993) *New Rules of Sociological Method*, Oxford: Polity.

Greenwood, R. and Hinning, C. R. (1988) 'Organizational design types, tracks and the dynamics of strategic change', *Organization Studies*, 9, 3: 293–316.

Hampden-Turner, C. (1990) *Corporate Culture: From Vicious to Virtuous Circles*, London: Hutchinson.

Handy, C. (1993) *Understanding Organizations*, London: Penguin.

Hays, S. (1994) 'Structure and agency and the sticky problem of culture', *Sociological Theory*, 12, 1: 57–72.

Itzin, C. and Newman, J. (1995) *Gender, Culture and Organisational Change*, London: Routledge.

Juckes, T. J. and Barresi, J. (1993) 'The subjective-objective dimension in the individual society connection: a duality perspective', *Journal for the Theory of Social Behaviour*, 23, 2: 197–216.

Manicas, T. (1993) 'The absent ontology of society: response to Juckes and Barresi', *Journal for the Theory of Social Behaviour*, 23, 2: 217–28.

Martin, J. (1992) *Cultures in Organisations*, Oxford: Oxford University Press.

Martin, J., Feldman, Hatch, M. J. and Sitkin, S. B. (1983) 'The uniqueness paradox in organizational stories', *Administrative Science Quarterly*, 28: 438–53.

Meek, V. L. (1992) 'Organizational culture: origins and weaknesses', in G. Salaman (ed.) *Human Resource Strategies*, London: Sage, 192–212.

Meyerson, D. and Meyerson, N. J. (1987) 'Cultural change: an integration of three different views', *Journal of Management Studies*, 24, 6: 623–47.

Mills, A. (1988) 'Organization, gender and culture', *Organization Studies*, 9, 3: 351–69.

Newman, J. (1995) 'Gender and cultural change', in C. Itzin and J. Newman (eds) *Gender, Culture and Organizational Change: Putting Theory into Practice*, London: Routledge, 11–29.

Parsons, T. (1960) *Structure and Process in Modern Societies*, Glencoe, IL: Free Press.

Pettigrew, A. (1985) *The Awakening Giant, Continuity and Change in ICI*, London: Basil Blackwell.

Pheysey, D. C. (1993) *Organizational Culture*, London: Routledge.

Popper, K. R. (1979) *Objective Knowledge*, Oxford: Oxford University Press.

——(1994) *Knowledge and the Body-Mind Problem*, London: Routledge.

Porpora, D. V. (1989) 'Four concepts of social structure', *Journal for the Theory of Social Behaviour*, 19, 2: 195–209.

Reed, M. I. (1992) *The Sociology of Organizations*, Guildford: Harvester Wheatsheaf.

Riley, P. (1983) 'A structurationist account of political culture', *Administrative Science Quarterly*, 28: 414–37.

Sayer, A. (1992) *Method in Social Science: A Realist Approach*, London: Routledge.

Schein, E. H. (1992) 'Coming to a new awareness of organizational culture', in G. Salaman (ed.) *Human Resource Strategies*, London: Sage, 237–54.

Smircich, L. (1983) 'Concepts of culture and organizational analysis', *Administrative Science Quarterly* 28: 339–58.

Stanley, L. and Wise, S. (1993) *Breaking Out Again: Feminist Ontology and Epistemology*, London: Routledge.

Thompson, J. B. (1989) 'The theory of structuration', in D. Held and J. B. Thompson (eds) *Social Theory of Modern Societies: Anthony Giddens and his Critics*, Cambridge: Cambridge University Press, 56–76.

Trigg, R. (1994) *Rationalism and Science: Can Science Explain Everything?*, Oxford: Blackwell.

Weick, K. E. and Sandeland, L. E. (1990) 'Social behaviour in organizational studies', *Journal for the Theory of Social Behaviour*, 20, 4: 323–46.

Whittington, R. (1989) *Corporate Strategies in Recession and Recovery*, London: Unwin-Hyman.

Willmott, H. C. (1990) 'Beyond paradigmatic closure in organizational enquiry', in J. Hassard and D. Pym (eds) *The Theory and Philosophy of Organisations*, London: Routledge, 4–60.

Willmott, R. (1996) 'Resisting sex/gender conflation: a rejoinder to John Hood-Williams', *Sociological Review*, 44: 728–45.

——(2000) 'The place of culture in organisation theory: introducing the morphogenic approach', *Organization*, 7, 1: 95–127.

Wittgenstein, L. (1968) *Philosophical Investigations*, Oxford: Blackwell.

Young, E. (1991) 'On the naming of the rose: interests and multiple meanings as elements of organizational culture', in P. J. Frost *et al.* (eds) *Reframing Organizational Culture*, London: Sage.

5 Connecting organisations and societies

A realist analysis of structures

Stephen Ackroyd

Introduction

In their activities and relationships people constitute societies. They also, simultaneously, constitute organisations and other groups. This paper is a consideration of the connections, overlaps and tensions between the processes by which societies and organisations are constituted. The paper argues that it is valuable to distinguish organisational processes of constitution from societal ones, to analyse these processes into their separate components and to consider the extent to which they are interconnected. To do this, a good deal of social theory (classical and contemporary) is reviewed and criticised, and then, following a critical discussion of some of the work of Anthony Giddens (1984; 1985; 1990; 1992), a realist analysis of organisation and their relations with society is developed (cf. Sayer 1992; 2000; Layder 1990; Ranson *et al.* 1980; Greenwood and Hinnings 1988).

The analysis is focused on the consideration of the relationships that produce and reproduce organisations and social structures. In an earlier paper (Ackroyd 1994a) structural processes were somewhat arbitrarily distinguished, by distinguishing *organisational constitution* (in which organisations are produced and reproduced) as distinct from *societal structuration* (in which organisations are implicated in the processes of production and reproduction of society). This usage will be continued because, in addition to being consistent, it draws a firm distinction between processes that are too often conflated.

Contemporary theorists, even those influenced by Giddens, whose work has been a critical stimulus in the present essay, do not see the point of distinguishing sharply these different aspects of social (re)production. It is perhaps not so surprising to find social theorists wishing to discuss general social processes. On the other hand, a failure to distinguish organisational constitution from more general social processes also affects organisational theorists. Such omissions are surprising when it is clear that organisations are produced and reproduced just as larger structures are, and the involvement of people in these processes is both more direct and consequential.

It is argued that one of the interesting applications of Giddens' work involves distinguishing organisational and societal structuration and considering the relationships between them. It is argued specifically that the imbricated character of the processes of organisational constitution and societal structuration is a subject of theoretical and substantive significance. This analysis in fact opens out for consideration a potentially large subject area which has hitherto been substantially ignored by social and organisational theorists alike. There are only one or two examples of students of social organisation being willing to take the relationship between organisation and society seriously and to consider the question of whether 'organisational constitution' is substantively more important in shaping the character of contemporary social life than processes of general societal structuration (see, for example, Ahrne 1990; 1993). More generally considered, what is being explored here is the applicability of organisational analysis to social regulation in the context of economic globalisation (cf. Peck and Tickell 1994).

The relevance of general social theory

The starting point for the present argument is in propositions that are, sociologically speaking, prosaic. Organisations, unlike many traditional structures, are more or less self-consciously and rationally constructed. They represent a significant development in the capacity of people to construct and reconstruct social institutions. The rationality which is a significant aspect of organisations, and the limited, instrumental nature of the characteristic engagements of participants in them, distinguish organisations from other kinds of social group prevalent in Western society. Moreover, it is mainly these new types of institutional relationships which are the starting points for processes of transformation to modern social relations and social formations. If Durkheim's idea of social differentiation has empirical reference, it is because large numbers of specialised organisations have been produced which augment traditional social relations. At this point, sociologists may start shifting moodily in their seats. Is this not simply the stuff of elementary sociology, yet another gloss on the proposition that modernity has ushered in a fundamental change of social relations? Since Toennies, the emphasis has been away from ascription towards achievement, from community to association, etc.

The argument of this paper, however, is to depart from the standard sociological account of social development. Instead it will be argued that, too often, sociologists have assumed that the augmentation of traditional groups by formal organisations results in a relatively stable and more or less permanent social arrangement in modern societies. According to this view, for all their dynamism, modern societies are relatively stable from a historical point of view. Alternatively, for those theorists where commitment to order and stability has been less strong, there is usually some idea that, with the onset of modernity, changed relations move out from organisations to other kinds of institutions at a rapid rate, to affect all social groups in relatively uniform ways. Theorists of modernity frequently attribute a seamless or unbroken quality to it, such that all institutions everywhere – the city, communities, families and organisations – are, or rapidly become, equally exemplary of modernity.

Against this it is argued that the appearance of modern organisations in otherwise traditional societies can occur in different ways, and so combine the modern with the pre-modern in different ways, engendering different social processes. It is not so much that modernity (cf. Habermas) is an uncompleted project but that it is intrinsically and irredeemably flawed. Formal organisations, themselves often assumed to be quintessentially modern, have pre-modern elements woven into them (Ackroyd 1994a). Thus, organisations frequently embody atavistic elements which persecute the individuals in them and/or function inhumanely on the people they process. The most extreme example of the latter is the holocaust which was thoroughly organised (Bauman 1989). Finally, as will be argued here, organisations can evade effective control by society, by, for example, escaping its physical boundaries and legal regulations, leaving little in the way of stable society behind them.

The thrust of this paper, then, is not to tell the conventional sociological story. It will be argued that despite their general familiarity to sociologists, the effects of the differentiation of institutions, and particularly the behavioural consequences of their presence, has not yet been well understood. One of the reasons for this is that theoretical sociologists tend to be focused on the character of modern social relations *per se* and the general processes that lead to the phenomenon of society as some kind of totality. Even when, as with Bourdieu and Giddens, theorists are aware of the importance of activities of human agents, their main concern is with the implications of these for social relations in general; that is, for social processes and for society. This is an unfortunate focus. New forms of relationship introduced by organisations have transformed social structures so that there is a need to think of them and their relation to social processes and the constitution of society fundamentally differently.

Theories of social organisation that allocate the production of society a less and less significant role in the shaping of behaviour and the reproduction of social relations are needed. This is because the organisation and organising have become so important as forms of social relation that they have inverted the relationship between institutions and societies which had previously become normal in the modern period, where structuration of society was in many ways a more significant set of processes than the constitution of organisation. Giddens does some important work in arguing that the constitution of societies has been often much less definite than appears appropriate to many contemporary sociologists who tend to treat the nation state and society as being synonymous (Giddens 1984: 165–8). In fact, in the current context, for large numbers of people, organisational relations have become much more salient than societal ones. In effect organisational relations have pulled the society inside out. What we are looking at in the contemporary transformation of social relations is the atrophy of specifically social structures and their substitution with little except the articulation of relations produced and reproduced by processes of organising. What contemporary sociologists are theorising about is organisational society (cf. Presthus 1978; Ahrne 1990). This is what makes possible the conflation of organisational and societal structuration and a general confusion of organisational with social processes.

In the following discussion of social theory, it is argued that there are obvious differences between the concerns of two groups of theorists. The first group, which is thought of as contributing to classical theory (including Weber, Marx, Durkheim and Parsons), is seen as recognising and having as part of its concern the relationship between organisations and society. The question of the interconnections between organisations and the society generally has considerable meaning for these theorists, however different their proposals are in detail. In contrast with this, for a second group of authoritative writers identified here as contributing to contemporary theory (and including Bourdieu, Habermas, Foucault and Giddens), concern with the question of the relationship between organisation and society has almost entirely disappeared. Instead there is a concern to identify key processes on the constitution and reproduction of society so that the centre of attention is processes which are thought to typify the social. It is not that the new theory has resolved the problem of classical theory, but that new social relations, to all intents and purposes, have abolished the problem. In this type of theory, society *per se*, as something capable of containing all institutions and social relationships, has a more problematic existence. Its place has been taken by accounts of recurrent but co-ordinated chains of action and reaction in which organisations and organising practices are elements, steps and conditions. This is what is now inevitably theorised as 'society'. Contemporary theory recognises the attenuated character of social relations, and resolves them into arrangements that are as much cultural as structural, as much voluntary as obligatory.

Classical theory: partial connections

That organisational theorists are preoccupied with the work of Weber is not difficult to understand (cf. Burrell 1994). Weber is the theorist of institutions who recognised both the historical singularity of modern organisations and their material and cultural potency. Other classical social theorists found a place for organisations, but Weber gives them special prominence. For Weber, institutions are the main stuff of social fabric, and formal organisations, in the shape of bureaucracies, in the modern world will settle the fate of modern society. Weber's legacy can be seen as involving neglect of society in preference for organisation. Almost no other significant theorist has taken the view that organisations are the primary component of social life in this sort of way. Marx, for example, had far less to say about organisations either in the economy, or in other spheres, than Weber.

The central thrust of Marx's analysis does, of course, implicate organisations in the connection he makes between the processes of capitalist accumulation and the tensions that are engendered in the social structure. Marx's ideas imply a good deal about the way factory organisations work, without arguing about such processes in great detail. As money is converted into commodities in the valorisation process, management in factories is at work, and the factory system developing. Moreover, the institutions of the state have a role in regulating the capitalist order. Latter day structural conflict theorists, working with both Marx's and Weber's ideas, have endeavoured to construct a satisfactory synthesis showing the systemic connections between the organisational networks of economy and the institutions of the polity and civil society.

Durkheim's stance towards social development postulates progressive internal differentiation of society. A naïve reading of his ideas finds a good deal of place for organisations, since organisations have been the predominant form of specialised institution in industrial society as it has developed. But Durkheim is of the view that institutional differentiation is not of itself a guarantee of social development. Durkheim gives the impression of preferring pre-modern forms of organisations – professions and other collegiate forms – and suggests that these are what is needed for the development of collective solidarity in the modern era. While Durkheim is, at best, equivocal about the desirability of modern organisations, there is little doubt that their existence has salience within his system of thought. The functionalist analysis of society that is often seen as developing from Durkheim involves the loss of a critical evaluation of social organisation and development.

Parsons' analysis of system needs – adaptation, goal-attainment, integration, pattern maintenance, which he used in almost all his work after 1950 – was made equally applicable by him to the family, organisations, subsystems of society and to the social system. Any and all of these 'systems' have analogous system needs, and although organisations contribute to the subsystem (the economy or the political system, for example) of which they are part, and also to society, this contribution is constitutive rather than causal. It is possible to study the system needs of organisations without considering the implications of system needs at this level for social organisation more generally. The pattern variables that Parsons uses to characterise the voluntary aspects of human action are also used in ways that do not allow the identification of linkages between the processes working at one level of social organisation to be connected with any other.

In sum, contributors to classical social theory do locate organisations and social collectivities in relation to each other. Marx and Weber share a conviction that the effect of organisations on society is likely to be more important than the other way around. Durkheim is of the opposite view, but is insufficiently specific about how organisations of different types will feature in these relationships. Classical theory can be understood as reaching some kind of resolution in the systematic functionalism which subsides theoretically into a bland and often presumptive bi-directionality of causation. Organisations are part of society and societies have organisations in them. One can move up and down the levels of analysis, but not connect systematically causes at one level with causes at another. In its Parsonian summation, classical theory may fail to resolve in any satisfactory way the place of organisations in society, but it does always locate them conceptually and grants the question of their relations considerable substantive importance. With contemporary theory the radicalism is back, the conjuring with freedom and morality as live issues that once animated the classical theorists. But the organisation, to all intents and purposes, has disappeared.

Contemporary theory: a neglect of organisations

Authoritative theorists since 1960 represent different attempts to work through the legacy of classical theory. Bourdieu, Habermas, Foucault and Giddens, for example, represent sophisticated responses of the theoretical problems of the earlier generation. Their intellectual merit is, however, inversely related to the applicability of their insights to organisations. Secondary commentators have made attempts to apply the insights of these writers to contemporary organisations. However, it is actually a feature which these systems of thought have in common that they resist attempts to constitute organisations as distinctive social entities. These perspectives dissolve the organisation as something distinctive and formative, and make organisational processes relatively unimportant aspects of social relations. These writers are concerned with social organisation. Although their ideas do illuminate particular organisational practices, their work specifically does not yield systematic theorisations of organisation and the connection of this to society.

Bourdieu has little to say about organisations as such in his published work. His work applies only incidentally to particular processes of organising in specialised institutions. Some of his work specifies linked groups of organisations and other institutions in culturally defined connections. Apart from the infrequent citations by institutionalists, his work has been little used by organisation theorists in the Anglo-Saxon world. Major concepts of Bourdieu, particularly 'habitus', do not illuminate contemporary organisation. The habitus refers to a system of regulated improvisation or generative rules that is constituted by the affective and evaluative ideas internalised by actors. It might therefore be taken to describe the culture of the factory or office, but, as Bourdieu himself suggests, 'class fractions' bear similar habitus creating similar patterns in aspiration, mentality and taste.

Habermas has a somewhat different solution to the problems of social theory. His notion of system is strongly reminiscent of functionalist theory in its underlying episteme, though it is transformed into a hyper-functional, rational and technocratic apparatus. This is in tension with the 'lifeworld', which has its origins in a quite different philosophical and analytical tradition. The Weberian vision is preserved in its pessimistic extreme, as the bureaucracy is no longer an organisation, but has become consolidated into a web of interlocking broadly based interests. The systemic elements of advanced society are seen as being technologically co-ordinated and, although this system is, in a sense, a system of institutions, it is not specified in sufficient detail to be resolved into a small number of generic types of organisation.

Amongst the writers considered in this section, the one who has most often inspired students of organisation has been Foucault. The paradox is that Foucault, in common with the other 'new theorists' considered here, says almost nothing about organisations as a class of social phenomena. His work teems with descriptions of fragments of organised activity – instances of administrative, legal, medical and other (typically professionally constituted) organising procedures and devices. Actually, as Burrell (1988) rightly affirms, Foucault's way of thinking is inimical to describing such entities as organisation, if not actually incapable of constituting them. He is the theorist who deconstructs and disembodies social entities so that they exist as a multiplicity of particularities of practice and relationships which are of interest because they supposedly reveal or demonstrate the characteristics of whole eras. Recent examples of supposedly Foucauldian analysis of organisations range widely across different kinds of examples of generic processes of surveillance supposedly found in (all?) organisations. In a much quoted paper by Sewell and Wilkinson (1992) for instance, examples of organisational practices are sampled across a range of organisations from supermarkets to factories, with not the slightest concern for the representativeness of the surveillance techniques cited. Similar methodological insouciance characterises other Foucault-inspired analyses of organisations. Foucault's categories so cut across organisation structures and boundaries, disassembling them into practices, that they do not exist in recognisable forms within his system of thought.

Giddens

At first sight Giddens' work has some similar mapping problems to those identified in the work of Bourdieu, Habermas and Foucault, in that organisations do not have an obvious place. There is a similar general lack of direct reference to organisations. But it is more accurate to say that there is an apparent reluctance to discuss organisations which at some points is much more noticeable than at others. There are several points here. In Giddens' work there is much discussion of institutional complexes more general than, but clearly implicating, organisations – such as industrialism and capitalism. There is also quite a lot of discussion which involves oblique and indirect recognition of organisations, as when, for example, the relations between commodities and money are discussed as 'structural sets' within capitalism. There are other discussions of processes within organisations, as when interaction between pupils and teachers in schools are mentioned, or, more rarely, when the workings of managerial regimes are discussed.

Giddens has a developed sense of the diversity of organised social life, in which there are yet extremely influential sequences and effects that produce patterning. It will be argued here that organisations and organisationally based processes, although making some appearance in the analysis, are actually more important than has yet been realised, and that further development of Giddens' ideas as they apply to organisations is a valuable undertaking.

The extent to which organisations feature in Giddens' numerous books varies a good deal. Only in *The Nation State and Violence* (1985) does there seem to be much sustained use of the term organisation, and here the argument is concerned with the powers and formative effects of the state. The use of the idea of organisation features prominently in the way modern state power is configured and deployed. Organisations feature as mediators of political and economic power of dominant groups in class societies. It is obvious that the different kinds of organisations are specialised arrangements mediating social and economic power. Institutions of the state were the prototype for most types of specialised organisation (Poggi 1978). However, in much of Giddens' other work, this crucial insight gives way to other emphases. At the same time, the term 'institution' is a more common subject for comment, indicating interest in a broader range of groups and the characteristic relationships found in and between them. Organisations as such are not fully discussed. In passages of *The Constitution of Society* (1984), for example, at a point where the extended discussion of organisations is clearly called for, Giddens couples organisations with 'associations' and 'social movements' (1984: 199–200) and gives organisation the briefest of summaries which is highly derivative of the work of Tourraine. Organisations, then, particularly as contributors to social change and transformation, are discussed rather little by Giddens, and clearly are given far less attention than their substantive importance merits. 'Social movements', Giddens complains, have been 'vastly under-represented' (203) within the social sciences, whilst there is a 'vast literature' (203) on organisations and organisation theory.

Organisations are more likely to feature in Giddens' writing in discussions of the effect of centralised power on people than in discussions of the capacity of people to influence society. The 'vast literature' is not out of proportion to the relative importance of organisations as the dominant institutions of modern society. Considered purely substantively, for much of recent history, organisations have involved more people for more significant proportions of their time than social movements. Moreover, the development of organisations has contributed rather little to social equality and the equalisation of wealth. As organisations have spread themselves across space, often protected and nurtured by nation states, they have not removed differences of wealth and status. In their latest phase of development organisations have decisively escaped national confines. Today, large organisations have more capital assets than governments, and the balance of power, between states and companies, has changed dramatically in favour of the companies.

In *The Constitution of Society*, Giddens formulates a key theoretical question as follows: 'Is the expansion of a diversity of different forms of organisation – in which the conditions of reproduction are reflexively monitored – a medium of emancipation from pre-established modes of exploitative domination?' To this he gives an indirect but broadly sceptical answer. It is interesting that he does not give more attention to the question of why it is necessary to be sceptical. In the view developed here it is, in fact, extremely unlikely that organisations will contribute to emancipation in any but very restricted forms. In addition, to gain understanding of the effects of organisations, it is necessary to disentangle and think more critically about the way that organisations relate to societies. In this project, the work of Giddens does no more than offer some useful but scattered building blocks.

Constituting the organisation

Whether Giddens has neglected to consider organisations thoroughly because of omission or conceptual inadequacy is an open question. Critics have pointed to the lack of adequate specification of mechanisms connecting abstract concepts such as structure and system (Urry 1982), and strategy and institution (Mouzelis 1989). Thompson (1989) suggests at one point that Giddens' concepts cannot account for the differentiation of specific organisational forms – publishers as opposed to car manufacturers.

It seems to be the case that when Giddens' concepts are applied to organisations they usually arrive at accounts which describe the activities of key actors within organisations, rather than organisations as such. A common product is accounts of management rather than organisation (Willmott 1981; Whittington 1992; Reed 1985). Yet it is important to understand how organisations achieve their characteristic forms, and the effects of their location on these forms. Using similar terms to those Giddens uses to characterise the constitution of society, the constitution of organisations can be analysed as something distinctive. Consideration of the process of organisational constitution has important implications for organisational theory, and because the constitution of organisations is so deeply implicated in the constitution of societies, what has been revealed has wider implications. In brief, individuals may constitute societies, but where there is a significant development of organisations, societies are constituted mainly by the mediation of organisations.

Despite the attention paid to Giddens' ideas (Morgan 1990; Reed 1985; Whittington 1992; Willmott 1986), there have been few attempts to use Giddens to provide an account of the organisation. However, in a paper of

1980, Ranson *et al.* hazard a first assay at constituting the organisation in a way that they take to be implied by Giddens. This attempt was immediately and severely criticised by Hugh Willmott (1981) on the ground that these authors had misunderstood Giddens' ideas. Willmott's point in one way is undoubtedly correct. Ranson *et al.* display a rather mechanical understanding of structuration, thinking of structures in a way that is alien to Giddens' conception. But, although technically correct in this criticism, Willmott overlooks a valuable contribution by these authors. This is to distinguish organisational from societal structuration – the former will hereinafter be called organisational constitution. For Willmott, the organisation, to the extent that it exists (for in his work the organisation is seldom precisely specified as to type or specific configuration, see, for example, Willmott 1987; 1981; 1994), is much more significantly the site of generalised processes of social control exerted by managers than something general, let alone something real. This is because, in common with many contemporary social theorists, Willmott does not think of organisations as being real structures, but merely as instantiations of general social processes. In sum, he does not work with a realist ontology.

Subsequent writers have often tended to concur with Willmott, and not to see a need to understand the organisation as something separate and really constituted. Thus Whittington (1992) applauds Willmott for his criticism of Ranson *et al.* and in particular on the way they insist on the consideration of 'organisational structuration' from organisation as a formative social process. This is again held to be untrue to Giddens. But although Whittington has an admirable sense of the plurality of the rules that can be evoked by management and other groups of actors, he fails to see how the rules and resources that management exploit also help to produce specific types of organisational roles and relationships, and that these social systems have a constraining effect on managers as well as other organisational participants. The idea of the organisation as something constituted in definite ways effectively disappears from view. For Whittington, the central problem of 'putting Giddens into action' is to open sufficient conceptual space to account for the existence and role of 'managerial agency'. The chief value of Giddens, in this view, is to account for the (effective) agency of some agents, not systematically for the full consequences of the agency of all agents, and the way that they collectively constitute the organisation as a structure. Thus, in this analysis, the organisation becomes a nominal entity 'cross cut' with social influences which set up a diversity of social rules and resources.

For both Willmott and Whittington, there is a relatively exclusive emphasis on general social processes against which organisations *per se* are indistinct if not unimportant. But bringing into focus the formative effects of society on key groups within the organisation has the tendency to attenuate any sense of the organisation as something real and adopting distinctive forms, and which, in virtue of these features, has had definite, indeed historically fateful, effects. If this is the case, the insights gained from using

Giddens are achieved at considerable cost. It follows from the indistinctness of the organisation that aspects of the organisation and the manner in which organisational processes work are left implicit. By implication, then, the organisation is constituted by the formal power of organisational controllers (managers and key professionals such as accountants) who, presumably, directly or indirectly manipulate organisational participants into conformity. Certainly in some of the work of Willmott (1993) and Knights and Willmott (1989) there has been attention to the transition in organisational control mechanisms as allegedly they have moved from coercion to other means of compliance – from degradation to subjugation. But there is too much emphasis on power and too little on the role of organisation in integrating the individual. Much more research effort has to be placed in understanding the way that behaviour contributes to the production of organisation.

An approach which takes significant steps in an appropriate direction draws heavily on ethnomethodology, and argues that talk and routine interaction are key mechanisms by which organisational continuity is sustained and individuals are integrated into organisations (Anderson *et al.* 1989; Boden 1994). Boden uses some of the theoretical ideas of Giddens to link together the analysis of conversation with some of the central themes and propositions of organisation theory; in particular suggesting that talk is the key mechanism in the production of routines and the reproduction of organisational relationships. There can be no doubt that talk is highly significant. Talk is the main activity of managers – as much expensive empirical research has shown. In Gowler and Legge's memorable formulation, 'the meaning of management is the management of meaning', and the management of meaning requires persistent efforts (Gowler and Legge 1983).

But an obvious objection to placing too much emphasis on the integrative aspects of talk is that this is also a means through which opposition and dissent are orchestrated. Talk is obviously an accompaniment of actively *dis*organising activities (Ackroyd and Thompson 1999), as well as organising. Clearly, talk is not all that goes into constituting the organisation. Management and professionals are not the only groups within organisations that are capable of organising, and using rules and other symbolic resources drawn from outside as well as inside the organisation to develop and to defend distinct positions. But the capacity of all groups within the organisation to formulate and defend their own agendas and programmes generally does not impair the routine constitution of organisations. The constitution of organisation has to be seen as in part the result of differential access to assets and is therefore to an extent grounded in material differences, but it is also a special quality emerging from the interaction of individuals and groups and to which they contribute actively. In this respect organisation can be seen as a distinctive social ability.

Organisation, in this account, is to an important degree a property of the action of agents (and groups acting as agents), which is engaged in actively and orchestrated by people. Thus, also, although organisations are sites of energetic contestation between groups, this is often associated with strong and persistent organisational forms. The most enduring and in many ways the most important instance to be considered here is, of course, contestation over the control of the capitalist labour process (Braverman 1974; Thompson 1984; Littler 1982). It is now clear that organisations in themselves are robust enough to accommodate and, to a considerable degree, buffer and absorb the contestation surrounding these fundamental tensions. In view of this it should hardly surprise us that, although the contestation between groups of workers is endemic in organisations, other kinds of conflicts are easily accommodated by organisations.

How organisation is effectively and routinely produced — despite, sometimes, almost equal access to resources between different groups of professionals, none with any obvious or prior claim to authority — is an important question for a realist research programme. Different professional groups in the health service, for example (Ackroyd 1994b), or engineers and accountants (Ackroyd and Lawrenson 1996), can be seen to be achieving organisation in broadly similar patterns over decades. Organisations may fail as a result of what is external to them — adverse market conditions, hostile government policies or predatory banking — but they seldom do so because their participating groups pull them apart from the inside.

... and structurating the society

In strong contrast to the short-term contestation between groups in organisations, over long time periods organisations nonetheless appear to be stable patterns of relationships (they have distinct organisational structures) which are slow to change, and which do not change the social structure very much. As Braudel (1983) suggests, organisations are strongly implicated in the 'longue durée'. Braudel's consideration of economic history documents the existence of the European company over long tracts of time. One does not have to be a population ecologist, therefore, to accept the idea that organisational structures have considerable inertia, and that they are seemingly unable to adapt, in certain fundamentals, rapidly (Hannan and Freeman 1989). Moreover, despite some periods of dramatic exception, there is a recurrent tendency for the production of organisation to lead to more organisation: as structures are reproduced they proliferate. Now it could be that the only reason for this is simply that the formal power monopolised by some groups is sufficient to keep dissent within bounds. On the other hand, clearly, the rational calculation of groups of actors combined with the idea of the organisation as structure necessarily comprising limited forms of collaboration are also important.

Because of this, amongst other things, organisations have precluded and limited the influence of people on their society. More often than not, organisational analysis and case studies show that despite the reality of agency, organisations do not change themselves very much, except in response to economic demands. They leave the class and elite structures of societies substantially unchanged in their normal functioning (Scott 1986). Organisations, for all their capacity for technical innovation and their indirect but considerable influences on culture through the promotion of consumerism, have made little contribution to structural transformation. This is true, despite the fact that it is actually organisations that are the providers of so many of the features of modernity that Giddens rightly finds compelling. Organisations, for example, have put in place the communications that have compressed time and space, and it is organisations that use them most fully and effectively; to use Giddens' own terms, they have 'bitten deeply into space and time' over the 400 years of modern Western history. But it is important to note, in addition, that they are the principal beneficiaries of the new kinds of control made possible by information technology; that is, control-at-a-distance.

Structurally considered, the organisation poses considerable problems for a theorist interested in effective human agency. As a context for action, organisations illustrate the scope of groups to display relative independence in action. Organisations are the sites for effective agency. But this does not yield much change either in organisations themselves or in the society of which they are part. The structural sets of relationships which Giddens identifies, and which centrally involve organisations, accomplish the business of production, distribution and exchange and many other processes as well. In so doing organisations involve the active engagement of people, but the result of much of this action is the perpetuation of society and its characteristic inequalities. On one side of the organisational divide are economic elites, on the other are the increasing numbers excluded from participation in organisations and therefore from everything but the remaining vestigial society (Mann 1992; Murray 1990). For reasons that have to do with their role as mediators of social and economic power, then, organisations consolidate and extend themselves as a condition of their reproduction. They do not at the same time become democratised. Historically speaking, no sooner had ordinary people gained some rights of representation in the state than the locus of significant power was removed by the development of huge multinational organisations.

Although they are arenas in which agents actively formulate and prosecute distinct projects and agendas, and they function in this way more clearly then other types of institution, organisations also manage to remain stable patterns of interaction over long periods of time, and so to sustain relations at the societal level in much the same form. Organisations contain the shocks and collisions of contestation by groups of agents very effectively. Whether or not this involves overt dissent, and/or failure to co-operate over a limited range of activities, the agency of actors in organisations is implicated in the production of traditional patterns of behaviour – both in the organisation and, by extension, in the society. To account for such things, a more adequate theory of organisational constitution is needed.

The main phases in the process of organisational constitution and its relation to societal structuration are out in a schematic way in Figure 5.1.

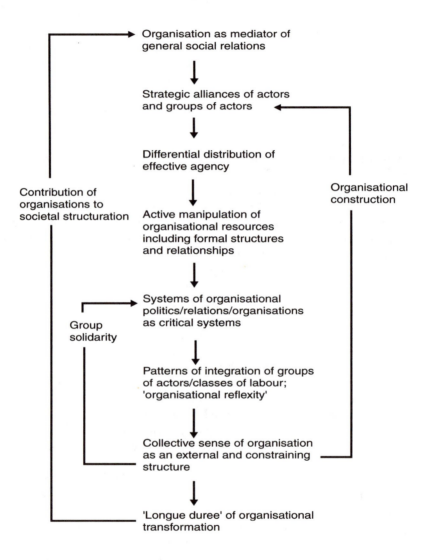

Figure 5.1   The connectedness of organisational constitution and societal structuration

What kind of organisation theory?

Organisational studies lack an adequate theorisation of the constitution of organisations, and, without this, the field is prevented both from developing in itself and from making a significant contribution to general social theory. Surprisingly, contributions to organisational analysis, drawing strongly on recent social theory, have not made organisation and organising subjects of interest in their own right (Willmott 1981; Whittington 1992). This is scarcely an improvement on the traditional view of organisation in which the view of the organisation is that it is something produced by external pressures. The leading schools of organisation theory (neo-contingency theory, institutionalism) emphasise, in one way or another, the importance of factors external to the organisation in producing organisations and determining their fate. If the argument of this paper is correct, however, and organisations are actively constituted by their members (and may well in many circumstances produce and transform what is external to them), such views are in need of fundamental revision.

At the centre of the view developed here is the proposition that organisations are indeed constituted by their members. Organisations should be analysed as configurations of different groups (with their own distinct priorities and agendas). What has been considerably neglected is that despite inevitable contestation in organisations, this occurs in ways which also produce significant integration of the organisational structure. Hence, organisational analysis needs to go back to look at the contribution of action theories, which also identified organisations as the product of groups with different orientations. But, this time around, more attention must be paid to the complexity of the processes through which organisation is constituted. The organisation that is produced seems to be a system of relations which: (a) express and embody conflict, but which also (b) exhibit the capacity to integrate behaviour and render it co-operative and yet (c) buffer and redirect more general social conflicts. To use Giddens' terminology, although agents in organisations are active, there are special features of the recursiveness of their actions which contribute to organisational stability and societal reproduction as well as change.

How this occurs may be considered the central problem of organisational theory. How is it that patterns of behaviour which involve so much self-reference and behavioural innovation in pursuit of the discrete agendas of groups also contribute to so much order and stability at the level of the organisation, and in terms of their connections with society?

There is tacit acknowledgement of some of this in Giddens' work, in that some of the examples he is fond of citing feature the way organisations achieve the accommodation of dissent. Examples here are Willis's (1977) account of working class socialisation and Burawoy's (1979) treatment of the game-like features of industrial relations. In a recent book (Ackroyd and Thompson 1999), this point has been generalised: organisations are to a considerable degree constituted by the misbehaviour they (partially) allow.

These works show how dissent from organisational regimes is nonetheless central to their social reproduction. To adopt this sort of approach is to depart significantly from the analytical traditions of much organisation theory, which attributes the systemic features of organisations to functionality and efficiency. The predominant approach, which attributes only limited effectiveness to the action of particular agents (strategic managers), ignores the agency of most other groups. (See Child 1972; Child *et al.* 1983.)

This is not to deny that the institutionalised self-monitoring of subordinate groups is shaped by the power of managerial groups to grant or deny material rewards, frame rules and to mobilise symbolic resources. The recognition of alternative views held by subordinate groups entails the capacity to discount them, push them to the periphery and render them essentially contested. The fact that organisations mediate general economic and political power achieves concrete expression in differential abilities of this kind. However, that dissenting views are perpetuated itself contributes to the production of organisation as a limited and distinctive kind of collaborative activity. In particular, such encapsulation of partially dissenting views effectively contributes to a strong sense of the organisation as something beyond the *de facto* powers of ideas and the agents dissenting from it. Dissent as much as conformity, therefore, contributes to the experience of the organisation as something real – and certainly beyond the powers of subordinated groups to alter. The label critical system (Garnsey 1993) describes this aspect of organisational constitution, in which systems of organisational politics contribute a collective sense of the externality of organisation, through the mediation of distinctive forms of organisational reflexivity. By such mechanisms organisations are constituted as something quite distinctive. Organisations are experienced as real – often at the very moment they are being challenged and contested.

To use Giddens' term, it is clear that organisations produce reflexivity in distinctive forms. Again there is some acknowledgement of this in Giddens' work. In his response to some critics of the arguments in *New Rules of Sociological Method*, he distinguishes between reflexivity as a quality of human interaction in general and 'institutional reflexivity'. This is an important qualification, suggesting that there may be significant variations in the modality of attachment of people to groups of different kinds (see Giddens 1990: 16, where organisational reflexivity is referred to). In view of the argument of this paper, it should be recognised that organisations contribute to and also alter reflexivity in ways that encourage the active engagement of participants in organisational processes, but at the same time entail a generally low level of affective attachment to them. The experience that has been described elsewhere as 'normalised alienation' is widespread in organisations: it is common for organisational participants to share a sense of detachment from the organisation and low general expectations (Ackroyd 1994a; Ackroyd and Thompson 1999). Management shares some of these features of detachment. Managers have superior access to the organisational resources and the levers of symbolical power, but they also are habitually instrumental and affectively neutral in their outlook. The attachment of both managers and managed to organisations shares a similar modality and managers and managed share similar degrees of reflexivity.

Institutional theorists share some of the emphases outlined here. Their work is concerned with giving precise shape to different kinds of organisations (DiMaggio and Powell 1991; Scott and Meyer 1994), and to implicate the ideas of participants in such processes. A recurrent emphasis of institutional theorists is on the influence of the social matrix as the source of the organisation, and this is seen to be the basis for the explanation of the characteristics of organisation. There is also a recurrent emphasis on conformity being reproduced by other means, such as myths and other kinds of symbols. But how and why conforming behaviour occurs must be further debated, and a place found for it within the theory of organisations. It is also clear that institutional theory misunderstands the role of agency in the reproduction of organisations. It is true that organisations are embedded in society (Granovetter 1985), but the organisation is also in some ways actively disembedding as well. There is a large difference between organisations and traditional institutions in this respect.

It cannot be too strongly emphasised how different organisations are from the majority of traditional institutions. There are striking limitations on the involvement of participants in organisations. There are several dimensions to this – among the most obvious is the temporal one, in that hours of work are limited; but there are distinct limits also on the physical and mental demands that organisations make on the powers and resources of participants. The crucial point is that emotional identification is limited. As has been argued, our detachment from organisations is integral to the way that we constitute them as objects and this reinforces our subjective detachment from them. Organisations are structures we are in but not necessarily of. In this respect organisations are the antithesis of traditional institutions. In the West, organisations are actively also disembedding mechanisms in society. They corrode the social matrix from which they spring. The formative influences that remain are few: the influences of owning and controlling groups for example and the conditions of capital supply, access to consumer markets and so on. Apart from these influences, organisations are substantially detached from the social matrix. It is easy to mistake these for substantial links because the development of the organisation itself produces an attenuated, disaggregated society, in which fragile social supports are all that there are. In a society in which institutions established in the last few decades are seriously postulated as having distinct 'cultures' (Peters and Waterman 1982), the social supports of general social life have become very attenuated indeed.

Giddens writes perceptively about disembedding as part of 'the dynamism of modernity' (1990). But his unwillingness to focus on organisations is apparent here as elsewhere. Almost everything cited as mechanisms of disembedding – 'money' and 'expert systems' – originate and have their principal usage in organisations. Organisations are significant concentrations of both money and expertise. In addition, although organisations did not create money, they have created the dense and layered markets in which money becomes the ubiquitous and indispensable basis for exchanges, driving out all other forms. Organisations also centrally involve expertise, either by disassembling it as in Taylorism/Fordism or by concentrating it as in professional bureaucracy and the knowledge-intensive firm. There is a school of economic theory which makes the value of knowledge central to the analysis (Penrose 1980; Casson 1991). In sum, the several key features attributed by Giddens to 'modernity' are also attributable to organisations and a society constructed out of nothing more than reticulated organisations.

Organisations have to be thought of as new kinds of institutions – as distinctive structures. Organisations are not basically neutral towards, and content to coexist within, traditional society. On the contrary, as a necessary feature of their existence, organisations entail anti-relationships, actively producing the corrosion and dissolution of traditional social relations. The markets which the organisation creates and which surround it – specifically, the labour and product markets – are the most potent forms of this anti-relational social correlate of organisation. However, all organisations have similar socially corrosive effects, as when welfare services and charities actively break down the social responsibility embodied in traditional social arrangements based on kinship relations or other customary social support. To adapt the concept of Geertz (1973) organisations replace 'thick' traditional relationships with 'thin' market relations, in which the palest of cultural colouring is retained. These are the fragile social supports which institutionalists seek to make the basis for their accounts of organisations.

Clearly, there are different ways in which organisations can relate to what is outside of them. Theory in this area will have to be constructed with international comparisons in mind. The American 'Fordist' model, in which product markets and labour markets are dominated by one huge producer, is but one pattern in which the organisation can produce self-reinforcing subjugation and control of its markets. It can be contrasted with the 'industrial districts' which were so important to British industrialisation (Marshall 1890) and which have inspired the neo-liberal ideas of Piore and Sabel (1984). These are different again from the hierarchical structures of firms that are at the core of the Japanese economy (Morishima 1982; Sasaki 1981). Given this it is clear that the inter-organisation relations which mediate control by owning elites and affect the supply of capital are also an important point of reference for the theorist. Arguably this question – that of the nature of the organisational infrastructure of economy and society – ought to be more important to both sociologists and organisation theorists. (However, see Lash and Urry 1987.)

In sum, a kind of institutional theory of organisations needs to be developed that sees organisations as the result of the powers and resources that different groups of agents can mobilise. It also needs to be recognised that the projects of agents will be differentially effective in their realisation of their objectives (and so constituting organisation of which they are part and, at a higher level, the form of the society in which they exist), according to their access to critical contingencies such as access to capital. Analysis is cast much more in terms of the material powers and resources of groups of agents than symbolic ones. Instead of the idea of an organisational field made up of organisations of similar size and type and perhaps some regulatory agencies, we have to see organisations as being made up of more and less powerful groups of agents, and fields being made up of more or less powerful organisations.

A summary conclusion

The basic argument of this paper can be formally constructed as a number of logical steps. Firstly, the constitution of organisations has been an extremely formative aspect of the structuration of societies. Secondly, because organisations are not neutral in respect of traditional social relationships, this development has initiated change processes that have their own self-reinforcing dynamics of social disintegration. Thirdly, a stage is reached in the 'organisational society' in which relations in organisations are more significant as contributions to social life and to the subjective sense of participants in them than processes of societal structuration. Theoretically speaking, what has happened is that the tensions between organisational and societal process have pulled the social structure inside out. Whereas organisation was formerly an element in social structure, now organising has subsumed and subordinated more general social relations. On the one hand organisations are in the direct control of incredibly wealthy elites (Scott 1986), on the other exclusion from engagement in organisations amounts to being excluded from society – and to being unloaded into what has been called the underclass (Mann 1992). If the present argument is correct, this condition might equally be labelled the under-society. However, if the effects of organisation are beyond control, it is not yet clear that organisations themselves are beyond control. However, a first step in taking control of them, or rendering it a possibility, is to understand better how far organisations are already in control of participants, but, also, how participants are persuaded that they are not.

Bibliography

Ackroyd, S. (1994a) 'Re-creating common ground: elements for post-paradigmatic organisation studies', in J. Hassard and M. Parker (eds) *Towards a New Theory of Organisations*, London: Routledge, 270–97.

——(1994b) 'Nurses, management and morale: a diagnosis of decline in the N.H.S. hospital service', in L. MacKay *et al.* (eds) *Inter-Professional Relations in Health Care*, London: Edward Arnold, 222–38.

——(1996) 'Organisation contra organisations: professionals and organisational change in contemporary Britain', *Organisation Studies*, 17, 4: 599–622.

Ackroyd, S. and Lawrenson, D. (1996) 'Manufacturing decline and the managerial division of labour', in I. Glover *et al.* (eds) *The Professional-Managerial Class*, Aldershot: Avebury, 171–93.

Ackroyd, S. and Thompson, P. (1999) *Organisational Misbehaviour*, London: Sage.

Ackroyd, S. and Whitaker, A. (1990) 'Manufacturing decline and the organisation of manufacture in Britain', in P. Stewart *et al.* (eds) *Restructuring for Economic Flexibility*, Aldershot: Avebury, 9–32.

Ahrne, G. (1990) *Agency and Organisation: Towards an Organisational Theory of Society*, London: Sage.

——(1993) *Social Organisations: Interaction Inside, Outside and Between Organisations*, London: Sage.

Anderson, R. J. *et al.* (1989) *Working for Profit: The Social Organisation of Calculation in an Entrepreneurial Firm*, Aldershot: Avebury.

Bauman, Z. (1989) *Modernity and the Holocaust*, Cambridge: Polity Press.

Boden, D. (1994) *The Business of Talk: Organisations in Action*, Cambridge: Polity Press.

Braudel, F. (1983) *Civilisation and Capitalism Vol. II: The Wheels of Commerce*, London: Collins.

Braverman, H. (1974) *Labour and Monopoly Capital*, New York: Monthly Review Press.

Burawoy, M. (1979) *Manufacturing Consent*, Chicago: University of Chicago Press.

Burrell, G. (1988) 'Modernism, postmodernism and organisational analysis 2: the contribution of Michel Foucault', *Organisation Studies*, 9, 2: 221–35.

——(1994) 'Modernism, postmodernism and organisational analysis 4: the contribution of Jurgen Habermas', *Organisation Studies*, 15, 1: 1–20.

Casson, M. (1991) *The Economics of Business Culture*, Oxford: Clarendon.

Child, J (1972) 'Organizational structure, environment and performance: the role of strategic choice', *Sociology*, 6, 1: 1–22.

Child, J., Fores, M. and Glover, I. (1983) 'A price to pay? professionalism and work organization in Britain and Germany', *Sociology*, 17, 1: 63–78.

DiMaggio, P. J. and Powell, W. W. (eds) (1991) *The New Institutionalism in Organisational Analysis*, Chicago: University of Chicago Press.

Garnsey, E. (1993) 'Exploring a critical systems perspective', *Innovation in Social Science Research*, 6, 2: 229–56.

Geertz, C. (1973) *The Interpretation of Cultures*, New York: Basic Books.

Giddens, A. (1984) *The Constitution of Society*, Cambridge: Polity Press.

——(1985) *The Nation State and Violence*, Volume 2 of *A Contemporary Critique of Historical Materialism*, Cambridge: Polity Press.

——(1990) *The Consequences of Modernity*, Cambridge: Polity Press.

——(1992) *New Rules of Sociological Method* (Introduction to the Second Edition), London: Hutchinson.

Gowler, D. and Legge, K. (1983) 'The meaning of management and the management of meaning: a view from social anthropology', in M. J. Earl (ed.) *Perspectives on Management*, London: Oxford University Press.

Granovetter, M. (1985) 'Economic action and social structure: the problem of embeddedness', *American Journal of Sociology*, 91, 3: 481–510.

Greenwood, R and Hinings, C. R. (1988) 'Organisational design types, tracks and the dynamics of strategic change', *Organisation Studies*, 9, 3: 293–316.

Hannan, M. and Freeman, T. (1989) *Organisational Ecology*, Cambridge, MA: Harvard University Press.

Knights, D. and Willmott, H. (1989) 'Power and subjectivity at work: from degradation to subjugation in social relations', *Sociology*, 23, 4: 535–58.

Lash, S. and Urry, J. (1987) *The End of Organised Capitalism*, Cambridge: Polity Press.

——(1994) *Economies of Signs and Spaces*, London: Sage.

Layder, D. (1985) 'Power, structure and agency', *Journal for the Theory of Social Behaviour*, 15, 2: 131–49.

——(1990) *The Realist Image in Social Science*, Basingstoke: Macmillan.

Littler, C. R. (1982) *The Development of the Labour Process in Capitalist Societies*, London: Heinemann.

Mann, K. (1992) *The Making of an English Underclass: The Social Divisions of Labour and Welfare*, Milton Keynes: Open University Press.

Marshall, A. (1890) *Principles of Economics*, London: Macmillan.

Morgan, G. (1990) *Organisations in Society*, London: Macmillan.

Morishima, M. (1982) *Why Has Japan Succeeded?*, Cambridge: Cambridge University Press.

Mouzelis, N. (1989) 'Restructuring structuration theory', *Sociological Review*, 35, 2: 144–66.

Murray, C. (1990) *The Emerging British Underclass*, London: IEA Health and Welfare Unit.

Peck, J. and Tickell, A. (1994) 'Searching for a new institutional fix: the after-Fordism crisis', in A. Amin (ed.) *Post Fordism: A Reader*, Oxford: Basil Blackwell, 280–315.

Penrose, E. (1980) *The Theory of the Growth of the Firm*, Oxford: Basil Blackwell.

Peters, T. and Waterman, R. H. (1982) *In Search of Excellence*, New York: Harper and Row.

Piore, M. J. and Sabel, C. F. (1984) *The Second Industrial Divide: Possibilities for Prosperity*, New York: Basic Books.

Poggi, G. (1978) *The Development of the Modern State: A Sociological Introduction*, London: Hutchinson.

Presthus, R. (1978) *The Organisational Society*, London: Macmillan.

Ranson, S., Hinings, C. R. and Greenwood, R. (1980) 'The structuring of organisational structures', *Administrative Science Quarterly*, 25: 314–37.

Reed, M. (1985) *Redirections in Organisational Analysis*, London: Tavistock.

——(1989) *The Sociology of Management*, Brighton: Harvester.

Sasaki, N. (1989) *Management and Industrial Structure in Japan*, Oxford: Pergamon.

Sayer, A. (1992) *Method in Social Science: A Realist Approach*, second edition, London: Routledge.

——(2000) *Realism and Social Science*, London: Sage.

Scott, J. (1986) *Capitalist Property and Financial Power*, Brighton: Wheatsheaf.

Scott, W. R. and Meyer, J. W. (eds) (1994) *Institutional Environments and Organisations*, London: Sage.

Sewell, G. and Wilkinson, B. (1992) 'Someone to watch over me: surveillance, discipline and the just-in-time labour process', *Sociology*, 26, 2: 271–89.

Thompson, J. B. (1989) 'The theory of structuration', in D. Held and J. B. Thompson (eds) *Social Theory and Modern Societies: Anthony Giddens and his Critics*, Cambridge: Cambridge University Press.

Thompson, P. (1984) *The Nature of Work: An Introduction to Debates on the Labour Process*, London: Macmillan.

Urry, J. (1982) 'Duality of structure: some critical issues', *Theory, Culture and Society*, 1, 2: 100–6.

Weick, K. E. (1969) *The Social Psychology of Organising*, Reading, MA: Addison-Wesley.

Whittington, R. (1992) 'Putting Giddens into action: social systems and managerial agency', *Journal of Management Studies*, 26, 6: 693–712.

Willis, P. (1977) *Learning to Labour*, Farnborough: Saxon House.

Willmott, H. (1981) 'The structuring of organisational structure – a note', *Administrative Science Quarterly*, 26: 470–4.

——(1986) 'Unconscious sources of motivation in the theory of the subject: explanation and critique of Giddens' dualistic models of action and personality', *Journal for the Theory of Social Behaviour*, 16, 1: 105–22.

——(1987) 'Studying managerial work: a critique and a proposal', *Journal of Management Studies*, 24, 3: 249–70.

——(1993) 'Strength is ignorance, freedom is slavery: managing culture in modern organisations', *Journal of Management Studies*, 30: 515–52.

——(1994) 'Theorising agency: power and subjectivity in organisation studies', in J. Hassard and M. Parker (eds) *Towards a New Theory of Organisations*, London: Routledge, 87–130.

6 Structure, agency and Marx's analysis of the labour process[1]

Stephen Pratten

Introduction

The past twenty years have seen a fundamental questioning and critique of traditional positions in the philosophy of science and the emergence and elaboration of a perspective known as transcendental realism, which is sustainable in the face of this increased questioning and critique. The specific version of transcendental realism that has been developed for the social realm, usually gathered under the heading critical realism, has in the last ten years increasingly been adopted in social and psychological research. However, there are two areas, surprisingly, where there has been rather little recognition of the importance of critical realism. These are: the area of organisation and management studies known as labour process theory and orthodox economics. Recently, critical realism has begun to gain ground in economics,[2] but there is as yet little recognition of it in many areas of organisation and management studies.

And yet there is at least one area in which critical realism seems to have an obvious application within organisation and management studies: this in the analysis of the capitalist labour process. It may be because critical realism has so far concentrated on the nature of social structure, human agency and their mode of interaction at a rather abstract level that little progress has yet been made making the connections between general processes and specific social structures or mechanisms. On the other hand, it is really quite remarkable how little interest there has been in critical realism from existing labour process writers and researchers, especially when one considers that critical realism is a philosophy which embodies elements of materialism. Not only are there similar intellectual emphases, but the growth to contemporary importance of both critical realism and labour process analysis can be traced from much the same period – the early 1970s. Critical realism and labour process analysis have developed alongside each other, but with very little contact or connection having been developed between them. Whatever the reason, it can be argued that there are many potential benefits to accrue from utilising critical realism specifically for the analysis of the labour process.

This paper attempts to move towards demonstrating this by focusing upon Marx's analysis of the labour process. Rather than relating the analysis to the existing work in the labour process tradition, this paper aims to demonstrate the consistency of Marx's account of enduring social relations to critical realism. It argues for a much more adequate theoretical account of the labour process than has been provided for labour process theory hitherto, from Braverman (1974) onwards. To this end the paper is divided into two main sections. In the first section the transcendental and critical realist positions are briefly elaborated. In the second section the correspondences are traced out between critical realism and Marx's method in general, his analysis of the labour process more specifically and his account of the organisational and technical transformations of capitalist production in particular. Some final comments and conclusions are contained in the last section.

Structures and events

Transcendental realism: structured ontology and conception of science

While transcendental realism resonates with certain much older traditions and positions in the philosophy of science, its emergence in the mid 1970s can be seen as a response to the crisis and demise of the formerly dominant positivist view and the failure to assimilate the insights which provoked this crisis into a consistent account of science.

The attack on positivism had two major components. The first questioned its view that science develops in a linear, or monistic, fashion, growing remorselessly, unproblematically accumulating knowledge. The second criticised its deductivist account of scientific structure. The first anti-monistic tendency, exemplified by the work of Bachelard, Popper, Kuhn, Lakatos and Feyerabend, while usefully stressing the ideas of scientific change and discontinuity, found it difficult to incorporate these new insights within an adequate account of the generally progressive character of scientific development. Some of these authors, such as Kuhn and Feyerabend, suggest that the phenomena of scientific change necessarily obscure any possibility of rational development in science, and at the extreme propose that we create and change the world along with our theories – in Kuhn's phrase scientists operating within different theoretical frameworks occupy different worlds.

Similarly, while authors such as Hanson, Hesse and Harré played a decisive role in undermining the deductivist theory of scientific structure, their attack remained incomplete. Such philosophers reacted sharply against the standard deductivist theory, which was firmly rooted in the Humean theory of causality. Against the long dominant Humean conception that causal relations may be analysed only as constant conjunctions of events, the anti-deductivists highlighted the lack of sufficiency of the Humean criteria of causal laws. Recognising that scientific statements cannot be tested in isolation, in a direct confrontation with experience, these authors suggested that they get their meaning from the complex networks of metaphors, models and theories in which they are located. Harré, for example, criticising the Humean conception of causality and recognising the role of metaphors, analogies and similes in science, located the necessity of laws in the models at the heart of theories. Thus, in contrast to Hume for whom laws were just empirical regularities, for Harré there is a dual criteria for the establishment of a law – the Humean condition, i.e. empirical invariance, is treated as necessary but insufficient, with the second condition relating to the plausibility, coherence, etc., of the model. However, there is a crucial ambiguity in these accounts, namely the question of what the model refers to. What are the ontological commitments of this school? Do the models possess a referent other than events and their conjunctions? To the extent that they do, this position moves towards a transcendental realist stance; to the extent that they do not, then it is left open to empiricist counter-attack (Harré 1970).

Thus, despite the major insights the anti-monistic and anti-deductivist streams provided, they failed to weave these into a convincing and coherent account of science. The source of this failure can often be traced to the implicit acceptance of the empiricist ontology presupposed by the positivist position. Bhaskar, by drawing out the ontological implications of scientific activity such as experimentation and the practical application of knowledge based upon scientific laws outside of experimental situations, produces a critique highlighting the lack of necessity of the Humean criteria for laws and related theories and propositions. Developing this critique, Bhaskar isolates the crucial realm of the non-actual and non-empirical, metaphorically, 'deep' which allows him to explicitly reject the empiricist ontology and advance a more adequate account of scientific development (Bhaskar 1978; 1986; 1989; 1991).

Positivism, according to transcendental realism, effectively conflates three separate domains of reality:

(1) the 'deep' (made up of structures, mechanisms, powers, tendencies),
(2) the actual (comprising events and states of affairs), and
(3) the empirical (constituted by experiences, impressions and perceptions).

These domains are distinct and only exceptionally coextensive, with moves from (1) to (2) and (2) to (3) being contingent. That is to say, events can occur without being experienced, causal mechanisms can counteract one another, and there can be real mechanisms in nature which never have effects, though they would under certain circumstances. Here constant conjunctions at the actual level, or their observations at the empirical level, are neither necessary nor sufficient to establish causal relations. Causal tendencies may neutralise each other such that there is no change to be observed, but the tendencies are no less real. That is, powers may be exercised without being manifest in states of the world. The notion of a power being exercised and yet unrealised in manifest phenomena is usually designated a tendency. For transcendental realists it is the ascription of a tendency that is interpreted as a statement of a law. Laws are seen as setting limits rather than prescribing uniquely fixed results. A key aspect of the transcendental realist ontology is, then, its *structured* nature. The world is seen as stratified in the sense that the objects of reality are not all of one kind.

Following on from this ontological stratification, the logic of scientific discovery must be situated in the movement from the identification of regularities (in general these are likely to be only partial) to the classification of the structures or mechanisms which generate them, rather than in the search for strict event regularities as on the positivist account. This characteristically involves three phases. First an effect is identified and described: the classical empiricist does not move beyond this phase. Second, a hypothetical mechanism is postulated, which, if it existed, would explain the effect. Thus against empiricists' invocation of the brute facts of experience, transcendental realists insist on the need for complex theoretical redescriptions of reality. These models are developed by drawing upon antecedent knowledge such as theories of scientific method and types of explanation learnt from an existing science and applied to a new subject matter. As we have seen, many anti-deductivists suggest that these models are necessary but claim they cannot really tell us what the world is like independently of us. For the transcendental realist there is a third stage where an attempt is made to demonstrate the existence and operation of the mechanism – both positively through experimental activity designed to isolate the mechanism and negatively by the elimination of alternative explanations. If the explanation stands then it becomes the subject of enquiry itself.

On this account *retroduction* not induction or deduction constitutes the characteristic mode of inference deployed in science. As Lawson (1997: 24) describes it, retroduction

> consists in the movement, on the basis of analogy and metaphor, amongst other things, from a conception of some phenomena of interest to a conception of some totally different type of thing, mechanism, structure or condition that, at least in part, is responsible for the given phenomena.

Further, on this view, knowledge is understood as the product of a social practice rather than arising out of passive experience. This does not carry the implication that scientific knowledge gravitates towards complete and unrevisable knowledge. On the contrary Bhaskar distances himself clearly from such a stance by stressing the necessity of distinguishing between the object of scientific analysis that exists outside the scientific process – the intransitive object of science – and the changing cognitive objects that are produced within science, as a function of scientific practice – the transitive object. It is a condition of the possibility of science that the objects of knowledge exist and act independently of their identification, i.e. constitute intransitive objects. But it is only when both dimensions are recognised that we can understand how changing knowledge of possibly unchanging objects is feasible. The intransitive object remains what it is whatever our theories about it. The transitive object is what we can say about it at any stage of the history of science. As deeper levels of reality are successively identified, described and explained, previously existing knowledge is typically revised, corrected or more or less drastically recast. To repeat, then, science involves the essential movement from knowledge of manifest phenomena (in the intransitive domain) to knowledge, produced by means of antecedent knowledge (in the transitive domain), of structures which generate them (in the intransitive domain), discovery of the new (growth) proceeding with criticism and correction of the old (change). The implications of these realist positions for the social sciences are the focus of the next section.

Critical realism, social structure and human agency

Recently a set of perspectives on the social realm, grounded in a transcendental realist account of science, has been systemised under the heading of critical realism. Critical realism argues that there are knowable structures at work here, partially analogous but irreducible to those identified in nature. That is, social phenomena are seen as being conditioned by and dependent upon, and only manifest in, natural phenomena but causally and ontologically irreducible to them.[3] The central themes of the critical realist position respecting the nature of social structure and the connection between society and people can be elaborated by outlining what Bhaskar terms the *Transformational Model of Social Activity* (T.M.S.A.).

A starting point here is the insight, emphasised by various authors, that societies and economies depend upon human agents and their conceptions. Social structure is conceptually and linguistically mediated implying that *verstehen* (or the attempt to grasp subjective interpretations) is necessary for social science. All social practices depend upon intentional human agency so that reference to beliefs, opinions, interpretations, attitudes, etc., is, in general, clearly necessary for any adequate social explanation. But, equally, attention to such conceptual matters will not be sufficient. Social structure cannot be read off from agents' conceptualisations. Human action almost always has a material aspect which cannot be reduced to its conceptual component. As Lawson (1994a: 141) notes, to an individual agent,

> being unemployed, on strike, living in poverty, and so on is not just (and sometimes perhaps not at all) possessing a particular idea of what one is doing: it involves being physically separated from the means of 'earning a living', being party to industrial conflict, and being separated

from (adequate) forms of health care, shelter and nutrition with all the material problems that involves.

The social is inescapably embedded in the material/physical basis of reality. Indeed we intervene in, and both manipulate and are conditioned by, nature in all our causal interactions with the world including those with other agents.

Furthermore, not only does social structure almost always possess a material dimension but also individual conceptions are characteristically inadequate as accounts of social structures (rules, relations, resources) which depend upon but are irreducible to them. That is, while human action does not in general take place independently of some conceptualisation, it does occur independently of its adequate conceptualisation. Specifically, social science may reveal as a necessary real condition of some actual social activity a level, or aspect, of reality which, although again not existing independently of agents' conceptualisations, may itself be quite unknown, or at least inadequately or misleadingly comprehended. Such a feature or level of reality may consist of real relations, processes, or structural complexes that are really generative of social life but unavailable to direct access by intuition or the senses. Agents need have no understanding of the totality of structures that make certain actions possible. In relying upon the interpretative understandings of the actors themselves we would expect too much of agents. There is, for example, no need to defer to a woman's own explanation for engaging in low-paid casual employment as 'only natural' or because this constitutes 'women's work'. Rather social explanation would, perhaps, entail detailing the structural constraints, patriarchal relations, etc., giving rise to gender bias in education, unequal family responsibilities and so on that tend to lead to a concentration of female workers in certain secondary labour markets.

Another important consideration here is that social structure is dependent upon not only individual concepts, but equally individual activities and practices. It is through human actions that social structures come about and endure when they do, whether or not individuals have a conscious or reflective awareness that or, how precisely, this is so. Thus, for example, irrespective of whether or not individuals are discursively aware of the rules of grammar of their language, the existence of any endurability of such rules is undoubtedly dependent upon the speech acts in which agents engage. Thus tacit aspects of knowledge may be important. Equally, not only tacit aspects of knowledge may be relevant but so too may unconscious motivations, needs and desires. In short, the immediate intentions of agents and the meanings of their own acts can be opaque to themselves.

To summarise then, an actor's account of his or her own activities while clearly important is never final or definite: he or she provides no more than a provisional starting point for explanation. As Bhaskar (1986: 162) notes:

what an agent does not make (what it must take to make) it can have no privileged understanding of … we do not make the conditions or consequences, skills or motives of our intentional making … we never start, cognitively or more generally socially, any more than we can biologically, from scratch … we are always in the predicament of the tinker, having to mend our cognitive tools on the job; we learn to swim in the water, not on the beach.

This leads us on to the consideration that if social structure depends on human conceptions and actions, then equally social structures, such as the rules of language, are a condition for intentional human action. Without social structure, action would not possess the *means to agency*. Society and social structure, as provider of the materials for action, constitute its precondition. Bhaskar writes:

all activity presupposes the prior existence of social forms. Thus consider *saying, making* and *doing* as characteristic modalities of human agency. People cannot communicate except by utilizing existing media, produce except by applying themselves to materials which are already formed, or act save in some or other context. Speech requires language; making materials; action conditions; agency resources; activity rules. Even spontaneity has its necessary condition the pre-existence of a social form with (or by means of) which the spontaneous act is performed.

(Bhaskar 1989: 34)

That is, all human action presupposes the pre-existence of society and makes no sense without it.

At issue, here, is a specific conception of the nature of the relationship between human agency and social structure. Because social structure depends upon human agency it cannot be conceived of as some fixed, external environment or container within which behaviour takes place; it represents the means to action and can itself be changed through such action. At the same time, neither can it be treated as the *creation* of individuals, for individual intentional action presupposes its prior existence. Social structure, then, can be neither reified nor interpreted as a creation of individuals. Rather it must be recognised that people and society refer to radically different kinds of things. The nature of society cannot be read off from the nature of people and, in turn, their nature cannot be inferred from that of society. The relevant conception of the connection between the two must be one of reproduction and/or transformation: individuals reproduce or transform social structure which at the moment of any individual act only can be taken as given. To elaborate, as actors draw upon social structures in their activities they effectively reproduce, reinforce and/or transform them. However, such reproduction is rarely (although it may sometimes be) deliberate: it is usually the unintended consequence of independently motivated actions: 'people do not marry to reproduce the nuclear family or work to sustain the capitalist economy. Yet it is nevertheless the unintended consequence (and inexorable result) of, as it is also a necessary condition for, their activity' (Bhaskar 1989: 35). Of course, if the transformation of social structures is not normally the reason that agents have for acting in the way they do, this is not to deny that they will always have some conception of what they are doing in their activity. Human acts are always intentional under some description. The point though is that, whatever the motivation and intentions of each and any individual, human action taken in total is always reproductive/transformational. Social structure is neither created by, nor independent of, human agency but rather is the typically unintended condition of all our intentional productions – the non-created but drawn upon and reproduced/transformed condition for our daily economic and social activities.

To take the example of language again, unless we had learnt a preexistent language with rules that exist independently of us we could not talk at all. While their effectiveness as a system of communication depends upon their collective acceptance (if in many cases at a tacit level), these rules do not determine the actual words used. That is, we usually talk, not to reproduce or transform the language, but for personal ends of which we are conscious. However, our language only continues to exist because we talk, for it has no existence apart from people taken in total talking. To the extent that we conform to established rules in choosing our words we reinforce/reproduce the prevailing linguistic conventions: on the other hand, as we strive to communicate novel ideas in new ways we help transform these rules.

With this transformational conception of social activity in place various consequences easily follow. One obvious implication of this view of the relation between agency and society is the geo-historical specificity of social structures. That is, because of the ever-present transformative potential of human agency on which social structure depends, the latter will, at most, be only relatively enduring. As Bhaskar notes, 'social theory treats of structures which are spatio-temporalised (geo-historically restricted), dynamic (and open, i.e, unbounded, unfinished and ongoing) and subject to (praxisdependent) change' (1986: 212). Change or at least its potential is always present. The reproduction of social structures is never automatic – structures are in process and constantly evolving.

Closely associated with the T.M.S.A. is a stress on the relational character of the material of social reality. Bhaskar writes that social theory

> is not concerned, as such, with large scale, mass or group behaviour (conceived as the behaviour of large numbers, masses or groups of individuals). Rather it is concerned, at least paradigmatically, with

persistent relations between individuals (and groups), and with relations between these relations (and between such relations and nature and the products of such relations).

(1989:28–9)

It is useful, here, to distinguish between two types of relation: external and internal. A relation is external in the case where the individuals so related do not change their category or type when they cease to stand in that relation, e.g. two passing strangers. Meanwhile two or more individuals are internally related when they are wholly or partly constituted as beings of a certain type by virtue of standing in that relation. For example, a person is constituted as a 'husband' by virtue of marriage with another person as 'wife'. The relation of marriage is internal to and a constitutive part of the meaning of 'husband'. Internal relations appear to be of particular importance in the social realm suggesting that social life must often be grasped as a totality whose 'various moments may be asymmetrically weighted, primed with differential causal forces' (Bhaskar 1989: 43). Furthermore it seems necessary to conceive of such relations as holding between *social positions* and not between the individuals who occupy or engage in them. As Lawson notes:

> If it is the case, say, that presidents exercise different rights, obligations, tasks, duties, powers, etc., to the rest of us, or that, say, teachers exercise different rights and obligations, etc., to students, it is equally the case that the relevant rights, tasks, powers and so on, exist independently of the particular individuals fulfilling these roles. At issue then is a system of relationally defined position-practices, a system of positions, with associated practices, obligations and powers, etc., defined in relation to other such positions, and into which agents essentially slot. With reflection it should be clear that all social structures and systems – the economy, the state, international organisations, trade unions and households, etc., – depend upon or presuppose social relations of this form.
>
> (Lawson 1994b: 521)

This position–practice system, then, and specifically the concept of a position into which individuals slot, provides the contact point between human agency and social structure. The causal effect of social structures on individuals is manifest in the interests, duties, resources, powers, constraints, rules, conventions and obligations built into, or associated with, such positions by the web of relationships. Various positions afford agents certain definite powers, obligations, etc., which they deploy, expand, augment and transmit in their interactions. However, these systems of positions are rarely tightly discrete and do not provide unambiguous courses of action to the individuals occupying them. While it is the case that some rules of interaction and production, say, might have relatively fuzzy boundaries (such as taking a walk) while others sharper ones (like behaviour at traffic lights), there will, in general, always remain some space for individual decision. Indeed, it is essential to the enabling and constraining, rather than determining, nature of social structure stressed by critical realism that the translation of particular rules, obligations, rights, etc., into corresponding actions be denied any smooth or automatic inevitability. The position of teacher does not enable us to say how this or that particular teacher will perform the tasks associated with the position in any given circumstance. Agency requires that motives for action should not be imposed by any single position. At any one time a particular individual will occupy a plurality of positions. As members of firms, families, religious groupings, political parties, ethnic communities, agents occupy a diversity of positions and have available a range of rules and a variety of resources for action. As Bhaskar insists, the relation between structures is complex and potentially contradictory:

> The theory of complex determination, in situating persons as comprehensive entities whose behaviour is subject to the control of several different principles at once, allows the possibility of genuine self determination (subject to constraints) and the special power of acting in accordance with a plan or in the light of reasons.
>
> (Bhaskar 1978: 111)

Agents are not faced with just one sort of structure from which definite actions follow, rather, they are confronted by the confusing and ambiguous array of positions — husband, boss, political associate, member of a religious group — in which they are likely to find themselves at any given time.[4]

Thus, for critical realism, providing an explanation for some human activities will typically entail not only identifying the unacknowledged structural conditions of these practices, but also understanding their conscious and unconscious motivations. Just as in the natural realm, in the social sphere explanations must be understood as the (socially produced and fallible) accounting of the previously unknown mode of existence of some phenomena of interest. This is not, of course, to deny that there are significant respects in which social structures differ from purely natural ones, indeed critical realism clearly identifies such differences. The chief ontological differences are their activity and concept dependence, their relatively greater space–time specificity and social relation dependence. Meanwhile the most significant epistemological feature of the social sciences is that social phenomena only ever occur in *open systems* characterised by the presence of numerous countervailing tendencies, whereas in the natural sphere it is sometimes possible to contrive *closed systems* where constant conjunctions hold. It follows from this that decisive test situations are in principle impossible, so that the criteria for theory choice and theory development must be exclusively explanatory and non-predictive. These differences do not block the possibility of social science. Rather scientific explanation can be achieved in the social realm on account of these differences, giving rise to a set of sciences as different from the natural sciences as are their objects.

Marx's analysis of the labour process

Bhaskar suggests that 'Marx's work ... illustrates critical realism; and critical realism is the absent methodological fulcrum of Marx's work' (1991: 143).[5] In the remainder of the paper I examine this claim and suggest that Marx's discussion of the labour process and account of the organisational and technical transformations characteristic of capitalist production can indeed be seen as consistent with a critical realist position.[6] Before turning to Marx's substantive analysis it is necessary to provide some background regarding his ontological commitments.

Marx's method and critical realism

Critical realism at the level of generality at which it operates can isolate only fairly abstract features of Marx's scientific practice. Here I wish to highlight the points of convergence between critical realism and the implicit ontological presuppositions embedded in Marx's later writings.[7, 8]

A central distinction for Marx is that between the real movement of things and their apparent movement or between essential relations and surface appearance. Appearances relate to those forms in which the phenomena of the material and social world represent themselves in people's experiences, impressions and perceptions. As Sayer (1979: 9) notes, this

> does not imply that what is presented is not already conceptually mediated, merely that at any given point there exists a constituted world whose phenomena have achieved what Marx calls 'the stability of natural, self-understood forms of social life' and which in the first instance confronts its participants as a simple datum.

Essential relations are those relations whose existence explains why the phenomena should take such forms. That is, they constitute the set of conditions which must prevail if experience of a particular kind is to be possible.

In establishing this distinction Marx adopts a particular view of science. According to Marx 'all science would be superfluous if the form of appearance of things directly coincided with their essence' (1981: 956). More specifically with regard to political economy he notes:

> [T]his much is clear: a scientific analysis of competition is possible only if we can grasp the inner nature of capital, just as the apparent movement of the heavenly bodies are intelligible only to someone who is acquainted with their real motions, which are not perceptible to the senses.
>
> (Marx 1976: 433)

The task of science for Marx is to understand the essential relations and show how they manage to operate in ways that give rise to the phenomena we observe. He notes, for example, that it is 'something fairly familiar in every science, *apart from political economy*' that 'in their appearances things are often presented in an inverted way' (1976: 677, italics added). For Marx it is simply a matter of recognising not only that the essential relations are distinct from, and normally out of phase with, appearances but also that they are often in opposition to the phenomenal forms they generate. He writes:

> The finished configuration of economic relations, as these are visible on the surface, in their actual existence, and therefore also in the notions with which the bearers and agents of these relations seek to gain an understanding of them, is very different from the configuration of their inner core, which is essential but concealed, and the concept corresponding to it. It is in fact the very reverse and antithesis of this.
>
> (Marx 1981: 311)

This distinction which Marx draws between essence and appearance, and the implications he argues follow from it for the nature of science, of course, lie very easily with the transcendental realist divisions between the realms of the empirical (the domain of human subjectivity) and the realm of the deep. However, this is clearly a very abstract feature of Marx's social ontology. At a less abstract level Marx conceives of the social world as constituted by social relations and human representations and motives. In order to trace out the link between Marx's analysis and specifically critical realism it is to these emphases and discussions that I now turn.

It is useful, here, to start with Marx's emphasis upon social relations. Marx insists in the *Theses on Fauerbach* that 'the human essence is no abstraction inherent in each single individual. In its reality it is the ensemble of social relations' (Marx and Engels 1975: 423). Society is not, then, a self-acting subject *sui generis*. That is, Marx is concerned to avoid reifying society. Similarly, in the *German Ideology* he attacks Stirner for treating 'society as a person, a subject' (Marx and Engels 1976: 206) and criticises Matthai, noting: 'Society, the "totality of life" is conceived by our author not as the interaction of the constituent "individual lives", but as a distinct existence, and this moreover separately interacts with these individual lives' (Marx and Engels 1976: 475). Equally, Marx is careful not to suggest that society is reducible to individual agency considered independently of the network of social relations. That would be to consider individuals abstractly and *ahistorically*. Marx attacks this kind of reductionism in the *Grundrisse*:

> the human being is in the most literal sense a [social being], not merely a gregarious animal, but an animal which can individuate itself only in the midst of society. Production by an isolated individual outside society

... is as much an absurdity as is the development of language without individuals living *together* and talking to each other.

(Marx 1973a: 84)

According to Marx, society's only agents are 'individuals but in mutual relationships, which they produce and reproduce anew' (1973a: 712). Individuals on this view are irreducibly social and cannot adequately be described independently of their social context. Society constitutes the set of relationships and associated positions that link individuals. Individuals acquire social characteristics in virtue of their position within this network of relationships. Marx writes:

> so-called contemplation from the standpoint of society means nothing more than the overlooking of the differences which express the social relation (relation of bourgeois society). Society does not consist of individuals, but expresses the sum of interrelations, the relations within which these individuals stand. As if someone were to say: seen from the perspective of society, there are no slaves and no citizens: both are human beings. Rather, they are that outside society. To be a slave, to be a citizen, are social characteristics, relations between human beings A and B. Human being A, as such, is not a slave. He is a slave in and through society.

> (Marx 1973a: 265)

Similarly he notes in *Wage, Labour and Capital*:

> A negro is a negro. He only becomes a slave in certain relations. A cotton-spinning jenny is a machine for spinning cotton. It becomes *capital* only in certain relations. Torn from these relationships it is no more capital than gold in itself is money or sugar the price of sugar.

> (Marx and Engels 1968: 81)

Thus Marx is not concerned with isolated individuals or material things as such, or in reified social structures, but addresses individuals who are, amongst other things, the bearers of particular roles defined by the social relations in which they stand.

Associated with this stress on social relations is an acknowledgement of the reproductive/transformative nature, and historical specificity, of social structure. Because human activities always take place in preconstructed social contexts people are not free to act entirely as they wish: they enter into relations which are 'independent of their will' (Marx 1970: 20). Nevertheless it is precisely through the activities of agents taken in total that the network of social relations is reproduced or changed, 'Just as society itself produces man as man, so is society produced by him' (Marx and Engels 1975: 298). Since these activities are at least potentially transformative, society is inherently changing and dynamic with a particular history. That is, history and change do not simply happen to society, they are part of its very nature. As Meikle (1991) notes, for Marx people are the sole makers of history, desire and intelligence are the motor and means of social development but at the same time agents never make history *ex nihilo*. Marx famously remarks:

> Men make their own history, but not of their own free will; not under circumstances they themselves have chosen, but under the given and inherited circumstances with which they are directly confronted. The tradition of the dead generations weighs like a nightmare on the minds of the living.
>
> (Marx 1973b: 146)

Marx's more specific discussions of historical development and social change, briefly set out below, must be understood as being grounded in these perspectives.

People, of course, are related to one another within society in numerous ways. For Marx certain kinds of relations are fundamental and provide the basis for distinguishing different forms of society. More particularly, the most basic social relations, according to Marx, are the *relations of production* – those social relations established within the production of material life itself. While relations of production far from exhaust the complex of relations, rules, roles, etc., which make up actually existing societies, they nevertheless, in terms of explanatory weight, constitute the most significant. In fact, other social relations are the very condition of existence of capitalist relations, e.g. the relations between men and women and those governing domestic life. He claims that social life as a whole cannot be understood without considering this materialistic connection and in fact suggests that production relations are nothing less than the core relations of social life.

To elaborate, according to Marx, all production involves two kinds of relations: 'the production of life, both of one's own in labour and of fresh life in procreation ... appears as a twofold relation: on the one hand as a natural, and on the other as a social relation' (Marx and Engels 1976: 43). Production always involves, first, relations between people and nature. The concept Marx uses to analyse this is that of the labour process. For Marx this represents 'first of all ... a process by which man through his own actions, mediates between himself and nature. He confronts the materials of nature as a force of nature' (Marx 1976: 283). The labour process is 'the everlasting nature imposed condition of human existence' and is thus 'independent of every form of that existence, or rather it is common to all forms of society in which human beings live' (Marx 1976: 290). Here labour consists of active practical interaction involving both the appropriation of nature and the transformation of human capacities. According to Marx what distinguishes human beings is that between their needs and environment and what they do comes the mediating stage of planning:

> At the end of every labour process, a result emerges which had already been conceived by the worker at the beginning, hence already existed ideally. Man not only effects a change of form in the materials of nature; he also realises his own purpose in those materials. And this is a purpose he is conscious of, it determines the mode of his activity with the rigidity of a law, and he must subordinate his will to it.
>
> (Marx 1976: 284)

The product created by the agent embodies his or her intentions or purposes. At the same time this activity of transforming objects also transforms the agent. For example, in realising his or her purposes through labour, the agent comes to recognise his or her capacity to effect this purpose and thereby recognise themself as a different kind of agent, possessing new skills and in consequence capable of new modes of action.

Social production, equally, involves relations between people themselves: 'All production is appropriation of nature on the part of an individual *within and through a definite form of society*' (Marx 1973a: 87, italics added). Whatever else it may comprise, every society includes such a materialistic connection, i.e. a set of social relations of production. He writes:

> it is quite obvious from the start that there exists a materialist connection of men with one another, which is determined by their needs and their mode of production and which is as old as men themselves. This connection is ever taking on new forms, and thus presents a 'history' irrespective of the existence of any political or religious nonsense which would especially hold men together.
>
> (Marx and Engels 1976: 43)

So, for example, by identifying a society as capitalist, Marx, while not reducing it to the set of relations he sees as characteristic of capitalist production, is stressing that a great deal of social life is organised around the reproduction (and transformation) of these social relations of production.

People's materialistic connection, to repeat, is essential according to Marx for understanding any society and different types of society are distinguished by the particular forms this connection takes. More specifically, the relations through which the social surplus over subsistence is extracted are the fundamental components of social structure and constitute Marx's primary substantive focus. He writes:

> The specific economic form in which unpaid surplus labour is pumped out of the direct producers determines the relationship of domination and servitude, as this grows directly out of production itself and reacts

back on it in turn as a determinant. On this is based the entire configuration of the economic community arising from the actual relations of
production, and hence also its specific political form. It is in each case
the direct relationship of the owners of the conditions of production to
the immediate producers – a relationship whose particular form naturally corresponds always to a certain level of development of the type
and manner of labour, and hence to its social productive power – in
which we find the innermost secret, the hidden basis of the entire social
edifice, and hence also the political form of the relationship of
sovereignty and dependence, in short, the specific form of state in each
case. This does not prevent the same economic basis – the same in its
major conditions – from displaying endless variations and gradations in
its appearance, as the result of innumerable different empirical circumstances, natural conditions, racial relations, historical influences acting
from outside, etc., and these can only be understood by analysing these
empirically given conditions.

(Marx 1981: 927–8)

If for Marx social structure essentially consists of the social relations which
make particular forms of production possible then the 'immanent laws' he
identifies relate to the tendencies of a particular form of society deriving
from its structure. It is worth noting, here, certain features of Marx's depiction of these social structures and laws. First Marx appears to be sensitive to
the idea that structure and agency relate to different kinds of thing:

As the conscious representative of this movement, the possessor of
money becomes a capitalist. His person, or rather his pocket, is the
point from which the money starts and to which it returns. The objective content of the circulation we have been discussing – the
valorization of value – is his subjective purpose, and *it is only in so far as
the appropriation of ever more and more wealth in the abstract is the sole driving
force behind his operations, that he functions as a capitalist, i.e., as capital
personified and endowed with consciousness and a will* … This boundless
drive for enrichment, this passionate chase after value, is common to the
capitalist and the miser; but while the miser is merely a capitalist gone
mad, the capitalist is a rational miser.

(Marx 1976: 254, italics added)

While it is the case that *if* capital as a social relation is to be reproduced
certain kinds of activities have to be undertaken, these requirements need
not in any way automatically determine the conduct of a particular capitalist. Throughout *Capital* Marx is concerned to identify the capitalist in
terms of the incentives, constraints, opportunities, obligations, etc., that
define his or her position within the system of social relations. The position
capitalist affords them particular motives and resources for action but this

does not imply that this exhausts their motives or resources. In short, Marx's account is not inconsistent with the view that agents possess internal complexities and are afforded a variety of motives for action.[9] Moreover, Marx is careful to isolate the coercive forces which act on different agents limiting the options available to them and compelling them to play certain broadly defined roles. Marx conceives of competition very much in these terms, suggesting that 'competition is nothing more than the way in which the many capitals force the inherent determinants of capital upon one another and upon themselves' (Marx 1973a: 651). Again this does not imply that competition forces capitalists to adopt specific courses of action.

This leads us to a second feature worth noting: the laws Marx refers to are laws of tendency that derive from the incentives, motives, constraints, duties and so on established by the structural relations characteristic of capitalism as a particular form of society. In particular, Marx holds that the 'laws' he identifies operate as tendencies which always meet contradictory influences. Thus, for example, laws relating to a particular social formation at a certain level of development first arise as tendencies hindered by relations belonging to the stage superseded (Marx 1981: 275, 297–8). Further, Marx characterises social laws operative within the capitalist mode of production itself as tendencies that may be offset by a multitude of different factors. Marx's argument for the tendency of the rate of profit to fall is, of course, a famous example of his conception of laws as tendencies. In advancing this law he recognises that other forces at work in the economy offset this tendency: 'Counteracting influences must be at work, checking and cancelling the effect of the general law and giving it simply the character of a tendency, which is why we have described the fall in the general rate of profit as a tendential fall' (1981: 339). Later on, in considering that a rise in the rate of surplus value will affect the drop in the rate of profit, he notes: '[this factor] does not annul the general law. But it has the effect that this law operates more as a tendency, i.e., as a law whose absolute realisation is held up, delayed and weakened by counteracting factors' (1981: 341–2).[10]

Now if, for Marx, society is a network of relations and associated rules, rights, obligations, etc., he is quite adamant that it does not always appear as such to its participants – and here we broach his discussion of fetishism. Marx identifies within capitalism an illicit and spontaneous substitution of relations between commodities or things for social relations. For Marx, to conceive of the social properties of objects as deriving from their material attributes is simultaneously to universalise them, i.e. to deny their specific historical character and lose sight of the transformative potential of human agency. The basis of these illusions lies in the forms in which society presents itself in the experience of its participants. Society's essential relations may not be transparent to the actors and experience may be systematically misleading. What is required, then, is a critique of actors' commonsense conceptualisations of the social world and a demystification of the 'natural, self-understood forms of social life' – the phenomenal forms –

on which these conceptions are founded. Such a critique would both explain why people's commonsense consciousness takes the form it does and show where and why it is erroneous.

To take a central example, capital appears 'on the surface of society' as money which when productively deployed is capable of increasing value – of making a profit. According to Marx this represents a fetishistic form, for the ability to command surplus value (which is, in fact, dependent on particular, historically specific, social relations) appears to be inherent in the material form of capital itself. Surplus value originates in the capital/labour exchange. It is not capital itself which generates the additional value, rather it comes from the divergence between the value the labourer is paid and the value he or she creates when productively employed. Underpinning this is, of course, what Marx calls the 'double freedom of labour'. The process supposes first that workers are free to sell their labour-power to employers (unlike, for instance, slaves or serfs) and second, that they are 'free from' any means of production of their own (unlike peasants or independent craftsmen). Means of production, in short, must have become the private property of the employers. The essential relation expressed in the phenomenal form of capital is the relation between a propertied bourgeoisie and a dispossessed working class: 'It is in fact this divorce between the conditions of labour on the one hand and the producers on the other that forms the concept of Capital' (1981: 354). Capital thus emerges, not as the mysterious thing it appears to be, but as

> a definite social relation of production pertaining to a particular historical social formation, which simply takes the form of a thing and gives this thing a specific social character. It is the means of production monopolised by a particular section of society.
>
> (1981: 953)

To summarise, it is apparent that for Marx the objects of scientific activity are real structures, mechanisms or relations ontologically irreducible to, normally out of phase with, and perhaps in opposition to, the phenomenal forms, appearances or events they generate. In addition Marx holds that causal laws are tendencies which always meet counteracting influences. Marx sees the social realm as a complex network of internal relations. He acknowledges the activity and concept-dependent nature of social structures together with their historical specificity and appears to respect the ontological distinction between society and people. Not surprisingly, then, Marx utilises T.M.S.A. where the reproduction and transformation of the social process is achieved in and through human praxis, while human praxis is, in turn, conditioned and made possible by that process.

The analysis of the labour process

I wish now to argue, at a more substantive level, that Marx's analysis of the labour process and account of the organisational and technical changes characteristic of capitalist production represents an attempt to isolate particularly important and enduring social relations or social structures and account for their reproduction and transformation over time. In pursuing this objective the argument developed within this section is that Marx deploys a methodology consistent with that of critical realism. That is to say, he adopts a methodology which remains sensitive to the historical specificity of social structures, deploys something approximating a position–practice system as a way of understanding the point of contact between structure and agency, identifies a series of structural tendencies and is careful to consider the interpretations of implicated agents.

In his discussion of the labour process Marx begins by identifying some general features of social production, i.e. certain necessary preconditions of all social production. This procedure enables him first to isolate some set of phenomena as pertaining to production and second to distinguish within these attributes which relate to production as such from those which stem from a more space–time restricted set of social relations. While referring to these general characteristics of production Marx makes it quite clear that this takes us only so far. He is careful to say that to conceptualise the labour process in this manner is to view it *ahistorically* and thus these 'general preconditions of all production are nothing more than ... abstract moments with which no real historical stage of production can be grasped' (1973a: 99). Referring to the general region of social production is helpful only in so far as it highlights the unique features of the production process under the particular social relations characteristic of capitalism. The implication here, one which is fully consistent with critical realism, is that any study that is formulated without sufficient regard to time and place is likely to miss connections crucial to the phenomena targeted for explanation. In guarding against such a methodological mistake, Marx moves from an abstract and general discussion to a more specific and grounded analysis of the labour process under capital. Here the focus shifts from viewing the labour process as the material process of production to viewing it as a social process. The labour process under capitalism is not simply a labour process, it is also and at the same time a '*valorization*' process – a process of adding value. Explicitly he notes that the 'capitalist process is the unity of labour process and valorization process' (1976: 995). The capitalist 'wants to produce a commodity greater in value than the sum of values of the commodities used to produce it, namely the means of production and the labour power he purchased with his good money on the open market' (1976: 293).[11]

Marx traces the origins of capitalist production to a change in social relations and more particularly to the emergence of a class of propertyless wage labourers. Marx, at a methodological level, remains acutely aware of the need to identify how these key social relations emerged in the first place. What is required according to Marx is an account of *primitive accumulation* – that is, an explanation for the very genesis of capitalist relations. Marx is particularly critical of political economists for their failure to provide an adequate account of the emergence of capitalist social relations:

> This primitive accumulation plays approximately the same role in political economy as original sin does in theology ... Its origin is supposed to be explained when it is told as an anecdote about the past. Long, long ago there were two sorts of people; one the diligent, intelligent and above all frugal elite; the other, lazy rascals, spending their substance, and more, in riotous living ... And from this original sin dates the poverty of the great majority who, despite all their labour, have up to now nothing to sell but themselves, and the wealth of the few that increases constantly, although they long ceased to work. Such insipid childishness is everyday preached to us in the defence of poverty ... In actual history, it is a notorious fact that conquest, enslavement, robbery, murder, in short force, play the greatest part.
>
> (Marx 1976: 873–4)

Now, Marx is not satisfied to give an account of how capitalist social relations emerged, as if once established they could be assumed to reproduce themselves smoothly or automatically. On the contrary he is concerned to examine the conditions within which the reproduction of these relations, once established, take place. In fact, Marx is especially eager to explore the tensions between the developing social relations and the conditions within which they operate. It is precisely as Marx elaborates upon these tensions and the transformations they promote that further connections with critical realism come to the fore.

At first Marx suggests that 'capital subordinates labour on the basis of technical conditions within which labour has been carried on up to that point in history' (1976: 425). Characteristically, this takes place when previously independent artisans who had produced goods on their own account are forced to become mere paid employees. The *social relations* within which they work have thus changed substantially while the technical content of their work typically remains the same. This Marx describes as the *formal subsumption of labour* to capital. It is formal in that it involves a change in social form (that is to say precisely the imposition of the valorisation process) without a corresponding, valorisation-inspired transformation in the content of the labour process. The *formal subsumption* of labour, Marx writes,

> does not in itself imply a fundamental modification in the real nature of the labour process, the actual process of production. On the contrary, the fact is that capital subsumes the labour process as it finds it, that is to say, it takes over an existing labour process developed by different and more archaic modes of production ... For example handicraft, a mode of

agriculture corresponding to a small, independent peasant economy. If changes occur in these traditional established labour processes after their takeover by capital, these are nothing but the gradual consequences of that subsumption. The work may become more continuous or orderly under the eye of the interested capitalist but in themselves these changes do not affect the character of the actual labour process, the actual mode of working.

(Marx 1976: 1026)

These traditional received forms of the labour process are limited in terms of their potential to contribute to the valorisation process associated with the emergent social relations. Within the constraints imposed by these inherited forms of the labour process, capitalists can increase surplus value primarily through the route of, what Marx calls, 'absolute surplus value' involving, amongst other things, the lengthening of the working day. However such manoeuvres are not always successful. Workers are in a position to resist – at its most straightforward workers can simply refuse to keep regular hours. The way capitalists sought to overcome these constraints and limitations on valorisation imposed by the traditional forms of the labour process is the subject of part four of Volume 1 of *Capital*.[12]

The first strategy that Marx discusses is 'simple cooperation'. This occurs when capital brings individual workers together in accordance with a plan. There is, in fact, nothing specific to capitalism about simple cooperation, it relates to the situation in which 'numerous workers work together side by side in accordance with a plan, whether in the same process, or in different but related processes' (1976: 443). Marx argues it corresponds to the power of social labour as opposed to individual labour. Marx isolates certain requirements associated with large-scale cooperation, in particular the need for authority at the point of production:

All directly social or communal labour on a large scale requires to a greater or lesser degree a directing authority in order to secure the harmonious cooperation of the activities of individuals, and to perform the general functions that have their origin in the motion of the total productive organism, as distinguished from the motion of its separate organs. A single violin player is his own conductor: an orchestra requires a separate one.

(Marx 1976: 448–9)

At first then, according to Marx, capital is simply an organising principle; the capitalist adopts, by virtue of the ownership of the means of production, the role of directing authority.

It is easy to see why simple cooperation offers substantial advantages from the point of view of valorisation. Moreover, the nature of these advantages highlights that valorisation involves the creation and maintenance of a social relation. Certainly, productivity is increased (the 'combined working day produces a greater quantity of use-values than an equal sum of isolated working days' (1976: 447)). Cooperation not only allows for greater possibilities than individual labour – people working together being able to lift a weight each individually could not – but reduces costs because a portion of the means of production are consumed in common. But equally important, the authority and position of the capitalist are strengthened since the individual workers who are brought together by capital are subordinate to capital. The coordinating role is filled by capitalist command. Thus, while the relation of authority existed in previous social formations where simple cooperative production was undertaken, the basis for that relation was different. Capital performs this function by virtue of its ownership of the means of production. Marx writes: 'It is not because he is a leader of industry that a man is a capitalist; on the contrary he is a leader of industry because he is a capitalist. *The leadership of industry is an attribute of capital*' (1976: 451, italics added). The physical concentration of workers under the one roof together with capital's augmented authority greatly facilitates the down-to-earth tasks of supervision: enforcing rules, timekeeping and preventing embezzlement. The implicit adoption by Marx of something approximating the position–practice system clearly is suggested by this kind of argument. He is engaged in the task of elaborating the tasks, rights, etc., that the position of capitalist has associated with it. It is precisely by elaborating upon the relations between positions, and the rights, rules and so on tied to them, that he identifies the objective possibilities for action of the individuals who stand in them and their differential access to resources and opportunities.

Marx is careful to spell out how these changes appear and affect the workers' own representations of the processes they are engaged in. He writes: 'the interconnection between their [the workers'] various labours confronts them, in the realm of ideas, as a plan drawn up by the capitalist, and, in practice, as his authority, as the powerful will of a being outside them, who subjects their activity to his purpose' (1976: 450). The enhanced collective capacity associated with cooperative production is seen as the power of another – the capitalist.

As noted above, the analysis of simple cooperation relates to some very general features of social production. More historically specific is the development of manufacture proper and the detailed division of labour. Marx, in tracing out the way in which capitalist relations help to mould the production process, distinguishes manufacture from the elementary forms of cooperation by the strict differentiation of work tasks associated with the former. Manufacture arises in two ways, first by bringing together separate trades under the same roof and second by the production process itself being broken down so that an item which used to be produced in its entirety by a single handicraft worker is decomposed into separate operations. The division of labour involved in manufacture was often extreme. The advantages in terms of the valorisation process of such a division are clear. Productivity is increased through specialisation and the increased continuity and intensity of work. The detailed division of labour in manufacture further reinforces the subordination of the worker to the capitalist. Again, Marx details how these processes feature in the representations of agents. Under manufacture the worker is unable to perform or even comprehend the total process of production. The manufacturing worker loses the intellectual command over production that the handicraft worker had possessed and this command is appropriated by capital:

> What is lost by the specialised worker is concentrated in the capital which confronts them. It is a result of the division of labour in manufacture that the worker is brought face to face with the intellectual potentialities of the material process of production as the property of another and as a power which rules over him.
>
> (Marx 1976: 482)

Despite all this, manufacture and the detailed division of labour were not fully adequate vehicles for valorisation. The foundation of the manufacturing labour process remained handicraft skill, and that skill was a resource that could be drawn upon in struggles against capital. Thus Marx suggests 'capital is constantly compelled to wrestle with the insubordination of the workers' and 'the complaint that the workers lack discipline runs through the whole of the period of manufacture' (Marx 1976: 490). As MacKenzie (1984: 486) notes, Marx's discussion of the formal subsumption of labour under simple cooperation and manufacture serves to highlight that these essentially organisational changes created the 'social space' for the machine. Within early forms of capitalist production a tension continuously arises between, on the one hand, the inherent tendency of capital to maximise surplus value and, on the other, a production process that has not been transformed to maximise surplus value. This tension, together with the power that comes from capitalist ownership of the means of production, gives rise to a further tendency for capitalists to initiate more radical transformations of the labour process. With machinery capital promotes and furthers the valorisation process by technological means rather than as previously through the sole means of reconfiguring social organisation:

> In manufacture the organisation of the social labour process is purely subjective: it is a combination of specialised workers. Large scale industry on the other hand, possesses in the machine system an entirely objective organisation of production which confronts the worker as a pre-existing material condition of production.
>
> (Marx 1976: 508)

Technology is here seen as itself moulded by the now established social relations. According to Marx one aspect of the machine's contribution to the valorisation process is that it facilitates the accrual of absolute surplus value. For example, by undermining the position of key groups of skilled workers and opening up the possibility of drawing in new sectors of the labour market the machine undercuts resistance to a lengthening of the working day. Moreover, since the pace of work can now be set by the machine its intensity can be increased. However, perhaps the central way in which the machine contributes to the valorisation process is through the medium *of relative surplus value*: the reduction in the labour time required to produce the equivalent of the worker's wage.

The formal subsumption of labour here gives way to its real subsumption. The real subsumption of labour is related to this change in the mode of exploitation from increasing absolute surplus value to increasing relative surplus value. Prior to the machine, the worker still commanded the tool and used this command as a resource in struggles against capital. The technical foundation of the detailed division of labour, embedded as it was in the skills of the labourers, had created a hierarchy of specialised workers; in contrast, through the adoption of machinery in large-scale industry there is a tendency to equalise and reduce to one and the same level every kind of work. It is not merely their lack of ownership of the means of production, but the concrete forms of the actual labour process itself – large-scale, mechanised production processes – that prevent the labourers from working for themselves. This, for Marx, in contrast to the formal subsumption of labour to capital, represents the development of a specifically capitalist mode of production, 'capitalist production proper' (Marx 1976: 1027).

Smith usefully highlights how Marx's account of technical change is most appropriately interpreted as referring to a series of structural tendencies:

> the owners and controllers of capital necessarily tend to introduce innovations that decrease the amount of time workers engage in necessary labour ... while increasing the amount of time they spend in surplus labour, which produces the surplus value appropriated in the form of profits. There is thus an inherent tendency in capitalism to introduce machinery with the potential to increase labour productivity. There is also a tendency to introduce technologies that allow a less skilled – and thus less expensive – workforce to be employed. Further, there is a necessary tendency to seek innovations that restructure the labour process so as to lessen the pores in the working day ... Finally, there is a tendency to seek technologies that enhance capital's control over the production process in order to reduce waste, lessen the opportunities for sabotage, and so on. How these various tendencies interact in given socio-historical contexts is a complex and contingent matter.
>
> (Smith 1997: 118)

This emphasis upon the identification of structural tendencies which can be consistent with a variety of actual outcomes[13] remains very much in line with critical realism. As Lawson notes, a statement of a tendency, according to critical realism,

> is not about long run, 'normal', usual, or average outcomes at the level of events. Nor is it reducible to a counterfactual claim about events or states of affairs that would occur if the world were different ... It is not a claim about anything at the level of the actual course of events at all. Rather it is a transfactual statement about the typically non-empirical activity of a structured thing or agent ... A statement of a tendency ... is about a power that is being exercised whatever events ensue.
>
> (Lawson 1997: 23)

As with the earlier changes in the production process Marx details how these processes, involving the machine, present themselves to the agents concerned. In particular he argues that the conceptions, already diagnosed as being associated with simple co-operation and manufacture, achieve a technical embodiment in the machine. For 'along with the tool, the skill of the worker in handling it passes over to the machine' (Marx 1976: 545). The machine is seen as embodying the power of the capitalist:

> The special skill of each individual machine operator, who has now been deprived of all significance, vanishes as an infinitesimal quantity in the face of the science, the gigantic natural forces, and the mass of social labour embodied in the system of machinery, which, together with those three forces, constitutes the power of the master.
>
> (Marx 1976: 549)

Meanwhile in the *Grundrisse* he notes that: 'The accumulation of knowledge and of skill, of the general productive forces of the social brain, is thus absorbed into capital as opposed to labour and hence appears as an attribute of capital' (Marx 1973a: 694). Class struggle within capitalism can take the form of a struggle between worker and machine. With the introduction of the machine workers blame machinery, an apparently non-human process, for either or both their own lack of employment or the extremely intense nature of their actual labour. In other words employees may only partially or inadequately perceive the nature of the relationships in which they stand with the implication here that sometimes the means for more efficient domination and extraction is mistaken for the source. Marx writes: 'It took time and experience before the workers learnt to distinguish between machinery and its employment by capital, and therefore to transfer their attacks from the material instruments of production to the form of society which utilises those instruments' (1976: 554–5). For Marx, as also acknowledged within critical realism, many of the fundamental conceptions agents hold can be inadequate to the situations they inhabit.

The focus of this section has been on the structure of Marx's account of the labour process *not* its explanatory power.[14] The aim has been to suggest that this account, with its emphasis upon essential social relations, structural tendencies and the stress upon accounting for agents' own representations, sits comfortably with critical realism.

Concluding remarks

Marx's analysis of the labour process seems consistent with a transcendental realist account of science and critical realist social ontology. Thus, in line with transcendental realism, he proceeds from what experience shows to be the case to the conditions that must prevail if experience of that kind is to be possible. He reasons from the phenomenal to its grounds of possibility. Marx appears committed to the view that social structures or essential relations are distinct from, normally out of phase with, and often in opposition to, the phenomena they generate. In addition, his treatment of both people and society corresponds to critical realist elaborations, his analysis of the capitalist production process providing an example of a social structural explanation compatible with the acknowledgement of human agency. None of this should be taken to imply that critical realism is tied to Marx's account of the labour process. If Marx's account of the labour process can be seen as consistent with critical realism there may conceivably be many other accounts of the labour process which are also consistent with this perspective and further it may be found that Marx's account is incomplete or inadequate in comparison to these competing accounts. Nor should it be assumed that drawing out the connections between critical realism and Marx's analysis exhausts the methodological lessons that can be recovered from a close analysis of Marx's work. Rather Marx's analysis of the labour process has been outlined here as an illustration of the kind of analysis facilitated by a critical realist approach. Marx's analysis of the labour process represents a useful example of what a substantive analysis consistent with the critical realist perspective can look like.

Notes

1   This paper represents a substantially revised version of Pratten (1993). I would like to thank Steve Fleetwood, Clive Lawson, Tony Lawson, Pat Northover and the original referees of the *Review of Political Economy* for very helpful comments on earlier drafts of the paper. The usual disclaimer applies.
2   Critical realism is *critical* because, amongst other reasons and as we shall see, it allows for ideology-critique, which, in turn, can be generalised to the critique of social systems on the grounds of their incapacity to sponsor structures which are wanted, needed and generally emancipatory.
3   At issue here is a theory of 'emergence', whereby entities or powers found at some level of organisation can be said to have risen out of some lower level, being conditioned by and dependent upon but not completely determined by properties found at the lower level.
4   Such a conception of the contact point between agency and structure also carries implications at a more specifically psychological level. As they participate in

society agents are afforded a plurality of social selves with different principles for action associated with each. The complex character of society adds powerfully to the complexity of the agent. Physiological principles add to human complexity simply by virtue of their potential opposition to psychological and sociological principles – at the dinner table, guests may be torn by the physiological drive of hunger, psychological tendencies towards greed and social pressures for polite good manners. Incorporating social rules multiplies internal complexity not only through its opposition to the other strata, but also by introducing all the conflicts and self-contradictions of society as a whole. On this see Bhaskar (1989: 80–119).

5 The specifically Marxist pedigree of Bhaskar's work has only gradually become evident. In his *A Realist Theory of Science* there is no direct discussion of Marx; however, in his more recent contributions Marx's influence is more explicit, culminating in Bhaskar's book on *Dialectics*, 1993.

6 Marx, of course, has been characterised as a positivist, pragmatist, humanist, structuralist, functionalist, critical theorist and so on. Therefore the suggestion that Marx, in fact, at least at times holds to a critical realist position is likely to be contentious and a full defence of such a reading would have to engage these competing interpretations more explicitly than is possible here. See Sayer (1979) for an extended argument supporting a realist interpretation of Marx and Bhaskar (1993) for an attempt to situate critical realism within a modified dialectical philosophical tradition helping to facilitate the task of defending a critical realist interpretation of Marx against various alternatives. There also exists an important literature drawing out the essentialist character of Marx's methodology and elaborating on the connections between Marx and Aristotle (see Meikle 1985; 1991; Pike 1999). To the extent that critical realism too can be seen as rooted in an Aristotelian essentialism then this reading of Marx would seem complementary to the one being offered here.

7 The ontological correspondences picked out here do not exhaust the links between Marx and critical realism. In particular, important epistemological ties could be drawn out. See Ollman (1993) for a valuable discussion of certain epistemological aspects of Marx's use of abstraction consistent with a critical realist perspective.

8 Although emphasis is placed on the later writings some reference is also made to earlier works, especially the *German Ideology*.

9 This is not to suggest, of course, that Marx provides much insight on human agency. As Harré remarks, 'Marx has no psychology worthy of the name' (in Morss 1984). The 'subjective' facets of action which condition the reproduction and transformation of social structures do appear to have been backgrounded in his critique of political economy and this has led to some recent criticisms (see Willmott 1993).

10 The term tendency is ambiguous but the weight of evidence taken together with other aspects of Marx's method suggest he means by tendency statements normic statements involving the exercise of tendencies which may not be realised. See Cartwright (1989).

11 As MacKenzie emphasises, it is important to recognise that the distinction between the labour process and the valorisation process holds, not between two different types of process, but between two aspects of the same process; the difference relates to the level of abstraction adopted. Mackenzie writes:

> Take a simple example the production of yarn. Looking at that as a labour process means examining the particular concrete ways in which people work, using specific technical instruments, to transform given raw materials into a product with given properties. In all societies that produce yarn it would be meaningful to examine in this way how it is done. But that is

not all there is to the production of yarn under capitalism. The production of yarn as a valorisation process is a process whereby inputs of certain value give rise to a product of greater value. The concrete particularities of the inputs and product, and the particular techniques and forms of work used to turn the inputs into the product, are here relevant only to the extent that they effect the quantitative outcome of the process. Capitalist production processes, but not all production processes, in all types of society, are valorisation processes.

(Mackenzie 1984: 481)

12 See MacKenzie (1984) for a detailed and insightful discussion of Marx's analysis of the labour process. Here the objective is to draw out the methodological points of contact between it and critical realism.
13 Thus, for example, it should be noted that while the imperative of valorisation and introduction of machinery does bring about changes in the labour process that do away with capital's dependency on many human competencies previously necessary, these changes can also create the need for new competencies and create new groups of skilled workers. That is to say the deskilling process associated with the introduction of new machinery must be recognised as nothing other than a tendency. For a balanced review of the deskilling debate which arose in the wake of Braverman's (1974) study see Elger (1979).
14 Since the social realm is necessarily open the empirical evaluation of theories requires something other than simple prediction. Theories can be judged in terms of, for example, their adequacy in accounting for a range of phenomena – other things being equal the greater the number of independent phenomena a theory can explain with its postulated causal framework, the better the theory. See MacKenzie (1984) for one attempt to assess the explanatory adequacy of Marx's account of the capitalist production process and its transformation.

Bibliography

Bhaskar, R. (1978) *A Realist Theory of Science*, Brighton: Harvester Press.
——(1986) *Scientific Realism and Human Emancipation*, London: Verso.
——(1989) *Reclaiming Reality*, London: Verso.
——(1991) *Philosophy and the Idea of Freedom*, Oxford: Basil Blackwell.
——(1993) *Dialectic: The Pulse of Freedom*, London: Verso.
Braverman, H. (1974) *Labour and Monopoly Capital: The Degradation of Work in the Twentieth Century*, New York: Monthly Review Press.
Cartwright, N. (1989) *Nature's Capacities and their Measurement*, Oxford: Oxford University Press.
Elger, T. (1979) 'Valorization and deskilling', *Capital and Class*, No. 7.
Fleetwood, S. (1999) *Critical Realism in Economics: Development and Debate*, London: Routledge.
Harré, R. (1970) *The Principles of Scientific Thinking*, London: Macmillan.
——(1977) 'Rules in the explanation of social behaviour', in P. Collett (ed.) *Social Rules and Social Behaviour*, Oxford: Basil Blackwell.
——(1979) *Social Being*, Oxford: Basil Blackwell.
Harré, R. and Secord, P. (1972) *The Explanation of Social Behaviour*, Oxford: Basil Blackwell.
Lawson, T. (1994a) 'Realism and Hayek: a case of continuous transformation', in M. Colana, H. Hageman and O. F. Hamouda (eds) *Capitalism, Socialism and Knowledge*, Aldershot: Edward Elgar.

——(1994b) 'The nature of Post Keynesianism and its links to other traditions', *Journal of Post Keynesian Economics*, 16, 4.

——(1997) *Economics and Reality*, London: Routledge.

MacKenzie, D. (1984) 'Marx and the machine', *Technology and Culture*, 25, 3: 473–502.

Marx, K. (1970) *A Contribution to the Critique of Political Economy*, London: Lawrence and Wishart.

——(1973a) *Grundrisse: Foundations of the Critique of Political Economy*, trans. M. Nicolaus, Harmondsworth and London: Penguin Books and New Left Review.

——(1973b) *Surveys From Exile, Political Writings, Vol. 2*, trans. D. Fernbach, Harmondsworth and London: Penguin Books and New Left Review.

——(1976) *Capital, Vol. 1*, trans. B. Fowkes, Harmondsworth and London: Penguin Books and New Left Review.

——(1981) *Capital, Vol. 3*, trans. D. Fernbach, Harmondsworth and London: Penguin Books and New Left Review.

Marx, K. and Engels, F. (1968) *Selected Works in One Volume*, London: Lawrence and Wishart.

——(1975) *Collected Works, Volume 3*, London: Lawrence and Wishart.

——(1976) *Collected Works, Volume 5*, London: Lawrence and Wishart.

Meikle, S. (1985) *Essentialism in the Thought of Karl Marx*, London: Duckworth.

——(1991) 'History of philosophy, the metaphysics of substance', in T. Carver (ed.) *The Cambridge Companion to Marx*, Cambridge: Cambridge University Press.

Morss, J. R. (1984) 'The dialectic of personal growth – theory, practice and human being: an interview with Rom Harre', *New Ideas in Psychology*, 5, 1: 127–35.

Ollman, B. (1993) *Dialectical Investigations*, London: Routledge.

Pike, J. E. (1999) *From Aristotle to Marx*, Aldershot: Ashgate.

Pratten, S. (1993) 'Structure, agency and Marx's analysis of the labour process', *Review of Political Economy*, 5, 4.

Sayer, D. (1979) *Marx's Method: Ideology, Science and Critique in Capital*, Brighton: Harvester Press.

Smith, T. (1997) 'The neoclassical and Marxian theories of technology: a comparison and critical assessment', *Historical Materialism: Research in Critical Marxist Theory*, No. 1.

Willmott, H. (1993) 'Breaking the paradigm mentality', *Organization Studies*, 14.

Part II

Substantive contributions

7 Critical realist ethnography

The case of racism and professionalism in a medical setting

Sam Porter

Introduction

In the wake of general acceptance of the role of qualitative methods within social science, recent criticisms of ethnography have tended to emanate from sympathetic rather than ideologically opposed commentators. This, however, does not make their observations any the less telling.

While attention was fixed on the motes in the sociological eye of quantitative positivism, the moral entrepreneurs of ethnography could afford to gloss over the inevitable inconsistencies within their own philosophy. However, with the battle won, and ethnography accepted into mainstream sociological method, its own optical beams are coming increasingly under scrutiny.

I propose here to frame a discussion of the criticisms faced by ethnography around the ideas contained in two papers by Martin Hammersley: 'What's wrong with ethnography?' (1990) and 'Ethnography and realism' (in Hammersley 1992). I will argue that one possible solution to the problems posed is the adoption of critical realism as an under-labouring philosophy for ethnographic research. Substantive support for this claim will be given in the form of an ethnographic study of the effects of racism and professionalism on occupational relations between nurses and doctors.

What's wrong with ethnography?

Hammersley's (1990) argument centres around the epistemological claims that are made for ethnography. In particular, he notes that a basic assumption behind much ethnography is that description, in and of itself, can generate theory. Moreover he charges ethnographers with being committed to a 'reproduction model of research', which claims to be able to describe the social world as it really is. Hammersley observes that truth underdetermines descriptions and that other values and concerns also play a role in their production. Acceptance of the validity of the reproduction model leads to a failure to make explicit the theoretical assumptions and values upon which research is predicated.

Without rehearsing the intricacies of Hammersley's (1990) critique, we can distil from it three significant problems that he raises for the aspiring ethnographer:

1   There is a need to explicate the representational claims of a study and to make apparent the assumptions and values that underlie it.
2   There is a need to focus empirical research on the theoretical issues that it is designed to illuminate.
3   There is a need to examine the explanatory status of a methodology which rejects determinism.

One issue not developed by Hammersley (1990) is the relationship between structure and action in ethnography. Many micro-sociological theorists adopt a methodological individualist stance. For example, Collins (1981) argues that social structures are merely abstractions bereft of causal power.

It would, of course, be a travesty to equate unproblematically micro-sociology with methodological individualism. It is explicitly rejected, for example, by Knorr-Cetina (1988). Nevertheless, 'methodological situationalism', while giving analytic priority to the social situation of individuals, rather than to the individuals themselves, still contains the assumption that macro-phenomena ultimately refer to micro-scale transactions; that structures consist of 'interrelationships between micro-episodes' (Knorr-Cetina 1988: 39).

Given the fundamental importance of the structure/action antinomy, it is appropriate to add a fourth ethnographic problematic:

4   There is a need to make explicit the ontological status ascribed to social structures.

The pertinence of critical realism

It is my contention that the use of Roy Bhaskar's critical realism is one way to solve these problems. Critical realism is an attempt to explain the relationship between social structure and human action. It rejects both individualist voluntarism and collectivist reification of social entities. Instead, it is argued that

> [T]he existence of social structure is a necessary condition for any human activity. Society provides the means, media, rules and resources for everything we do ... It is the unmotivated condition for all our motivated productions. We do not create society – the error of voluntarism. But these structures which pre-exist us are only reproduced or transformed in our everyday activities; thus society does not exist

independently of human agency – the error of reification. The social world is reproduced and transformed in daily life.

(Bhaskar 1989a: 3–4)

According to critical realism, social phenomena are the result of a plurality of structures (Bhaskar 1989a). These structures cannot be perceived. Therefore, they cannot be identified except through examination of their effects. Nor indeed can they exist independently of them (Bhaskar 1989b). However, if we accept the causal criterion for reality – that to be is to be able to do (Bhaskar 1978) – then the very existence of these effects demonstrates the reality of structures. Social analysis consists of a synthetic a priori production of hypotheses about the nature of structures, and the subsequent testing of them through empirical examination of their effects.

Thus far, three of the issues identified earlier have been addressed. The basic theoretical assumption of critical realism is that human action is enabled and constrained by social structures, but this action, in turn, reproduces or transforms those structures. Acceptance of the reality of social structures entails the rejection of methodological individualism as a sufficient mode of explanation. Similarly, methodological situationalism is seen as providing too weak a conception of structure.

Theoretical analysis of the nature of structures is an essential prerequisite to the understanding of social phenomena. In turn, theories about the nature of social structures and their effects upon human action need to be empirically tested. This testing is complicated by the fact that the subject matter of social science is conceptual. This limits the explanatory power of quantitative measurement. As Bhaskar puts it: 'meanings cannot be measured, only understood' (1989b: 46). Thus there is a need for the qualitative testing of hypotheses about the nature and effects of generative structures upon human action and vice versa. It is at this stage that ethnographic techniques can play a role. The purpose of ethnographic investigation here is not to idiographically illuminate small-scale social events, but to use examination of human agency to shed light on the relationship between agency and structure. It is therefore necessary explicitly to focus research on effects of the structural phenomena that are thought to be involved. This concentration on structures, rather than events *sui generis*, facilitates comparative testing of conclusions drawn.

It has to be conceded that the exposing of prior theoretical assumptions, while it entails rejection of naïve realist pretensions, does not exhaust the thorny problem of representation. The issue is not simply how the researcher perceives data, it is also how s/he portrays it. Betwixt interaction and publication, data is subjected to several stages of translation and transcription (Atkinson 1990). This process tends to involve manipulation of the data so that it fits with the arguments that are being promulgated (Williams 1990). The great danger here is that the events being described will be 'subverted by the transcending stories in which they are cast' (Crapanzano 1986: 76).

Given the transcendental aspects of critical realism, it would seem that it is especially prone to this error. Nevertheless, I would argue that recognition that critical realist ethnography, as any other, is not written in a neutral descriptive language does not lead us to the relativist view that regards every ethnography as an invention of its author (Clifford 1986). Rather, I would concur with Atkinson (1990) that awareness of the processes by which our understandings are fashioned can only strengthen our critical reflection.

I now turn to the third problematic: Hammersley argues that because ethnographers do not accept the existence of deterministic social laws, the theories they generate can be nothing more than teleological or ideal typical. He notes that it is only on the assumption

> that there are scientific laws of human social life (and deterministic rather than probabilistic ones at that) ... that reconstruction of theory in the face of conflicting evidence makes any sense.
>
> (Hammersley 1990: 60–5)

In contrast, Bhaskar argues that the belief that deterministic laws can be identified through the study of constant conjunctions, occurring within the artificially enclosed environment of the experiment, fails to recognise the reality of both the social and natural worlds; namely that they are open systems. He argues that in open systems, constant conjunctions do not pertain. Therefore:

> causal laws must be analysed as the tendencies of things, which may be possessed unexercised and exercised unrealised, just as they may of course be realised unperceived ... Thus in citing a law one is ... not making a claim about the actual outcome which will in general be co-determined by the activity of other mechanisms.
>
> (Bhaskar 1989b: 10)

The aim of science, both natural and social, therefore, becomes the identification of the structures and mechanisms which generate tendencies in the behaviour of phenomena. While the reflexive nature of humanity may entail qualitative differences between methods of studying people and other phenomena, this does not mean that we are forced to choose between crude positivism and the abandonment of any nomothetic pretensions whatsoever.

To summarise, ethnographic techniques can be used within the model of critical realism to investigate the nature of generative structures through examination of social phenomena. While such a use of ethnographic techniques involves stripping ethnography of much of its epistemological baggage, it has the merit of surmounting many of the weaknesses of that epistemology. Put another way, this approach abandons the *methodology* normally associated with ethnography, but continues to use ethnographic methods of data collection (cf. Brewer 1991).

Critical realism is, of course, not the only attempt to come to terms with the complex relationship between structure and agency. Notable alternatives include Berger and Luckmann's (1971) thesis on the social construction of reality, Giddens' (1984) structuration theory, and the work of Rom Harré (1979). Bhaskar (1989b) criticises the former model for its attempt to relate dialectically structure and action as two moments of the same process, which results in a failure to identify the radical differences between them. Structuration theory is closer to critical realism. However, an important difference lies in interpretation of the significance of structure. While structuration theory emphasises the autonomy of social actors, critical realism underlines the pre-existence of social forms, thus giving structure a stronger ontological grounding (Bhaskar 1983). This emphasis on structure provides a useful antidote to the micro-sociological tendencies of much ethnography. For similar reasons, I did not select Harré's work as the theoretical foundation for this study. While Harré seems to accept the existence of social structures, he is rather dubious about our ability to understand them. In his own words, 'We enter what is plainly a theatre, but we have to guess what play is being performed' (Harré 1979: 139). Contrary to this position, one of the contentions of this paper is that social structures are epistemologically amenable.

Critical realism versus subtle realism

Critical realism has a good deal in common with Hammersley's (1992) prescription for a 'subtle realism' in ethnography. However, a major difference between them relates to evaluation of subjects. Hammersley argues that the aim of ethnography should be to understand the perspectives of others rather than to judge them. He advises ethnographers to suspend any beliefs that conflict with those being described in order to avoid misunderstanding. By contrast, Bhaskar (1989a) is explicit in his assertion that critical realism logically entails evaluation, which he sees as an imperative for social research.

This disagreement is associated with differing conceptions of the role of social analysis. Hammersley (1992) takes the view that sociology is largely insulated from its subject matter. Conversely, Bhaskar (1989a) contends that social theory and social reality are causally interdependent. Because social analysis may have practical consequences in society, the evaluation that analysts put upon specific social phenomena is crucial.

There are dangers in adopting either side in this controversy. While it is important to realise that 'the social world may be opaque to the social agents upon whom it depends' (Bhaskar 1989a: 4), distinguishing between clarity and opacity is problematical, given that analysts themselves cannot have direct contact with the reality of social structures. It has been argued that acceptance of the interpretations of social actors avoids the danger of legislating social structure by fiat (Dingwall 1977). However, while there may be difficulties in gaining knowledge of structures, in that they can only be identified through examination of events, this does not mean that they do not exist. By ignoring the possible constraining nature of social structures, commentators are in danger of giving consent, through silence, to their oppressive effects.

Consider, for example, an ethnographic study of British soldiers (Hockey 1986), part of which involves an account of combat duty in rural Ireland (offensively described as 'bandit country'). While the soldiers' everyday lives in XMG are lavishly portrayed, there is no discussion at all about why they are there in the first place. More generally, while the study provides us with ample evidence that the outlook of British soldiers is largely mediated through sexist frames of reference, it makes little attempt to analyse critically this phenomenon, beyond portraying it as part of the aggressive masculinity that is seen as necessary for military effectiveness. Nor was it the aim of the author to make such an attempt. He is quite clear about the scope of his research, which involved stressing 'the importance of interpreting the behaviour of people *in terms of their subjectively intended meanings*' (Hockey 1986: 10, my emphasis).

Exclusive concentration on, and uncritical acceptance of, subjects' own accounts is the Achilles heel of phenomenological ethnography. It is the *reductio ad absurdum* of the valid hermeneutical point that the social world cannot be fully understood without taking account of the interpretations of the social actors in it. Understanding actors' viewpoints may be a necessary condition for social knowledge, but it is not a sufficient one. The ontological assumption that individual interactions and interpretations are ultimately all there are, leads to analytic superficiality. As Marx pithily remarked, 'all science would be superfluous if the outward appearances and essences of things directly coincided' (1966: 817).

The structure of racism

The deliberations of this paper thus far have been highly abstract. While ruminations such as these on theory and methodology may be important, on their own they are not enough; they tell us nothing substantive about the social world (Bulmer 1989). The utility of theoretical constructs can only be assessed through their application to concrete examples. The usefulness claimed by critical realism rests on its ability to act as an 'underlabouring' philosophy for social science (Bhaskar 1989a). The Lockean conception of underlabouring involves 'clearing the ground a little, and removing some of the rubbish that lies in the way of knowledge' (Locke 1894: 14), so that the builders of science can go about their task less encumbered. Whether this exercise in ideological refuse disposal has been successful will be judged according to its utility in helping us to understand specific aspects of the social world with greater clarity. It is therefore incumbent upon me to demonstrate the practical applicability of my theoretical position through examination of a particular social situation.

The substantive example to be addressed is a study of the influence of structural racism and professionalism on occupational relationships between nurses and doctors. Before going any further, however, it is necessary to demonstrate that it is valid to describe racism in structural terms, and to discuss how structural racism articulates with racist attitudes and behaviour.

The two core features of social structures, according to critical realism, are that they are *relational* – they involve enduring relations between the societal positions of actors – and that they possess *ontological depth* – their existence lies behind, and affects, manifest phenomena (Craib 1984).

Racism certainly involves enduring relationships between agents in different social positions. Being black in a racist society entails being categorised in numerous disadvantageous ways. Racist-engendered positions predate any of the individual actors now situated within them, and may well outlast them, albeit in modified forms. Moreover, *mutatis mutandis*, it is experienced by people in diverse social situations (including that of Ireland) (McVeigh 1992).

This persistence over time and space also indicates ontological depth. Beneath manifestations of racism is an underlying set of social relationships. Racist acts cannot be adequately explained solely through elucidation of the attitudes of the individuals involved. Such an empiricist psychological approach, because it fails to address the origins of individual attitudes, leads to their reification (Rex 1970). In order to avoid this static conception of racism, the articulation between racist acts, racist attitudes and structural racism needs to be considered.

The first thing to note is that their relations are not invariant. Because social phenomena occur in open systems, social and psychological 'laws' can only be analysed as tendencies (Bhaskar 1989b). Individuals' attitudes and actions are not predetermined by the social structures within which they live. Rather, the practices they engage in will be influenced by the social position which they occupy, in that social position provides the means, media, rules and resources available to enable or coerce action (Bhaskar 1989a). Thus, individuals will enjoy more or less powerful and enabling positions in a society which displays structural racism, depending upon how they are categorised in racist terms. However, this does not mean that because someone lives in a racist society, they will necessarily display racist behaviour, or even possess racist attitudes. Nonetheless, there is pressure on them to do so, especially if they reside in the empowered camp of a racist divide, in that racist attitudes can provide an ideological rationalisation for the structural inequalities from which they may benefit.

The links between the ideology and practice of racism are even closer than this. Bhaskar (1989b) observes that specific ideologies are associated with specific practices, which in turn are associated with structural positions. Indeed, it should be noted that racism is entirely premised upon an ideological category, 'race' being nothing more than a reified social construction (Miles 1982). This does not mean, however, that it can be reduced to the status of superstructural epiphenomenon. Racism, although founded upon ideological assumptions which have little bearing on reality, nevertheless has real effects upon social relations.

In mapping out the relationship between material activity and ideology, Bhaskar attempts to avoid the twin errors of idealism and material reductionism. Rather than viewing ideas and actions as separate entities, he argues that:

> all activity ... necessarily has an ideational component, that is to say that it is unthinkable except in so far as the agent has a conception of what s/he is doing and why s/he is doing it (in which of course s/he may be mistaken),
>
> (Bhaskar 1989b: 66)

The parenthetic qualification is an important one in that it allows for the possibility of unintentional racism. Because the social world may be opaque to the actors within it, it is possible for actions to have the effect of maintaining racist structures without actors realising that they are doing so. Nevertheless, if we allow that individuals act with reflexive intentionality, we must assume that there is often a connection between racist acts and racist ideas.

There is, however, another qualification that requires to be made in relation to the connection between thought and action – the possession of racist beliefs does not necessarily entail the performance of racist acts. By dint of the fact that the human psyche is an open system, attitudes should be regarded as tendencies, rather than iron determinants. To this end, it will be my contention that racism will usually only be manifested in circumstances which the racist actor regards as auspicious for its display.

In sum, racism is a structural phenomenon, displaying both relational power and ontological depth. Its effect upon action, however, cannot be construed in terms of constant conjunction. Rather the relationship between structure and action can better be described as generative – with the former providing the conditions for the latter. Conversely, structural racism is dependent upon the consciousness and motivated action of agents, because it is that consciousness and action which maintains or transforms it.

Method

Empirical evidence about the manifestation of racism in a medical setting was gathered over a period of three months in 1989, during which I was employed as a staff nurse in the intensive care unit of a large metropolitan hospital in the north of Ireland. The number of subjects observed were 'thirty-three nurses, all of whom were white Irish; and twenty-one doctors,

six of whom belonged to racialised minorities – groups to which the ideological category of "race"' has been attributed' (Miles 1982).

Data was obtained through participant observation. While the subjects
were aware that I was conducting research into communication between
nurses and other health workers, they were not aware of my interest in race.

Pressure of work, and the need for discretion, meant that there were occasions when a considerable period of time elapsed between observation of data
and its recording (which was usually done in privacy). The data was recorded
manually in a notebook.

My method of analysis was largely conventional, involving prior formulation of general hypotheses, followed by cycles of empirical testing and
hypothetical reformulation. The process was, of course, not as mechanical as
this; serendipity and imagination played a considerable part in the work's
evolution. The cycle of testing and refining continued to the point of 'theoretical saturation' (Strauss 1987).

The hypotheses I commenced with were:

1   The structural phenomenon of racism would to some degree inform
    relationships between white health workers and those belonging to
    racialised minorities.
2   The occupational situation would affect the way in which racism was
    expressed.

'Race' and power

My work was essentially an attempt to engage with David Hughes' (1988)
ethnographic study of nurse–doctor interaction in a British casualty unit.
Hughes had noted that a significant variable affecting the nurse–doctor relationship was the geographical origin of the doctor. Many of the doctors he
studied were recent immigrants to Britain from the Asian sub-continent.
Interactions with these doctors frequently involved a breakdown of nurses'
deference.

Such was not the case in my study. The interaction of nurses with black
or Asian doctors elicited little observed alteration in the balance of power.
Indeed, the doctor in the unit most respected for his clinical knowledge was
African. With a background in medical research which had furnished him
with an impressive fund of information, he was frequently quizzed by nurses
on the more esoteric aspects of the medical corpus. It was noticeable,
however, that he made conspicuous efforts to ensure that his superior grasp
of formal occupational knowledge was recognised. An example of this self-
assertive strategy involved a demonstration of the diagnostic limitations of
nurses. Much to his own amusement, the doctor asked in turn every nurse
present in the unit to try to interpret a patient's chest X-ray. After several
had failed to grasp the import of the image they were examining, he even
provided a clue that the patient had suffered from tuberculosis about fifty

years previously. To the evident satisfaction of their interrogator, not one nurse noticed that the patient had had half a lung removed! To my eternal shame, I was one of those tested.

That episodes such as this were part of a deliberate strategy, rather than an unselfconscious display of clinical knowledge, can be inferred from the following field notes of a conversation between myself and this doctor.

Transcript 1

I asked him what it was like coming to work in a place like this. He went over some of the pros and cons of his move ... [One con he identi- fied was] that every time he got a new post, he had to start all over again. People automatically assumed that because he 'wasn't from here' he wouldn't know anything. Every time, he had to go through the same old routine before they accepted that he was good at his job. He wryly concluded: 'but I think people soon get the message'.

Another strategy adopted by some doctors from ethnic minorities was the utilisation of formal occupational power. For example, one Asian consultant was noted for his authoritarian manner. His attitude was normally one of distant superiority. He rarely talked to his nursing colleagues, and made little attempt to involve them in decision-making processes about patient care. Indeed, when he did communicate with nurses, it was almost exclu- sively to gain information upon which to base his own decisions. Indeed, if he could get the information he needed from clinical recordings, he eschewed even this mode of interaction. Once he had made a decision, he rarely felt it necessary to explain the rationale behind it:

Transcript 2

The consultant enters the side room, without greeting either nurses or patient. He stands for a considerable period of time staring silently at the monitors. The nurses, who curtailed their conversation on his entering, wait in silence for him to speak.

CONSULTANT: Inotrope up to ten.

He turns and leaves the room without any further communication. The nurse does his bidding, though not without a sigh and shake of the head.

His demeanour was not simply one of social distance. He was prepared to exercise his occupational authority in more direct ways. He did not balk at demonstrating his power to the point of chastising nurses in front of their patients, as the following field note demonstrates:

Transcript 3

In the process of a 'ward round', the consultant comes across a heavily stained dressing.

CONSULTANT: Who is looking after this patient?

STAFF NURSE: I am.

CONSULTANT: This is a disgrace. This dressing should have been changed hours ago.

(The staff nurse reddens, but does not reply.)

SISTER: The wound's been giving us a lot of trouble. There's a lot of exudate and we're having to change the padding almost continually.

CONSULTANT: Mmm. Is he pyrexial?

This authoritarianism was rarely openly challenged by nurses. Overt demonstrations of dissatisfaction were restricted to some nurses withholding help or information from the consultant unless and until he specifically asked them. This exacerbated communication problems and increased mutual resentment (to say nothing of the effect it had upon clinical efficiency). Nevertheless, interactions between nurses and this doctor displayed an aura of starched propriety, where nurses gave the outward appearance of 'knowing their place' in the occupational hierarchy.

The reality of racism

One possible explanation for the deference found in my study, in contrast to Hughes' (1988), is that racism is absent from Irish society. Such a hypothesis was, however, belied by the private complainings of nurses amongst themselves which indicated that the conceptions of 'race' and racial inferiority were utilised by at least some of them. When nurses were on their own, or 'backstage' to use Goffman's (1969) term, the mask of professional propriety was dropped. During tea and meal breaks, and on other occasions when they were out of earshot of both doctors and patients, nurses often complained about what they regarded as unfair behaviour on the part of some of their medical colleagues. These complaints served as 'secondary adjustments' (Goffman 1968), allowing nurses temporarily to shed institutional assumptions about how they should think and behave. On occasion, they were expressed in racist terms:[1]

Transcript 4

STAFF NURSE: Who does he think he is, coming over here from the arse end of the world and telling us who were born and reared here what to do?

Racism was frequently elided with gender issues, as can be seen in a nurse's reaction to the consultant's behaviour recorded in Transcript 3:

Transcript 5

STAFF NURSE 1:   Jesus, [Surname] was really nasty to you on the round.
STAFF NURSE 2:   Yea, but at least [Sister] stood up for me.
STAFF NURSE 3:   It's out of order, treating us like that. They may treat women like skivvies in Pakistan, but I don't see why he should get away with it here.

This introduction of gender is cautionary; isolating the effects of individual structural mechanisms such as racism upon specific phenomena is, to a degree, an artificial exercise, providing only partial explanation.[2] Ironically, the other doctor whose perceived authoritarianism was complained about in racist terms was female:

Transcript 6

STAFF NURSE: I think she thinks that that dot on her head makes her a maharaja or something. Someone should tell her we're not Indian peasants.

However, backstage racism was not simply a pathologised reaction to heavy-handed authoritarianism. More egalitarian doctors were also subject to prejudice:

Transcript 7

A staff nurse opens the door to enter a clinical room where she discovers a Palestinian doctor at prayer. After mumbling polite apologies, she retreats from the room. However, almost immediately the following interaction occurs.

STAFF NURSE: That bloody Arab is praying again in the treatment room. How am I supposed to get my work done?
DOMESTIC ASSISTANT: Huh, if he wants to go down on his hands and knees every ten minutes, you'd think he'd stay in his own country and do it.
STAFF NURSE: Arabs.
She moves off, shaking her head.

Even the African clinical expert was not totally immune:

Transcript 8

·STAFF NURSE: He's the smartest black person I've ever met.

Moreover, with the exception of the clinical expert, the relationship of white nurses and black doctors was considerably cooler and more formal than between white nurses and white doctors, irrespective of whether the nurses characterised the doctors as authoritarian.

However, this undercurrent of racism in the attitudes of some of the nurses did little to undermine the authority of the doctors concerned in face-to-face interactions. This is not to say that nurses were unproblematically subservient (cf.Porter 1991), rather that the negotiating tactics that they used did not differ qualitatively to those they used with white doctors. Specifically, I saw no evidence of the types of interactions that were noted in Hughes' (1988) study: nurses in my study were not seen to abandon outward shows of deference to black doctors, to direct them to perform specific tasks, to reprimand them for their behaviour, or to openly criticise their professional competence.

Another possible reason for the differences between these two studies is that while the doctors in Hughes' study were not familiar with the cultural cues of the host culture, those in my study were. This is largely the explanation given by Hughes. He argues that their unfamiliarity leads immigrant doctors to be dependent upon nurses for cultural translation, allowing nurses to be far more actively involved in therapy than they would otherwise be. This alteration in the balance of power is exacerbated by the loss of status resulting from nurses observing doctors to 'misconstrue events or omit to make seemingly "obvious" inferences concerning particular cases' (Hughes 1988: 14).

If this explanation is accepted, the differences in power between doctors and nurses in these two studies can be seen in functional terms: those doctors who are competent at their job are given the status usually accorded members of that occupation; those who are perceived as incompetent are not. What worries me about such an explanation is that it excises the issue of racism altogether, and as we have already seen, racist attitudes were certainly evident in my study at least.

Hughes implicitly deals with racism by introducing E. C. Hughes' (1945) concept of status dilemma. E. C. Hughes observes that a complex of auxiliary characteristics tends to grow up around a particular status. He identifies whiteness as an auxiliary characteristic of high-status occupations such as medicine. A dilemma in status occurs if this expected characteristic is missing. Thus D. Hughes explains the relationships he observed in the following terms: 'relations between young, inexperienced Asian [doctors] and mature, experienced, Anglo-Saxon *(sic)* nurses almost inevitably involve dilemmas in status, and some departure from expected role relationships' (Hughes 1988: 17).

Though neither of the authors (Hughes 1988; Hughes 1945) states it, the issue being dealt with here is the effects of a structurally constituted racism. Status is being denied some people because of what others see as their inferior 'racial' characteristics.

It can be seen that D. Hughes is positing two separate explanations for the phenomena he observed, one functional and one racialised. He attempts to synthesise these by stating that:

> Everett Hughes's analysis is capable of marriage to contemporary socio-logical perspectives. Hughes, admittedly, was concerned with contradictions of status primarily in terms of combinations of personal characteristics that violate normative expectations regarding occupational incumbency, but such contradictions are also likely to have direct implications in terms of interactional performance ... [D]ifferential competence in utilising relevant bodies of social knowledge is perhaps the most salient interactional manifestation of 'status' characteristics.
>
> (Hughes 1988: 17–18)

I would argue that the connection between these two factors is only contingent. It may be the case in Hughes' study that 'status differentiation' or, in more critical language, racist discrimination is mediated through 'differential competence'. However, it would be naïve to assume that manifestations of racism are limited to such circumstances. Racism is not suffered exclusively by people who are unattuned to British or Irish culture. The experiences of second- and third-generation black British people testify to the contrary (Brown 1984).

Nevertheless, the case of members of high-status occupations suffering from racism is significant. In E. C. Hughes' words:

> membership of the Negro *(sic)* race, as defined in American mores and/or law, may be called a master status-determining trait. It tends to overpower, in most crucial situations, any other characteristic which may run counter to it. But professional standing is also a powerful characteristic ... In the person of the professionally qualified Negro *(sic)* these two powerful characteristics clash.
>
> (Hughes 1945: 357)

In other words, there are two contradictory social mechanisms at work here. Racism tends to reduce social status, while professional power enhances it.

The influence of professional ideology

We must now ask why the tendency of racism was 'exercised unrealised' (or latent, in Merton's (1968) terminology) in my study, but realised in D. Hughes' (1988) study. It will be remembered that Bhaskar (1989b) observes that the actual outcome of a tendency will generally be co-determined by the activity of other mechanisms. In this case, the other mechanism is that of professionalism.

Professional power is based on the ability of professions to maintain occupational closure by such means as credentialism and legal licence (Parkin 1979). These methods of closure, in turn, depend upon the justificatory ideology of professionalism, central to which are the pattern variables identified by Parsons (1951).

I realise that an attempt to resuscitate Parsonian sociology will be met with some scepticism. However, it is my contention that radical critics of Parson's theory of professions (for example, Freidson 1972; Johnson 1972) may have thrown the baby out with the bathwater. Turner (1985) has noted that the sociology of professions exemplifies the tendency of the discipline as a whole to lurch from one exaggeration to another. The Parsonian definition of professions emphasised knowledge as the dominant criterion, dismissing the salience of power. In reaction to what they saw as the sanguine naïvety of this position, later commentators asserted that occupational dominance was central, knowledge and ethics being irrelevant. Turner argues that an adequate conception of professions must take both dimensions seriously.

While it may be the case that professional ideology is adopted by professionals for self-serving purposes, namely the maintenance of occupational control, this does not mean that the ideology is non-existent. Notwithstanding the dubiety of its material referent, because ideology has effects it cannot be dismissed as an illusion (Hirst 1979). Indeed, because nurses hanker after a professional status that they have not attained, and which they see so close to them in the form of medicine, they take professional ideology very seriously indeed (Porter 1992a).

It was in his study of the medical profession that Parsons first developed the notion of pattern variables (Holton and Turner 1986). Three of these are of direct relevance to the issue of racism. They are linked together by their emphasis of the importance of rationality. Acceptance of universalistic achievement values entails doctors being regarded as having attained their occupational status through their ability, independent of ascriptive qualities such as 'race'. Affective neutrality is also pertinent. It assumes that judgements should be made on the basis of scientific rationality rather than affectivity. The final variable is that of functional specificity, which only allows doctors to be judged on their skills as doctors, rather than on factors extraneous to the job.

This rationalistic conception of professionalism is largely accepted within the culture of nursing (Porter 1992a). As a consequence, the variables outlined above are criteria by which actions are judged within the social setting I have described. Naked racism, being irrational, ascriptive, particularistic, diffuse and affective, is therefore not justifiable as an open form of social interaction between nurses and doctors. To be acceptable in this social milieu, racism needs to be cloaked in a 'rational' veneer. This is what is happening when differential competence is married to 'race'. Criticism on the grounds of competence can be portrayed as rational, affectively neutral, universalistic, achievement oriented, and specific to the skills of medicine. Yet, the racism is there. From such a perspective, criticisms of immigrant doctors' competence can be seen as the vehicle through which racism is expressed. However, the connection between knowledge of social cues and race is not a necessary one. It follows that if a black doctor is culturally literate, an important avenue for the expression of racism is closed off. This does not mean that racism ceases to exist, just that the mechanisms for its articulation are limited – it is submerged in the public arena, but continues to find expression backstage. Thus, in a discussion bewailing the infiltration of non-Christian religions, the nurse who deferred publicly to the Palestinian doctor's religious observances, but complained about them privately in racist terms (Transcript 7), explained her behaviour in the following terms:

Transcript 9

STAFF NURSE 1:　Why didn't you say something to him about it?

STAFF NURSE 2:　Well, it wouldn't be proper. It would be a bit unprofessional.

STAFF NURSE 1:　It's not exactly professional to get down on your knees in the middle of the clinical room.

STAFF NURSE 2:　Yea, but you couldn't just say 'Listen you, you're not in Arab land now'. I suppose I could have told him that clinical areas have to be open to staff at all times.

The sifting of structures

To return to critical realism, we can see the complex interpolations that exist between social structures and social phenomena. While structural racism exists, it is modified by the professional ideology to which the actors adhere. This counter-balancing effect is in the nature of open social systems. There is no reason to suppose that the *matrix* of structures within which agency occurs will not contain contradictory elements. Actors are therefore often faced with incongruent structural variables. This does not imply that actors have total discretion in choosing which structural tendencies to take notice of and which to ignore; it is possible to rank hierarchically structures in terms of their explanatory significance for any specific social event (Bhaskar 1989a). Nevertheless, the openness of the social world attenuates the determinant power of social structures in favour of agents' reflexive volition. Agents are faced with the task of collapsing structural variables into categories that can inform interactional practices. Goffman (1983: 11) has argued that this is done by means of 'a set of transformational rules, or a membrane selecting how various externally relevant social distinctions will be managed within the interaction'. Thus, in a social situation where nurses deemed open expressions of racism as inappropriate, they filtered them out, selecting instead professional modes of interaction.

This process of filtering out racism in favour of professionalism was encouraged by the possible victims of that racism. Their success in utilising professionalism to negate the effects of prejudice varied according to the tactics used. The authoritarian consultant relied on the status ascribed to him by dint of his occupational position, and did not adopt more subtle justificatory strategies. While his authority was not formally challenged, it was accepted with bad grace. Onstage, this was evidenced by the sullen manner by which nurses interacted with him; backstage, by the frequency of racist remarks.

Some indication that this doctor's behaviour was a response to racism was given by a nurse who had worked in the unit since its foundation:

Transcript 10

> SISTER: It's not all his fault. When he came here first he had a hard
> time of it. People were a bit cheeky. It's not a wonder he closed up.

A more successful strategy was adopted by the knowledgeable doctor. By portraying himself as a paragon of scientific rationality, he was more closely attuned to the presumptions of professionalism, by which the nurses set such store. As a result his authority was not only formally, but also conatively accepted.

Conclusion

The aim of this paper has been to demonstrate the possibility of using critical realism to overcome some of the epistemological weaknesses associated with ethnography. Firstly, by emphasising social structure, I have attempted to counterbalance the micro-sociological tendencies often associated with ethnography. Secondly, rather than attempting to reproduce the social situation studied, the theoretical values were identified upon which the research was predicated, and which determined the focus of empirical enquiry. The aim was not primarily to describe events, but to explain why they occurred. This explanation involved identifying the influence of structural factors on human agency, in this case the influence of racism and professionalism upon the interactions of nurses and doctors. Equally, explanation focused on how agency maintained or transformed those structures. This was most striking in doctors' use of occupational advantages to ensure that the disempowering effects of racism were minimised.

The variable manifestations of racism, which occurred overtly in Hughes' study and covertly in mine, provide an example of the inadequacy of explanatory models founded upon the premise that the identification of constant conjunctions is essential to 'scientific' explanation. Instead, racism can be seen as a tendency that is realised in certain circumstances, but exercised unrealised in others.

Finally, a critical realist approach to ethnography facilitates subsequent comparative or critical work. Firstly, because the emphasis is on structural mechanisms rather than unique events, conclusions about the effects of those structures can be tested through empirical examination of events in other settings. Secondly, because the research is explicitly founded on a clearly articulated philosophical position, it is possible for critics to engage with the assumptions inherent in that position and to assess their validity. Thirdly, explicit identification of an underlabouring philosophical model enables critics to examine whether the substantive research properly utilises the theory upon which it purports to be predicated.

Acknowledgements

I would like to thank Robbie McVeigh, John Brewer, and the editors and anonymous reviewers of *Sociology* for their help and encouragement in the construction of this paper.

Notes

1   In fairness to the nurses, racist was rarely uttered. Nevertheless, the fact that a few nurses felt able to use it with impunity indicates that racism was at least tolerated in backstage culture.
2   For a fuller discussion on the influence of gender relations upon this social situation, see Porter (1992b).

Bibliography

Atkinson, P. (1990) *The Ethnographic Imagination: Textual Construction of Reality*, London: Routledge.

Berger, P. L. and Luckmann, T. (1971) *The Social Construction of Reality*, Harmondsworth: Penguin.

Bhaskar, R. (1978) *A Realist Theory of Science*, second edition, Brighton: Harvester Wheatsheaf.

——(1983) 'Beef, structure and place: notes from a critical naturalist perspective', *Journal for the Theory of Social Behaviour*, 13, 1: 81–95.

——(1989a) *Reclaiming Reality: A Critical Introduction to Contemporary Philosophy*, London: Verso.

——(1989b) *The Possibility of Naturalism: A Philosophical Critique of the Contemporary Human Sciences*, second edition, Hemel Hempstead: Harvester Wheatsheaf.

Brewer, J. D. (1991) 'The ethnographic critique of ethnography – or how sectarian is the RUC?', unpublished paper given at the Conference on Systematic Aspects of Qualitative Research, University of Surrey, 22–24 November.

Brown, C. (1984) *Black and White in Britain*, London: Heinemann.

Bulmer, M. (1989) 'Theory and method in recent British sociology: whither the empirical impulse?', *British Journal of Sociology*, 40: 329–417.

Clifford, J. (1986) 'Introduction: partial truths', in J. Clifford and G. E. Marcus (eds) *Writing Culture: The Poetics and Politics of Ethnography*, Berkeley, CA: University of California Press, 1–27.

Collins, R. (1981) 'On the micro-foundations of macro-sociology', *American Journal of Sociology*, 86: 984–1014.

Craib, R. (1984) *Modern Social Theory: From Parsons to Habermas*, Brighton: Harvester Wheatsheaf.

Crapanzano, V. (1986) 'Hermes' dilemma: the masking of subversion in ethnographic description', in J. Clifford and G. E. Marcus (eds) *Writing Culture: The Poetics and Politics of Ethnography*, Berkeley, CA: University of California Press, 51–76.

Dingwall, R. (1977) *The Social Organisation of Health Visitor Training*, London: Croom Helm.

Freidson, E. (1972) *Profession of Medicine: A Study of the Sociology of Applied Knowledge*, New York: Dodd Mead.

Giddens, A. (1984) *The Constitution of Society: Outline of the Theory of Structuration*, Cambridge: Polity.

Goffman, E. (1968) *Asylums: Essays on the Social Situation of Mental Patients and Other Inmates*, Harmondsworth: Penguin.

——(1969) *The Presentation of Self in Everyday Life*, Harmondsworth: Penguin.

——(1983) 'The interaction order', *American Sociological Review*, 48: 1–17.

Hammersley, M. (1990) 'What's wrong with ethnography? The myth of theoretical description', *Sociology*, 24, 4: 597–616.

——(1992) *What's Wrong with Ethnography?*, London: Routledge.

Harré, R. (1979) *Social Being: A Theory for Social Psychology*, Oxford: Blackwell.

Hirst, P. (1979) *On Law and Ideology*, London: Macmillan.

Hockey, J. (1986) *Squaddies: Portrait of a Subculture*, Exeter: University of Exeter Press.

Holton, R. J. and Turner, B. S. (1986) *Talcott Parsons on Economy and Society*, London: Routledge & Kegan Paul.

Hughes, D. (1988) 'When nurse knows best: some aspects of nurse/doctor interaction in a casualty department', *Sociology of Health and Illness*, 10, 1: 1–22.

Hughes, E. C. (1945) 'Dilemmas and contradictions of status', *American Journal of Sociology*, 50: 353–9.

Johnson, T. J. (1972) *Professions and Power*, London: Macmillan.

Knorr-Cetina, K. (1988) 'The micro-social order', in N. G. Fielding (ed.) *Actions and Structure: Research Method and Social Theory*, London: Sage, 21–53.

Locke, J. (1894) *An Essay Concerning Human Understanding*, Volume 1, ed. A. C. Fraser, Oxford: Clarendon.

McVeigh, R. (1992) 'The specificity of Irish racism', *Race and Class*, 33, 4: 331–45.

Marx, K. (1966) *Capital*, Volume 3, London: Lawrence and Wishart.

Merton, R. (1968) *Social Theory and Social Structure*, third edition, New York: Free Press.

Miles, R. (1982) *Racism and Migrant Labour*, London: Routledge & Kegan Paul.

Parkin, F. (1979) *Marxism and Class Theory: A Bourgeois Critique*, London: Tavistock.

Parsons, T. (1951) *The Social System*, London: Routledge & Kegan Paul.

Porter, S. (1991) 'A participant observation study of power relations between nurses and doctors in a general hospital', *Journal of Advanced Nursing*, 16: 728–35.

——(1992a) 'The poverty of professionalisation: a critical analysis of strategies for the occupational advancement of nursing', *Journal of Advanced Nursing*, 17: 720–6.

——(1992b) 'Women in a women's job: the gendered experience of nurses', *Sociology of Health and Illness*, 14, 4: 510–27.

Rex, J. (1970) *Race Relations and Sociological Theory*, London: Weidenfeld and Nicholson.

Strauss, A. L. (1987) *Qualitative Analysis for Social Scientists*, Cambridge: Cambridge University Press.

Turner, B. S. (1985) 'Knowledge, skill and occupational strategy: the professionalisation of paramedical groups', *Community Health Studies*, 9, 1: 38–47.

Williams, A. (1990) 'Reflections on the making of an ethnographic text', *Studies in sexual politics*, No. 29, University of Manchester.

8 Routines, strategy and change in high-technology small firms

Neil Costello

Institutions and routines

Ideas about routines or rule-bound behaviour are used increasingly in attempts to understand the behaviour of organisations. Routines are seen, at a common-sense level, as predetermined, unchanging patterns of behaviour exemplified by the kind of activities which workers carry out on production lines. Thus, passing partially completed sets of components from one worker to another, with each adding a small contribution to the finished product, is the common image of routine. A broader definition is more helpful, however, since the idea of a routine is generally used in the analysis of behaviour which requires some thought even though the behaviour may be, in some senses, automatic. A stimulus may prompt the firm towards a particular form of analysis or other form of complex behaviour. The behaviour is routine in the sense that those sorts of problems are always analysed in that way but it is not simple. Here the concept of routine is used to look at the taken-for-grantedness of behaviour and it has close links with the concepts of institutions and culture.

One of the fundamental premises of institutional economics is that the determination of whatever allocation occurs in society arises from the organisational structure – the institutions – which change through 'non-deliberative' (habit and custom) and 'deliberative' (legal) modes (Samuels 1995). Nelson defines institutions as 'a complex of socially learned and shared values, norms, beliefs, meanings, symbols, customs, and standards that delineate the range of expected and accepted behaviour in a particular context' (Nelson 1995). This is consistent with the broader approach to institutions which comes out of anthropology. Douglas (1987), for example, sees an institution as a convention, which she defines, following Lewis (1968), as arising 'when all parties have a common interest in there being a rule to ensure co-ordination, none has conflicting interest, and none will deviate lest the desired co-ordination is lost'. Such conventions are self-policing and Douglas refers to an institution as a legitimised social grouping. The legitimacy can come from many places but specifically excludes any purely instrumental or practical arrangement that is recognised as such. Nelson's 'expected and accepted' behaviour is close to Douglas' legitimacy. For the new (economic) institutionalists, institutions are 'the rules of the game' (North 1990) where for North the emphasis is on the self-reinforcing nature of institutionalised behaviour, a form of self-policing convention. Path dependency is an important implication of these definitions.

Broadly within this same framework, Nelson and Winter's classic text (Nelson and Winter 1982) sees routines as a response to the quantity and complexity of information faced by firms. Routines are not a conscious-maximising choice, on these arguments, but are where the firm's organisational knowledge is stored. They are a source of difference among firms which, through a selection mechanism, drives the evolutionary process. In practice, rules and procedures cannot be too complicated because of the bounded rationality of firms, but modelling the firm requires modelling routines and observing how they change over time.

Such concerns are based upon a world possessing an excess of information (excessive, that is, in relation to the ability of individuals or organisations to process it) which was the focus of the seminal work of March and Simon (1958). They define routinised behaviour:

> Activity (individual or organisational) can usually be traced back to an environmental stimulus of some sort ... The responses to stimuli are of various kinds. At one extreme, a stimulus evokes a response – sometimes very elaborate – that has been developed and learned at some previous time as an appropriate response for a stimulus of this class. This is the 'routinised' end of the continuum, where a stimulus calls forth a performance program almost instantaneously.
>
> (March and Simon 1958: 139)

This definition is important in insisting that firm differences matter and therefore that analysis of firms as unique and important institutions in themselves is a valuable activity. March and Simon discuss a continuum which describes behaviour moving from completely routinised to 'problem-solving' where new performance programmes may be constructed. A set of activities are regarded as routinised 'to the degree that choice has been simplified by the development of a fixed response to defined stimuli' (March and Simon 1958: 142). The research reported here will show that this is too stark a distinction in practice. Penrose (1959) pre-figured this form of analysis by distinguishing between resources and services (that resources render). It is the services which are a function of the experience and accumulated knowledge of the firm and that are the source of the firm's distinctiveness. Dynamic capabilities (Teece *et al.* 1990) which are sticky, i.e. not easily changed, acquired or passed on, build on Penrose's distinction. Such capabilities are inherited from and constrained by the past and from them the firm develops a set of skills, assets and routines which become its core competencies. Such soft assets cannot be traded and so must be built, often over decades.

Teece's resource-based approach to the firm has many similarities to an approach which concentrates on routines. In the resource-based approach firms with superior organisational structures and capabilities are profitable because they have lower costs, higher quality or higher product performance. Their strengths are related to the experience inherent in management effectiveness and co-ordination. Intra-firm differences in performance are found to be greater than inter-industry differences (Teece *et al.* 1990). This is another way of saying that the routine (in the way the term is used here), or taken-for-granted practices in management, are an important source of difference between firms.

Rules or habits are advantageous for human decision making or action (Hodgson 1997). Even conventional profit-maximising models require the adherence to a rule and Hodgson sets out an exhaustive taxonomy of the circumstances in which habits and rules are beneficial. This is a helpful orientation. An important distinction is then that between rules and habits. Rules are deliberative and usually consciously adopted; habits, according to Hodgson's definition, are characteristically unexamined. Rules can become habits. Routines, as used here, draw on both rules and habits.

Consistent with a taxonomy of this kind, it is argued here, routineness exists at all levels. Taken-for-granted, skilled responses – routines – are called forth by complex stimuli at operational levels and at strategic and policy-making levels. Conceptually, routines can be categorised as operational and strategic, where operational routines are concerned with the maintenance of structure – the nature of the organisation – and strategic routines are concerned with the organisation's ability to operate in its environment but, in practice, the two are linked and empirical routines frequently contain some element of both. Routines, however, are not determining. They are a tendency to act in a particular manner. That is to say, firms are predisposed to act in that way but at any given time there may be other social or economic factors operating upon them which override the tendency.

For analytical purposes, established practices at a societal level – institutions – can be distinguished from those within the organisation – routines. *Routines are seen here as established, significant, sanctioned and recurrent practices within organisations.*

The focus of the study is on the dynamic aspects of a particular firm's behaviour, not on a comparative series of static pictures. The goal is to try to discover the ways in which the firm generates and deals with change. Time is not simply elapsed time, but has a chronology and a history. Events are essentially historical and influence activities in a path-dependent way. As Thomas (1991) shows, this is not a new idea. It was a problem with which Marshall struggled in writing his *Principles*. There are also very clear practical implications, frequently at a detailed, technical level, well demonstrated, for example, by the history of the QWERTY keyboard (David 1985).

The research focuses on the different perceptions of individuals in different structural positions within the case study company. In looking through their eyes, the objective is to find the key events, beliefs and symbols they use in making sense of the organisation. There is a need to look at events and processes as the subjects perceive them (Boland 1985; Johnson 1987; Walsham 1993). The organisation is the output of the processes under study and is not an entity that has opinions of its own or one that can carry out its own actions. In order to understand the organisation, it is crucial to gain an understanding of the perspectives of the members of the organisation. Their combined understandings are essentially the organisation's understandings. Such a focus is an interpretative one.

Development of the interpretive approach in institutional and evolutionary economics links closely to ideas coming from organisational and sociological theory. Giddens' notion of structuration can be helpful (Giddens 1982). Giddens defines structure as recursively organised rules and resources (Giddens 1982: 35) while structuration is seen as conditions governing the continuity or transformation of structures, and therefore the reproduction of systems (Giddens 1982: 35). What this comes down to in simplified terms is the need to conceptualise a structure that is constantly being changed by the actions of the individuals who operate within it. The individuals are not necessarily aware that their actions both confirm the existence of the structure and change it. Such an approach is consistent with the evidence drawn from the case examined here. However, in dealing with technologies it became clear that the material nature of the world and the inextricable connections between the social and the technical required a realist methodology.

The categories used here to understand routine behaviour are not all accessible to observation. Using a broadly critical realist framework is helpful in sorting this out. Critical realism's structure of three domains, the actual and the empirical (which are well known from conventional empirical realism) and the non-actual, provides a way forward. The actual is the events and states of affairs themselves. The empirical is our experience of these events. The non-actual or deep domain refers to the structures, mechanisms, powers and tendencies which govern events. Explanations of the kind used here refer to such categories, though, in empirical work, it is frequently difficult to make the tight distinctions which a list of this kind implies. Here the interconnection of human agency, social structures and practices, and technology has been analysed in this way. Routines are manifestations of tendencies. Human agents and technologies have powers which operate recursively within social structures.

The approach adopted in this paper argues that the persistence of social structures is dependent on the practices or activities which the structures help to constitute. Structures do not exist independently of the conceptions or definitions made by individuals. And social structures are only *relatively* enduring. People can change them; hence the dynamic nature of social life. But these structures can have an existence which is independent of any individual and the actions in which that individual is involved. Rules and the hierarchy of relationships associated with them – the structure – interact in a recursive way with human agency. Social rules are drawn upon as generalised procedures of action. They govern, condition, limit and facilitate but cannot be reduced to action (Lawson 1997).

This approach does not adopt inductive and deductive law-like statements but makes use of retroduction (or abduction, an idea drawn from, among others, Peirce (Mirowski 1987), one of the founding figures of old institutionalism), in which explanation is made by drawing attention to metaphors or analogies with mechanisms which are familiar, in order to understand new phenomena. The metaphor can never be complete. It is a way of using existing knowledge to contemplate explanations of phenomena less understood. In this formulation metaphors are essential to the conception and development of scientific theories (Lewis 1999). However, in this account, metaphors are not used in the manner of some of the relativist contributors to organisation studies (Morgan 1986).

The interpretation of case studies

Interpretive work has been carried out in the social sciences for many years, and it has relatively recently returned to prominence as doubts have arisen over the epistemological claims of the crude use of quantitative methods. A rigorous methodology has slowly evolved. By its nature, each interpretive study will be different, but there is now a corpus of practice upon which economists can draw in order to acquire a rich picture of economic institutions. In using case studies as one form of the interpretive method, the detail will be specific and relate to a particular case, but it can be used to build theory (Eisenhardt 1989) and to improve understanding (Van Maanen 1979). It is not incompatible with other research methods (Hari Das 1983; Bryman 1989). An interpretive approach is also consistent with a critical realist methodology (Tsoukas 1989; Sayer 1992).

The research process adopted here is clearly different from that typically carried out in orthodox, econometric methodologies. In particular, analysis is not primarily carried out in the last phase of the research (Tesch 1990). Analysis and data gathering are carried on in parallel and the research is focused on object of study. There is a need for the researcher to be self-conscious about the nature of the research and to reflect on it as it proceeds (Layder 1998; Sayer 2000). The researcher is attempting to make sense of the interpretations of others and must be aware of the influence of him- or herself on the research process. Awareness of the context of the research and the cognitive models held by those contributing are vital. Once collected, data – in this case research, interviews and documents – are segmented, categorised and compared. The comparative method is used to find conceptual similarities and to refine categories that grow out of the data. Manipulation of the data is relatively eclectic though there are systematic procedures (many now computerised) that can guide the analysis to a higher-level synthesis identifying patterns, themes or fundamental structures. One such structure could be a system of routines, but it is important in work of this kind not to impose that framework on the data collection. Patterns arise from the data and are interpreted by the researcher using retroduction, i.e. building analysis on experience or knowledge of previous cases or institutions.

The research focus

The research on which this paper is based involved a longitudinal study of a number of high-technology small and medium-sized firms in the Cambridge area of the UK. The aims of the study were to examine the relationship between electronic systems and economic change, in particular the impact of these systems on organisational routines and learning. The research findings have challenged the idea that electronic systems 'impact' on routines, as will be shown.

Four companies from different sectors were studied over a two and a half year period. A diagonal slice of staff in each company (a sample of staff which covers the width and depth of the organisational structure, but ideally where each member of staff is functionally independent of the others in the sample) was interviewed approximately every six months, to obtain a rich picture of the organisation's changing internal structures and its relationships with its suppliers and customers/clients in the market.

The focus of the analysis was, firstly, the production, reproduction and modification of routines in the context of rapid technological change and, secondly, the way in which routine behaviour was a constitutive part of the behaviour of the firm. Established, significant, sanctioned and recurrent practices were evident in all the organisations studied. Those practices are called routines. Each of the firms, however, experienced a great deal of change. The firm which is particularly reported on here was operating in the new market for internet products. It underwent a number of mergers and takeovers, its product became a commodity (in the marketing sense) and its environment is now unrecognisable in comparison with the company's beginnings in this market in 1992.

Technology, in the form of electronic systems, was implicated in all the changes observed. For all the companies it was a significant feature but was then used and interpreted in different ways in the different companies. The technology cannot be interpreted independently of the people who work with it (Latour 1996a). Different views existed about the value of the technology and the companies found themselves pulled in different directions. Disagreements were not usually explicit. They arose as grumbles or comments on how things might be. In some cases the use of modern information technology was so much a part of the way of doing things that no alternative approach was even considered. Technology in this sense was not a technical feature but a demand for service or a form of relationship. Technology as artefact and technology-in-use (Orlikowski 1995) were inextricably mixed. The technology did not have an impact on organisational routines, rather it was constitutive of them.

Technology is a major focus because technology is a key exogenous variable used in both orthodox economics and organisation theory to account for change in firms. It is also of interest because strongly technological–determinist accounts are commonplace in common-sense discourses about change in advanced economies, and such views require investigation.

Some commentaries imply that we are undergoing a new industrial revolution. Does technology drive – or is it merely an enabler? Could the changes we see have occurred (differently) without electronic systems? A fascinating and thoughtful reflection on this discussion is given by Zuboff (1988). She shows how the potential of information systems makes visible previously hidden aspects of organisational processes and may have a significant effect on the way individuals learn about their work:

> To fully grasp the way in which a major new technology can change the world ... it is necessary to consider both the manner in which it creates intrinsically new qualities of experience and the way in which new possibilities are engaged by the often conflicting demands of social, political and economic interests in order to produce a 'choice'. To concentrate only on intrinsic change and the texture of an emergent mentality is to ignore the real weight of history and the diversity of interests that pervade collective behaviour. However, to narrow all discussion of technological change to the play of these interests overlooks the essential power of technology to reorder the rules of the game and thus our experience as players.
>
> (Zuboff 1988: 389)

But how does technology reorder the game? How does it combine with social, political, economic (and individual) interests and practices? Information theorists have no simple answers. Orlikowski (1992) sets out the argument for using a structurationist approach (Giddens 1984) in carrying out this kind of analysis. She looks at the dualism, represented by the human use of technical systems, of material and the social, and shows how the relationship between agency and structure is a recursive one. In this analysis routines can be considered as (incompletely) institutionalised practices formed and changed within a structurationist interpretation. The duality of technology identifies technology as a product of human action. Technology is physically constructed by actors working in a social context and socially constructed by actors through the meanings they attach to it and by the ways in which they choose to use and deploy it.

There are difficulties here, however (cf. Jones 1998). Technology is a material entity which is more than, or different from, the traces in the mind as in Giddens' account of structures. The material nature of technology, whilst still open to interpretation, cannot be solely reduced to ideas or constructions in people's minds. Routines, norms or rules which are *embedded* in the technology, but which are recursively flexible, similarly have a real existence.

A case study

INTERVIEWER: Well OK, what hasn't changed? What's the same, or what's identifiably Uninet that was here two or three years ago and is still here?
BEN: To give you a rather devious and nasty answer, what hasn't changed is our ability to change everything at the turn of a hat, at the drop of a hat.

The answer to my question given by Ben Rogers, a senior manager at Uninet-Inline (the names of the company and its staff have been invented), encapsulates the view of the company from most, if not all, of the people connected with it. Uninet-Inline was an extraordinary company. It was involved in the formative development of a new industry. The changes it underwent were large, and sometimes appeared dramatic. If Ben Rogers is right and the company had an ability 'to change everything ... at the drop of a hat', can this be considered a routine which the company had acquired or learned or was the company simply forced to change because of the turbulent environment it faced? How did the company acquire those competencies, if it did; and how was technology implicated in this change? These are the questions which this case study helps us to address.

Change as routine

Uninet-Inline was undoubtedly experiencing change. Some of that change was directly its own creation: for example, the company had merged two quite separate product categories, Uninet and Inline, into one organisational structure; Uninet sold network software and associated products, Inline was an internet service provider. Some change arose from its own behaviour in the external environment; some arose from the turbulence of the environment in which it operated. The company culture was aggressive and fast moving. Uninet and Inline were different. Whilst Uninet faced frequent changes in software specifications and a rapidly growing market, its environment possessed regularities. Uninet had created established, significant and sanctioned practices using formal and informally developed relationships as well as technologically driven processes via its databases. Inline, on the other hand, saw itself as a mission to establish a new product – the internet – driving hard with few holds barred.

The different cultures manifested themselves in the practices of the company. To give a sense of how this worked, and to gain an insight into routine practices in Uninet-Inline, requires a story-telling approach which does more than give the thought-through interpretations of the researcher. The company lived change. Its style and responsiveness is part of the research evidence. I would like to describe events as they appeared to me during one set of visits to the company. Those events encapsulate the culture and routines of Uninet-Inline. It is important to go through the detail of the visit in order to capture the subtlety of the firm's practices and to feel what the firm and the events were like. There are other ways of reporting research of this kind, but for this company at the stage it was when the visit took place, such an open account is very revealing. Van Maanen (1988) would call this an impressionist tale.

The meetings took place in July. I visited the company on consecutive days. The company was expanding fast. It had doubled its number of employees since my previous visit at the end of January and now employed nearly 200 people. A new building was being opened in a nearby location and the merging of Uninet with Inline was underway.

'Action Man mode'

The company's offices are in a prestigious location. The architecture is modern with high-tech design predominant. In general the buildings are low rise with car parks and small gardens dividing them. There is an atmosphere of modernity, advanced technology and youth. It was a very hot day. The grass outside was scorched and everybody was working in shirt sleeves in the air-conditioned building. Andrew Davis, the CEO, came down to meet me in reception and took me upstairs. The building was busy. People's desks were pushed up against each other. Andrew's room was a glass-partitioned office in one corner of a larger room covering perhaps half the first-floor area of the building. The room was relatively small, big enough for a desk and table and a few chairs. Nobody else in that area had a room. It was completely open plan. Andrew could see, and be seen by, the people working all around him.

Andrew was welcoming and very open. He seemed even more full of energy than when I had last seen him. I began by asking what had happened since my previous visit to the company. Andrew explained there had been something of a watershed. The group had switched its focus away from products to particular market sectors and had merged Uninet with Inline. The conversation moved to the difficulties of managing these changes. Andrew's manner remained relaxed but with lots of nervous energy. He seemed to want to talk about the issues concerning him. He had split up the

Inline sales team the previous week and used the meeting with me as an opportunity to get things off his chest.

ANDREW: Well, basically, I pretty much forced the issues with them. And where there were missed decisions I faced them. ... On a couple of occasions I have had to just tell them. You know, 'You've got to do this.' ... The Director of Sales was really upset about it on the day. Cut the legs off him. 'Completely eroded my authority' and then sort of after a couple of days he confessed 'I should have done that, shouldn't I?'

Andrew had claimed previously that he wanted to delegate more. Going over the head of the Director of Sales irritated him. He did not want to do that, he claimed, but was forced into it. But this was not good practice:

ANDREW: Yes. I should have talked through that before I put it down to his managers, I'm sure. But it was one of those things that, sort of, one of my little ... I occasionally get into a mood, which I call Action Man, and it's awful in that I tear up all the rule books and just kind of do things. You know. Unfortunately when I'm in that mode I don't actually think about it. I've thought about what the actions that need doing. OK, I've got frustrated that they haven't happened, right. When I go into Action Man mode I don't, I say 'Well that's got to happen, damn the consequences, what's the quickest way of doing it?' OK? I don't think about, OK I'm going to do this but at least tell the manager first, sort of stuff. And it trips me up occasionally.
INTERVIEWER: But you're learning too?
ANDREW: Well, I wish I was learning but. I know I shouldn't do it but when I'm in Action Man mode I still do it. Grrrrrrrrrrrr.

This was an extraordinary meeting. Andrew had met me several times and saw me in some respects as a confidant. He seemed to find the process of being interviewed relaxing and status enhancing. He was literally acting out his 'Action Man mode', growling and expressing his frustration at his colleagues for not integrating and at himself for dealing with them in a way he regretted. The atmosphere felt electric. I wanted to hear more about his sense of how he should behave and how he did behave:

INTERVIEWER: As the company grows, of course, it's going to become more of a problem for you, I suspect.
ANDREW: I get more frustrated at things going on. There are times when I think 'Well, what do you have to do?' And that can be important little things. I have to complain OK .... And there are occasions when I think 'What the. I get really frustrated. And I get doubly frustrated because I shouldn't be doing that. That is well below my horizon, or should be. And uses up so much energy. And occasionally I lose confidence in our

success ... I try desperately to delegate. But my impatience and what have you gets in the way of it. I think. I keep on telling people 'Don't come and ask me what to do. Tell me what you want to do.' Get affirmation, but they don't seem to believe me all the time. It continually gets better. I go on about the company but it continually gets better.

Andrew had now relaxed. The tension had drained out of him and he started to stand back a little from the specific things which frustrated him:

ANDREW: ... Fundamentally we have to reinvent the company every 6 months, changes in market place and so on, changing size, what have you. All but a bit of it is changing. Well, a bit of it changes all the time. And quite often people think that. We're a relatively open company and we're open in our thought processes, and so we've got this awful rumour mill going. If you ask a question the rumour mill makes it policy ... If we could get some of the positive messages of the company around the company as fast as some of the rumours, you know, it would be amazing. And, of course, if I ask a question it's definitely policy. You know it doesn't confine to me ... But, if I could get rid of some of the downsides of Action Man mode but OK you want to do something, you talk to a manager first. That's all I've got to do, and Action Man – to get through some red tape, if you like – that's what you have to do, you have to occasionally, you just have to change gear and push through, OK. And it's, it is not the wrong thing to do, it's just that my character makes it that, it's more painful than it should be. I shouldn't be Action Man all the time, 'cos then I would be doing everyone's job. And you've got to allow people, got to allow people to make mistakes. It's this thing, you don't allow, can't allow people to make mistakes on an ongoing basis...

This conversation gives a sense of change, the way it was managed and the way in which it manifested itself at Uninet-Inline. Change was occurring continuously in the company: 'Fundamentally we have to reinvent the company every 6 months' was the way in which Andrew Davis put it. The use of the term 'reinvent' reflects both his image of himself as an innovative technocrat and the reality he and others perceived of a company which in many respects transformed itself and yet remained identifiably the same company. A routine was developing – a hard-driven style with little self-reflection. The rate of change was uncomfortable and the ability to live with discomfort was an important part of routine behaviour for all members of staff during the period of the research. An aggressive and rapid response focusing on the main strategic agent is in many respects an absence of a developed routine. It is simply a working through – almost a caricature – of an entrepreneurial style. But the Inline side of the company had begun to adopt a pattern of behaviour which also had energetic and aggressive characteristics. This was not simply a routine adopted by one individual. One interviewee described how the Sales Director of Inline made decisions about the sales portfolio, dumping many products other staff were working on, without consultation, and how Inline sales staff worked in competition, taking business from their colleagues in Uninet. This was the routine at Inline which felt uncomfortable to the more conventional approaches of Uninet. It was recognised as the way Inline did things. They coped with change by moving fast and hard, pushing objections out of the way.

Andrew Davis's behaviour was therefore not only a function of his personality but drew from the culture and relationships in the company he had established.

The modem story

The company drove change externally. It continually tried to keep ahead of its rivals and in some cases changed the perception of the external world about the nature of the internet business. In the same set of interviews in which Andrew Davis described his 'Action Man mode', Ben Rogers showed the tension for him of creating a completely new business.

Ben Rogers was a senior technical manager. He had wide experience in the computing industry. On the day following the conversation with Andrew, I met Ben in an animated state. He was wearing overalls instead of his usual suit. Ben always struck me as someone who was concerned about his appearance and his clothes were usually fashionable, so this was a surprise. The weather remained exceptionally hot and he looked uncomfortable. The company was expanding into a second building. He had been instructed to arrange major changes to the cabling that had been put into the building because it was now to be used for a new product, Link. Ben was quite literally getting his hands dirty. Link was the Uninet-Inline product which brought the internet into the domestic and single-user market and was a brand-new area of work for the company. Ben had been given responsibility for Link a few weeks earlier. Ben's manner was urgent and abbreviated, rather like Andrew's. In my notes of the meeting, I described Ben as a personification – almost a caricature – of the company culture. I asked him why the company had moved so fast into the single-user market when six months earlier they had claimed no interest in it:

BEN ROGERS: Today [the company is] going for a mix of things, but at the end of the day the Internet market's growing very very fast. We have 80% of that market place today in UK corporate connections market and if you extrapolate the growth, the projected growth in the market place and what we're planning to do we will actually lose market share by growing as fast as we possibly can. So there's more business out there, enough there for everyone. But we don't want to lose out too much. We've really got to strive as hard as we can to keep pace with that.

Couple that with the fact that, yes, we can sell what it is we have today, usually what we have today isn't what we're going to be selling tomorrow. An opportunity comes along. Experience has told us that if it's not something we've done before we still need to look at it very, very carefully, because another two or three will be along in no time at all...

INTERVIEWER: Do you feel that if you didn't grow so fast and keep up that you might be swamped and just disappear? Is that the sort of threat? It's either keep up or disappear? I guess it is exciting.

BEN: It's frustrating, it's exciting, it's annoying, it's irritating, it provides you with adrenaline, it becomes the reason why you get out of bed, it becomes the reason why you couldn't sleep when you were in your bed, it becomes all encompassing. ... Yes, and one of the problems is in trying to move forward many areas of technology whilst still addressing the growth and the new opportunities that clients are throwing at us with the solution to creative takes an awful lot of skill and an awful lot of time. Having anyone left who can pick the phone up and say 'Yes, Mr Customer, I'll sell you one of those today' is hard work. 'Cos everyone's ricocheting off the walls.

It seemed to me that Ben wanted to be seen as an important, go-getting manager, as a big shot. I wanted some examples of why 'everyone's ricocheting off the walls'. His answer set out a dramatic change.

BEN: We produced [Link] at the tail end of last year which was, as its name would imply, a single user dial up connection to the Internet. The intention was, bearing in mind that we were almost entirely in Inline area, and I wasn't involved at all in Inline at that time, not at all. I mean Inline was those guys downstairs in inverted commas. Maybe not quite that step but you understand what I'm saying, my day to day activities ... it was outside my field of vision. But it was intended to be used in the corporate market place for two reasons. One is as a taster for the key decision makers who we were trying to influence, who couldn't even spell Internet but they'd heard of it but didn't really 'My IT guy tells me that we want this. Convince me.' And the other was for those people that had taken the corporate connections to use for tele-working. Now that addresses two nice areas in the market place. One as a hook for those people to take on the eleven thousand pound a year connection and the other into tele-working, very much an area of interest. So we produced this product called Inline Link. Suddenly it looks very appealing to everyone from the key decision maker in British Gas at board level right down to little Jimmy in his bedroom with his Amstrad PC and a modem and his mum and dad haven't got a clue what he's doing, but he's certainly on the net, sending E-mail to his girlfriend, OK? And that product, by accident rather than design, fitted those roles perfectly. Nothing else like it on the market place, time was

right, the market was right. Part of the marketing machinery meant
that PC Answers magazine caught onto this and put a cover disc on
their magazine and it hosed our network. We were in the middle of
some upgrades, so we weren't too worried about the extent of that and
fairly shortly after we did one for the Internet magazine, a cover disc,
and again it just destroyed our network through sheer volume of
demand. So then that was the point at which we said 'Look, we're
getting lots of these enquiries, we're getting dragged into this, we've
got a product, it's here now, we need network infrastructure, we either
disappear into complete and utter chaos saying "We can't cope with
this" or we put our minds against it and we say "We can cope with this
by doing this, this and this".'

Rather like Andrew the previous day, Ben was animated. He was describing
actions taken by the company more or less to test the water which 'hosed our
network'. The network staff and the marketing and sales people were
screaming. How would the company react? What would the routine
response be? The company had taken a small step and suddenly found itself
in a new world. What could it do? Ben continued:

Part of that was Andrew's command. His command from on high to me
'Ben do this.' And I built the network. On the day that he gave me that
I had no idea what to do. Didn't know what the technology involved
was, what the modem racks looked like, what bits and pieces I'd need,
what Lego bricks I'd need to put in place. Where the suppliers were,
how it all fitted together, what space we had. We didn't have space to
put it anywhere. Just knock a few walls down, move a few things
around and it all comes together. But, you know, Andrew and I put our
minds round it and we came up with an attitude of mind that said 'We
can do it. The only things that'll stop us are things that'll get in our
way so we move them out the way.'

Ben described these changes with a sense of pride. He had been given a task
far bigger than he had expected in an area new to him and it had gone live.
At the beginning he did not know what 'Lego bricks' he would need but
when things got in the way he would 'move them out of the way'. He was
operating according to the rules of the Uninet-Inline strategic routine. The
big investment had been in network capacity. Network capacity determines
the speed of response which users receive when they dial in to their internet
service provider. It is a major measure of quality. Uninet-Inline seemed to
have got it right. They were able to upstage their main competitor because
they could give a quality response. What I had not realised at the time of
the conversation with Ben, but was revealed to me much later in a conversation with Andrew Davis after he had left the company, was the sheer scale of

the investment Uninet-Inline had made. I'll let Andrew tell it in his own words:

> there was no-one spare apart from Ben so I went to Ben and said 'Go and get more modems, modems in four to six weeks. How quickly can we do it? Find out as fast as you can. So anyway we came out of that, five hundred new modems in about six weeks and he came back after two or three weeks and said right 'Well, I've got 250 modems ordered and I've got 250 lines' and I was so cross. 'I said 500. And when you've got those 500 go and get another thousand.' And all of a sudden he thought 'Ah. You're not kidding, are you, about this?' It's a case of if you're going to do it, go for it. OK, and he went off and got 500, got the 1000, didn't need the whole 1000. Cost us a million pounds that mistake. It actually sort of points to the expenses. It cost us a million pounds and probably made that business. There's a lovely post-justification for it. Because he'd gone, the key thing is that those events, Ben all of a sudden understood that we were in this business, you know, we weren't playing around. And we've got to make a success. You know, you make the decision and you've got to make it work. Of course, one of the consequences of that, going from 120 lines to 1600, is that you actually need ten times more customers. So all of a sudden it was no longer a problem of lines, it was a problem of customers, we had to go and get customers. 'Cos the money was going out the door. So that those events kicked Ben in. He got belief in himself, he actually did it as well, OK so he got belief in himself, a nice self fulfilling, up the spiral for Ben. And the other interesting thing though is that because Ben went in for 500 and then asked for a thousand all of a sudden the Telcos took us seriously in this business. Mercury, Energis, BT what have you all of a sudden they started talking to us about discounts and you know. Occasionally people come for a 500 order. No one ever goes 500 then two weeks later asks for another 1000. Doesn't happen. So all of a sudden it kicked over the Telcos into realising that it was a serious business and that Uninet was a serious player. And that goes for the modem manufacturers. All of a sudden we went from being a customer to being a strategic partner.

The last point here is very important. By expanding ludicrously fast by industry standards – buying 1500 high-speed modems at a cost of several million pounds in a very short time-scale – Uninet-Inline changed the perception of the industry. It enacted its own environment. The Telcos (industry-speak for large telecommunications companies) such as BT and Energis suddenly took notice and the world had changed. This is symptomatic of the Uninet-Inline approach. A marketing opportunity was recognised and taken up at a large scale very quickly. The company strategy was continually to take steps into the unknown. In this case it transformed Uninet-Inline from seeking capacity to seeking customers and made it a major player in this market. Rogers did a good job. At the end of the research period he was the only remaining contact still working for the company and was in charge of the Link project.

A routine

'Action Man mode' and the modem story tell us about emerging routines at policy levels in response to change and as a generator of change. There is a consistency of behaviour and a regularity which reveals itself in many aspects of the company's practices.

If the company had been unable to incorporate change, it is likely that it could not have survived. And the way of doing things was in an aggressive, go-getting, abrasive style. This is the beginning of a routine. It is a tendency to act in a particular way which is established and sanctioned within the company. The routines here were rooted in the history and culture of the company, the company's structure (and changes in its structure) and the changing market, plus the skills and competencies of the main agents and their search for security. The technological context was implicit in all that was done.

Analysis

The routine which was adopted at Uninet-Inline was thus a fast-moving, aggressive response based upon an immediate assessment of the relevant circumstances and a belief that it was important to move faster than the competition. The company continually took decisions which redefined the environment and moved into unknown, and indeed unknowable, territory. The routine was adopted by managers throughout the company and for the Inline side of the company operated at operational as well as strategic levels. It was the way things were done and taken for granted. This is a practice of the company. It is not the same as company culture. Culture establishes shared meanings (Hall 1997), and is deeply implicated in practices, but the two are separate.

The routine arose from a range of factors: the culture, which partly drew from the personal style of the key agent, Andrew Davis, the rate of change of the environment and the insecurity this created in the company's staff. The routine developed recursively. It seemed to work and provided a route map through uncertainty. The modem story is a rich example of this and also illustrates well how the routine itself changed the environment: Uninet-Inline suddenly became relevant to the major companies in the industry. In the modem story the company responded fast to the unexpected demand for its new product. The opportunity was perceived and followed through. Davis saw the need to enter at a large scale. This was based partly on his knowledge of the market place and partly on his 'Action Man' style, which had become part of the company way of doing things. His style had become locked in to the routine. It became difficult for him to operate in any other way. People would not come to him for 'affirmation'. Other staff also operated in similar ways to him. Ben Rogers then drove the changes through but expected the environment to change and was continually looking out for new and 'unexpected' events. This produced the adrenaline which got him out of bed in the morning.

Internal company structures and relationships played a part, recursively, in developing the routine through interacting with each other and the external world. Andrew Davis's overriding of the Sales Director, in breaking up the Inline team, and in his discussion of the rumour mill exemplify this mechanism: his relationship with the Sales Director illustrates a company structure which is loose. Little respect is paid to established reporting lines. As a result rumours became extensive as a means of communication, partly because conventional reporting lines seemed unreliable. These things were happening throughout the company, however, and were not peculiar to Davis. The Director of Sales, himself, reportedly took decisions which rode roughshod over his staff, for example. The company was not anarchic nor driven by Davis in the guise of an archetypal, single-minded entrepreneur. Both those images – anarchy or single-minded dominance by an individual – miss the sense in which this company hung together through the co-operation of and competition between its members, running all the time to survive by staying ahead of the rest of the market.

The routine then incorporated change. It did not respond to change nor reflect on change but took change as the norm and, in doing so, was itself implicated in many of the changes facing the company. Environmental structures and norms, both external and internal, changed as the company or staff members interacted with them.

Technology played a part in this. It cannot be identified as a separate factor contributing in its own particular way. Without the new network technologies there would have been no Uninet. The exploitation of those technologies was its *raison d'être*. Davis was driven by a desire to be an industry leader. But a focus on technology also drove many day-to-day activities, so that staff, whilst apparently autonomous, had relatively little room for manoeuvre. Informating (Zuboff 1988) – the automating of information previously held as part of an individual's knowledge or skill – was widely apparent at operational levels. Uninet had, in fact, used relatively sophisticated databases for most of its history. These databases enabled staff to manage their work in an information-rich environment. The database provided them with an enormous amount of detail about transactions they and others were undertaking. The information was public to the company and constrained the manner in which activities took place. Autonomy was thus severely circumscribed. The precise manner in which an activity took place was under the control of the staff member but the basic task was highly routinised.

The use of such a system gave Uninet effectively a very clear set of operational routines. They were not written down in a conventional way. The routine was built into the software. Uninet's memory of what had been done and how its activities were carried out, at a practical level, were also embodied in the software. For a company at the raciest end of the high-tech business this was not a problem. Staff expected, indeed wished, it to be that way. The technology in some respects drove the detail of people's lives and was the dominant force in the strategic vision of the company. In terms of relationships within the company, the things spoken about and difficulties perceived, however, technology was barely mentioned. It was taken for granted.

The company thus focused on technology in a deep sense. Technology formed part of its way of doing things which was unquestioned. Informating was taken for granted and operational routines were embedded in the technology.

Orlikowski's distinction between technology as artefact and technology-in-use is revealing (Orlikowski 1995). The artefact was continually being reinterpreted in use as the modem story shows. The technologies which Rogers was then using were commonplace. E-mail systems and advanced telephony were no longer the state of the art. The product enhancements he used to attract custom, he admitted, were not sophisticated. Value was added for customers by giving multiple e-mail addresses or more web space in the standard package. But the technology was everywhere. It was pervasive and part of the Uninet-Inline world. The social and the technical were thus inseparable. They are different units in a network (Latour 1996b; Walsham 1997) which, through their relationship with each other and the organisational and social structures in which they were nested, interacted in the reproduction and transformation of routine behaviour.

Conclusions

Two key points can be drawn from the analysis. Firstly, that routines can exist at a strategic level. This observation runs contrary to some conventional assumptions (March and Simon 1958). In addition, in practice, it is difficult to disentangle operational routines from strategic routines. Routine behaviour contains elements of each. Even primarily operational routines have strategic importance and strategic routines influence operational activity. The use of sophisticated technology in its operational routines partly gave the secure base from which, at a strategic level, Uninet-Inline leapt. It is not possible therefore, in trying to understand the behaviour of small and medium-sized firms, to separate completely the analysis of strategic behaviour from a consideration of more mundane operational activities.

Secondly, the research has shown that routines exist which can accommodate change or which are predicated on change. The value of routine as a concept with which to understand the behaviour of firms is enhanced if it can incorporate change. It is not simply a static phenomenon but can help in understanding lived experiences. The routine will not always operate in precisely the same way. Sometimes it may be counteracted by other powers and tendencies but underlying the work of this firm we can see a recurrent pattern which enables us to understand its strategic direction and the particular way in which it went about achieving its strategy.

The concept of routine is thus a helpful one in understanding the behaviour of small, high-technology companies. The case study has enabled us to develop the concept in a rich context and can be tried as an analytical device in gaining an understanding of other firms with different cultures and histories.

Bibliography

Boland, R. J. (1985) 'Phenomenology: a preferred approach to research on information systems', in E. Mumford *et al.* (eds) *Research Methods in Information Systems*, New York: North-Holland.

Bryman, A. (1989) *Research Methods and Organization Studies*, London: Unwin Hyman.

David, P. A. (1985) 'Clio and the economics of QWERTY', *American Economic Review*, 75: 332–7; reprinted in Witt, U. (1993) *Evolutionary Economics, The International Library of Critical Writings In Economics 25*, Aldershot: Edward Elgar.

Douglas, M. (1987) *How Institutions Think*, London: Routledge & Kegan Paul.

Eisenhardt, K. M. (1989) 'Building theories from case study research', *Academy of Management Review*, 14: 532–50.

Giddens, A. (1982) *Profiles and Critiques in Social Theory*, London: Macmillan.

——(1984) *The Constitution of Society*, Cambridge: Polity Press.

Glaser, B. G. and Strauss, A. L. (1967) *The Discovery of Grounded Theory: Strategies for Qualitative Research*, Chicago: Aldine.

Hall, S. (1997) 'The work of representation' in S. Hall (ed.) *Representation: Cultural Representations and Signifying Practices*, London: Sage.

Hari, Das T. (1983) 'Qualitative research in organizational behavior', *Journal of Management Studies*, 20: 301–14.

Hirschman, A. O. (1970) *Exit, Voice and Loyalty: Responses to Decline in Firms, Organisations and States*, Cambridge, MA: Harvard University Press.

Hodgson, G. M. (1997) 'The ubiquity of habits and rules', *Cambridge Journal of Economics*, 21: 663–84.

Johnson, G. (1987) *Strategic Change and the Management Process*, Oxford: Blackwell.

Jones, M. R. (1998) 'Structuration theory', in W. J. Currie and R. Galliers (eds) *Rethinking Management Information Systems*, Oxford: Oxford University Press.

Latour, B. (1996a) *Aramis or The Love of Technology*, Cambridge, MA: Harvard University Press.

——(1996b) 'Social theory and the study of computerized work sites', in W. J. Orlikowski, G. Walsham, M. R. Jones and J. I. DeGross (eds) *Information Technology and Changes in Organisational Work*, London: Chapman and Hall.

Lawson, T. (1997) *Economics and Reality*, London: Routledge.

Layder, D. (1988) *Sociological Practice: Linking Theory and Research*, London: Sage.

Lewis, D. (1968) *Convention: A Philosophical Study*, Cambridge, MA: Harvard University Press.

Lewis, P. (1999) 'Metaphor and critical realism', in S. Fleetwood (ed.) *Critical Realism in Economic: Development and Debate*, London: Routledge.

March, J. G. and Simon, H. A. (1958) *Organisations*, New York: Wiley.

Mirowski, P. (1987) 'The philosophical bases of institutional economics', *Journal of Economic Issues*, 21, 3: 1001–38.

Morgan, G. (1986) *Images of Organization*, Beverly Hills, CA: Sage.

Nelson, R. R. (1995) 'Recent evolutionary theorising about economic change', *Journal of Economic Literature*, XXXIII, March: 48–90.

Nelson, R. R. and Winter, S. G. (1982) *An Evolutionary Theory of Economic Change*, Cambridge, MA: The Belknap Press of Harvard University Press.

North, D. C. (1990) *Institutions, Institutional Change and Economic Performance*, Cambridge: Cambridge University Press.

Orlikowski, W. J. (1992) 'The duality of technology: rethinking the concept of technology in organizations', *Organization Science*, 3: 398–427.

——(1995) 'Action and artifact: the structuring of technologies-in-use', Unpublished paper, Sloan School of Management, Massachusetts Institute of Technology, Cambridge, MA.

Penrose, E. T. (1959) *The Theory of the Growth of the Firm*, Oxford: Basil Blackwell.

Samuels, W. J. (1995) 'The present state of institutional economics', *Cambridge Journal of Economics*, 19: 569–90.

Sayer, A. (1992) *Method in Social Sciences: A Realist Approach*, second edition, London: Routledge.

——(2000) *Realism and Social Science*, London: Sage.

Teece, D. J., Pisano, G. and Shuen, A (1990) 'Firm capabilities and the concept of strategy', CCC Working paper No. 90–8, Consortium on Competitiveness and Co-operation, Center for Research in Management, University of California at Berkeley.

Tesch, R. (1990) *Qualitative Research: Analysis Types and Software Tools*, Basingstoke: Falmer Press.

Thomas, B. (1991) 'Alfred Marshall on economic biology', *Review of Political Economy*, 3: 1–14.

Tsoukas, H. (1987) 'The validity of ideographic research explanations', *Academy of Management Review*, 14, 4: 551–61.

Van Maanen, J. (1979) 'The fact of fiction in organizational ethnography', *Administrative Science Quarterly*, 24, December: 539–49.

——(1988) *Tales of the Field: On Writing Ethnography*, Chicago and London: University of Chicago Press.

Walsham, G. (1993) *Interpreting Information Systems in Organizations*, Chichester: Wiley.

——(1997) 'Actor-network theory and IS research: current status and future prospects', in A. S. Lee, J. Liebenau and J. I. DeGross (eds) *Information Systems and Qualitative Research*, London: Chapman and Hall.

Zuboff, S. (1988) *In the Age of the Smart Machine: The Future of Work and Power*, Oxford, Heinemann.

9 Managers' innovations and the structuration of organisations

John Coopey, Orla Keegan and Nick Emler

Introduction

In this paper we offer a theoretical framework for understanding processes of innovation in organisations. This framework is developed by integrating various research perspectives within an envelope of 'structuration theory' (Giddens 1984). We focus deliberately on the actions and self-perceived innovations of individual managers, an approach which contrasts both with most of the studies reviewed by King (1990) which favour an organisational level of analysis, and much of the creativity literature, which has emphasised personality traits and the products of creative behaviour (e.g. Barron and Harrington 1981). Ours is an attempt, therefore, to respond to the need defined by West and Farr (1990) for more research into the everyday ways in which people express themselves creatively in the workplace, rather than to the research agenda suggested by Wolfe (1994), which makes almost no reference to personal agency.

Our objectives are to make sense of the innovation process from the point of view of different individual actors, to amalgamate their various stories and to relate the key themes to the proposed theoretical framework. The data used stems largely from narratives derived from interviews with managers drawn from a university (Uni), an IT manufacturer (ITC), and the social work department of a regional council (SWD). The diversity of organisations and of managers within them — and hence the diversity of types of innovation reported by them — is consistent with principles set out by Campbell and Fiske (1959) in defining validity, reflected in Patton's (1987) term 'maximum variation sampling'. He argues that when similar patterns emerge from diverse contexts they are more likely to be of value in capturing 'core phenomena', providing in the present case a potentially robust basis for theorising the relationship between modes of innovative behaviour, social relationships and organisational context.

Research sample

Interviewees were recruited following a survey in which fifty managers in each of the three organisations were invited to 'give an example of a recent innovation of yours'. For the purposes of the survey a manager was defined as:

> a person in a formal position involving some responsibility for the work of other people and for other resources, especially financial.

Innovation was defined as:

> a particular form of change characterised by the introduction of something new. This 'something' may relate to a product, service or a technology or it may involve the introduction of new managerial or administrative practices or changes in other elements of the organisation. Innovations may vary in magnitude from those which affect only the manager's own role to others which have major implications for the whole organisation. Ultimately innovations bring about beneficial change.

The term 'beneficial' is typically part of definitions of creativity used in psychology. It was included in this definition to encourage the reporting of only innovations that had been or were likely to be implemented and, hence, could more probably be verbalised. In a second stage of the survey respondents provided information on their perceptions of their innovations and the organisational setting. From this stage we selected for interview ten respondents in each organisation who had described an innovation, seeking to ensure that we sampled all hierarchical levels and functions and a wide range of experience, while maintaining the gender balance. Despite the difficulties involved in relying on volunteers, this sub-sample did not differ in age or years in present position from the total group reporting innovations.

In open-ended, tape-recorded interviews lasting about an hour managers were encouraged to give freely their account of the innovation project. The 'attributes' of their innovations differ considerably, for example in terms of Wolfe's (1994) dimensions of centrality, complexity, magnitude, focus (i.e. technological, managerial or administrative) and radicalness (see Appendix 1).

Each interviewee was asked to nominate for interview two individuals crucial to the progress of the innovation. Not all were able to do so and it was not possible to interview all of those nominated. But except in one case at least one such 'collaborator' was interviewed. In all, forty-four collaborators' narratives were generated and analysed in addition to those of the thirty innovators.

Emergent themes and their interpretation

In using a qualitative methodology we acknowledge our active involvement in choosing the organisations, defining the terms 'innovation' and 'manager' against which accounts of innovations were elicited, and in shaping 'a causal description' of underlying individual and social processes. The research process moved from level to level of 'analytical abstraction' in three broad steps: (a) the creation of texts and the categorisation of the data therein, (b) the drawing out of themes and of relationships between them, and (c) the synthesis of those themes and supporting data into an explanatory framework (Miles and Huberman 1994).

The interviews were framed by our definitions and shaped by our invitation to talk 'about your experience of imagining, developing and implementing the innovation', and by various follow-tip prompts. Like Watson (1994a; 1994b), therefore, we are likely to have influenced those who took part in the research.

Narratives were analysed using some of the procedures of a grounded theory approach (Glaser and Strauss 1967; Strauss and Corbin 1990), a cumulative, iterative procedure for defining categories that capture overlapping accounts of specific contexts, people or events. An initial analysis of fifteen innovator narratives yielded over eighty separate categories of data, of which the fourteen most 'saturated' (i.e. those to which a high proportion of the separate narratives contributed) provided a framework for analysing the remaining data.

'Fragmenting' narratives can cause the text segments to become 'decontextualised' such that narrative and its implicit process of change are lost (Dey 1995). To avoid this we returned regularly to original texts and to case summaries of how the process seemed to have evolved, using collaborators' narratives to complement those of innovators. Hence, we are more confident that linkages created between the categories reflect explicit and implicit connections within the flow of the narratives.

We did not, as suggested by Glaser and Strauss, expect theory to 'emerge' from the data unprompted. Instead, we were involved actively in an 'interplay' between the narratives and their interpretation. By employing practical strategies for close, detached qualitative analysis provided by grounded theory we were able to adopt the perspective in the research process of 'an outsider within', creating the possibility of seeing 'what is ordinarily invisible from within a dominant order' (Henwood and Pidgeon 1994: 17).

The insights of the forty-four collaborators helped, and since twenty-seven of them did not meet our definition of 'manager' they were, presumably, less likely to share closely in any managerial discourse. Additional data was provided by our principal contacts in each of the three organisations, including documentary evidence – on policies, planning frameworks, etc. – supplementing that received from many respondents. Further data arose from feedback meetings with participants at which preliminary findings were discussed. Finally, vital contextual knowledge was gleaned from our own involvement in the university, from site visits and from published accounts of extensive external pressures to which, from our data, the three organisations appeared to be subject (e.g. Cowen 1991; Storey 1992; Wilson and Game 1994).

Hence, by applying grounded theory approaches, supplemented by these other sources of data, we were enabled – like other researchers such as Currie (1988) – to address questions of structure and process despite the personalised, subject-centred interview mode. This is consistent with Silverman's (1993) view that interview data can give access both to 'cultural particulars related to the patterns of social organisation' as well as 'displays of members' artful practices in assembling these particulars during interviews. Thus we have been able to shape, from the analytical categories and the connections between them, a 'generic, cultural and social account' of the initiation and development of an innovative idea from origins through to implementation and eventual institutionalisation (see Figure 9.1).

A generic account

This account is structured within a framework of 'levels' of phenomena in one dimension and an implicit timescale in the other, running from the past (as 'memories drawn from experience'), to the origination of the innovation and then through its development to implementation and institutionalisation. The levels start with the self in social interaction with others throughout the timescale. To a greater or lesser degree, the participants in the interactions perceive themselves as subject to various internal, systemic influences at the next level. Possibly moderated by higher levels of management engaged within the innovation process, these include pressures to work within ever tighter resource constraints, to increase flexibility, to improve control, to import new ideas and so on. Some pressures are perceived to emanate directly or indirectly from more distal sources within the environment external to the organisation, such as legislation, the market and technology. In some cases innovators, collaborators and other organisational members involved in the process deal directly with representatives of external organisations, such as the parent company, charitable foundations and government agencies.

The process that connects these levels along the time axis derives first from feelings experienced by one or more of the various actors, especially the self-nominated innovator – of dissatisfaction, anxiety, anticipation and so on – promoted by perceptions of a problem to be resolved or an opportunity to be grasped. Those perceptions and the associated feelings are usually related in some way via memory to experience.

The innovation is carried forward through various social interactions, especially between the innovator and other actors, in relationships subject to structural constraints of resource allocation and rules, procedures and norms which regulate resource use. Actors benefit from the intimacy of relationships but have the potential to exploit positional power within social

Levels

Environmental

(Distal 'forces' – legislation,
competition, etc.)

(Influencing the environment)

Systematic

Internal 'pressures' (resources
flexibility, control, etc.)
and 'constraints' (resources,
rules, norms)

(System modification)

Interactive

Others

Self

Feelings → Remembering → Problem/opportunity → Interactions → Revision/recycling

(Mediated by internal management
and/or external partners)

(Relationships of intimacy/power)

Sequence → Origination → Development → Implementation → Institutionalisation

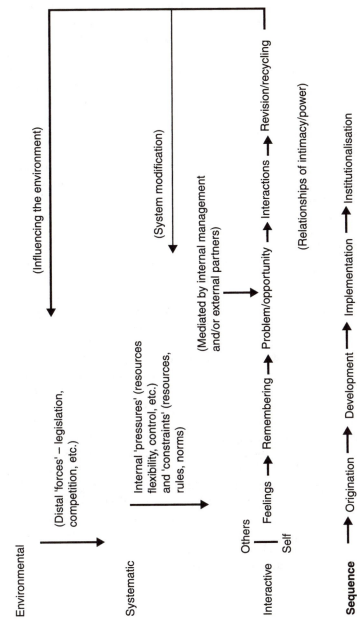

Figure 9.1 A generic account

networks, dependent on their capacity to mobilise appropriate social and political skills.

Once an innovation is implemented and, in time, becomes institutionalised, the cycle of reciprocal influence between individual and system is closed. The revised pattern of resource allocation and of the controlling rules and norms brought about by the innovation become embedded at the level of the system, now experienced as constraint or opportunity by various members of the organisation in their everyday or innovative activities.

Our main purpose in this paper is to suggest an integrative theoretical framework within which these cyclical processes can be better interpreted. Unfortunately, much of the literature on psychological and social theory is not yet up to this task, leaving unresolved the dualism of collective and individual perspectives. This is true in two branches of literature most relevant to our particular focus: that on innovation research, described in Wolfe's (1994) review as yielding 'a relatively undeveloped' and 'fragmented' understanding of innovative behaviour, and the decision-making literature, a source of only partial frameworks (Zey 1992).

Taking Wolfe's advice to build on 'extant research and theory', we use Giddens' theories of structuration (1984) and of the self (1991) to reconcile the continuity and potential for transformation that stem from both individual actors and the social system of which they are members.

Crucial to structuration theory is the proposition that the very rules and resources on which actors draw in producing and reproducing social action are at the same time the basis for reproducing the social system within which those actors relate to each other. Hence the theory promises a flexible approach to integrating the behaviour of individual agents and the social relationships and institutional structures that constitute organisational forms, an integration that is implicit in the narratives, made more explicit in the 'generic account' of the innovation process represented in Figure 9.1.

For the purposes of this paper we extend and elaborate Giddens' theory in a number of ways. The concept of self-efficacy is introduced to account for the confidence with which innovators launch their projects and the persistence they show in carrying them through. More explicitly than Giddens, we include the discursive, rhetorical process within social relations through which the ambiguities of complex organisational life are exploited. Account is also taken of the quality of intimacy that characterises social relationships to varying degrees and is a vital influence on people's behaviour. Finally, we focus on the reciprocal, generative development of both social relationships and the substance of the innovation.

Three case studies

Discussion of the narrative data within this framework is developed using three case studies, one from each organisation. They illustrate and focus the discussion, providing lines of reference along which to structure its flow and connections. Each case is not the most radical from its organisation and its effects are not likely to be the most far reaching. Together they encompass all of the analytical categories, provide much of the attribute variety referred to earlier, and illustrate some less usual aspects of the total set. Where relevant, references to other cases will be made.

Ian's 'umbrella management' within ITC

ITC, part of a large US multinational corporation, manufactures computer-based products. The research was conducted at its main location, where about 1,500 people are employed.

Following a row with the CEO of his previous company, Ian joined ITC, where he set up and managed a new plant separate from the main location. On taking up his present post managing a key assembly department, Ian concluded that it had been subject to considerable interference. Resolved to change the managerial style, he confronted a director to stop him interfering, an intervention that provided an 'umbrella' under which reorganisation could proceed.

Ulrich and managerial accounting in Uni

Uni is a small university with approximately 5,000 students and 1,500 staff. Its form is conventional: academic departments within faculties and a tiered policy-making committee system.

Ulrich, an academic department head, was keen to prepare for delegation to departments of greater responsibility for resource management. He wanted to relate departmental accounts more transparently to the complex resource flows within the department, to reduce sub-discipline compartmentalisation, and to resolve several 'moral' issues including the responsibilities and rights of tenure compared to temporary staff.

Ulrich developed a spreadsheet accounting format as a vehicle to persuade colleagues to accept a new approach to departmental management that would resolve these various difficulties. In parallel he tried to persuade the finance department to adapt to his format the monthly data they provided.

Susan and the sex offenders programme in SWD

The region's dispersed population is served by SWD's 3,000 staff. Most managers moved into their positions as a natural progression within a social work career.

Susan, a division manager, reported the creation of a three-member team to run a sex-offenders treatment programme but, unlike Ian and Ulrich, did not lay claim to the original idea. The innovation process started when divisional staff became interested in the new approach and received Susan's agreement to attend an outside training course. Afterwards, with her encouragement, they set up a 'self-help' group, supporting each other in the difficult task of dealing with offenders. About a year before our interview the group had appreciated the great demands the new approach made on staff and proposed that a special team be set up to take a lead in the offender programme.

Interpretation and theoretical connections

We now turn to our interpretations of the data and links made between those interpretations and relevant theoretical formulations. First we consider the context of the three organisations and their internal 'logics of action' (Whittington 1992), related in the second section to the origins of the innovations in the sense of identity anti-personal agency of those most closely involved in the process. From that point on, the discussion focuses on social and political processes: the rhetorical process through which arguments are developed to a state where they can serve as the basis for action; how the development of the innovation is mediated by social and political relationships in which intimate mutual knowledge is important; the reciprocal effects of the innovation's social and substantive strands and, lastly, the institutionalisation of the innovation.

Organisational flux and competing 'logics of action'

In considering organisational settings we employ Giddens' (1984) notion that a 'social system' is constituted by the patterning of social relations. System integration depends on reciprocal interrelationships between individuals or collectivities. Its maintenance depends on the use made of sets of rules that guide action and resources that empower action – rules and resources which also constitute the organisation's structure. Actors draw on rules and resources in their social relationships, generally with the effect of maintaining the order and continuity of the system. In times when that order is disrupted they draw on the same rules and resources to re-establish that order or – consistent with the main focus of our research – they attempt to transform it.

In each of the organisations managers had experienced a considerable degree of disruption to the ordering of the social systems within which they were positioned. Any sense of continuity experienced earlier had been giving way progressively to one of change. The management of ITC, for example, had embraced a wide range of modern techniques designed to reduce costs, maintain quality, enhance flexibility and bring new products to market rapidly. References were made by our respondents to approaches which litter the management literature such as just-in-time, total quality management, process re-engineering and project management control systems.

Most ITC narratives refer to a closely choreographed, top-down culture change programme such as Peters and Waterman (1982) popularised;

British examples have been reviewed by Williams *et al.* (1989). Innovation was a key value, supported at the research site by various programmes. In parallel, ITC's long-standing interest in human resource management – consistent again with the literature (e.g. Legge 1995; Storey 1992) – had prompted a playing-down of managers' authoritative role, emphasising teamworking instead. Managers were called 'coaches', symbolising their new role in facilitating improved employee performance.

In common with most UK higher education institutions, Uni had for many years been responding to a government strategy since 1979 to disrupt academic values and practices which, it was alleged, had reinforced national cultural patterns based on social status which were inimical to the needs of the modern economy. The goal of such initiatives is the 'entrepreneurial university', strongly linked to business and more accountable to its clients (Cowen 1991).

To some extent Uni's management systems had been adapted to conform more closely to models proposed by the likes of Jarratt (CVCP 1985) and Sizer (e.g. 1987; 1988). A strategic and resource planning process had been introduced, greater resource management responsibility was being delegated to departments; more formal systems existed for evaluating performance, and a body of specialists had been recruited to assist decision making.

In this context it was not surprising that many respondents perceived themselves as coping with pressures caused by reduced government funding, increased competition for students and research grants, and the audit of academic outputs. Key issues were raising revenue, improving research and teaching ratings, and enhancing management quality, all areas subject to frequent changes in government policy.

In SWD, managers were also caught up in a dynamic created during the 1980s and 1990s when, under legislative and other pressures, innovation became endemic in local government. By the time our research project started SWD seemed to have undergone most of the transformations experienced in local authorities across the UK (Leach *et al.* 1994; Wilson and Game 1994).

Like other local authorities, SWD had been expected to become a purchaser as well as a provider of services, and to tighten up its policies and practices following widely publicised major social work debâcles throughout the UK. Most recently, in anticipation of the NHS and Community Care Act, SWD had been reorganised radically. The directorate's role had been modified to enable it to deal better with strategic issues, central policy units had been strengthened, and structures had been 'flattened' by removing layers of management and delegating more responsibility to field units. Attempts had also been made to transform SWD's culture to correspond with this new reality. Narratives of those nearer the apex do make reference to changes in values, policies and styles that may have facilitated some of the innovations, whereas others organisationally and/or geographically further from the directorate tell of the burdens of new rules.

In such fluid contexts, organisations are probably less 'monolithic and determined' than they have ever been, becoming ever more open to external influence. Hence strategic efforts to influence the way in which the social system is reproduced or modified are unlikely to be complete, leaving the organisation vulnerable to transformation through deliberate action by people within and outside its boundaries (Whittington 1992).

ITC illustrates well the ambiguities of 'the large, diversified and managerially controlled firm ... [that] have fragmented the simplicity of the profit-maximising rule into a plethora of competing managerial "logics of action"' (Whittington 1992: 705). Meanwhile, in the flux of externally prompted change, organisations traditionally not measured against profit, such as Uni and SWD, have become ever more difficult to model and manage. Their logics of action proliferate providing an ambiguous field of information out of which innovations emerge through the deliberate choices of individual agents.

For example, in Uni there were several different rationales for the management of a university ranging from a traditional 'logic' – a form of 'collegiality' that enabled academics to 'do their own thing' – through to an 'enterprise culture' logic that universities should be subject to a form of 'executive management'. Ironically, in ITC, top-down control stemming from the executive management model competed with something nearer a 'collegial' model based on notions of 'delegation', 'empowerment' and 'autonomous work groups'. In SWD, pressure for devolved forms, giving managers more scope to take initiatives, conflicted with a bureaucratic tightening up of service accountability.

Changes external to an organisation – whether attributed to government, competition or technology – become operative internally only when the basis for such change exists there. Similarly, internal change, as with the development within ITC of a less autocratic style of management and Uni's greater delegation to departments, prompts 'knock-on' change only if, again, the basis for further change exists or can be created. At both levels nothing happens if individuals who can choose freely, such as Ian, Ulrich and Susan, do not feel cause within themselves for wishing to create the change. If a person has no choice about undertaking a project, as was the case in a small minority of the innovations reported, we hypothesise that its success will depend on how much of that individual's self is invested in the project. In either situation the essential element is personal agency, a theme to which we now turn.

The basis of innovation in personal agency

Self identity A key concept in our interpretation and attempt to build theory is 'self-identity', used in a sense similar to that employed by other researchers using qualitative methods – e.g. Maclure (1993) and Watson

(1994a) – for whom identity serves as an organising principle in under-standing, respectively, the jobs of teachers and managers. Self-identity is concerned with being 'an individual to and for oneself', and how that indi-viduality is presented in the sense-making process through which people position themselves within discursive practices (Harré and Gillett 1994). To have and to be able to present this uniqueness of self requires a sense of spatial location that yields a 'point of view', of existing at a moment in time along one's life trajectory, of being a responsible agent within a network of mutual obligations and commitments, and of being socially situated according to criteria such as status, age and reputation.

The continuity of an individual's self-identity is safeguarded by his or her feeling of *ontological security*, established early in life as part of mechanisms to control anxiety (Giddens 1984). Security of being is maintained through the predictability of routine discursive practices such as tactful behaviours which sustain mutual trust. Even while acting as an agent of transformation, as in our cases, an individual behaves in ways that both sustain 'continuity of the personality' as he or she 'moves along the paths of daily activities' (Giddens 1984: 60) and reproduce the structures to which he or she is subject.

Central to our theme, however, is how individuals transform those struc-tures by repositioning themselves discursively in attempts to make sense of some disruption to everyday routines or, spontaneously, to promote some innovative idea. Engaged as they are in the flux of organisational activity, those individuals are able to tap into its 'flows of social and psychological information about possible ways of life'. In attempting to make sense of and influence that flux in innovative ways they are faced with the question 'How shall I live?' (Giddens 1991: 14). An organisation's members can address this question by drawing on experience, not just from the work context but as social beings in various other domains. Through membership of other bodies managers may be able to import into their imaginings and actions alien values, rules and resources (Whittington 1992).

References to seemingly key aspects of identity are common in the narra-tives. Ulrich's innovation was motivated by an overall concern for his academic discipline, probably a more important contributor to his sense of self than his managerial role. However, from his positioning in that role Ulrich realised that Uni could survive without his discipline, especially as the department was subject to high levels of uncertainty and therefore diffi-cult to manage. So he accepted responsibility for initiating steps to secure an improvement.

Ulrich also revealed strong security needs in admitting that what had sustained him through eighteen difficult months was 'the avoidance of chaos and the need for a tidy world ... a degree of anxiety sometimes, fear about things being out of control'. But an academic collaborator, in describing how Ulrich took risks as a mountain climber under severe conditions, and in challenging authority within the university, provided evidence that Ulrich

could quell his anxiety in critical situations. Moral issues also seemed important to Ulrich, illustrated by his hope that whether or not colleagues agreed
with him, they would say he 'was fair and treated them properly, with
respect'.

Ian exhibited a great need for personal autonomy, reacting strongly when
its security was threatened by the unreasonable exercise of authority by
superiors. His identity as a manager, especially after his new plant experience, hinged on capability to enable others to exercise their personal agency
with greater independence. These values were rationalised and made potent
in ITC's setting by his attachment, as a professional manager, to the ideas of
various gurus (e.g. Peters and Waterman 1982). While it may be that
company policies on greater empowerment were consistent with guru literature, perhaps ITC directors might not have wished to move as quickly or as
far as Ian did.

Susan's sense of self was buttressed by very strong convictions about good
social work practice that may not have been consonant with what was
managerially efficient as defined by civil servants responsible for her division's funding but which were probably shared by colleagues in the
judiciary, the police and the prison service. Reputation seemed important,
too. A collaborator noted that Susan 'is quite a career person' and the project
would be 'something for her to be seen doing' – reflected perhaps in her own
comment, 'another first for the Region'.

Drawing on the evidence that these case studies illustrate, as framed by
the context of organisation and external environment discussed earlier, we
hypothesise that our respondents, in making the various interventions
recounted to us, were exhibiting what Giddens (1979) calls 'transformative
capacity'. This is concerned with the capability of agents to achieve certain
outcomes, a function of the freedom to choose between alternative ways of
behaving, expressing how they are 'willing to exist as particular subjects';
their deployment of knowledge and other resources, and their self-efficacy.

Within the structuration framework we are proposing, a person's self-
identity is shaped and confirmed by adherence to routines that ensure
organisational continuity. Conversely, in attempting to forge his or her
own work-based identity, the same individual contributes to reshaping the
organisation, exerting social influences which, potentially, have wide consequences. Innovative initiatives can thus be conceived as having reciprocal
effects, through personal agency, on both the organisation and the agent's
sense of self. This seems to mirror how Watson (1994b) interprets the stories
told by his sample of managers; in attempts to shape their organisations they
'shape themselves as individual human beings ... continually having to
realise themselves and make sense of their place in a potentially chaotic
world' (82).

Drawing on experience　The 'trajectory' of life's experiences along which identity is formed is also a source of the knowledge and understanding that

managers can mobilise in developing their innovation. Some had long-standing interests which endowed them with expertise. For example, Susan's work with sex offenders had made her aware of the severe problems of recidivism associated with traditional modes of treatment. Even Ulrich's limited interest in spreadsheets was of practical and symbolic value.

Experience had sensitised some individuals to current problems, as when an SWD manager recognised that an organisation he had inherited was likely to be a particular 'hot spot' of trouble with NHS consultants. More specific still, some imported the basic idea of an innovation directly from their experience, as with Ian's creation of a flat departmental structure and radical 'ethos', building on his achievement at another ITC plant.

Crucial, too, is what Giddens (1984) calls 'discursive penetration', referring here to the depth of managers' understanding of and degree of fluency with key discourses which shape their own and other organisations. Such understanding and fluency enables managers to direct their energies and to form their arguments effectively. The three case managers had deep discursive penetration of their own organisations, while Susan, out of painful experience of dealing with a government department and its civil servants, used her understanding of that context to good effect in the negotiation of funding.

Experience also provided for many the foundation of self-beliefs which yielded a sense of confidence that they would achieve successful outcomes, examples of what Bandura (1986) calls 'self-efficacy', based on the person's judgement of their 'capabilities to organise and execute courses of action required to attain designated types of performances' (391). Hence, 'the successful, the innovative, the sociable, the non-despondent, and the social reformers take an optimistic view of their personal efficacy to exercise influence over events that affect their lives' (Bandura 1989: 418). Moreover, in critical situations, as Ulrich showed strongly, when the security of everyday routines is disrupted, such people are able to think ahead and risk choosing from alternative courses of action rather than suffer a collapse of the will.

There is evidence in our data that some managers were not entirely reliant on their own capacity to recall from experience. Instead, they and their collaborators drew on 'community memory', a coping strategy similar to that of photocopier technicians who collaborated to solve seemingly intractable problems (Orr 1990). Like the technicians, our respondents – such as Susan and her colleagues wrestling with issues related to sex offenders, university managers attempting to establish a leading-edge research centre, and the ITC team charged with introducing new micro-chip technology – seemed to have been involved in 'the reflective manipulation of a set of resources accumulated through experience ... piecing together an understanding from bits of experience, their own and others, in the absence of definite information' (Orr 1990: 184–5).

Freedom of action and command over resources   Narratives also provided evidence that most managers had some choice as to where and how they channelled their energies, an essential element of 'agency'. They seemed to be on a relatively light rein, with scope to manipulate their roles (cf. Fondas and Stewart 1994; Katz and Kahn [1966] 1978). Our three cases provide clear examples, and in other narratives even quite junior managers claimed that, provided they got the 'bread and butter work' done, their own superiors let them get on with local innovations.

Capacity to transform social situations is also a function of resources of two forms: 'allocative', which facilitate command over raw materials, production methods and products, and 'authoritative', yielding command over persons (Giddens 1984). But it is neither necessary nor sufficient to have formal authority. The narratives revealed that only about six of the thirty innovators interviewed were able to implement the innovation within the sphere of their own authority. The remainder seemed to feel constrained to consult and negotiate with some set of peers, bosses and external agencies. Even those who had direct authority to command resources consulted or negotiated with those over whom they had nominal command. This behaviour may have been part of an 'education strategy' intended to overcome resistance (Kimberly 1981). It is also consistent with two other arguments: that the managerial role can be legitimised only through co-operation (Hales 1993; Kaplan 1984), or that followers can make a contribution to effective leadership (Hollander and Offermann 1990). In general our data suggest a greater incidence of co-operation and joint contribution strategies.

Even so, command over resources – which, for example, gave Susan scope to rebalance social work teams without agreement from bosses – is seen as a useful asset in furthering an innovative initiative. But the evidence from the narratives places the mobilisation of that advantage clearly within the constraints of social and political relationships, to which we now turn.

Furthering innovation through social and political relationships

The narratives are replete with stories of a great variety of social interactions within which the focal managers and others used their intrinsic and acquired capability to transform situations. Many refer to *meetings*, regular and irregular, formal and informal, including those related to the procedures managers had to follow in order for their project to be sanctioned by others. For example, internal departmental meetings and those with the finance department were particularly crucial to the success of Ulrich's project.

One-to-one exchanges   These feature frequently, being used to persuade someone to join an alliance; to 'chat up' people before a key meeting; and to deal discreetly with some difficulty, as when Ian told his director to stop interfering. Some managers are revealed as good networkers, facilitating access to unusual sources of information and other forms of support, enhancing their discursive penetration of different settings, and enriching the range of exotic perspectives and arguments they are able to import into the workplace.

Anchored relations   West (1990) hypothesises that 'innovation is more likely in situations of high psychological safety' (312). This notion implies a degree of interpersonal intimacy consistent with what Goffman (1971; 1983) called 'anchored relations', anchored in mutual knowledge which comes from regular face-to-face interactions, along a continuum from mere 'acquaintanceship' through degrees of increasing intimacy.

Anchored relations, as the source of non-sexual friendship bonds, provide the 'preconditions for something crucial: the sustained intimate co-ordination of action, whether in support of closely collaborative acts or as a means of accommodating closely adjacent ones' (Goffman 1983: 3). It is through such relations that 'intersubjective meanings' emerge, a level of social reality created when 'individual thoughts, feelings, and intentions are merged or synthesised into conversations during which the self gets transformed from "I" into "we"' (Weick 1995: 71).

How well we are known by others can be crucial in many senses as revealed in narrative examples. One SWD manager, new in his role, felt that his boss did not know him well enough to trust him to progress an innovative idea without taking it 'up the line' into the bureaucracy. So he went ahead with his project without consulting his boss in advance. Conversely, close and trusting relationships were revealed which, while implicitly providing 'a traffic' of relatively 'unthinking, routine actions that maintain order and integrate existing social systems' (Goffman 1983: 3), are drawn on by those involved in developing an innovative project. Ulrich made clear that he traded on his good working relationship with the finance officer. Ian and his senior supervisor, Tom, built up a degree of trust that served them well in the arm's-length nature of their formal relationship under 'umbrella management'. Susan's assistant manager, involved with her in all stages of the offender project, claims that: 'We get on well professionally and that makes a whole lot of things possible ... we can go together to these meetings [with civil servants] in the knowledge that we will cover each other ... because we trust each other.'

Within the narratives, anchored relations seem to facilitate easy acceptance of each other's ideas and plans. But there is evidence to the contrary, as when Ulrich and the finance officer, and Ian and his supervisor, Tom, disagreed strongly on issues central to their innovations. Probably more important then is the development of trust within the relationship so that each person can believe 'that relinquishing some degree of control over a situation to one or more others will not lead to personal loss or harm' (Moingeon and Edmondson 1996: 2).

Each example of anchored relations referred to above corresponds to what

Goffman (1971) calls a 'two-person', formed by friends for various kinds of social participation. There is a suggestion in the narratives that, adapting the term used by Bandura (1986; 1989), the reciprocal effect of the partnership is one of 'mutual self-efficacy'. From their shared experience of each other's support they derive beliefs that bolster their own sense of self-efficacy.

The importance of anchored relations as the source of 'structure building entities' − as reflected in our data − tends to have been ignored by Giddens in his structuration theory (Cohen 1987). We argue, therefore, that the theory needs to be extended to include the structural potential of such relations if it is to be used as a framework for interpretation of innovation in organisations.

A rhetorical process   Though friends and other close acquaintances share the goals to which change is directed, they may still need to be persuaded of the wisdom of the action proposed, engaging rhetorically in a form of social dialectic through which arguments can be refined and agreed on as a basis for action (Billig 1989).

The novelty of an argument seems to depend on two creative streams, one more cognitive and reflective, the other social and interactive. Creative insights help us to reframe circumstances that constrain into ones that enable and facilitate opportunities to transform social systems (cf. Giddens 1984; Shotter 1993). The products of those insights are processed in the social challenge of argumentation, through which differences are revealed and conflicts resolved, potentially generating sufficient creative energy to sustain action. In practice, as the narratives reveal, it is difficult to separate these two creative activities.

The individual actor reflects on his or her perceptions of contextual ambiguities. Strongly motivated to resolve any inherent problems, or to translate them into opportunities, he or she draws on 'domain relevant knowledge and skills' which are cognitively processed (Amabile 1983). Yet thought, like talk, is subject to strong social influences − constrained by the thinker's reliance on culturally derived discursive practices and the need to justify memories and ideas as the basis for future action in a social setting where other people's attitudes and expectations are crucial (Middleton and Edwards 1990).

The three case managers talk of their perceptions of such constraints: of colleagues whose meanings cause them to compartmentalise their academic lives, or to await instructions from outsiders before acting, or to consider it more important to provide services to the victims of crime than to deal with the perpetrators. These constraints operate within, and sometimes flow from, the ambiguities of competing 'logics of action' at higher levels of the organisation.

In shaping arguments intended to change existing meanings in such constrained contexts, those with sufficient cognitive flexibility, sense of self-efficacy and knowledge of their audience may be in a position to exploit the very ambiguities that cause the confusion, especially if they are able to import values and cultural props from other domains as Ian and other respondents did. Ulrich, more than the others, provides indirect access to an internal dialogue in which 'the same arguments which we use in persuading others when we speak in public, we employ also when we deliberate in our thoughts' (Billig 1989: 110). Ulrich reveals how he rehearsed, in an internal dialogue facilitated by the symbolism of the spreadsheet, a narrative to present to his colleagues that he knew would be questioned. He realised that only if his arguments were perceived by others as authoritative would they be acceptable, capable of turning the audience to new meanings (Shotter 1990). A more vivid example is the boast of an SWD manager, confirmed spontaneously by a collaborator, that when 'I know the person that I am going to speak to ... [I am] able to change and adapt and communicate in a way that person ... feels at ease with'.

Finally, although the narratives are not a rich source of actual 'talk' within the innovation process, there is evidence of the creative use of rhetoric to win key people over. Susan and one of her collaborators, for example, tell from their different perspectives how members of SWD's top policy-making committee were persuaded to sanction, despite strong reservations, the use of scarce resources to help the perpetrators rather than the victims of abuse. It was argued that perpetrators would go on behaving in the same way and creating yet more victims unless they could be persuaded to behave differently. So, in the long run local politicians' constituents would lose out. Meanwhile, Susan and her collaborator put reciprocal pressures on civil servants and area managers. The former were told, if you want to spread the costs of our service this project is the route and a lot hangs on it in the region; on the other side managers were pressed to yield one member each from their teams to service the project because it was argued, if they did not, government would insist on savings anyway and they might well lose people without compensating support from a project team.

Of Ulrich's crucial meeting with the finance department he said:

> Not only was I able to convey the importance I attached to this in the long term, but also to understand one or two of the things that had been getting in the way ... interfaces with their systems that hadn't been explained to me in a way that I could see as anything other than inertia. It was a sort of 'translation of the context to each other' without which 'energy is lost in the friction between central services and departments'.

Reciprocal, generative effects of the social and substantive   This extract exemplifies parallel series of changes that take place, each implicated in the other. As the meaning evolves through the dialectic, the relationship moves on; and the developing relationship assists in freeing up the dialectic. Arguments that flow from the 'old logic' are kept in dialogue with the 'new logic' long enough for some resolution to be achieved, so that 'the innovation process enacts and is enacted by the relational patterns which commit the different parties as they deal with the diversity, difference and ambiguity which surround them' (Steyaert *et al.* 1996: 83). Exchanges of feeling within the relationship provide a release of tension that eventually helps the partners rethink their personal values and interpretative frames.

Many of the narratives illustrate the interweaving of social process and the construction of the substantive elements of the innovation, and the importance of expressions of feeling to that development. This is particularly well portrayed in reports by Ulrich and a collaborator of how departmental colleagues presented serious challenges to Ulrich's reasoning, both technical and moral. Tensions were released as some of them indulged in vituperative outbursts, spilling over into the wider university. It was claimed that this led to a show of support from others, securing a movement towards Ulrich's position. On another level both Ulrich and his other collaborator spoke of how the relationship between his department's administrative assistant and finance department staff 'began to oil the wheels between the two parts of the system', bringing substantive progress.

Synergy between relational events and the substance of the innovation was also evident in Ian's case. Only by challenging early the authority of the director, he believed, could he begin to help the supervisors change the meanings that constrained them. This act ensured that he did not get caught up in the earlier meaning and practices; it also symbolised new meanings in a very dramatic way, modelling how he wished the supervisors to behave. As Tom, the senior supervisor reported, Ian provoked them to start doing things their own way. There were frictions and disputes and those who could not accept the transformed meaning of what it was to be a supervisor dropped out of the team, their need for security threatened by the lack of assurance from external authority and internal structure. Within the team that survived, strong relationships developed based on a robust openness that could tolerate difference and argument. At this stage Ian was able to trust the team more fully, allowing him to achieve another substantive end, greater autonomy for himself.

In the case of the sex offender project the substantive proposal to set up a special team arose only after the relations between members of the *ad hoc* mutual support group had matured. Susan spoke of how the support group, having collected data about departmental attitudes to the new approach to treating offenders, put their interpretation to her, proposing the creation of a mechanism for supporting those involved in dealing directly with offenders. In partnership with her assistant manager, a collaborator, Susan was then able to develop existing relationships with directorate colleagues, elected members and civil servants to the position where they were willing to endorse the proposal for a special team.

Conclusion: institutionalisation of the innovation

At such a stage an innovative proposal can be converted into a 'working innovation', becoming institutionalised, overlapping with and integrated into the existing social system and related structures of the organisation (Steyaert *et al.* 1996). In Susan's case she and her collaborators report on steps taken to rebalance resources by transferring staff from the area teams to the project team, and to define the team's role and to establish rules which would sustain that role in practice.

Formal implementation is only one, if a key, stage of institutionalisation, a process that evolves, as paths of the innovation's development converge on and link into ongoing operational routines (Steyaert *et al.* 1996). In the sex offender project we assume, for example, based on our interpretation of the data, that the proposals put to the policy-making committee would have been screened to ensure that the resource implications and any new rules envisaged for controlling the proposed service meshed with existing arrangements.

Similarly, Ulrich and a collaborator reported how, prior to final implementation of the management accounting system, agreement had already been reached with the finance department to change its monthly reporting practices. But this was possible only after Ulrich's original proposal had been modified to take account of constraints within which the finance department operated. Convergence had been assured by a willingness of each party to accommodate to the other's objectives and practices.

In Ian's case it was necessary to ensure that any changes in practice proposed by the supervisory team were consistent with the company's normal operating procedures. In the extended period during which the innovation was consolidated and built upon – for example, in achieving ISO 9001 status for the quality of the department's operations – it is likely, according to our interpretation, that the substantive changes were also linked more closely to the institutions of both the company and external agencies.

In Giddens' (1984) terms, for these three and all the other cases researched, steps taken to implement the innovation had the effect of reconstituting the established systems of social relations and the structure of rules and resources that are implicated in the reproduction of those systems. Collaborators spoke of how members of area teams in Susan's division had to build up new sets of social relations with the new project team, the members of which had similarly to create relationships with other parties such as offenders, police officers and members of the judiciary. The data also suggest that Susan herself controlled the use of resources that had previously been subject to the direct authority of area team leaders. We also assume that all of the participants in the offender programme were constrained by rules published as part of the innovation and any norms which evolved as the revised programme was implemented. All those affected by the innovations were, in effect, repositioned to some degree within the discursive practices which evolved in the development and implementation of the innovative idea and in the subsequent operation of the 'live' programme.

We have come full circle as envisaged in the crucial relationship between individual agency on the one hand and the organisation's social system and structure that sustains it, on the other (Giddens 1984). Our interpretation of the data, consistent with the methodology discussed in the early part of the paper, is that, through the innovative project agents spontaneously used their capacity to transform circumstances, producing definite outcomes by influencing the actions of others in ways that disrupted everyday routines. To achieve this outcome they drew on knowledge, social skills and access to resources they already had or could acquire. In mobilising and expressing power in this way their actions had an effect on both the social system and structure on the one hand and their own identity on the other. But, once implemented and operational, the new arrangements constrained, admittedly in new modes, the behaviours of all of those affected, including the agents involved in the creation of the innovative product. The 'reality' of the changed arrangements was now part and parcel of the context which these organisational members would monitor in their attempts to sustain control reflexively over their everyday conduct. And through the mutual deployment of skilful behaviour as they collaborate with others to maintain both the routine order of daily life and the continuity of their own personality, they continually reconstitute the organisation's newly modified system of social relations and its sustaining structure of rules and resources.

So, in effect, our conclusions emphasise the duality of the shaping process referred to by Watson (1994b). Yes, managers in shaping the organisation also 'shape themselves as human beings' in the process. But in doing so they also create new structures which, in turn, serve to constitute – no less directly but in more subtle ways – the identities of the organisation's members, including the innovators.

Appendix 1

Interviewers' innovations, listed by organisation

The number in brackets at the end of each line indicates the number of analytical categories that are referred to in the narrative. The hash sign (#) indicates one of the three cases described in the paper.

University

U1	Structures to improve functioning of a department's academic board (11)
U2	Postgraduate diploma course for language teachers in region's secondary schools (14)

U3	Restructuring of departmental accounting format to facilitate better use of resources (13) #
U4	Establishment of new research centre funded by major medical charity (14)
U5	Masters' course in surgery based on self-directed learning (12)
U6	Neurosurgical programme for treating chronic mental disorders (12)
U7	Devolved department management as part of strategy for improving teaching and research performance (12)
U8	'Well-being' programme for staff and students with potential for raising revenue from public (12)
U9	New budget system for academic departments (13)
U10	Management system for halls of residence to deal with overspending and vandalism (11)

IT company

IT1	New management style and structure introduced by manager of core production department (13) #
IT2	Visible work in progress system introduced into a production department (11)
IT3	Team of recently recruited graduate engineers formed to conceive, propose and implement an innovative project (11)
IT4	Incorporation of new 'application specific integrated circuit' into major product range (12)
IT5	Training programme for customers' help-desk personnel to optimise use of new generation of hardware (11)
IT6	Delegation of performance appraisals to project leaders in conjunction with peer input into the process (8)
IT7	Formal system to evaluate and screen projects for process improvement (12)
IT8	A new-generation desktop publishing system in a department controlling product information (13)
IT9	Computerised system for employee records (10)
IT10	Market research for, and specification of, equipment to deal with various types of 'smart card' (14)

SWD

| S1 | Specialised service in support of field workers charged with dealing with sex offenders (13) # |

S2	Flexible scheme for the care of children of parents affected by HIV/AIDS developed in partnership with a national charity (12)
S3	Policies, roles and systems for consultation with carers and agencies involved in community care (14)
S4	Restructuring of care roles to support elderly clients in hospital (12)
S5	Restructured roles and rules for the work of a duty social work team responding to initial client contacts from an extensive city area (13)
S6	Criteria introduced to facilitate parental attendance at case conferences concerning their children (14)
S7	System of group supervision for a set of social workers new to a team (12)
S8	Mission and rules of community centre revised so that parents whose children no longer attended could continue to receive support at the centre without eroding its principal service to families (13)
S9	A team of social workers were transformed into care managers able to deliver services consistent with community care legislation (13)
S10	A newsletter designed for all women in SWD (12)

Acknowledgements

The authors acknowledge the support of the ESRC, through grant no. R000221 143, for the conduct of the research on which this paper draws. They also wish to thank the *JMS* referees for the many positive criticisms and suggestions which served to prompt considerable improvements in the paper.

Bibliography

Amabile, T. M. (1983) *The Social Psychology of Creativity*, New York: Springer-Verlag.

Bandura, A. (1986) *Social Foundations of Thought and Action*, Englewood Cliffs, NJ: Prentice Hall.

——(1989) 'Perceived self-efficacy in the exercise of personal agency', *The Psychologist*, 2, 10: 411–24.

Barron, F. and Harrington, D. (1981) 'Creativity, intelligence and personality', *Annual Review of Psychology*, 32: 439–76.

Billig, M. (1989) *Arguing and Thinking: A Rhetorical Approach to Social Psychology*, Cambridge: Cambridge University Press.

Campbell, D. T. and Fiske, D. W. (1959) 'Convergent and discriminant validation by the multitrait-multimethod matrix', *Psychological Bulletin*, 56: 81–105.

Cohen, I. J. (1987) 'Structuration theory and social praxis', in A. Giddens, A. and J. H. Turner (eds) *Social Theory Today*, Cambridge: Polity, 273–308.

Cowen, R. (1991) 'The management and evaluation of the entrepreneurial university: the case of England', *Higher Education Policy*, 4, 3: 9–13.

Currie, D. (1988) 'Re-thinking what we do and how we do it: a study of reproductive decisions', *Canadian Review of Sociology and Anthropology*, 25, 2: 231–53.

CVCP (1985) *Report of the Steering Committee for Efficiency Studies in Universities* (Chairman: Sir Alex Jarrett), London: CVCP.

Dey, I. (1995) 'Reducing fragmentation in qualitative research', in U. Kelle (ed.) *Computer-aided Qualitative Analysis*, London: Sage, 69–79.

Fondas, N. and Stewart, R. (1994) 'Enactment in managerial jobs: a role analysis', *Journal of Management Studies*, 31, 1: 84–103.

Giddens, A. (1979) *Central Problems in Social Theory: Action, Structure and Contradiction in Social Analysis*, London: Macmillan.

——(1984) *The Constitution of Society*, Cambridge: Polity.

——(1991) *Modernity and Self-identity*, Cambridge, Polity.

Glaser, B. G. and Strauss, A. L. (1967) *The Discovery of Grounded Theory: Strategies for Qualitative Research*, New York: Aldine.

Goffman, E. (1971) *Relations in Public*, New York: Basic Books.

——(1983) 'The interaction order', *American Sociological Review*, 48: 1–17.

Hales, C. (1993) *Managing Through Organization*, London: Routledge.

Harré, R. and Gillett, G. (1994) *The Discursive Mind*, Thousand Oaks, CA: Sage.

Henwood, K. and Pigeon, N. (1994) 'Grounded theory: a resource for reflexive and deconstructive analysis?', submitted to a Special Issue of *Journal of Community and Applied Social Psychology*, 4, 1, 225–38.

Hollander, E. P. and Offermann, L. R. (1990) 'Power and leadership in organizations: relationships in transition', *American Psychology*, February: 179–89.

Kaplan, R. E. (1984) 'Trade routes: the manager's network of relationships', *Organizational Dynamics*, 12: 37–52.

Katz, D. and Kahn, R. L. ([1966] 1978) *The Social Psychology of Organizations*, second edition, New York: Wiley.

Kimberly, J. R. (1981) 'Managerial innovation', in P. C. Nystrom and W. Starbuck (eds) *Handbook of Organizational Design*, New York: Oxford University Press, 84–104.

King, N. (1990) 'Innovation at work: the research literature', in M. A. West and J. L. Farr (eds) *Innovation and Creativity at Work: Psychological and Organizational Strategies*, Chichester: Wiley, 15–59.

Leach, S., Stewart, J. and Walsh, K. (1994) *The Changing Organization and Management of Local Government*, London: Macmillan.

Legge, K. (1995) *Human Resource Management: Rhetorics and Realities*, London: Macmillan.

Maclure, M. (1993) 'Arguing for your self: identity as an organizing principle in teachers' jobs and lives', *British Educational Research Journal*, 19, 4: 311–22.

Middleton, D. and Edwards, D. (1990) 'Conversational remembering: a social psychological approach', in D. Middleton and D. Edwards (eds) *Collective Remembering*, London: Sage, 23–45.

Miles, M. B. and Huberman, A. M. (1994) *Qualitative Data Analysis*, Thousand Oaks, CA: Sage.

Moingeon, B. and Edmondson, A. (1996) 'Trust and organizational learning', paper presented at a Symposium on Organizational Learning and the Learning Organization, Lancaster University, 1–3 September 1996.

Orr, J. E. (1990) 'Sharing knowledge, celebrating identity: community memory in a service culture', in D. Middleton and D. Edwards (eds) *Collective Remembering*, London: Sage, 169–89.

Patton, M. Q. (1987) *How to use Qualitative Methods in Evaluation*, Newbury Park, CA: Sage.

Peters, T. J. and Waterman, R. H. (1982) *In Search of Excellence*, New York: Harper & Row.

Shotter, J. (1990) 'The social construction of remembering and forgetting', in D. Middleton and D. Edwards (eds) *Collective Remembering*, London: Sage, 120–38.

——(1993) *Conversational Realities*, London: Sage.

Silverman, D. (1993) *Interpreting Qualitative Data Methods for Analysing Talk, Text and Interaction*, London: Sage.

Sizer, J. (1987) 'Universities in hard times: some policy implications and guidelines', *Higher Education Quarterly*, 41, 4: 354–72.

——(1988) 'In search of excellence – performance assessment in the United Kingdom', *Higher Education Quarterly*, 42, 2: 152–61.

Steyaert, C., Bouwen, R. and Van Looy, B. (1996) 'Conversational construction of new meaning configurations in organizational innovation: a generative approach', *European Journal of Work and Occupational Psychology*, 5, 1: 67–89.

Storey, J. (1992) *Developments in the Management of Human Resources: An Analytical Review*, Oxford: Blackwell.

Strauss, A. L. and Corbin, J. (1990) *Basics of Qualitative Research: Grounded Theory Procedures and Techniques*, Newbury Park, CA: Sage.

Watson, T. J. (1994a) *In Search of Management: Culture, Chaos & Control in Managerial Work*, London: Routledge.

——(1994b) 'Managing crafting and research: words, skill and imagination in shaping management research', *British Journal of Management*, 5, Special Issue: 77–87.

Weick, K. E. (1995) *Sensemaking in Organizations*, Thousand Oaks, CA: Sage.

West, M. A. (1990) 'The social psychology of innovation in groups', in M. A. West and J. L. Farr (eds) *Innovation and Creativity at Work: Psychological and Organizational Strategies*, Chichester: Wiley, 309–33.

West, M. A. and Farr, J. L. (1990) 'Innovation at work', in M. A. West and J. L. Farr (eds) *Innovation and Creativity at Work*, Chichester: Wiley, 3–13.

Whittington, R. (1992) 'Putting Giddens into action: social systems and managerial agency', *Journal of Management Studies*, 29, 6: 693–713.

Williams, A., Dobson, P. and Walters, N. (1989) *Changing Culture*, London: Institute of Personnel Management.

Wilson, D. and Game, C. (1994) *Local Government in the United Kingdom*, London: Macmillan.

Wolfe, R. A. (1994) 'Organizational innovation: review, critique and suggested research directions', *Journal of Management Studies*, 31, 3: 405–31.

Zey, M. (1992) 'Criticisms of rational choice models', in M. Zey (ed.) *Decision Making*, Newbury Park, CA: Sage: 9–31.

10 Case research as a method for industrial networks

A realist apologia

Geoff Easton

Introduction

Few researchers involved in research in the business or marketing areas spend much time thinking about research methods or methodology. Fewer still show any concern with, or interest in, the philosophical bases for their knowledge claims. To an outsider this state of affairs might seem strange. After all, such researchers would, if asked what they were doing, make claims such as 'we seek to gain understanding' or 'we are pushing back the frontiers of knowledge'. It is even stranger that we, who research what managers do, and often criticise them for making decisions based on few or dubious data, do not apply the same criteria to our own activities.

It would be interesting to speculate at length on why this anomaly has occurred. However, for the purposes of this paper it will suffice to offer just one or two observations. It may be that we are so embedded in our own paradigm that we simply take for granted that the methodologies we employ are correct because we are doing what everyone else does. Someone else has done the thinking for us. It may be that the research training we receive is inadequate, apprentices learning from masters who themselves have little background in methodology. All this is, perhaps, the result of being involved in immature disciplines. Another contributory factor may be that to many researchers the philosophical justification of their work is self-evident. What you see is what you get. I collected these data and this is what they mean. So what is the fuss all about? Finally, for those who have dipped their toes in the waters of philosophy, they may seem very cold indeed. There are no tight little prescriptions. It is hard work and much of what is written appears incomprehensible. It does not help that philosophy proceeds by way of argument and controversy. It is much easier to call a plague on all your houses and get back to the practicalities of getting research monies, finding and supervising research assistants, designing research methods and writing papers.

However, the issue will not go away. The coming and going of postmodernism, if nothing else, raised the consciousness of many to the problems of demonstrating that we do know what we claim to know. And if the diffusion of innovation model continues to operate in the social sciences in the way that it has in the past, then the death of positivism seen in the basic social sciences should and is beginning to have an impact on the more applied disciplines. An attack on, for example, the prevailing positivist position has been going on in marketing for a decade. Hunt (1991) and Anderson (1986) have been assaulting the bastions of the key journals from two different directions and some argue that there is evidence that breaches are beginning to appear in the walls. Others are convinced the damage is purely cosmetic. It is noticeable, moreover, that consumer behaviour rather than marketing academics are in the forefront of the battle. Nevertheless a generation of doctoral students is aware of the arguments and the revolution may occur quicker than we think.

Closer to home, I would claim that we have a particularly acute problem in the field of industrial networks research. The traditional methodology, inspired by the IMP (Industrial Marketing and Purchasing) Group, has been a mixture of relationship or focal organisation surveys and case research. The former fits quite well into the current paradigm though misses out by not, in general, offering the level of operationalisation of variables and randomness of sample required by the more prestigious US journals. Hallen *et al.* (1992) offer one of the few exceptions although the analysis was dyadic rather than network in form. Anderson *et al.* (1994) provide another but the case material in this latter paper was suitably diluted by more traditional material. As a result of this espousal of a rather restricted form of positivism by traditional journals, case-based writing appears mainly in books.

Yet I wish to argue in this chapter that case research is perhaps the most appropriate method for research into industrial networks and that there exists a philosophical defence for case research which is at once powerful and appeals, certainly at the most superficial level, to our common-sense notions of the world. This philosophical position is a sophisticated form of realism developed by, among others, Bhaskar, Harré and Sayer and brought to bear on case research by Tsoukas (1989). One way of describing it would be as critical perceptual transcendental realism. All that this portmanteau phrase means is that it is a realism that has been modified and articulated to take account of the many philosophical attacks made on naïve realism in the past.

The paper begins with a description of the features of the realist position that I wish to build upon. It continues by defining a particular mode of case research and aligning it with the realist position. In the third section I briefly show how case studies do or do not fit in with other philosophical orientations, particularly positivism in some of its many forms. Finally, an attempt is made to identify some of the 'realistic' causalities that appear to underpin industrial network phenomena.

A realist philosophy

In a recent work on methodologies for industrial networks research (Easton 1995), I argued that four key philosophical orientations can be identified in social research. I used the label orientation to indicate a cluster of schools or positions which have certain aspects in common but which also have, within them, much heterogeneity. The four orientations are: realism, positivism, conventionalism and constructivism. I will deal with the issue of how the last three orientations relate to case research in a later section. In this section I wish to set out the structure of, and the arguments for, the particular brand of realism, hereafter simply realism, that can be used to justify knowledge claims arising out of case research.

What is it that we are trying to do when we do research? The realist position is that we seek valid explanatory knowledge. Explanation is a contentious issue in philosophy and there are many alternative views about what explanation comprises. However, what should be apparent is that each meaning of explanation can only be understood in the context of the philosophical position that is being employed. What a valid explanation means in terms of realist epistemology will only become apparent when the basic postulates of the system have been described. However, suffice it to say that it differs sharply from the deductive–nomothetic form of explanation that occurs in many forms of positivism. It has been argued, by positivists, that the ultimate aim of research is prediction. Again realists would argue that prediction, apart from the atheoretical predictions produced by forecasting techniques, is very rarely possible even in closed and well-understood systems and that its value is, in any case, not easy to justify (Sayer 1992: 130–8).

The fundamental assumption of the realist position is that there is a reality 'out there' waiting to be discovered. This may not seem a very radical notion but there are many adherents to constructivist and conventionalist positions that may make it seem so. They would argue that what reality there is, is merely socially constructed, or that there is no reality and that all knowledge claims are relative to the system that produced them. What is not being assumed, however, is a naïve realism implying that reality is obvious or self-evident or easy to discover. In fact, precisely the opposite is claimed. 'Our knowledge of that (real) world is fallible and theory laden ... Nevertheless it is not immune to empirical check and its effectiveness in informing and explaining successful material practice is not mere accident' (ibid.: 5). We see through a glass darkly but there is something there to see. Or, using another metaphor, there is land below the aircraft but we get only occasional glimpses of it.

Bhaskar (1978) provides a more articulated view. He distinguishes between the real, the actual and the empirical domains. The real domain contains the independent-from-observer mechanisms that create events. The actual domain is where the events created by the interaction of the real mechanisms appear. Events can occur, of course, without their being observed. The empirical domain is where events are experienced by observers. Bhaskar's schema is shown in Table 10.1.

Table 10.1   Bhaskar's (1978) classification of the real, actual and empirical domains

	Domain of real	Domain of actual	Domain of empirical
Mechanisms	✓		
Events	✓	✓	
Experiences	✓	✓	✓

The events, and the experiences that stem from the events, may be out of phase with the mechanisms that create them. It is partly this quality of being out of phase that distinguishes between the realism described here and naïve realism. It represents one of the forms of complexity which researchers have to decipher. In addition, events may be one-offs or patterned in particular ways. Realism accounts for both types of occurrence. In one sense it might be argued that much of the operationalisation of the positivists is an attempt to bridge the gap between the actual and the experienced. The crucial link is, however, between the real and the actual. How these two domains are linked provides the basic *raison d'être* of realism.

Starting in the real domain, Bhaskar argues that mechanisms are 'nothing other than the ways of acting of things' (Bhaskar 1978: 14). Sayer (1992: 5) puts it slightly differently. 'There is necessity in the world: objects – whether natural or social – necessarily have particular causal powers or ways of acting and particular susceptibilities'. The central concept is that of causality. This is not the causality as correlation or sequence of positivism but a realist causality inherent in the nature of things, or objects. Gravity makes apples fall from trees. People build houses. Firms downsize. Individuals create personal networks. This is not only everyday causal language but also the kind of language we use when we theorise and report results. It should, however, be noted that in none of the cases above is the causal power of the initial object sufficient of itself to cause the event to occur, though it may be necessary. It is therefore the realist project to discover what causal powers act in what ways.

For those who may be sceptical, it is quite easy to demonstrate that causal language is indispensable to everyday life. When we put pen to paper it makes a mark. More convincing for the theorist, however, is the extreme difficulty that adherents to other epistemologies have in describing their work without recourse to causal language. Positivists rarely stick to correlation when they report their work. Explicitly or implicitly they equate correlation or invariant sequence with causality. Constructivists argue that reality is social constructed, i.e. that humans cause a reality to occur and describe how these realities are created. Conventionalists argue that there is no reality except that agreed by convention but such conventions are caused to occur by human actors.

Sayer has elaborated Bhaskar's original model and the concepts are summarised in Figure 10.1.

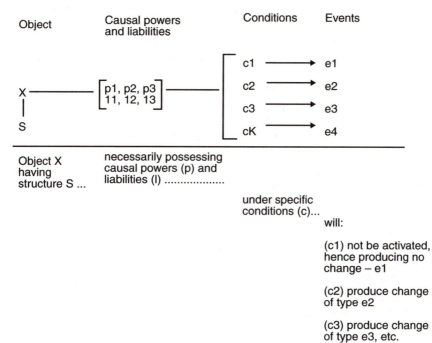

Figure 10.1 The structures of causal explanation
Source: Sayer (1992)

Objects, in Sayer's terms, may be simple or complex, social or material, abstract or concrete and are characterised by their relations. But 'neither objects nor their relations are given to us transparently: their identification is an achievement and must be worked for' (Sayer 1992: 88). Similarly relations are of various types: substantial and formal; contingent and necessary; symmetric and asymmetric. Thus networks comprising firms have a whole set of relations and it can easily be demonstrated that their internal relations provide examples of all of Sayer's kinds of relations. Similarly structures can exist which are comprised of internally related 'objects'. For example, social networks overlay economic and communication networks and have relations with them. But while understanding the nature of objects and their structures is important, their causal powers are more important to explanation. 'On the realist view, causality concerns not a relationship between discrete events ("cause and effect"), but the "causal powers" or "liabilities" of objects or relations, or more generally their ways-of-acting or mechanisms' (Sayer 1992: 105). Causal powers may also be attributed to the structures that objects are involved in. If firms are objects, networks of firms (their structures) have emergent causal powers above and beyond the causal powers of the simple aggregation. Objects not only have causal powers but also liabilities, i.e. ways in which they themselves are acted upon by other causal powers: their susceptibilities. It is tempting to argue that causal powers define objects (a manager controls subordinates) but that should not be the case. The key distinction is to be clear what it is about a manager that allows him or her to control subordinates and not to allow explanation to descend into tautology. Another issue in this conceptualisation is that of agency. Realism is eclectic on this point. People clearly have causal powers but they do not control all the events they are involved in. Conversely people's behaviours are not simply the result of causal powers of objects outside of their control.

A vitally important aspect of the realist view of the action of causal powers is that they are contingent. Events occur as the result of causal powers of an object acting in certain contexts and under certain conditions. In general the conditions take the form of other objects with their associated powers and liabilities or else in terms of the structure of the object itself. For example, in the former case the atmosphere in any relationship between two firms in a network will usually depend upon the relationship that each has with other firms. In the latter case the nature of the relationship itself will also impact upon the atmosphere in terms of its history, the actors involved and the technology of interrelating.

It seems strange that this realist view of the operation of causality is attacked for being particularistic and too complex. However, it is vital that the contingencies are used as explanations via causal mechanisms. It is not enough, for example, to show that networks operate differently in service and product-defined industries. It is essential that the mechanisms that lead to this observation are uncovered. Thus valid explanatory knowledge in this realist perspective requires the researcher to identify the contingent causal powers that are operating in the particular situations under research and the ways in which they combine and interact in order to create the particular events observed in the empirical domain. The generalisation of this type of explanation will be dealt with later in the paper.

Case research and realist epistemology

The term case research is generally used very loosely even among seasoned researchers. However, in adopting a realist position, the nature of case research can be made much clearer although other uses of the word cannot be denied to those who want to use the term to mean something else. Authors have discussed the definition of case research for some years. The holistic nature of case research has been emphasised by Goode and Hatt (1952): 'It is a way of organising social data so as to preserve the unitary character of the social object being studied' (331). Hakim (1987) offers another important, discriminating dimension. 'Case studies take as their subject one or more selected examples of a social entity' (61). A case is a single example or instance. Of course we may use more than one case but, as will be made clear, case research cannot depend upon numbers for its epistemological justification.

Yin, who has written what many believe to be the definitive work on case research, defines a case study in the following terms: 'A case study is an empirical enquiry that: investigates a contemporary phenomenon within its real life context; when the boundaries between the phenomenon and context are not clearly evident; and in which multiple sources of evidence are used' (Yin 1989: 23). The notion of multiple sources of evidence can be extended to include different types of data: qualitative and quantitative. Even quite seasoned researchers make the mistake of conflating qualitative and case research (e.g. Bonoma 1983). The vast majority of case studies will largely comprise qualitative data because the data available to examine complex, rich, 'contemporary phenomena' are of this kind. But it is possible to conceive of largely, or even wholly, quantitative case studies and it could be argued in closed and metric systems these do occur. Of course, in one sense, every piece of research is a case study if the boundaries of the case are taken as the time and space limitations of the particular study.

Yin offers a further important qualification when he describes the use of case studies for explanatory purposes, though his use of the concept explanatory is rather different from that a realist would use:

> how and why questions are more explanatory and likely to lead to the use of case studies, histories and experiments as the preferred research strategies. This is because such questions deal with operational links needing to be traced over time, rather than mere frequencies or incidence.
>
> (Yin 1989: 18)

Case studies need to be concerned with dynamics and time if they are to be explanatory in either Yin's or a realist sense. A realist can only identify casual mechanisms if they operate to cause events to happen, a time-based phenomenon. The use of the word contemporary in the original definition is thus explained. Cases are different from histories, where data cannot be created or events followed, and from experiments where the system is closed and if/then effects observed.

We are now in a position to compare case research and the realist philosophy. Realists argue that the world is composed of real objects and their relations, though they cannot be directly apprehended, which have structures but, more importantly, causal powers which combine in complex ways to create events which occur in the actual world and may be researched in the empirical domain. Case research can, in theory, be used to describe empirical events and, by its use of multiple data sources, trace out links over time, digging ever deeper, and following through the actual to the real domain. A useful, though not entirely appropriate metaphor, is that of peeling off the layers of an onion. The 'peeler' in this case is the use of the question why consistently and continually. Why did this network change structure at this time? Because a key actor merged with a competitor. But why did that lead to this new structure and not another? Because some of the customers of both firms decided to find new suppliers. Why did they do this? Because ...

The inappropriateness of the metaphor quickly becomes apparent. This is no easy or mechanical process. What happens at any one stage of researching the case depends upon what is found at the previous stage. The process is reactive. It may be necessary to go back over old ground but in a different way. It is also apparent that simply peeling away will not necessarily reveal 'reality'. There are acts of creation and retroduction (Sayer 1992: 107) to be carried out. 'Real' concepts have to be induced from the data or, alternatively, already existing concepts need to be employed to see if they provide some sort of match with reality. The complexity is compounded when the realist notion of the ways in which causal powers combine contingently is taken into account. The non-occurrence of events does not imply that a particular causal power is not operating but simply that the configuration of other objects and their casual powers is such that it remains a potential unactualised. For example, a new IT system may have the potential to increase the interaction between a customer and its suppliers but the software is not designed to help this happen.

Earlier it was stated that 'case research can, in theory, be used ...'. Implicit in this statement is the idea that case research, in practice, often lacks any explicit epistemological base. Some case studies are simply rich descriptions of events from which readers are expected to come to their own conclusions. Others are really examples of data that appear to provide, at best, partial support of particular theories or frameworks and are used in a quasi-deductive theory testing way. A third kind employs multiple 'case studies' in a way that suggests that they are relying on some notion of statistical generalisation. Case research which would wish to lay claim to a realist philosophy should be carried out in a different way: to be inquisitive, to look for the roots of things, to disentangle complexities and to conceptualise and reconceptualise, test and retest, to be both rigorous and creative and above all to seek for the underlying reality through the thick veil which hides it.

Case studies and other philosophical positions

The most obvious philosophical orientation that provides a useful contrast with, and alternative to, realism is *positivism*. There are many schools of positivism and what I present here is a simplified and lowest common denominator version. One of the crucial distinguishing features of positivism is that the basis for explanation must spring from empirical data. It was, put crudely, a response to pre-scientific armchair theorising and asser-tion and, in that sense, offered a significant advance in scientific thought. However, it led to the notion that unobservables must be rejected, in sharp contrast to the realist view.

However, the sharpest distinction occurs in terms of the role of laws or invariance in the two epistemologies. This is clearest in the form of posi-tivism labelled logical empiricism though it is present in other forms. The resulting method has been labelled nomothetic/hypothetico-deductive. Law-like relationships are hypothesised among a set of operationalised, and therefore empirically measurable, constructs and data are collected, and anal-ysed, using the methods of statistical inference, to see whether the original variables are correlated. It is argued that the relationships are only law-like and not lawful because of problems of sampling and measurement and there-fore 100 per cent correlation cannot be expected. As a result rules have been evolved which help researchers decide whether the correlations, in whatever form calculated, are significant. If they are not significant then the hypotheses are rejected. If they are not (technically) rejected, it can be assumed that the original model/theory received some measure of confirma-tion. More tests of the same model/theory lead to increasing confirmation. Other forms of positivism use the logic of refutation but the principle is similar.

Realists would argue that the assumption that invariances exist anywhere outside fully closed systems is problematic: 'If positivistic claims about the natural and social sciences were true, scientific activity would not have been possible because most events in the natural world take place in open systems, in which events do not invariably follow a determined and recur-rent pattern' (Tsoukas 1989: 552). Positivists put their faith in regularity and conjunction. Their 'laws', to the extent that they can be found, reflect covariation and not causation. Since positivists cannot have recourse to unobservables they cannot explain in any meaningful sense. They may be able to show that there are complex patterns in the data that they collect based upon measuring techniques they have devised but they cannot say why. Their 'explanations' are simply summaries of relationships among a set of variables. It is acknowledged that this critique of positivism caricatures a broad, and often sophisticated, epistemology but it does identify some of the main issues.

What is the relevance of positivism to case research? Clearly, since posi-tivism relies on correlation to infer causation, the role of individual cases must be marginal. A case is a single instance; statistical inference requires many hundreds of cases in a sample, depending on the number of variables involved, in order to provide a powerful and sensitive test of the model. Cases are only useful as exploratory devices, identifying the likely variables and the relationships among them. And the qualitative data they include must be converted into metrical or logical form before they can be helpful.

This comparison between realism and positivism can also be used to explore, perhaps, the most contentious issue for case researchers: generalisation. What can one case tell you? is the way that the question is often posed. The answer for positivists is clear: very little indeed. The basis of the statistically based nomothetic approach is inferential. The form of generalisation, which is highly limited in practice, is generalising to the population from a sample. The larger the sample the more certain one can be about the nature of the population. However, if one accepts a realist view, one case is enough to generalise: not generalising to any population but to a real world that has been uncovered. Yin uses the term analytical generalisation:

> The short answer is that case studies, like experiments, are generalisable to theoretical propositions and not to populations or universes. In this sense, the case study, like the experiment, does not represent a sample and the investigator's goal is to expand and generalise theories (analytical generalisation) and not to enumerate frequencies (statistical generalisation).
>
> (Yin 1989: 21)

Unfortunately Yin is rather coy about the process of analytical generalisation. He need not have been so. It matches exactly the realist notions discussed earlier, i.e. research should be aimed at understanding and explaining the reality underlying any event or set of events (i.e. case) by unpacking and describing the contingent causal powers of the objects that brought them about. One case can create and/or test a theory to the extent that it uncovers reality.

Even enthusiastic case researchers often fail to appreciate the distinction that Yin makes. They seek to do a number of case studies as if greater numbers, by and of themselves, increased the explanatory power of what they have been doing. Eisenhardt (1989) for example argues that a minimum of eight cases seems reasonable but on what grounds? Yin's concentration on research designs for multiple cases betrays the same belief. Ragin and Becker (1992) offer a more sophisticated design that captures something of the notion of contingent causal powers. They suggest that by doing relatively large numbers of superficial cases and noting the presence or absence of particular factors, one can begin to see how contingent variables work in combination to create effects on a dependent variable. However, in this situation, there is no attempt to get behind the conjunctions to discover what the causal powers and mechanisms might be. Researching greater numbers of cases, with the same resources, means more breadth but less depth. One may be able to identify other contingent causal powers but at the expense of discovering how they operate 'in reality'. This is clearly an alternative research strategy but one which should build on deeper knowledge to start with.

Realists should not, however, reject positivist methods but rather consider reversing the normal role of case and, for example, survey work.

Surveys, given their superficial nature, might be used as the first stage of research to provide a broad overview of the research domain and to guide more in-depth explanatory studies: in a word to provide something to explain. They offer the chance to identify the contingent variables. An example from industrial networks would be a survey of the links between a net of firms and subjecting them to a clique detection programme. Case research would then seek to explain how, for example, one of the cliques came into being, how it has changed over time and, of course, why.

Constructivism is a set of beliefs that centre on the idea that the knowledge of the world is constructed, most usually socially. There is no reality to be discovered. What we regard as knowledge is that which we, as social animals, choose to accept as knowledge. When we collect data we use our perceptions of the world to decide what to collect and we only recognise what we have concepts for. When we analyse and interpret, we do so through language that is, in turn, a socially conditioned tool. Hegel was one of the first to argue that the world cannot exist independently of our perceptions of it. Berger and Luckman (1966) were among the first to coin the phrase – the social construction of reality. The movement has had an enormous influence on social research and, because it has represented a radical alternative to positivism, with its reliance on sense data, there have been mighty battles in the literature between the proponents of different views.

Constructivists would, of course, argue that the case study is as it is because of who has written it. Since there is no ultimate reality to guide us, many other case studies might have been written and while they are not all equally valuable, since there are other criteria one can use to judge, nevertheless there is not 'one true account'. *Interpretivism* is one form of constructivism and one can use it to show how cases might be used in this genre. A summary of interpretivist views might include the following: human beings construct multiple realities, the researcher and the researched are mutually dependent, cause and effect cannot be separated and research is never value free. Thus the value of case studies is minimal to interpretivists. The depth that they offer is a snare and a delusion. What is required instead is multiple interpretations of the same 'text'. Similarly the power of the case to combine material and social data is largely lost on the interpretivist. They would argue that there was no distinction anyway but concentrate on the worlds of those being researched. And, of course, the process of research, which is largely separate for the case-studying realist, is part and parcel of the content for the interpretivist.

While the constructivist might reject the case method except as one rather interesting way of producing text to analyse, the case researcher can and must learn from the constructivist. Sayer, for example, accepts the social nature of the realist project: 'Social phenomena such as actions, texts and institutions are concept dependent. We therefore have not only to explain their production and material effects but to understand, read or interpret what they mean' (Sayer 1992: 6).

The final orientation, *conventionalism*, is similar to constructivism but different enough to warrant separate consideration. Knowledge, in this view, is determined by convention. Conventionalists thoroughly reject realism and make either certain convention-based knowledge claims (e.g. each individual's own personal knowledge) or none at all (anything goes). The conventions for judging the worth of theory can be many and various and are often quite admirable: humanity, creativity, beauty, mode of production, etc. However, proximity to reality does not figure on the list.

One key concept that realists can accept from conventionalists is that of criticality. Sayer again offers a useful summary of how it might be incorporated in a realist epistemology: 'Social science must be critical of its object. In order to be able to explain social phenomena we have to evaluate them critically' (Sayer 1992: 6). Put another way, it is not enough to simply understand the world and accept it. Beyond understanding there are judgements to be made about whether that world is acceptable according to the criteria that we as individuals and/or we as society can agree on. Two of the issues in industrial networks that deserve critical attention are those of power and co-operation. Networks can act to distribute or concentrate power; should there be public policy initiatives to favour the former at the expense of the latter. Industrial networks involve both competition and co-operation of many kinds and at many levels. Should we make suggestions to managers as to how to increase co-operation and reduce competition? In other words, can industrial network researchers really claim that their work is value free and objective or should they recognise that the conventions that they use have values incorporated in them and strive not only to surface them but to judge whether they are personally or societally appropriate?

Case studies, realism and industrial networks

Having provided a description of a particular kind of realism and the underpinning it can provide for case research, the final step is, briefly, to apply both of these concepts to the special case of researching industrial networks. Industrial networks comprise large numbers of organisational actors where the boundaries between one net and another are, at best, indistinct. The connectedness among and between actors means that Yin's prescription that cases should be used where the boundaries between the phenomenon and the context are not clearly evident is wholly applicable. The notion, for example, of surveying networks as a sample of independent actors or links or dyads or triads is risible. The essential element of a network view is lost in this situation since connectedness is assumed away. Conversely a sample of one looks far more defensible if the one is a net comprising large numbers of actors. Similarly, the complexity of the links within and between actors requires a method that can handle rich sources of data and multiple forms of data collection. Networks have consistently been portrayed as dynamic forms. Again the case method with its attention to changes over time is well suited to providing longitudinal data. In summary, it is hardly surprising that much, if not most, research in the realm of industrial networks is case based. We have been driven to cases because they make sense of the phenomena we have sought to understand. We have a common-sense rationale, as summarised above, as to why we have been making the right choice. The thrust of this paper is that we now have an epistemological justification through new critical realism.

But can realism do more and provide a direction or strategy that we might adopt in carrying out research into industrial networks? I believe it can. First of all there are a whole series of process prescriptions that become apparent in the design and conduct of realist case research. These include: the acceptance of small sample numbers, the creative use of alternative data sources, an emphasis on process as the key area to be understood and, above all, the need to identify the causal mechanisms that underlie the processes that we are observing by continuing to ask the question why and collecting more data until we believe we have an explanation.

Perhaps even more importantly there are content implications which will be unique for industrial networks. What, for example, are the objects we seek to study? Håkansson and Johanson (1992) have put forward the actors, resources and activities (ARA) model which has been the basis of many recent studies. Although there could be alternative models it will be useful to examine how the ARA model can be treated in a realist fashion. Clearly actors and resources can be identified as objects that cause events to occur. Should we then identify events with activities? It would seem to be a reasonable first step to do so. After all, activities are caused by actors and resources. However, some activities also cause other activities and activities can have a causal impact on actors and resources. Perhaps all three concepts should be regarded as objects. Actors, resources and activities also have relations and combine to form structures which themselves have emergent causal powers.

A key step in terms of theory development is the identification of the causal powers of the objects we study. There are already a number of candidates in the set of dialectics that have been used to describe network processes: stability and change, centralisation and decentralisation, co-operation and conflict, hierarchisation and heterogenisation, structuring and destructuring. An important problem in using these dialectics has been to account for the end result of their operation in terms of some kind of combination or interplay among them. For example, do industrial networks grow more quickly if relations among actors are more co-operative than competitive? The crucial step in overcoming this problem is supplied by Sayer's realist notion of the varying combination of contingent causal powers. Thus a particular network, net or even relationship develops in a particular way because of a particular configuration of contingent causal powers. For example, hierarchisation is nullified by heterogenisation in a particular case because of the specific constellation of actor and resource structures that are involved, and so the network remains stable.

Conclusions

Case studies are a powerful research method and one particularly suited to the study of industrial networks. The prevalence of case study research in the industrial network field lends support to this assertion. However, up to the present the justification has been at the level of praxis. Case research has been carried out for a series of practical and common-sense reasons. In this paper I have attempted to show that there exists a justification for using case studies based upon a particular form of realism. However, the argument does not depend on the employment of all the details of, for example, Sayer's schema. The logic is more robust than that. It may be that case researchers would prefer to derive alternative views about how causality operates in detail. The key assumptions of realism would not be disturbed by such changes but would still remain in place providing, I would hope, industrial networks case researchers with a more secure feeling as they write up their methodology sections or chapters.

Bibliography

Anderson, J. C., Hakansson, H. and Johanson, J. (1994) 'Dyadic business relationships within a business network context', *Journal of Marketing*, 58, October: 1–15.
Anderson, P. (1986) 'On method in consumer research: a critical relativist perspective', *Journal of Consumer Research*, 13, September: 155–73.
Berger, P. L. and Luckman, T. (1966) *The Social Construction of Reality*, London: Allen Lane.
Bhaskar, R. (1978) *A Realist Theory of Science*, Brighton: Harvester Press.
Bonoma, T. V. (1983) 'Case research in marketing: opportunities, problems and a process', *Journal of Marketing Research*, 22, May: 199–208.
Easton, G. (1995) 'Methodology and industrial networks', in K. Moller and D. T. Wilson (eds) *Business Networks*, Norwell, MA: Kluwer Academic.
Eisenhardt, K. M. (1989) 'Building theories from case study research', *Academy of Management Review*, 18, 4: 532–50.
Goode, W. J. and Hatt, P. K. (1952) *Methods in Social Science*, New York: McGraw-Hill.
Håkansson, H. and Johanson, J. (1992) 'A model of industrial networks', in B. Axelsson and G. Easton (eds) *Industrial Networks: A new view of reality*, London: Routledge.
Hakim, C. (1987) *Research Design. Strategies and Choices in the Design of Social Research*, London: Allen and Unwin.
Hallen, L., Johansson, J. and Seyed-Mohamed, N. (1992) 'Interfirm adaptations in business relationships', *Journal of Marketing*, 55, April: 29–37.
Hunt, S. D. (1991) 'Positivism and paradigm dominance in consumer research: towards critical pluralism and rapprochement', *Journal of Consumer Research*, 18, July: 32–44.
Ragin, C. C. and Becker, H. S. (eds) (1992) *What is a Case? Exploring the Foundations of Social Inquiry*, Cambridge: Cambridge University Press.
Sayer, A. (1992) *Method in Social Science*, London: Routledge.

Tsoukas, H. (1989) 'The validity of idiographic research explanations', *Academy of Management Review*, 14, 4: 551–61.

Yin, R. K. (1989) *Case Study Research; Design and Methods*, Newbury Park, CA: Sage.

11 Structuring the labour market

A segmentation approach

Jamie Peck

The conception of the labour market as a complex, not to say contradictory, institutional structure could hardly be further from the neo-classical image of a self-equilibrating labour market in which individual actors pursue rational self-interest within a framework of free competition. In that neo-classical world, the labour market is a social space in which the actions of all actors are governed by a particular set of rules: those of competitive and optimising behaviour (Marsden 1986: 142). With its diverse origins in institutionalist labour economics, Marxian, and post-Keynesian approaches, segmentation theory has developed in recent decades into the leading alternative to the prevailing neo-classical orthodoxy. While disputes between segmentation theorists and orthodox economists often focus on empirical questions (such as the extent of occupational segregation or patterns of wage dispersal), they also reflect fundamental theoretical disagreements. In particular, these disagreements concern the *rules* governing labour market behaviour or how the labour market is regulated.

Crucially, segmentation theory holds that the social space of the labour market is not only divided into submarkets (a contention many orthodox economists are able to accept), but also that the rules governing the behaviour of labour market actors differ from one segment of the labour market to the other: 'What distinguishes segmentation from mere division is that each segment functions according to different rules' (Michon 1987: 25). This does not deny the existence of competitive rules, which segmentation theorists concede play an important role in some segments of the market. Rather, it represents a rejection of the bundle of claims made by orthodox theorists concerning this competitive state, namely that

- it represents the *prevalent* system of rules;
- it is historically and logically *prior* to other (more regulated or institutionalised) rule systems;
- it represents the *natural* underlying state to which labour markets are tending.

Segmentation theorists take issue with all these claims, arguing that labour markets are 'social constructs, incorporating within them *various rules and forms of organisation* which both condition their mode of operation and also structure to some extent the actors themselves and determine their behaviour' (Castro *et al.* 1992: 7, emphasis added). The competitive form is only one mode of labour market organisation, coexisting alongside other modes of organisation. The ideal–typical internal labour market, in which bureaucratic rules and organisational norms govern the allocation of labour, is one (albeit generic) example of a noncompetitive segment of the labour market. In contrast to the a priori reasoning of neo-classical economics, segmentation theorists begin with the proposition that:

> economic, social and political forces *combine* in determining how economies develop ... [T]he result is a dynamic non-equilibrium process which can only be revealed by empirical investigation. This is not to suggest that abstract reasoning has no role to play but rather to argue that *there are and can be no universal, pre-determined, 'true' systems* to *which underlying economic forces are tending* ... It is necessary at the outset to recognise that the abandonment of conventional economic theorising requires sacrificing the formality of its modelling and the surety of its conclusions.
>
> (Wilkinson 1983: 413, emphasis added)

Defining features of this approach include its root-and-branch rejection of orthodox equilibrium theory, its advocacy of theoretically informed empirical research and multi-causal explanation, and its openness to the role of contingency.[1] Contrary to the orthodox preoccupation with unilogical explanation, based on the empirically unassailable competitive model, this branch of segmentation theory has been concerned to examine the combined effects of technological, social, institutional, and economic forces in the generation of labour market structures. As Villa has observed, 'the crucial problem [for segmentation theory] is neither a problem of categorisation nor a question of competing explanations, but a *problem of explaining labour markets in terms of their different structures*' (1986: 24, emphasis added).

Emphasis on the nature and bases of labour market *structures* represents a considerable advance on the revisionist rendering of dualism in the labour market from which it drew initial inspiration. Emphasis in segmentation theory is placed on the roles of class struggle, institutional forms and processes, and the sphere of reproduction in labour market structuration, representing an increasingly credible and nuanced alternative to the orthodox paradigm. Let us briefly review the intellectual precursors of segmentation approaches.

First-generation segmentation approaches

Contemporary segmentation theories have their foundations in the notion of the dual labour market, developed by Doeringer and Piore (1971) to explain low pay and unemployment in ghetto labour markets and, more broadly, by institutionalist approaches to labour economics as exemplified by Kerr's (1954) path-breaking analysis of the internal labour market. Doeringer and Piore extended Kerr's approach by considering groups *excluded* from internal labour markets. Their work, which represents the first generation of segmentation theories, developed the concepts of primary and secondary sectors of the labour market.

Second-generation segmentation approaches

The second generation of segmentation theories stems from the American radical school, typified by Gordon *et al.* (1982). This approach emphasised the role of labour market segmentation as a capitalist control strategy. For the radical theorists, segmentation strategies became necessary with the advent of routinised production techniques in which the work force was increasingly deskilled and homogenised. Labour segmentation provided a means by which capital could overcome the contradictions inherent in deskilling: through a strategy of divide and rule, it sought to maintain control over the production process. The subdivision of clusters of work tasks and their integration with internal labour markets enabled capital to undermine the bases of class consciousness and solidarity in the work force while inducing worker motivation within an increasingly inhumane work system (Gordon 1972).

Dualist models

The dualist model represented a significant shift in labour market theory: first, they focused on characteristics of jobs rather than those of workers; and second, they sought to bring to labour market theories an understanding of institutional processes. The dualist model focuses on jobs as opposed to workers in the sense that jobs and job structures are seen to differ qualitatively, contrary to the assumptions of homogeneity in orthodox theory (Sorensen and Kalleberg 1981). Because the number of primary jobs is limited by demand-side factors, some form of rationing must occur. The mechanisms of job creation in the dualist model are treated as largely independent of the quality of the work force as measured in terms of education and skills. Certainly, the process of job creation is aided by the existence of a well-trained work force, but the degree of interdependence between the two is held by dualists to be grossly overstated by human capital theory.

In the dualist model, the process of job creation is treated as analytically prior to the mechanisms of job filling: the economy generates a certain set of jobs, a proportion of which are primary sector jobs, and these are then rationed out among the available work force. This rationing process could, of course, be responsive to human capital considerations, as individuals could be assigned places in a job queue according to their potential productivity. The dualist model, however, describes a different set of selection criteria. Access to the primary sector is conditioned by employer discrimination, the effects of union-imposed constraints on labour supply, information shortages, and the operation of feedback mechanisms. It suggests, too, that secondary sector workers develop behavioural traits deemed to make them unsuitable for primary sector employment.

For dualists, the distribution of labour market opportunities is highly sensitive to the ascribed rather than achieved characteristics of the work force. Access to labour market opportunity is systematically restricted for such groups as women, ethnic minority and migrant workers, the disabled, and young people, who bear the brunt of a bundle of labour market risks (Offe and Hinrichs 1985). While such groups are subjected to discrimination in the education and training systems, the scale and scope of their disadvantage in the labour market is greater than can be attributed to variations in human capital (Thurow 1975). In other words, there are forces at work *within the labour market itself* which are contributing to social inequality. The labour market does not simply mirror extramarket inequalities (as orthodox theorists would have it), but plays a part in the generation of inequality (Ryan 1981).

Perhaps the most important contribution of the dualists has been to introduce into mainstream debates the notion of the internal labour market. This was defined as an 'administrative unit, such as a manufacturing plant, within which the pricing and allocation of labour is governed by a set of administrative rules and procedures', in contrast to the orthodox model of the labour market in which 'pricing, allocation and training decisions are controlled directly by economic variables' (Doeringer and Piore 1971: 1–2). While orthodox theory can accept that labour markets are divided into submarkets, it is seriously challenged if any of these submarkets appears to operate under different sets of rules (Marsden 1986; Michon 1987).

Third (contemporary) generation segmentation approaches

Taking dualism as its inspiration, third-generation segmentation theory has begun to claim the status of a mature, alternative paradigm to economic orthodoxy (though this remains strongly contested). In so doing, it has shifted increasingly away from crude dualism. According to Rubery (1992: 246), 'there is now no single "model" of segmentation but more a cluster of models or theoretical approaches which have arisen out of labour market research in the 1970s and 1980s'. However, this is not merely an eclectic bundle of labour market literature, but one sharing both common misgivings about orthodox theory and methods, and a common set of analytical precepts. Contemporary segmentation theories share a concern with the following three phenomena:

1   Primacy is accorded to the demand-side of the labour market, as the area where job structures are shaped and the level and form of demand is determined. This contrasts with neo-classical approaches where individualised labour supply behaviour in terms of acquisition of human capital or in terms of job search and wage demands affects the form and level of demand.
2   Institutions and social forces are taken to be central determinants of the structure and organisation of employment. There is no division between the economic and the institutional as 'markets' are formed through institutions. Although primacy is accorded to labour demand, this demand necessarily has an institutional and social form.
3   There are no inherent tendencies towards convergence in employment organisation, either within or between societies. Segmentation, in the sense of inequalities in form and access to employment, is likely to be found both within and between societies; and this segmentation is as much created by market or economic conditions as by social organisation (Rubery 1992: 246–7).

The following overview of this diverse segmentation literature is organised in terms of a simple threefold breakdown, reflecting the different causal emphases of contemporary theories:

Segmentation of labour demand for example, the technical requirements of different labour processes, stability of different product markets, labour control strategies used by employers, and effects of industrial structure.
Segmentation of labour supply for example, the role of the household division of labour in shaping labour market participation, stigmatisation of certain social groups as secondary workers, processes of occupational socialisation, and the influence of labour unions in restricting the labour supply to certain occupations.
Segmentation and the state for example, the structure of welfare provision and its eligibility rules, industrial relations and labour contract regimes, the structure and emphases of the education and training system.

This is not to say that it is possible to isolate the tendencies for segmentation arising from the demand side of the labour market, the supply side, or the state. Concrete manifestations of segmentation processes are multiply determined, resulting from the *combined effects* of these three sets of causal tendencies. This threefold classification is therefore a heuristic framework, not intended to prioritise one set of factors over another.

The segmentation of labour demand

The processes surrounding the derivation of labour demand and segmentation are complex. The Labour Studies Group (1985) offers a succinct explanation: the overall level of market demand for labour is an outcome of the aggregate level of market product, while the structure of labour demand is determined by the combined effects of the technological requirements of the production process and power relationships. It is, of course, impossible to assign analytical priority to these determinants. The processes of technological innovation and diffusion are themselves conditioned by political structures and struggles, forces which are particularly accentuated at the point of the adoption of technologies (Coombs 1985; Zuscovitch *et al.* 1988). Technology is socially structured as well as socially structuring.

The two main determinants of the structure of labour demand – technology and power relationships – were fundamental in the development of the early dualist theories. Doeringer and Piore traced the causes of dualism to the structure of technology and especially to the particular labour requirements of different production systems, an approach Piore extended in later work. By contrast, Reich *et al.* (1973) rooted the differentiation of labour demand in the power relations between capital and labour in the context of struggles to maintain control over the labour process.

In *Segmented Work, Divided Workers* Gordon *et al.* (1982) went on to argue that patterns of labour segregation are integrated more closely with the structure and evolution of the US economy relating forms of segmentation to long swings in the development of US capitalism. Stable, primary labour markets are associated with the large, core corporations of monopoly capitalism. Stable employment in the core sector allows employers to 'organise job tasks more systematically in order to permit more control, greater differentiation among workers' tasks and greater fragmentation of internal work groups' (173). Large corporations at the core of the economy are able to pursue such strategies because of the considerable power and comparative stability following from their dominance of product markets. By contrast, peripheral firms exist in the shadow of the core firms, exploiting less stable and less profitable markets and absorbing many of the business risks of the core sector. Radical labour market theory continues to take the issue of control within the workplace as the underlying cause of segmentation and as a source of the labour market's fundamental dynamic. As Edwards (1979: 165) has argued, 'to understand why segmentation occurs, we must look to how labour power is consumed in the labour process'.

Segmented Work, Divided Workers has been criticised (amongst other reasons) on the grounds of the direct connections it asserts between industrial structure and labour market segmentation; while it is important to make these connections, it is equally important that they are not made too straightforwardly. Labour market structure (including segmentation) is more than simply a derivative of industrial structure (and segmentation). There is a complex and iterative relationship between the two.

While accepting the contention that stable patterns of labour utilisation are more likely to be sustained in core sectors where the degree of control over product markets is high, Jones (1983) suggests that the industrial structure and labour segmentation nexus needs to be rethought on two fronts. First, labour market segmentation is both an *intra-industry* and an *intra-firm* phenomenon; instances of secondary employment conditions are found in some core firms while primary jobs are found in some peripheral firms. Jones (1983: 28) maintains that such phenomena are not occasional aberrations, but rather 'are an integral and pervasive element of the capitalist labour process'. Moreover, as core firms shift towards the utilisation of core–periphery models and contingent labour strategies, distinctions between the primary and secondary sectors are becoming increasingly blurred. Second, it is necessary to recognise that the character of labour segmentation differs *qualitatively* between industrial sectors. Capital intensity and industry scale are particularly important sources of variation.

More recently, an essentially dualist conception of labour demand segmentation has informed the much-popularised 'flexible firm' model. Here, it is argued that pressures for flexibility and market responsiveness are inducing firms to segment their work forces into a core element for which employment is relatively secure (approximating the primary sector of the dualist formulation). In the core sector flexibility tends to take a functional form; deployment of workers within an organisation and the content of their jobs are adjusted in accordance with external demands. (Multi-skilling is an example of such functional flexibility.) In a less secure position are those peripheral workers who may or may not be employees of the flexible firm, but who are engaged in various kinds of contingent relationship (ranging from part-time or temporary employment, for those on the company payroll, to different forms of arm's-length employment via the engagement of self-employed workers or the use of subcontractors and employment agencies). In this segment of the labour market, flexibility is of the numerical type, representing a strategy for ensuring that the amount of labour input is finely tuned to (fluctuating) demand requirements. The case of the flexible firm illustrates one of the ways in which tendencies towards segmentation of labour demand, clearly emanating in this instance from firms' responses to (what is seen as) market uncertainty and fragmentation, might be reflected in the wider structure of the labour market.

Needless to say, core–periphery models grossly understate real-world complexities. It is perhaps more appropriate to regard capital as factionalised (Wilkinson 1983) and its fragmentation as the product of a host of causal processes, including industry scale and capital intensity. Wide variations in individual capital units also occur with regard to access to finance and other factor markets, which combine to produce a hierarchy of market power (Labour Studies Group 1985). Within this overall hierarchy, a complex web of interfirm relations develops, many of which act to reinforce the subordinate position of those firms in a weak market position. For example,

production subcontracting is commonly portrayed in terms of the exploitation of small firms by large, market-dominant firms.

Although labour market structure is not a direct product of industrial
structure, it remains less likely that stable employment patterns will be
found under conditions of product market instability, for the simple reason
that firms find it difficult to insulate themselves from the effects of
declining product demand (Craig *et al.* 1982). Nonetheless, the association
between industrial and labour market structures is not causally direct. The
complex relationships between the two are perhaps best understood as
tendential, being associated with tendencies that may or may not be realised
in the concrete circumstances of different industrial sectors (cf. Elmbaum
and Wilkinson 1979; Villa 1986). Demand-side factors remain the primary
but not exclusive determinant of segmentation in third-generation theories.
In effect, they define a differentiated structure of jobs which itself acts as
an essential precondition for segmentation. However, concrete forms of
segmentation are seen as forged by the *interaction* of demand-side factors and
the structures of the supply side along with the wider sphere of social reproduction.

The segmentation of labour supply

Examining patterns of wage-labour mobilisation on the supply side allows a
much fuller view of the dynamics of the labour market. Labour and capital
are mutually dependent (Wilkinson 1983). Even if capital did operate as a
fully coherent class, it could not control completely the labour market or the
means by which labour power is reproduced. The supply of labour is *socially*
produced and reproduced. Capital did not create the particular constellation
of social groups in the secondary work force, although it can and does exploit
those cleavages. To accord capital absolute control over the labour market is
to sidestep a rigorous examination of the complexity of labour market structures and their derivation.

Social phenomena can never be explained by the argument that their existence and preservation is 'in the interest' of a social power group:

> That something is 'in the interest' of the corporations (for example) does
> not mean that it becomes a permanent part of social reality; many
> things would be in the interest of corporations which have been success-
> fully prevented from becoming social reality because of the formation of
> opposing social power. Therefore social phenomena actually occurring in
> reality must be methodically screened not only for those interests which
> are orientated towards their *preservation*, they must also be examined as
> to why their preservation was not met by *resistance*, especially successful
> resistance.
>
> (Offe and Hinrichs 1977, quoted in Kreckel 1980: 538)

The gendered division of labour is a case in point. Though capital did not create the patriarchal social structures that underpin the marginalised role of women in the labour market, it exploits and thereby perpetuates gender divisions (Hartman, 1979). Moreover, Marshall (1994: 44) argues that there is now 'a recognition that men and women *supply* their labour on different terms', reflecting role specialisation within the family and the complex of social expectations attached to roles. A notable feature of recent segmentation research, representing a considerable advance on the dualist models, has been the specification of the role of labour-supply factors in structuring the labour market. Three areas merit detailed consideration: social reproduction and the role of the family, labour union structures and strategies, and the position of marginal groups in the labour market.

Social reproduction and the family

The institution of the family – 'the basic unit for the reproduction of labour' (Villa 1986: 259) – exerts a profound influence on patterns of wage-labour mobilisation, being focal in the dynamic between the spheres of production and reproduction.[2] The labour market is structured, third-generation theories insist, in ways reflecting the structures of the sphere of social reproduction and its attendant divisions of waged and unwaged work. Acknowledging that the domestic sphere and wage labour each have their own logics of organisation and change, segmentation theorists nevertheless argue that the two spheres interpenetrate, each conditioning the other. The family exerts an important influence on labour market activity in three ways: first, it plays a key role in the social conditioning and education of the young; second, it provides support for workers in the labour market as well as for other dependents (such as the sick and the old); and third, the sharing of income within the family unit impinges on both male and female roles in the labour market, as well as the distinctive functions fulfilled by younger and older workers (Garnsey *et al*. 1985).

The first is particularly significant. In tandem with the formal education system and wider community structures (in ways considered explicitly in Bourdieu's concept of habitus),[3] families play a crucial role in socialisation for work. As expectations about the world of work evolve, they affect the terms under which individuals will make their labour available. The pertinent process involves occupational socialisation, not occupational choice *per se*. As Willis (1977) has argued, the important questions concern how working-class youth come to want and how they are socialised into accepting working-class jobs. This process of occupational socialisation is related to 'other social affiliations, with the effect being that career paths are highly compartmentalised and dependent upon the social milieu that originally moulded the individual participant' (Seccareccia 1991: 48).[4] Through socialisation there is an 'occupational structuring' of the supply side of the labour market (Offe and Hinrichs 1985), which reflects not only labour market opportunities but also the domestic and labour market expectations of different social groups. These occupational orientations tend to be regarded in orthodox theory as preferences, a completely inappropriate term given their origin.

A second way in which the institution of the family serves to structure the supply side of the labour market is in the allocation of domestic responsibilities. Socially encoded divisions of labour are constructed around received notions of male 'breadwinner' and wage-earning roles and female domestic labour and child-rearing roles (cf. Marshall 1994). This division is reinforced by labour market structures in which career interruptions and part-time work are penalised. Even for those women who do not conform to the stereotypical work pattern, the very expectation among employers that they will, or may, serves to restrict their access to primary jobs.

The family's income sharing is a third way in which this institution impinges on the labour market. Socially, there is a continued ideological association between the male and the family wage, and between women's income and pin money. There is historical evidence that the family wage has exerted upward pressure on real wage rates as the household division of labour has effectively restricted the supply of labour (Humphries 1977), although this view has been disputed by those stressing the role of the family in enforcing women's oppression and dividing the working class (Barrett and McIntosh 1980).

Women are likely to remain trapped in the most unstable segments of the labour market until there is a change in their (real and perceived) position within the household division of labour; or until these household 'responsibilities' become more compatible with primary sector employment (Rubery 1988; Picchio 1992). The role of female labour within the secondary sector is crucial because segmentation theory holds that this sector acts as a structural safety valve for the labour market as a whole, facilitating the mobilisation or demobilisation of this group of workers in line with fluctuating demand requirements (Humphries 1976; Rubery and Tarling 1982). The secondary sector clearly does not disappear in its entirety during periods of recession. Similarly, female workers as a group cannot be regarded as constituting a completely disposable segment of the labour market. Nevertheless, flexibility in the secondary sector (which is not nearly so readily available in the primary sector) acts as an important determinant of the aggregate size and composition of demand for labour over the business cycle. Secondary workers do not have access to the shelters constructed by primary sector employers and workers as a defence against the vagaries of the labour market (Freedman 1976). Thus, the actions of both employers and organised sectors of the working class act to heap the burden of economic downturn upon those workers consigned to the secondary sector (Sengenberger 1981; Wilkinson 1988).

Labour union structures and strategies

In the process of workplace struggle, organised factions of the working class have performed a powerful function in defending, maintaining, and extending their employment opportunities in the primary sector. In so doing, labour unions exert an important influence on the structure of labour markets, processes of rule-setting, and patterns of labour mobility. Rubery (1978: 33) has argued that it is necessary to

> include more fully the effect of worker organisation in the development of structured markets. However, trade union development is not to be regarded as an exogenous influence on labour market structure. Rather worker organisation attempts to control the competition in the labour market that the capitalist system generates, and, further, adapts and restructures itself in response to developments in the economic structure.

Discontinuities in the distribution of power within the working class should be seen as a product of both the actions of workers *within* the labour market and uneven distribution of power *prior to* entry into the labour market. In other words, labour union power has both demand- and supply-side determinants. Collective exclusionary action on the part of suppliers of labour power is, of course, a logical strategy in the face of labour market competition (Offe and Weisenthal 1980; Offe and Hinrichs 1985). Trade unions and professional associations derive much of their power in the labour process from the restrictions they are able to place on the supply of labour to their particular niche of the labour market.

Such restrictive strategies are pursued through a variety of means, such as apprenticeship and other training systems, licensing, accreditation, and credential requirements. Through these and other means, groups of workers exert their collective power in an exclusionary way to bring about some degree of insulation from the external labour market, this being one of the principal means by which asymmetries of power in the labour force are formed and maintained (Freedman 1976). Of course, because the basis of these strategies is exclusion, labour's strategic disadvantage in the market is not reduced in an absolute sense but redistributed within the working class. Typically, excluded workers are concentrated in the secondary sector and drawn from a familiar cluster of social groups: women, ethnic minorities, the young, and the disabled. One of the defining features of disadvantaged groups in the labour market is, therefore, their lack of collective organisation (Craig *et al.* 1982). They are in a sense victims of the successful collective organisation of other (more powerful) groups of workers, their own organisational weakness being both cause and consequence of their marginal position in the labour market.

The ability to exercise control over the labour supply does not reflect the innate attitudes and abilities of collectively organised workers. Other factors are at work, creating an uneven terrain of possibilities for collective organisation. First, and on the demand side of the labour market, there is a long-standing debate over the extent to which labour union power can be explained by the uneven distribution of genuinely scarce production skills (Turner 1962; Dunlop 1964). Those with scarce production skills, it is suggested, are in a stronger position to organise and bargain collectively and to win concessions from management. Ultimately, this becomes a chicken-and-egg argument as skill does not refer just to physical and mental capabilities, but also has an important ideological component reflecting the distribution of power in the labour market and in the sphere of social reproduction. Second, it has been argued that certain industrial sectors are particularly vulnerable to disruption and thus have spawned powerful labour unions. For example, this may have been one of the factors behind unionisation of the newspaper industry, a sector especially vulnerable to strikes. It is possible (although, in practice, apparently not common) for workers from disadvantaged social groups to be located within one of these strategically vulnerable industries. Third, and on the supply side of the labour market, Offe and Hinrichs (1985: 37) have argued that marginal and unorganised groups tend also to be those which 'enjoy the licence to conduct a lifestyle outside the labour market'. These groups are denied access to primary jobs, and opportunities for collective organisation, because they are perceived to have an alternative role (or means of support) outside the waged sector.

Marginal groups in the labour market

While concurring with Craig and her colleagues (1982: 77) that 'the number of good jobs in the economy is mainly determined by the development of the industrial and technological structure, largely independent of labour supply', there also is a need to consider the cluster of related processes acting to generate the supply of labour considered appropriate for secondary work. One reason secondary work exists is the *prior* existence of a group of workers who can be exploited in this way.[5] The processes of job allocation in the secondary sector are governed, not by direct measures of productive potential as orthodox theory would have it, but by ascriptive criteria connected to the distribution of economic, social, and political power.

> Firms can claim labour from segments where pay is low relative to labour productivity in order to compete more effectively and can possibly retain otherwise obsolete techniques. The existence of segments of the labour force with different labour market status may also create the situation where jobs are classified not by their content but according to the labour market position of the workers normally undertaking the work. Thus jobs are secondary because they are performed by workers generally considered secondary: jobs are regarded as unskilled because they are feminised and not feminised because they are unskilled ...

[The] existence of non-competing groups may be of considerable social and political importance for the maintenance of labour force segmentation.

(Craig *et al.* 1982: 77)

Offe and Hinrichs (1985) take up this issue, arguing that the utilisation of contingent workers plays an important part in the wider process of labour regulation. The exploitation of social divides is one way in which fluctuating labour demands are reconciled with a comparatively inelastic supply of labour (the size and needs of which, in the short to medium term at least, are constant).

[R]ecourse to constituting ascriptive categories is the means by which industrial capitalist societies try to institutionally overcome a dilemma, namely, that they cannot possibly force the *entire* population into direct participation in the labour market, while, at the same time, they cannot make generally available the option of non-participation in the labour market (and thus dependence of means of subsistence external to it). If the latter option were available, a 'mass exodus' from market relations – which are also power relations – would have to be reckoned with. To overcome this dilemma ... these societies are dependent upon criteria of exclusion or exemption from the labour market that must have two qualities: (i) they may not be freely chosen individually and thus potentially useable as a means of strategic withdrawal from the labour market; and (ii) they must be selected in such a way that the exempted portion of the population ... is not in a position to place 'excessive' demands and politically effective expectations about its need for the means of subsistence on the production and occupational system.

(Offe and Hinrichs 1985: 36–7)

This approach is useful in that it locates domestic labour within the overall rationale of capitalist labour markets and their regulation. The existence of groups of workers with alternative roles provides a regulatory safety valve for the labour market. In fact, this is a mechanism of *social* regulation.

While alternative roles can account for much of the unevenness in the social distribution of labour market risks, it is just one among a range of factors structuring the labour supply. Not all marginalised workers have an alternative role on which to fall back. In the case of migrant workers, for example, the alternative role hypothesis is less appropriate in the British context than it is for the German guest-worker system (Kreckel 1980). The alternative role hypothesis alone is not sufficient to explain patterns of disadvantage in the labour market. The social structures of patriarchy and racism, though clearly mediated by labour market attachments, exert autonomous influences on labour market disadvantage. These factors, alongside the alternative role hypothesis and the few possibilities or low propensities of some social groups to organise collectively, form a constellation of causes of labour market disadvantage.

If there is a single, definitive characteristic of secondary sector workers, it is that they are stigmatised in some way. The roots of this stigma need to be traced carefully in specific contexts. The alternative role hypothesis, which shares a great deal with Piore's notions of weak labour-force attachment (Berger and Piore 1980), has been criticised for the way in which it separates the determinants of social and political power from labour market power relations (Humphries and Rubery 1984). Offe and Hinrichs (1985) were certainly thinking of these problems when they maintained that the limited access afforded disadvantaged groups to primary employment would lead, 'in a circular fashion, to a decline in their subjective hopes and expectations of strategically asserting themselves in the labour market, and to a strengthening of their subjective orientation to their "alternative role"' (40). However; this is little more than a reworking of the dualist conception of feedback processes. While the subjective orientations and material labour market positions of workers are clearly related, one cannot be reduced to the status of by-product of the other. The link is more dynamic: material experiences of work and the formation of labour market expectations are dialectically related and mutually constitutive (cf. Craig *et al.* 1982; McDowell and Court 1994).

Certainly, the participation of stigmatised social groups in the labour market often serves only to reinforce their lack of economic and political power. Although work in the secondary sector typically requires skill and discretion and though the secondary work force may exhibit stability and loyalty to an employer, it is by virtue of the very presence of low-status groups in such jobs that their skill and social status become devalued. Consequently, the subordinate position of stigmatised workers is both perpetuated and legitimated, illustrating one way in which segmentation on the demand and supply sides of the labour market becomes mutually conditioning. Labour segmentation does not result *only* from organisation of the labour process and related demand-side factors; it is also conditioned by the social actions of those who find their way into different kinds of jobs. Segmentation is partly a product of who does the jobs, social conventions concerning appropriate forms of waged and unwaged work undertaken by different social groups, and the relationship between the labour market and the sphere of social reproduction.

Segmentation and the state

Given their quite different structures, dynamics, and logics, the interface between the demand and supply sides of the labour market involves contradiction and mutual adjustment, not seamless coordination. Much of the responsibility for managing this jarring relationship (or, perhaps more precisely, dealing with its contradictions) falls to the state. State action in the labour market tends to be as continual as it is imperfect. The actions of states are bedevilled by inadequate analysis and prescription, the lagged nature of interventions, and the multiplicity of unintended consequences with which they are inevitably associated. It is this flawed and sometimes haphazard process which is charted in analyses of the state's regulatory role in the labour market. This regulatory role tends to be particularly intense and problematic around the sphere of social reproduction and supply of labour; which is not regulated by mechanisms indigenous to the labour market (such as expectations about potential saleability) as could be argued with other commodities.

De Brunhoff (1978: 11) maintains that the state is 'immanent in the process of capitalist accumulation at the same time as it is fundamentally external to it'.[6] Thus, the state's role in the labour market stems from a requirement to secure the necessary conditions for the reproduction of labour power and, more broadly, of market relations. De Brunhoff argues that although the state's role in the labour market is necessary, the form of its intervention is not determined directly in a functionalist manner. Its role is revealed in efforts to counteract, or at least to minimise, the negative effects of imbalances in the supply and demand of labour. Thus, in periods of labour market buoyancy, state initiatives tend towards mobilisation of segments of the labour supply from the margins of the labour market. For example, the British government's commitment to childcare provision peaked during the Second World War and quickly dissolved following the demobilisation of men after the war (Labour Studies Group 1985). More recently in the UK, policies for the incorporation of 'women returners' and disadvantaged groups entered into ascendancy in the late 1980s, as concerns grew over a looming demographic dip in the supply of young workers (Haughton 1990). Conversely, during periods of high unemployment, the state is likely to pursue policies aimed at temporarily restricting the supply of labour. Measures promoting early retirement, job sharing, and make-work often figure in such periods. It is also true, however, that states often take steps to reinforce the disciplining effect of the market during periods when labour is strategically weakened by high unemployment (Piven and Cloward 1993).

One of the principal means of state regulation of the labour market is institutionalisation of nonparticipation in wage labour. The requirement that this sheltered area of the labour market stop short of being attractive to wage labourers is met by the degrading and punitive way in which these groups are treated (Piven and Cloward 1971; Block *et al.* 1987). Wilkinson (1988) has described the process by which disadvantaged social groups are progressively excluded from the labour market during periods of recession; the demobilisation of segments of the labour supply is by no means a straightforward process. Moreover, structural change in the economy, and in particular long-run shifts in the job-generating capacities of some national economies, has meant that the state must construct institutional means by which elements of the marginal work force can be excluded from the labour market on a more or less permanent basis (Hinrichs *et al.* 1988). The result is that 'social "catchment areas" outside the process of production are required to ensure the reproduction of labour power even when no actual employment within the production process results' (Böhle and Sauer 1975, quoted in Offe and Lenhardt 1984: 99).

A key way in which labour supply is regulated is the imposition of controls on the initial entry of young people to the labour market. Child labour laws, compulsory education, the raising of school-leaving ages, and training programmes restrict the supply of youth. Thus, the state exerts a profound influence on both patterns of supply-side segmentation (its policies tending to focus on particular social groups) and the dynamic of the labour market as a whole (as it takes steps to combat or control imbalances between supply and demand). The state is drawn into the regulation of labour markets not only in terms of the maintenance of aggregate demand and the construction of welfare safety nets, but also in validating and repeatedly adjusting the social distribution of work.

This regulatory function has been thrown into particularly sharp focus under the current period of state-induced flexibilisation in the labour market. Couched in the rhetoric of deregulation and the liberalisation of market forces, these strategies in fact have served to underline the simultaneously central and problematic nature of the state's role in the labour market.

> Government policies to free-up the labour market have not resulted in the creation of a competitive labour market with the neoclassical hallmarks of competitive equalisation of prices, increased flexibility and mobility and real wages levels responsive to overall conditions of demand and supply ... *Deregulated* labour markets are ... not synonymous with *competitive* labour markets; they increase the scope for inequality primarily by removing protection from the weak and not by exposing all groups to competition. Moreover, deregulated labour markets have in practice required a more frequent recourse to the law in order to regulate the system of industrial relations.
>
> (Rubery *et al.* 1989)

Flexibilisation strategies need to be understood for what they are. They are not so much concerned with the restoration of labour market efficiency as with the *political re-regulation of the labour market* during a period of excess labour supply and weakened labour unions. Thus, the opportunity is seized by the state (and by neo-liberal nation-states in particular) to discipline the unemployed with the economic whip of market forces while further weakening labour unions and breaking up institutional structures used by labour (and employers) in defence against the market. In the process, contours of labour segmentation are profoundly reworked in the interests of capital.[7]

Contrary to the rhetoric of labour market flexibility, segmentation does not disappear under a supposedly free and fair flexible labour market, but instead social inequalities widen, power relations are reinforced and wage polarisation occurs. The labour market is just as unequal and it is still structured; the difference is that it is structured less on labour's terms. Ideologically, of course, the state must be represented as re-establishing market forces, not as disciplining labour on the part of capital. Hence the prevailing rhetoric of flexibility and competitiveness.

Explanation in segmentation theories

Segmentation theories are no longer concerned solely with patterns and processes of labour market inequality, but are increasingly moving to explore the fundamental dynamics and social foundations of the labour market. The conception of the labour market developed by third-generation segmentation theorists stands in sharp contrast to the orthodox model in which labour demand and supply mesh with one another in response to wage signals. The supply of labour is not governed simply by market forces, but also by demographic factors, social norms concerning the participation of different groups in wage labour (mediated through the institution of the family), and state functions in such areas as employment contracts, welfare provision, and training. While undeniably influenced by labour supply factors, labour demand is driven principally by a quite different set of forces – in particular, struggles over labour processes, technical change, patterns of competition in product markets, and state policies in areas such as taxation, monetary strategy, and public expenditure. The state's role in the labour market is also vital. Indeed, the ongoing regulatory activity of the state (which itself is mediated through political struggles and therefore not determined in a direct, functional way by the requirements of the labour market) constitutes one of the key means by which the inevitable discordance between labour supply and demand (which has quantitative and qualitative dimensions) is minimised, adjusted, and accommodated.

Thus, labour market structures and dynamics do not derive from a fully coherent inner logic, as the orthodox model would suggest. There is not one set of (competitive) labour market rules, embedded within an overarching (market) rationality. Rather, the labour market is a complex, composite structure bearing the imprints of a diverse range of influences. Some of these influences, identified in this chapter, have been grouped together in the spheres of labour supply, labour demand, and the state. Each sphere has its own characteristic structure and dynamic, and each brings with it *different tendencies towards segmentation*.

Consequently, one would not necessarily expect a close fit between primary and secondary jobs, primary and secondary workers, and core and periphery firms. Segmentation refers to *tendencies*, not a taxonomy of labour market positions (Gordon *et al.* 1982). For example, the allocation of social groups to different segments of the labour market is sensitive to the contingencies of time and space (Peck 1989; Hiebert 1994). Segmentation is the outcome of the contingent and dialectical interaction of several causal tendencies; the state, the sphere of social reproduction, and demand-side factors exert *relatively autonomous* influences on patterns and processes of labour market segmentation. The task of disentangling the forces at work in particular labour markets is, of course, largely empirical. Concrete labour market structures represent the product of a synthesis of causal powers; their precise form cannot be determined purely by a priori reasoning (cf. Wilkinson 1983).

Segmentation and causality

Segmentation theory seems destined never to exhibit the analytical purity of the orthodox model of perfect competition. In stressing the complexity of labour market processes and outcomes, however, it has a strong purchase on the concrete realities of the labour market. However, if segmentation theory is to rise above criticisms that it is no more than a descriptive, mid-level approach, more attention must be given to clarifying and refining its conceptual foundations. This task is not without difficulties, as Lever-Tracy's review of third-generation segmentation theories illustrates:

> It is not necessary for Marxists, or indeed for any school of sociology, to allow its problematic to be defined … by an adversary role vis-à-vis orthodox economics. Since we have never taken very seriously the view that inequality, wage levels, class structures, and so forth, were due to the laws of supply and demand, it is not necessary to group together labour market deviations from these laws as a single phenomenon.
>
> (Lever-Tracy 1984: 81)

On the contrary, although it should not be their entire rationale, segmentation theorists must engage in the struggle over labour market theory and attempt to break the hegemony of neo-classical orthodoxy. While segmentation theory must be more than reactive (in the sense that its scope is bounded by the flaws and questions of the orthodox approach), one of its fundamental goals must be the establishment of a credible and internally consistent alternative paradigm. Almost by definition, this requires the establishment of an analytical position which is both distinct from *and critical* of orthodox theory. The basis for such an alternative paradigm is already in evidence.

The segmentation approach represents an 'inclusive' treatment of the labour market, emphasising both the *necessarily social* nature of labour power and the *necessarily institutional* form of labour market processes. This can be contrasted with the 'exclusive' treatment in orthodox accounts where the competitive bases of labour market transactions are both exaggerated and abstracted from the social and institutional context in which they are embedded. It is this focus on social embeddedness[8] which has led segmentation theorists to investigate the differentiated form of labour market structures.

Thus, if we define segmentation as the separation of the market into different segments within which workers are treated differently, independently of their own characteristics, then we have to explain the different structures of the labour market as a complex phenomenon within which different structuring relations interact. What is needed is a comprehensive conceptual framework, capable of including different levels of analysis, from the social reproduction of labour power to the transformation of labour power and their interrelations (Villa 1986: 257).

The conceptual framework proposed by Villa concentrates on the interactions between four relatively autonomous social processes: the social reproduction of labour, determination of employment opportunities, allocation of workers to jobs, and transformation of labour power into labour (258–72). Labour market structures are viewed as multiply or conjuncturally determined; hence the emphasis on empirical investigation and the variability and unpredictability of outcomes (cf. Wilkinson 1983; Tarling 1987).

Regulation, institutionalisation, and contingency

Processes of institutionalisation are of particular importance in third-generation segmentation theories. Institutions and social factors captured here under a broad conception of social regulation represent a central analytical focus, being conceived as endogenous to the labour market and deeply implicated in its structures and dynamics (Castro *et al.* 1992). This is not merely to say that labour market processes are institutionalised (as in the original dualist conception of internal labour markets). Rather, it is to stress the ways in which the labour market is *itself* an institution, governed by a complex set of rules and evolving in a continuous and reciprocal way alongside other social institutions. Thus, labour markets bear the imprints of (and reciprocally condition) the institutional structures and dynamics of, for example, the education and training systems, the welfare and social insurance systems, and the industrial relations system. In this sense, the labour market does not have a single institutional dynamic, but is a composite of several institutional dynamics.

As institutionalised, codetermined, conjunctural phenomena, labour market structures vary over both time and space. Economists tend to privilege the former over the latter; reflecting perhaps their long-standing preoccupation with questions of history, evolution, and equilibrium (cf. Robinson 1979).

In the orthodox view, economic theory was synchronic: an abstraction from reality that isolated its trans-historical and universal aspects. [The] institutionalists asserted that the abstractions of economic theory were neither timeless nor placeless but instead were an ideal-type – an enhancement of features unique to modern Western capitalism ... [Their] empirical research led them to view [the distance between abstraction and reality] as substantial, at least for some parts of orthodox theory, as historically variable ... Hence, they insisted that diachronic analysis – how *the economy acquired its features and the conditions that cause those features to vary over time and place* – had to be part of economics, alongside synchronic abstraction.

(Jacoby 1990: 319–20, emphasis added)

Synchronic analysis – abstracting to that placeless, timeless world in which equilibrium rules – raises the danger of misspecifying labour market processes. Rejection of the synchronic abstraction of economic orthodoxy opens the door to both historical and geographic contingency, a defining feature of a realist approach.

The strongest and most developed realist feature of institutional SLM [segmented labour market] research is its use of historical analysis to understand the nature of any given labour market phenomenon by identifying the conditions of its emergence and subsequent mutation. In contrast, neoclassical theory relies ... on a synchronic form of analysis, in which abstraction is used to isolate factors independently of time and locality. Institutional SLM researchers do not object to the use of abstraction per se, but rather to the specific way in which abstraction is used to isolate only time- and place-independent aspects of observed economic phenomena. They argue that *labour market outcomes are historically contingent* and that this cannot be ignored without possibly biasing the explanations – i.e., identifying incorrect causal mechanisms.

(Iacobacci 1992: 28, emphasis added)

Thus, sensitivity to historical and geographic contingency raises fundamental explanatory issues in labour market analysis.

However, segmentation theorists have proved more comfortable with historical than geographic contingency. Their conceptual frameworks, conditioned by 'empirical and historical investigation' (Wilkinson 1983: 414), have been described as 'historically specific and non-functionalist' (Humphries and Rubery 1984: 33). Although geographic specificity is occasionally acknowledged, it is typically only at the level of variations between national labour systems or what Rubery (1994) terms 'societal-specific production regimes'. [9] Similarly, uneven development in labour markets is often recognised between the productive sectors of national economies, but rarely between different regions. Even when their philosophical critique of economic orthodoxy suggests the need to take account of temporal *and spatial* contingency, segmentation theorists remain largely space-blind. As Hiebert (1994: 9) puts it, 'segmented labour-market theory is aspatial, implying the same processes operate at all places simultaneously' and, one might add, with more or less the same effects. What is required, therefore, is a fourth generation of segmentation theory, one that emphasises the spatiality of the labour market and its underlying regulatory forms.

Notes

1   For methodological statements, see Labour Studies Group (1985), Woodbury (1987), Lawson (1989) and Iacobacci (1992).
2   This argument has been made most persuasively by Humphries (1977), Meillassoux (1981), Picchio del Mercato (1981), Humphries and Rubery (1984), Picchio (1992) and Marshall (1994).
3   Bourdieu (1973); cf. Bourdieu and Passeron (1977) and Mingione (1991).
4   These social milieux are structured in accordance with not only ethnicity, gender, and class but also *location*, contributing to the geographically distinctive process by which segmented labour supplies mesh with segmented job structures (Peck 1989; Hanson and Pratt 1995). This represents one of the ways in which labour markets are locally embedded, as job-filling mechanisms and conventions vary from place to place.
5   This is one of the ways in which processes of job generation and labour process change (and more broadly the course of industry restructuring) are shaped by the contours of the labour supply, including its geographies.
6   For a slightly different perspective, emphasising the mutual constitution of the state and market, see Block (1994).
7   Cf. Deakin and Mückenberger (1992), Standing (1992) and Streeck (1992).
8   Cf. Granovetter and Swedberg (1992) and Amin and Thrift (1994).
9   For example, cf. Elbaum and Wilkinson (1979), Michon (1992) and Rubery (1992).

Bibliography

Amin, A. and Thrift, N. (eds) (1994) *Globalization, Institutions and Regional Development in Europe*, Oxford: Oxford University Press.

Barrett, M. and McIntosh, M. (1980) 'The "family wage": some problems for socialists and feminists', *Capital and Class*, 11, 52–72.

Berger, S. and Piore, M. J. (1980) *Dualism and Discontinuity in Industrial Societies*, Cambridge: Cambridge University Press.

Block, F. (1994) 'The roles of the state in the economy', in N. J. Smelser and R. Swedberg (eds) *The Handbook of Economic Sociology*, Princeton, NJ: Princeton University Press, 691–710.

Block, F., Cloward, R. A., Ehrenreich, B. and Piven, F. F. (1987) *The Mean Season: The Attack on the Welfare State*, New York: Random House.

Böhle, E. and Sauer, D. (1975) 'Intensivierung der Arbeit und staatliche Sozialpolitik', *Leviathan*, 3: 123–46.

Bourdieu, P. (1973) 'Cultural reproduction and social reproduction', in R. Brown (ed.) *Knowledge, Education and Cultural Change*, London: Tavistock, 71–112.

Bourdieu, P. and Passeron, J.-C. (1977) *Reproduction in Education, Society and Culture*, trans. R. Nice, London: Sage.

Castro, A., Méhaut, P. and Rubery, J. (eds) (1992) *International Integration and Labour Market Organisation*, London: Academic Press.

Coombs, R. (1985) 'Automation, management strategies and labour process change', in D. Knights, H. Willmott and D. Collinson (eds) *Job Redesign: Critical Perspectives on the Labour Process*, Aldershot: Gower, 142–70.

Craig, C., Rubery, J., Tarling, R. and Wilkinson, F. (1982) *Labour Market Structure, Industrial Organisation and Low Pay*, Department of Applied Economics Occasional Paper 54, Cambridge: Cambridge University Press.

Deakin, S. and Mückenberger, U. (1992) 'Deregulation and European labour markets', in A. Castro, P. Méhaut and J. Rubery (eds) *International Integration and Labour Market Organisation*, London: Academic Press, 135–49.

de Brunhoff, S. (1978) *The State, Capital and Economic Policy*, London: Pluto Press.

Doeringer, P. B. and Piore, M. J. (1971) *Internal Labor Markets and Manpower Analysis*, Lexington, MA: D. C. Heath.

Dunlop, J. T. (1964) 'Review of Turner', *British Journal of Industrial Relations*, 2: 287–92.

Edwards, R. (1979) *Contested Terrain: The Transformation of the Workplace in the Twentieth Century*, London: Heinemann.

Elbaum, B. and Wilkinson, F. (1979) 'Industrial relations and uneven development: a comparative study of American and British steel industries', *Cambridge Journal of Economics*, 3: 275–303.

Fine, B. (1987) *Segmented Labour Market Theory: A Critical Assessment*, Birkbeck Discussion Paper 87/12, London: Department of Economics, Birkbeck College.

Freedman, M. (1976) *Labor Markets: Segments and Shelters*, London: Allanheld.

Garnsey, E., Rubery, J. and Wilkinson, F. (1985) 'Labour market structure and work-force divisions', in R. Deem and G. Salaman (eds) *Work, Culture and Society*, Milton Keynes: Open University Press, 40–75.

Gordon, D. M. (1972) *Theories of Poverty and Underemployment*, Lexington, MA: D. C. Heath.

Gordon, D. M., Edwards, R. C. and Reich, M. (1982) *Segmented Work, Divided Workers: The Historical Transformation of Labor in the United States*, Cambridge: Cambridge University Press.

Granovetter, M. (1981) 'Towards a sociology of income differences', in I. Berg (ed.) *Sociological Perspectives on Labor Markets*, New York: Academic Press, 11–47.

Granovetter, M. and Swedberg, R. (eds) (1992) *The Sociology of Economic Life*, Boulder, CO: Westview Press.

Hanson, S. and Pratt, G. (1995) *Gender, Work and Space*, New York: Routledge.

Hartman, H. I. (1979) 'The unhappy marriage of Marxism and feminism: towards a more progressive union', *Capital and Class*, 8: 1–33.

Haughton, G. (1990) 'Skills shortage and the demographic timebomb: labour market segmentation and the geography of labour', *Area*, 22: 339–45.

Hiebert, D. (1994) 'Labour-market segmentation in three Canadian cities', paper presented at the Annual Meeting of the Association of American Geographers, March, San Francisco.

Hinrichs, K., Offe, C. and Wiesenthal, H. (1988) 'Time, money and welfare-state capitalism', in J. Keane (ed.) *Civil Society and the State: New European Perspectives*, London: Verso, 221–43.

Humphries, J. (1976) 'Women: scapegoats and safety valves in the Great Depression', *Review of Radical Political Economics*, 8: 98–121.

——(1977) 'Class struggle and the persistence of the working class family', *Cambridge Journal of Economics*, 1: 241–58.

Humphries, J. and Rubery, J. (1984) 'The reconstitution of the supply side of the labour market: the relative autonomy of social reproduction', *Cambridge Journal of Economics*, 8: 331–46.

Iacobacci, M. (1992) 'The institutionalist approach to segmented labour markets: a realist interpretation', King's College, Cambridge, Mimeo.

Jacoby, S. (1990) 'The new institutionalism: what can it learn from the old?', *Industrial Relations*, 29: 316–59.

Jones, E. (1983) 'Industrial structure and labour force segmentation', *Review of Radical Political Economics*, 15: 24–44.

Kerr, C. (1954) 'The balkanization of labor markets', in E. W. Bakke (ed.) *Labor Mobility and Economic Opportunity*, Cambridge, MA: The MIT Press, 92–110.

Kreckel, R. (1980) 'Unequal opportunity structure and labour market segmentation', *Sociology*, 14: 524–49.

Labour Studies Group (1985) 'Economic, social and political factors in the operation of the labour market', in B. Roberts, R. Finnegan and D. Gallie (eds) *New Approaches to Economic Life: Restructuring, Unemployment and the Social Division of Labour*, Manchester: Manchester University Press, 105–23.

Lawson, T. (1989) 'Abstraction, tendencies and stylised facts: a realist approach to economic analysis', *Cambridge Journal of Economics*, 13: 59–78.

Lever-Tracy, C. (1984) 'The paradigm crisis of dualism: decay or regeneration?', *Politics and Society*, 13: 59–89.

Marsden, D. (1986) *The End of Economic Man? Custom and Competition in Labour Markets*, Brighton: Wheatsheaf.

Marshall, B. L. (1994) *Engendering Modernity: Feminism, Social Theory and Social Change*, Cambridge: Polity Press.

McDowell, L. and Court, G. (1994) 'Missing subjects: gender, power and sexuality in merchant banking', *Economic Geography*, 70: 229–51.

Meillassoux, C. (1981) *Maidens, Meal and Money: Capitalism and the Domestic Community*, Cambridge: Cambridge University Press.

Michon, E. (1987) 'Segmentation, employment structures and productive structures', in R. Tarling (ed.) *Flexibility in Labour Markets*, London: Academic Press, 23–55.

Michon, F. (1992) 'The institutional forms of work and employment: towards the construction of an international historical and comparative approach', in A. Castro, P. Méhaut and J. Rubery (eds) *International Integration and Labour Market Organisation*, London: Academic Press, 222–43.

Mingione, E. (1991) *Fragmented Societies: A Sociology of Economic Life Beyond the Market Paradigm*, trans. P. Goodrick, Oxford: Blackwell.

Offe, C. and Hinrichs, K. (1977) 'Sozialokonomie des Arbeitsmarktes und die lage "benachteiligter" Gruppen von Arbeitnehmern', in C. Offe (ed.) *Opfer des Arbeitsmarktes: zur theorie der strukturierten arbeitslosigkeit*, Neuwied-Darmstadt: Luchterhand, 3–61.

——(1985) 'The political economy of the labour market', in C. Offe, *Disorganized Capitalism: Contemporary Transformations of Work and Politics*, Cambridge: Polity Press, 10–51.

Offe, C. and Lenhardt, G. (1984) 'Social policy and the theory of the state', in C. Offe (ed.) *Contradictions of the Welfare State*, London: Hutchinson, 88–118.

Offe, C. and Weisenthal, H. (1980) 'Two logics of collective action: theoretical notes on social class and organizational form', *Political Power and Social Theory*, 1: 67–115.

Peck, J. (1989) 'Reconceptualizing the local labour market: space, segmentation and the state', *Progress in Human Geography*, 13: 42–61.

Picchio, A. (1992) *Social Reproduction: The Political Economy of the Labour Market*, Cambridge: Cambridge University Press.

Picchio del Mercato, A. (1981) 'Social reproduction and the basic structure of labour markets', in. F. Wilkinson (ed.) *The Dynamics of Labour Market Segmentation*, London: Academic Press, 193–209.

Piven, E. F. and Cloward, R. A. (1971) *Regulating the Poor: The Functions of Public Welfare*, London: Tavistock.

——(1993) *Regulating the Poor: The Functions of Public Welfare*, updated edition, New York: Vintage.

Reich, M., Gordon, D. M. and Edwards, R. C. (1973) 'A theory of labor market segmentation', *American Economic Review*, 63: 359–65.

Robinson, J. (1979) 'History versus equilibrium', in *Collected Economic Papers of Joan Robinson*, 5: 48–58, Oxford: Blackwell.

Rubery, J. (1978) 'Structured labour markets, worker organisation and low pay', *Cambridge Journal of Economics*, 2: 17–36.

——(ed.) (1988) *Women and Recession*, London: Routledge & Kegan Paul.

——(1989) 'Precarious forms of work in the United Kingdom', in G. Rodgers and J. Rodgers (eds) *Precarious Jobs in Labour Market Regulation: The Growth of Atypical Employment in Western Europe*, Geneva: International Institute for Labour Studies, International Labour Office, 49–74.

——(1992) 'Productive systems, international integration and the single European market', in A. Castro, P. Méhaut and J. Rubery (eds) *International Integration and Labour Market Organisation*, London: Academic Press, 244–61.

——(1994) 'The British production regime: a societal-specific system?', *Economy and Society*, 23: 335–54.

Rubery, J. and Tarling, R. (1982) 'Women in the recession', in D. Currie and M. Sawyer (eds) *Socialist Economic Review 1982*, London: Merlin Press, 47–76.

Rubery, J., Wilkinson, F. and Tarling, R. (1989) 'Government policy and the labor market: the case of the United Kingdom', in S. Rosenberg (ed.) *The State and the Labor Market*, New York: Plenum Press, 23–45.

Ryan, T. (1981) 'Segmentation, duality and the internal labour market', in F. Wilkinson (ed.) *The Dynamics of Labour Market Segmentation*, London: Academic Press, 3–20.

Seccareccia, M. (1991) 'An alternative to labour market orthodoxy: the post-Keynesian/institutionalist policy view', *Review of Political Economy*, 3: 43–61.

Sengenberger, W. (1981) 'Labour market segmentation and the business cycle', in F. Wilkinson (ed.) *The Dynamics of Labour Market Segmentation*, London: Academic Press, 243–59.

Sorensen, A. B. and Kalleberg, A. L. (1981) 'An outline of a theory of matching persons to jobs', in I. Berg (ed.) *Sociological Perspectives on Labor Markets*, New York: Academic Press, 49–74.

Standing, G. (1992) 'Alternative routes to labor flexibility', in M. Storper and A. J. Scott (eds) *Pathways to Industrialization and Regional Development*, London: Routledge, 255–75.

Streeck, W. (1992) 'National diversity, regime competition and industrial deadlock: problems in forming a European industrial relations system', *Journal for Public Policy*, 12: 301–30.

Tarling, R. (ed.) (1987) *Flexibility in the Labour Market*, London: Academic Press.

Thurow, L. C. (1975) *Generating Inequality*, New York: Basic Books.

Tomlins, C. L. (1984) 'Long swings and spatial yardsticks: directions in American labour history (2)', *Labour History*, 46: 128–41.

Turner, H. A. (1962) *Trade Union Growth, Structure and Policy: A Comparative Study of the Cotton Unions*, London: Allen and Unwin.

Villa, P. (1986) *The Restructuring of Labour Markets: A Comparative Analysis of the Steel and Construction Industries in Italy*, Oxford: Clarendon Press.

Wilkinson, F. (1983) 'Productive systems', *Cambridge Journal of Economics*, 7: 413–29.

——(1988) 'Deregulation, structured labour markets and unemployment', in P. J. Pederson and R. Lund (eds) *Unemployment: Theory, Policy, Structure*, Berlin: Walter de Gruyter, 167–85.

Willis, P. (1977) *Learning to Labour: How Working Class Kids Get Working Class Jobs*, Aldershot: Gower.

Woodbury, S. (1987) 'Power in the labor market: institutionalist approaches to labour problems', *Journal of Economic Issues*, 21: 1781–1807.

Zuscovitch, E., Heraud, J.-A. and Cohendet, P. (1988) 'Innovation diffusion from a qualitative standpoint: technology networks and economic evolution through case studies', *Futures*, 20: 266–306.

12 The British production regime

A societal-specific system?

Jill Rubery

Despite the recent change of government, Britain remains the European country least likely to endorse the high-skill, high-value-added model for the future of an integrated Europe. The notion of competitive advantage based on productivity and skill may be an ideal-type model to which no individual country conforms, let alone the European Union as a whole. Nevertheless, most European governments at least aspire to these goals, accepting that Europe can compete effectively in world markets only if it eschews the temptation of trying to undercut other European countries and Third World countries on the basis of low wages.

The UK is content to compete for jobs and for trade on the basis of low wage levels, even at the expense of productivity. In the early 1980s it directly endorsed the view that future jobs in the UK would not even be 'low tech' but in fact 'no tech' (Lawson 1984). These differences in approach came to a head over Maastricht when the UK government demanded an opt-out clause on the grounds that Britain would lose out in world competition if it was not able to offer inward investors the lowest pay and working conditions among advanced European countries. Minimum wage legislation notwithstanding, Britain is concerned not only to hold on to its current advantage in wage levels but also to enhance it by placing further pressure on wages and conditions in many parts of the employment system.

This distinctive British approach to competition within Europe provokes mixed reactions within the rest of the European Union. While at one level the UK can be, and often is, regarded as a maverick, pursuing its own very particular, but also self-defeating and destructive, model of economic development, there remains an underlying interest within all European states in the functioning of the UK production system. This arises out of the presumption, propagated by the Blair government, that the UK production regime is the most flexible in Europe, the closest to a pure market regime.

New Labour's continuing experiment in so-called free market economics underpins the interest in what might otherwise be considered a marginal and not very successful model of economic and social organisation, measured by indicators such as trade performance or productivity levels. Nevertheless, according to advocates of the free market approach, the UK may provide a pointer to the future organisation of Europe, once the historical baggage of a commitment to a welfare state and to national industrial policy is dispensed with. Even those who reject this model still feel obliged to pay attention to developments within the UK in order to better understand the enemy 'within' (not only 'within' the European Union, but also a potential model which may emerge within any of the individual nation states).

Societal system: the case of Britain

The purpose of this paper is to contribute to the continuing debate over the existence and persistence of different production regimes in Europe through the study of the specificities of the UK production and labour market system. The approach adopted is related to the societal system model, whereby the characteristics of a nation's production system are seen as inter-related with a whole set of social and economic conditions and institutions (Maurice *et al.* 1986). This societal system approach has developed in opposition to the notion of a universalist process of convergence between nation states as a consequence of international integration based on free trade.[1] From this perspective there is no organisation's one 'best way' of organising production, and economic organisation must be regarded as socially embedded, and not as 'distorted' by social factors and institutions. Each societal system is seen to have a certain internal coherence, which generates both the society's specific 'comparative advantage' within the international economy but also at the same time forecloses other options or paths of development and inhibits individual organisations from breaking free and developing alternative modes of operation. This societal systems approach, developed initially through comparisons between France and Germany but also applied to a limited extent to Britain (see, for example, Lane 1992; Sorge 1991), has the merits of the holistic approach to analysis. Factors and characteristics of an economic system are treated in context and the complex correlations between the economy and the society are fully understood. For example, a system of training is related not only to firms' production needs but also to the career paths and expectations of workers and indeed to the system of reproduction of skills that operates within the society.

However, a societal systems approach also has its dangers. Two in particular need to be highlighted here (Rubery 1992). First, there is a danger, as in any comparative analysis, of stressing the internal coherence and functioning of the productive system, and of thus paying less attention to the internal contradictions and tensions and the pressures for change inside and outside the system. An important source of these pressures and tensions will be the extent to which the system delivers an efficient and productive system of organisation as tested by world trade (Wilkinson 1983). The societal effect school in LEST has in fact paid relatively little attention to the issue of competitive success and to the tensions that arise under economic failure. Such tensions are now, for example, evident in Germany where a previously successful and coherent societal system may be unable to continue to deliver the economic prosperity on which the system is based. The responses to such pressures do not necessarily move a productive system in a direction in which the underlying problems may be solved. For example, short-term fiscal problems may push an economy to cut back on the social and economic infrastructure which may be a necessary precondition for the economic development necessary to resolve the long-term contradictions between aspirations and current output levels (Wilkinson 1983).

Comparative analysis also tends to overstress the functionalism of the aspects of societies that it identifies (as has constantly been identified as a problem within, for example, social anthropology). In developing society models to explore intercountry differences, the diversity within societies tends to be reduced to averages and norms which again may disguise as much as they reveal.

The second and related danger is a tendency to analyse societal systems as static and to pay insufficient attention to the ways in which systems evolve over time. The dynamic element in analysis is critical to the debate over European convergence and integration. What we need to distinguish between are differences in countries' production systems that exist at present but which may be expected to disappear over time (for example, differences attributable to stages of economic development or to the still incomplete integration into the wider European market), and differences that relate to inherently different ways of operation and organisation and which may be expected to increase as much as decrease over time.

The societal effect approach tends to emphasise the second over the first set of differences; if differences were primarily related to stages of development, then convergence may need to be orchestrated over a long time period (a two-tier Europe is often advocated, for example, to allow some countries longer to converge), but no long-term obstacles to convergence are held to exist. However, even if this convergence hypothesis is rejected, the question of change in societal systems over time must still be addressed. One important set of influences on this process of change will in fact be the process of international integration itself. These influences, as we discuss below, may create tensions and contradictions leading to transformations of societal systems. Yet such transformations will not necessarily bring about convergence – each particular societal system will respond in a different way to common forces[2] – but direct attention needs to be paid to the impact of internationalisation, not only of trade but also of technology, consumption patterns, intellectual and political ideas and ideologies. Societal systems that have previously been more isolated from the influences of the international community may experience relatively rapid and pervasive change as a consequence of these multi-dimensional influences.

This analysis of the advantages, disadvantages and shortcomings of the societal effect approach provides the basis for the following schematic analysis of the British productive system. Though this model has already been subject to much debate and analysis, we aim to contribute further to the discussion in two particular ways. First, we highlight some aspects of the interrelationships within the societal system which have been relatively neglected, at least in terms of the discussion of differences in labour market structures. Second, at the same time as highlighting these interrelationships and internal coherence, we will also focus on the tensions and forces for change, thus introducing a more dynamic element into the analysis of production regimes. We start the analysis by discussing the internal coherence of the system, and in particular the interrelations between production, consumption and social reproduction in the British context. In the second section we identify both the sources of tensions and conflicts within the UK system and consider the role of international influences on developments within the British system of production. We conclude by examining first of all the long-term prospects for Britain and, second, the impact on the European integration policy of Britain pursuing its policy of remaining outside the social dimension to Europe.

The British production system

The British production system is often characterised as a low-skill, low-value-added system of production, which competes in world trade and for foreign investment on the basis of low wages and lack of restrictions on the employment of labour (Finegold and Soskice 1988; Ashton *et al*. 1989; Keep 1989; Lane 1992). This production system has been described as a low-skill 'equilibrium'. The lack of a skilled labour force is argued not to be a problem from the perspective of individual British employers as they have in fact adjusted their systems of work organisation and production to make minimum demands on the work-force, other than acceptance of low wages and working-time patterns determined by management (short part-time work where necessary; long and flexible working hours where necessary (Marsh 1991)).

The literature on training and skills, which has grown extensively in Britain over recent years, has gone quite a long way towards explaining the basis of this low-skill equilibrium position. These analyses have argued that the low-skill labour force is a consequence of the long-term policy adopted towards training and education in the UK, reinforced by cultural attitudes and practices. Some analysts have also extended the debate to include the industrial relations system and particularly the absence of high-trust relations. These analyses have already identified the many faceted obstacles which confront individual firms or organisations which wish to break out of this mould and develop a more skill-intensive production system. However, the set of factors that interact to create a low-skill equilibrium production system can be identified as even wider than the labour market and industrial relations systems (Best 1990). Other aspects of the UK production regime identified as contributing to relative failure include a lack of managerial expertise inhibiting moves towards a higher value-added or higher skilled and more flexible production system, the historical limited role of the state and, of course, the influence of the finance system (Lane 1988; 1992; Williams *et al*. 1990).

All aspects of a country's production, consumption and social reproduction systems are necessarily interrelated. At one level this statement may be considered a truism, similar for example to the interdependencies of the circular flow of income. However, at another level these interdependencies are critical for understanding the ways in which different modes of operation are embedded in a societal system. It is not possible, for example, to look at the high share of women who work part-time in the UK without analysing the full set of reinforcing factors that have led to this outcome: favourable social security systems, the dominance of large firms in the service sector which have developed sophisticated working-time planning systems, the lack of child-care facilities and the establishment of standards of living based on a norm of a male bread-winner on long hours and a female part-time worker (Gregory 1991; O'Reilly 1992; Marsh 1991; Rubery 1989).

To understand how societies may move into self-reinforcing vicious or virtuous circles it is necessary to examine these interactions and interrelationships between elements of the societal system, instead of the alternative cross-sectional and a historical approach to data analysis. Yet it is also necessary, for purposes of analysis, to be selective about the components of the system which should be highlighted and at which interactions or links take on critical importance. This selection is necessarily subjective, varying according to the analyst's interests and competencies as well as between countries. For example, the dominance accorded to the educational system by the LEST would not necessarily be found in other societal systems where educational divisions may be less related to the structuring of employment than in France. The selection of areas for analysis also reflects the issue or question to be addressed. Our interest here is in the type of labour market organisation that the UK production regime generates, and this leads to a somewhat different list of criteria than analyses focused on, for example, differences in business systems (Lane 1992), although of course the two impact upon each other.

The interrelationships that we have chosen to highlight in the case of Britain are: first, the relationship between consumption, distribution and production systems; second, the relationship between the systems of education and training, career paths in the labour market and the production system; third, the relationship between the labour market system and the organisation of families and social reproduction (see Figure 12.1). The elements included here that are often neglected in discussions of, for example, UK training and skills policy or UK working-time patterns, are on the one hand the influence of the consumption and distribution systems and on the other the social reproduction system. Nevertheless other relevant elements, such as the industrial relations regime, the fiscal regime and the financial regime, which have been more fully discussed elsewhere, are either omitted from the discussion or alluded to only in passing.

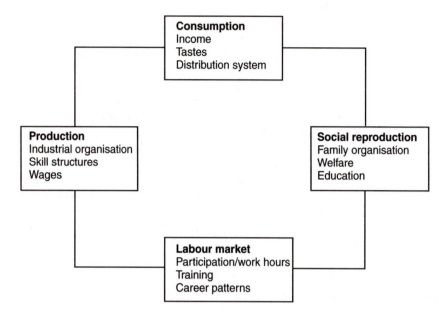

Figure 12.1   Selected elements of a societal system

Consumption distribution and the production system

Much of the debate around changing competitive requirements in the 1980s and 1990s has centred on the increased need for higher-quality output, more customised to meet consumer tastes and with the emphasis on non-price competition. Part of the economic convergence argument depended on the notion that increased penetration of markets had resulted in firms having to compete on variety and style and not simply on producing standard commodities at the lowest possible price (Piore and Sabel 1984; Best 1990). This argument assumed that the penetration of international markets would have similar impacts on consumption patterns in all countries. One of the main arguments that has been made explaining Britain's poor economic performance has been the absence of a suitably trained managerial and non-managerial labour force to meet these new production requirements. However, this argument presupposes that the main constraint on the UK production regime moving up-market was to be found in the labour market, and associated government policies towards labour.

Indeed, the emphasis on increasing quality in product markets has tended to confuse similarities in trends with similarities in outcomes and indeed levels. Search for higher quality in some markets certainly implied the development of designer-based luxury products, but in countries such as the

UK the trend to higher quality was still compatible with mass marketing of relatively cheap commodities. Studies of consumer goods industries in the UK have found that these changes in consumer tastes, far from providing manufacturing firms with the basis for moving towards a higher-value-added production system and creating scope for the development of new products, have instead acted as an additional constraint imposed upon organisations geared up to produce standard low-quality commodities (Rubery and Wilkinson 1989). Instead of being able to produce in large batch against stable demands, firms have had to provide goods against short-run and variable orders but priced on the basis of large-batch standard commodities. Flexibility in the production systems in many consumer industries has thus been used to provide flexibility to the large and dominant retail chains and not to enhance the market position of the producer.

The British low-wage economy has been reflected in the maintenance of low-price and low-quality distribution outlets. The dominance of large retailers, and indeed large companies in other service areas such as catering, has restricted the development of manufacturers and service producers designed to serve the higher end of the market; where demands for higher quality products develop, these are often in practice served by imports as the scale of the domestic market is too small or too fragmented for British producers accustomed to dealing with large retail chains. Thus, in the case of the footwear industry, we found the paradoxical position of the small flexible Italian firms receiving the large-batch advance orders from British retailers, with the larger and more Tayloristic UK firms expected to pick up the small, repeat and flexible orders as the season progressed (Courault 1992; Rubery and Wilkinson 1989). Similar findings in clothing, hosiery and furniture (Rubery *et al.* 1987; 1992; Best 1990) all suggest that in large areas of consumer production, British manufacturers have the 'worst of all worlds', lacking the independence and power to move into high-value-added, small-batch production but denied the stability and size of orders necessary to reap traditional benefits of economies of scale. However, as the experiments of industrial policy in the early 1980s revealed, there is no easy solution for the independent producer; the domestic market infrastructure appropriate for a higher-value-added production system may not be in place and a producer may well be adopting an entirely rational strategy in remaining within the network of the dominant retailers. These arguments provide important caveats to the debate about training; many studies have bemoaned the short-termism of UK producers and their unwillingness to invest in high skills and training. Such strategies may be a necessary condition for developing a more effective industrial strategy but they are by no means sufficient, and training staff in the absence of an effective industrial strategy is likely to lead both to the waste of resources and to frustration on all sides about the under-utilisation of skills.[3]

The vicious circle in which producers are trapped is only one part of the problems restricting the adjustment of the UK economy to modern training conditions. Another problem is that profitability of capital does not neces-sarily depend on the development of a strong manufacturing and servicing base. A particular feature of the UK government policy since 1979 has been the support for a profit-based strategy for firms at the expense of any consid-eration of the development of the real economy which may be necessary to sustain the profitability of the UK production system. Most British firms do not see themselves as producers but as asset managers; issues such as devel-oping new products and technologies to enhance Britain's long-term competitiveness are treated very much as second- or third-order importance to ensuring a decent return on capital even if this means divesting all direct manufacturing activities. This 'hollowing out' of the British economy is a further, and arguably equally important, reason why individual organisations will not necessarily take the steps needed to develop a high-value-added skilled production system (Williams *et al.* 1990; Cutler 1992). It is also a demonstration of one further feature of the UK production system often referred to in the literature: that is, the dominance of accountants over engi-neers in steering organisational strategy, a dominance that in turn can be related to historical trends in the education system and to the specific rela-tionships between the city and industry in Britain.

The current comparisons of the UK production system cannot take on board the analysis of the specific development of the UK, let alone an histor-ical analysis of how and why the development took a particular form. Our main focus here is on the various elements that contribute to the mainte-nance of a 'low-skill' production system, although some may argue the more interesting question is why there is so little concern with the real economy in all its aspects in the management of the British economy.

Skills, training and the labour market

Numerous comparisons of the UK and German and French firms in different industries have revealed not only a skill deficiency in the UK labour force but also a system of low skill embedded in industrial work organisation (see, for example, Steedman and Wagner 1987; 1989; Lane 1988; 1990). Firms minimise their requirements for skilled staff by using a detailed division of labour and by compensating for lack of skill on the production side by the use of supervisors and quality control inspectors. This alternative may be argued to be as cost-effective as a high-skill, mass-training system, particularly given the risk of labour poaching. However, the studies also make clear that the skill deficiencies are not fully compen-sated for: productivity is markedly lower per person employed, such that differences in pay between skilled and unskilled are likely to offset these productivity differences; UK firms are geared to the production of low-quality products; and UK firms are more likely to make more limited use of capital equipment, both by investing less and by making less effective use of such equipment as is installed. Managers and employees lack the basic educational knowledge necessary to program and implement the equipment effectively and the interactive capacities of office equipment and the like are under-utilised because of a lack of both trained staff and managerial expertise to implement such systems.

The reasons for this low-skill equilibrium have been variously attributed first to the voluntarist approach to training in the UK, which apart from a brief interlude from 1964 to 1981 has historically almost always been left to the market and to training within firms independently of the education system. The other major factor has been argued to be the negative attitude towards vocational education or training within the UK cultural system. The new vocational qualifications, NVQs, could be interpreted as an attempt to overcome this long-term historical disregard for vocational skills and training; the NVQs assess skills on the basis of actual competencies at work and are thus an alternative to academic study and abstract training on the route to qualification. This new approach to training could equally well be regarded as a method of consolidating the low-skill base of the British economy; the levels set by NVQs compare unfavourably to, for example, the standards expected in the German system and the emphasis on competencies alone means that there is no attempt to combine basic education in core subjects with vocational training, but instead an emphasis on narrow job-related competence testing unconnected to abstract knowledge and understanding (for a critique of firm-specific and narrow job training, see Streeck 1989).

The low-skill system in Britain can be argued to arise out of a number of strongly reinforcing factors. These include:

(i)   the maintenance of a large-batch, low-value-added production system as described above;
(ii) the influence of the elitist educational traditions in the UK which tend to divide children at an early age into those that are expected to achieve within academic subjects and those that are not, with the majority falling into the latter category;
(iii) the lack of government intervention in the training system, such that firms are not compelled to train and often are not able to make use of readily available training systems;
(iv) the prevalence of a low-wage system which reduces employers' incentives to train as more skilled workers may demand higher wage levels;
(v)   the relationship between vocational training and union craft organisation, such that training outside these areas has been neglected, and within them training has been regarded as akin to supporting trade union restrictive practices;
(vi) the low-trust industrial relations systems that exist in at least parts of the British production system and which therefore inhibit the development of a highly skilled flexible production system;

(vii) and, last but by no means least, the absence of a strong relationship between training and career prospects in Britain.

In many of the comparative case studies British workers have been implicitly criticised for their lack of interest in training and their desire to move out of trainee positions into a 'proper job'. Such attitudes may, however, be entirely rational and indeed forward thinking within a UK context. It is certainly clear that completion of a YT training course does not provide a passport to stable employment or to jobs with chances of advancement (Bynner and Roberts 1990). These problems also apply to those who stay within the education system to undertake education or training past the age of 18 but not related to higher education. Evidence suggests that members of the same cohort who succeed in obtaining a job at 16 fare better than those who seek to advance their education or training (Clarke 1991). One of the major problems for the new system of NVQs in gaining widespread acceptance by workers and employers is the question as to what benefit they will be in enhancing careers. If employers choose to ignore such qualifications, as they appear to do for a wide range of vocational qualifications at present, then the system itself will prove to be unworkable as there will be little incentive on the part of employees to obtain NVQ qualifications. Thus in Britain, outside the apprenticeship system which affected primarily craft, male, manual workers, the relationship between training and career opportunities has been at best indeterminate and at worst negative. In Germany we perhaps find the opposite system, which in some respects is no more rational than that found in the UK. Here because of the widespread use of the apprenticeship system as a credential for entry into intermediate- and higher-level jobs, young people are willing to take on and complete a lengthy training in an occupation where the prospects for employment are extremely limited (Bynner and Roberts 1990; Maier and Quack 1992). They use this training then as a passport to another occupation where they may have actually very limited opportunity to use the skills they have learnt, although the general education that goes with the apprenticeship may be more transferable and useful in all occupations.

The labour market and social reproduction

The features that distinguish the UK labour market from that of its European competitors are linked not only to the specific industrial organisation in Britain but to the specific firm of social organisation. Three schematic examples can be given.

First, the high levels of low-skill, part-time work among women are related to:

(i) the continuing tendency for women in Britain to quit the labour market at childbirth, which results in a large supply of female returners who are often unable to re-enter at a level equivalent to their qualifications;

(ii) the absence of child-care support, either from the state or from extended family arrangements;

(iii) the prevalence of a social norm that it is appropriate for women with children to work part-time but not full-time. This social norm may have even greater influence than the presence or absence of child care (see, for example, the comparison with the United States where women do work full-time in the absence of any state-provided child care). Alwin *et al.* (1992) provide evidence on differences in social attitudes towards mothers in full-time and part-time work in the UK, Germany and the US, which endorse the actual practices in those countries.

Second, the tendency for men to work long hours in Britain (Marsh 1991) is not only a consequence of employer policy in the absence of regulation. All evidence suggests that British men are willing to work long hours and often deliberately seek jobs with overtime opportunities. This preference may at least in part be related to family organisation and family budgets. First, the expectation that male full-timers will work long hours in the UK may restrict the opportunities for women to consider taking on full-time work. The norm of the woman in the partnership working part-time may then increase the willingness of men to seek overtime work as a means of supplementing family income. Thus, the model of men working long, full-time hours and women working part-time may be reinforced by the actions of individuals to increase family income. It is notable that this model of the nuclear family is taken to be the common-sense model within British society but bears little resemblance to the models adopted in other European states. For example, in the Scandinavian countries the model is more one of short, full-time work for both partners (Jonung and Persson 1993) or in France of medium, full-time work for both, with even part-timers effectively working a short, full week.

Third, the organisation of the UK labour market can be seen to be strongly related to the system of education and training and of income support for the young. The low participation in higher education in Britain has meant that the youth labour market is both large and consists of workers who are seeking entry into long-term employment on a full-time basis. In contrast, in other countries much of the youth labour market consists of people who are still partially in education or training and who may be seeking, for example, temporary or part-time work to provide income support for their education. One factor which has perhaps decreased the number of young people willing to train in Britain is that the family system is geared to young people making independent contributions to their upkeep at an earlier age than in many countries. There is considerable pressure on young people to find a 'proper job' when leaving school, and even within the higher education system support for young adults has up until recently been provided primarily by the state and not by the family system. The lack of a tradition of family-based support for education and training thus places an additional obstacle in the way of policies designed to increase the scale of further and higher education and training in Britain.

The British productive system: coherence or conflict?

The model we have presented so far has been of a coherent and interlocking system of consumption, production and social reproduction, all tending towards the establishment and reinforcement of a low-skill, low-value-added economy. In many aspects there is considerable validity in a vicious circle approach to the UK economy, but it would be wrong to present the system as a harmoniously and smoothly adjusting model, albeit in a downward direction away from a prosperous, skill-based system. Conflicts and tensions, whether suppressed or overt, are inherent in the UK system as indeed in any 'societal model'. In considering these conflicts, tensions and indeed pressures for change, it is useful to discuss first those that relate to what could be called the real economy – to disharmonies in the various balance sheets of the economy. In the second section we look at the British model and how it has survived, adapted and changed in response to more external influences, in particular, to the spread of ideas and ideologies across nation-state boundaries, including the increasing influence of, or knowledge of, other modes of operation.

Tensions, conflicts and imbalances

The British productive system could be, and is often described as, providing an alternative mode of competition to that of the highly regulated and high-wage economy. The advantages of the British system are identified in its supposed flexibility and in its ability to compete on the basis of labour costs. However, identification of a different mode of competition does not guarantee that this mode is capable of delivering competitive success when measured in terms, for example, of the balance of trade. It is in the relative failure of the British productive system to deliver competitive success on world markets that the strongest tensions and conflicts in the UK model arise. The imbalance in trade arises from both consumption and production patterns. British labour costs are not sufficiently low to allow successful competition in standard low-wage-cost commodities; British consumers have developed tastes for commodities that can often best be met from imports. This is either because they are high-quality and high-tech goods which British firms do not produce or because Britain, as a low-wage economy but with well-developed and internationalised consumption patterns, consumes high-fashion products produced at low cost, often imported from the Third World. These imbalances on the foreign exchange markets are kept in check by monetary and fiscal policy which restricts the level of employment, thereby causing tensions between the employed and the unemployed. Unlike the textbook model of competition between firms, competition between nation states will not necessarily result in the elimination of unproductive regimes. Nation states do not disappear under competitive pressure and will usually continue to survive even under conditions of great indebtedness. Thus long-term relative failure is still a possible outcome, even if this failure leads to internal tensions and conflicts.

In addition to these macro-economic imbalances there are conflicts and tensions at a micro-level. British firms have adjusted to a long-term low-skill equilibrium, but this does not prevent the emergence of skill shortages whenever the economy speeds up a little or even whenever a firm wishes to expand over and above its planned level.

Deregulation of the labour market has encouraged the growth of low-wage employment. It has also provided the opportunity for substantial increases in pay for those at the top end of the pay hierarchy, in both public and private sectors. These developments are likely to cause major problems in the future, particularly in the public sector. The system of national industry-level bargaining and national pay and grading scales was argued by Conservative governments to have led to the overpayment of wages for the less skilled relative to so-called market rates. However, perhaps the more important effect was to keep the lid on salaries of managerial and professional staff within the public sector. Deregulation and individualisation of pay has provided the opportunity for some cutbacks in wages for the low paid but the rapid rises in managerial salaries and in performance-related pay may be a long-term problem for public sector expenditure, and for the wage bill of private sector organisations. Of course, the most likely way within the current political context that these problems will be addressed is to exert further pressure on the middle and low paid in order to provide the funds for the increases for the higher paid. But there may be a limit to the cost savings that can be achieved through such strategies.

The UK has long been a low-wage, low-productivity economy with balance of payments problems. The long-term persistence of these characteristics does not mean that they did not generate tensions and conflicts. Indeed, it is arguable that the industrial relations reforms of the 1980s were designed to suppress the conflict that constantly evolved over the level of wages within the UK economy. The combination of high unemployment, industrial relations legislation and a weakened trade union movement and Labour Party may have acted to reduce the level of overt conflict. This does not mean, however, that there is not underlying tension and conflict over the distribution of both income and employment and that the British labour force has finally and forever accepted its role as the social dumping ground of Europe.

Nor is it the case that the 'model' of the nuclear family on which both labour market and social policy is based, that is of a male bread-winner and a female second-income or part-time worker, is either fully accepted or accepted by the majority of the population. True, most women who return to work in the context of the nuclear family do so on a part-time basis and rarely move back into full-time work. However, there are many households that do not conform to this model; there are more single parents, divorced and separated couples and more women staying on at work or returning to work very quickly after having children (McRae 1991). The current cohort of female returners may be keener to return to full-time work than the older cohorts, so it may be dangerous to predict future behaviour on the basis of past patterns. The result of these changes is increasing problems of poverty for women not embedded in the standard nuclear family, as women's wage and employment opportunities are still geared to second-income-earner status. There are other tensions over the long hours of work and lack of child care in the increasing number of families with two full-time workers. However, if women resist their use as a low-paid, part-time labour force, as is indicated by the higher share of women using maternity leave provisions rather than quit the labour force, changes in the educational system may be generated through an alternative labour supply for low-paid, part-time jobs. The switch from student grants to loans is increasing the number of students seeking to supplement their income while studying through work, and in the future Britain could follow the US route towards the use of youth rather than female labour in many catering and retail-type activities. Thus, adjustments can take place in the sources of labour supply for particular types of jobs, but the analysis of this adjustment process requires an understanding of institutional and non-market arrangements, such as the education and training system and the family system. The British production regime is as much conditioned by and related to forms of social organisation as other European regimes, even if these institutions increasingly lack coherence and stability.

Towards convergence or divergence

The British productive system has so far been analysed as if it has developed in isolation from the world economy and the international transmission of ideas, ideologies and modes of operation: in short, as if Britain was an isolated island whose only point of contact with the rest of the world was through trade. Instead, Britain has been the recipient of large amounts of inward foreign investment, which has brought with it not only capital but different managerial ideas and ideologies; it is integrated into the ideological and political debates of the international community; and it has itself sought to use the experience of other nations in designing and developing its own productive system. With these different but reinforcing channels of influence from the external community, it might be expected that the possibility of divergence in productive systems is being steadily eroded. If not forced to conform by the pressures of world trade, the international integration of firms and the spread of ideas freely across national boundaries might be expected to do the trick.

What is interesting, however, is the way in which these international influences can reinforce and increase as well as reduce differences. Contact with the rest of the world helps to highlight differences and indicate problems in the British productive system. For example, it is arguable that the current low level of interest in training in Britain would be even less if it were not for the role of foreign multinationals in stimulating interest in techniques of human resource management. Perhaps more significant is the adoption of the term human resource management in Britain to signify moves to minimise the role of unions in the work-force, but without the commitments to the investment in human resources and the associated employment guarantees that such a term implies.

A similar use can be seen to have been made of the concept of 'Japanisation'. Firms legitimate the changes they make to working conditions and modes of operation by reference both to the economic threat from Japan and to the established practices of Japanese firms (Marchington and Parker 1990: 100; Ackroyd *et al*. 1988). However, many of those changes are not towards a more skill-intensive production system but towards increased flexibility over working time and a reduced role for trade unions. No mention is made by employers of increased job security, and performance-related pay and internal competition between individuals is substituted for the Japanese model of team working achieved through job security and seniority-related pay.

There are many examples of how practice or policies pursued in other countries have been used in the UK context either to reinforce existing practice or to legitimate change. Even the neo-liberal experiment in the UK has been justified by reference to the fact that all European states have been concerned about the degree of labour market regulation and are seeking to deregulate their own systems; but this debate has ignored the differences in the starting points between Britain and other member states. Deregulation of the British labour market in the 1980s, when it started with a much lower degree of regulation than other European states, has acted to increase the degree of divergence between the economies even if their regulatory trends appear to be in the same direction. Even the European ideal of a social dimension to the labour market has been used internally within Britain for ends that are not directly related to the European issue itself. The British Labour Party espoused the social charter idea and the notion of individual employment rights in part to enable it to refuse to promise to re-establish the pre-Thatcher status in industrial relations legislation. This move was arguably as much connected with an attempt to distance itself from the trade unions in order to increase its chances of being elected as with any specific commitment to or interest in Europe.

In the area of training and education the use and misuse of international comparisons has been rife. The employer-led Training and Enterprise

Councils were apparently modelled on a successful American system, but in reality these systems in the US were both less successful and less important than the UK government would have us believe (Bailey 1990; Peck 1992). The establishment of NVQs has been justified as a move towards raising the status of vocational skills, following practice in Germany and elsewhere, but little attention has been paid to the setting of lower attainment levels in Britain or to the exclusive focus on competences without the simultaneous continuing extension of general education that is the hallmark of the German system.

From even these examples it is clear that the spread of international ideas and the process of learning from other countries does not necessarily lead to convergence, as it is the interpretation and implementation of the ideas within a specific community which matters. In fact, the whole international-isation and integration trend depends not on automatic and inevitable market forces, but on how these influences are taken up and used within specific consumption, production and social reproduction systems.

To take the spread of international consumption patterns, it is arguable that in the UK there has been a rapid internationalisation of tastes, especially in the area of food, partly because of the tendency of the British to seek the sun abroad during their annual holidays. Yet this internationalisation is firmly within the control of the large retailer, who determines which particular brand of Italian bread or French cheese will be the next to be introduced on a mass scale into British households. The more fragmented distribution systems in other European countries, and indeed perhaps a better cuisine, has reduced the spread of 'international' consumption patterns.

In production, as we have already argued, the international move towards more flexible production systems has also taken a specific form in the UK; just-in-time and small-batch production systems are being introduced, but to meet the demands of the retailer and not to enhance the producer's position within the consumer market. Flexible employment systems are being used not to enhance the skill level of the labour force but to increase work intensification (Brunhes *et al.*1989).

Social reproduction systems are also open to 'internationalisation'. In Britain, the spread of feminist ideas has, as elsewhere, been associated with the increased integration of women into the economy. But in a deregulated labour market women are facing decreasing wages in part-time jobs, and where employed in higher-level jobs, for example in the public sector, they are in practice providing a relatively cheap alternative to men who are leaving the public sector as pay and prospects decline.

Conclusion

The British productive system has not evolved in isolation from the international community. The need to trade and compete within the international community helps to expose the deficiencies of the system as a long-term answer to economic growth and prosperity. However, the adaptations to the system that are called forth by these failures are not necessarily those that will enhance the long-term success of the British economy or bring it into convergence with other European states. Some of the remedies that are called for to solve British economic ills, including increased flexibility of the labour force, and less government expenditure and intervention, are often justified in the name of practices and policies in other states. The different starting points and cultural and economic conditions in these states are glossed over. However, these adaptations may postpone the fundamental adjustments required by the system to move onto a virtuous path of upskilling and growth. The problem of European convergence is thus not a static one; it is not simply a question of how to eliminate current differences but also of how to stop countries moving onto different tracks, and competing against each other, not only in terms of current differences in costs but on their ability to drive costs even lower. The British productive system is not static but is constantly evolving, under the influence of international integration. Yet the specific form that the evolution takes is determined by the ways in which these international influences are taken in and embedded into British-specific institutions and practices. The responses made by British firms to changes in product market conditions are constrained by the presence or absence of other institutions and institutional arrangements by the power of the dominant retailers on the one hand and the absence of institutional arrangements to generate a supply of skilled labour on the other. Thus, the British production system demonstrates the danger of assuming that deregulation will lead to efficient and productive adaptations to changing market conditions. Yet demonstration of the unsuitability of the British productive system as a model of feasible future development for Europe is not sufficient. The European integration process does not have to result in long-term relative success but can equally well result in long-term relative failure and decline. In this context European states and European citizens may well be right to worry about the potential destabilising effect of the British productive system uncontrolled by even the minimum regulatory regime that may emerge out of the Maastricht treaty.

Notes

1   This societal effect school is perhaps the best known but by no means the only approach to stress the societal embeddedness of economic organisation. Other examples include the associated work by Lutz, who undertook the German part of the original French/German comparisons, the work by Sorge and Warner (1986) and the business systems approach developed by Whitley (1992), the productive systems approach of Wilkinson (1983) and the work of the International Working Party on Labour Market Segmentation (Castro *et al.* 1992; Tarling 1987; Wilkinson 1981).

2   The approach adopted here is similar to that advocated with respect to the analysis of the articulation between the spheres of production and social
reproduction. Instead of seeing social reproduction systems either as determined
by the economic production systems, or as in more culturalist arguments,
entirely independently determined, the argument has been made that each
sphere should be considered to be 'relatively autonomous'. For example, developments in the production sphere influence the path of development of social
reproduction, but the adaptations these bring about are not determined by the
economic system but arise out of the dynamic development within the social
reproduction sphere (Humphries and Rubery 1984).

3   In the study of skills and training in the clothing industry young people in
Britain were implicitly criticised for their lack of interest in training (Steedman
and Wagner 1989). Yet this could be regarded as an entirely rational approach,
given the concentration of the industry in low-value-added products and the
poor job prospects in the industry.

Bibliography

Ackroyd, S. *et al.* (1998) 'The Japanisation of British industry?', *Industrial Relations Journal*, 19, 1: 11–23.

Alwin, D., Braun, M. and Scott, J. (1992) 'The separation of work and the family: attitudes towards women's labour-force participation in Germany, Great Britain and the United States', *European Sociologist Review*, 8, 1: 13–37.

Ashton, D. *et al.* (1989) 'The training system of British capitalism: changes and prospects', in F. Green (ed.) *The Restructuring of the UK Economy*, Brighton: Harvester-Wheatsheaf.

Bailey, T. (1990) 'The mission of the TECS and private sector involvement: lessons from the PICS', conference on US and UK Education and Training Policy in Comparative Perspective, University of Warwick, June.

Best, M. (1990) *The New Competition*, Oxford: Polity Press.

Brunhes, B., Rogot, J. and Wasserman, W. (1989) *Labour Market Flexibility: Trends in Enterprise*, Paris: OECD.

Brynner, J. and Roberts, K. (eds) *Youth and Work: Transition to Employment in England and Germany*, London: Anglo-German Foundation.

Castro, A., Méhaut, P. and Rubery, J. (eds) (1992) *International Integration and Labour Market Organisation*, London: Academic Press.

Clarke, K. (1991) *Women and Training: A Review*, Manchester: EOC Discussion Series.

Courault, B. (1992) 'Footwear manufacturers and the restructuring of distribution in the shoe industry: a challenge to the flexible specialisation analysis', in A. Castro *et al.* (eds) *International Integration and Labour Market Organisation*, London: Academic Press.

Cutler, T. (1992) 'Vocational training and Britain's economic performance', *Work, Employment and Society*, June.

Finegold, D. and Soskice, D. (1988) 'The failure of training in Britain: analysis and prescription', *Oxford Review of Economic Policy*, 4, 3.

Gregory, A. (1991) 'Patterns of working hours in large-scale grocery retailing in Britain and France: convergence after 1992?', *Work, Employment and Society*, 497–514.

Humphries, J. and Rubery, J. (1984) 'The reconstruction of the supply-side of the labour market: the relative autonomy of the labour market', *Cambridge Journal of Economics*, December.

Jonung, C. and Persson, I. (1993) 'Women and market work: the misleading tale of participation rates in international comparisons', *Work, Employment and Society*, 7, 2: 259–74.

Keep, E. (1989) 'A training scandal?', in K. Sisson (ed.) *Personnel Management in Britain*, Oxford: Blackwell.

Lane, C. (1988) 'Industrial change in Europe: the pursuit of flexible specialisation in Britain and West Germany', *Work, Employment and Society*, June.

——(1990) 'Vocational training, employment relations and new production concepts in Germany: some lessons for Britain', *Industrial Relations Journal*, Winter.

——(1992) 'European business systems: Britain and German compared', in R. Whitley (ed.) *European Business Systems*, London: Sage.

Lawson, N. (1984) 'Mais lecture', reprinted as 'The British experiment', *Public Money*, September.

McRae, S. (1991) *Maternity Rights in Britain*, London: Policy Studies Institute.

Maier, F. and Quack, S. (1992) *Occupational Segregation of Women and Men in Germany*, Report for the EC Network on the Situation of Women in the Labour Market.

Marchington, M. and Parker, P. (1990) *Changing Employee Relations*, Basingstoke: Macmillan.

Marsh, C. (1991) *Hours of Work of Women and Men in Britain*, EOC Research Series, London: HMSO.

Maurice, M., Sellier, F. and Silvestre, J.-J. (1986) *The Social Foundations of Industrial Power*, Cambridge, MA: MIT Press.

O'Reilly, J. (1992) 'Banking on flexibility', *International Journal of Human Resource Management*, March.

Peck, J. (1992) 'TECs and the local politics of training', *Political Geography*, July.

Persky, J. (1992) 'Regional competition, convergence and social welfare – the US case', in A. Castro *et al.* (eds) *International Integration and Labour Market Organisation*, London: Academic Press.

Piore, M. and Sabel, C. (1984) *The Second Industrial Divide*, New York: Basic Books.

Rubery, J. (1989) 'Precarious forms of works in the UK', in G. Rodgers and J. Rodgers (eds) *Precarious Jobs in Labour Market Regulation: The Growth of Atypical Employment in Western Europe*, Geneva: Academic Press.

——(1992) 'Productive systems and international integration', in A. Castro *et al.* (eds) *International Integration and Labour Market Organisation*, London: Academic Press.

Rubery, J. and Wilkinson, F. (1989) 'Distribution, flexibility of production and the British footwear industry', *Labour and Society*, 14, 2: 121–40.

Rubery, J. *et al.* (1987) 'Flexibility, marketing and the organisation of production', *Labour and Society*, March.

Rubery, J., Humphries, J. and Horrell, S. (1992) 'Women's employment in textiles and clothing', in R. Lindley (ed.) *Women's Employment: Britain in the Single European Market*, Equal Opportunities Commission, London: HMSO.

Sengenberger, W. (1992) 'Future prospects for the European Labour market: visions and nightmares', in A. Castro *et al.* (eds) *International Integration and Labour Market Organisation*, London: Academic Press.

Sorge, A. (1991) 'Strategic fit and the societal effect: interpreting cross-national comparisons of technology, organisation and human resources', *Organisation Studies*, 12, 2: 161–90.

Sorge, A. and Warner, M. (1986) *Comparative Factory Organisation: An Anglo-German Comparison of Management and Manpower in Manufacturing*, Aldershot: Gower.

Steedman, H. and Wagner, K. (1987) 'A second look at productivity, machinery and skills in Britain and Germany', *National Institute Economic Review*, No. 122, November.

——(1989) 'Productivity, machinery and skills: clothing manufacture in Britain and Germany', *National Institute Economic Review*, No. 128, May.

Streeck, W. (1989) 'Skills and the limits of neo-liberalism: the enterprise of the future as a place of learning', *Work, Employment and Society*, March.

Tarling, R. (ed.) (1987) *Flexibility of the Labour Market*, London: Academic Press.

Whitley, R. (ed.) (1992) *European Business Systems*, London: Sage.

Wilkinson, F. (1981) *The Dynamics of Labour Market Segmentation*, London: Academic Press.

——(1983) 'Productive systems', *Cambridge Journal of Economics*, 7, 3/4: 413–30.

Williams, K. *et al.* (1990) 'The hollowing out of British manufacturing', *Economy and Society*, December.

Index

Ackroyd, S. 3, 4, 11, 16, 18, 20, 51, 65, 87, 89, 97, 98, 101, 102, 259
action reductionism 51, 54, 58, 67, 68, 120, 148
actor–network theory 47, 49, 51–2
adaptation 91, 218, 261
agency 14, 15, 18–21, 28, 29, 34, 42, 98, 99, 102, 103, 108–9, 113, 157, 181, 188, 190
agency, personal 190–4
agency/structure debate 45–62, 113–17,120, 124, 127, 142–3, 145, 156, 164, 165, 167, 190–2, 200, 266
Ahrne, G. 88, 90
Alvesson, M. 3, 50, 62, 265
Alwin, D. 255, 262
Amabile, T.M. 196
Anderson, R.J. 97, 206
Anthony, P. 20, 65
Archer, M.S. 9, 17, 45, 51, 52, 58, 66, 68, 71, 73, 74, 75, 77, 78, 79, 80, 81, 82, 84
Armstrong, P. 34
Ashby, R.W. 39
Ashton, D. 248
Atkinson, P. 143, 144
authoritative communication 33

Bandura, A. 193, 196
Barker, J.R. 51, 62
Barley, S.R. 58
Barnard, C. 26, 33
Barrett, M. 229
Barron, F. 181
Barry, A. 50
Bauman, Z. 89
Beer, S. 31, 39
belief system 17, 18, 74
Berger, P.L. 30, 70, 145, 215, 233

Best, M. 51, 248, 250, 251
Bhaskar, R. 5, 9, 10, 13, 14, 28, 53, 54, 55, 67, 68, 69, 266
Billig, M. 196, 197
Bittner, E. 48
Block, F. 234, 268
Bloor, D. 82
Boddy, D. 29
Boden, D. 97
Bonoma, T.V. 74, 211
Bourdieu, P. 89, 90, 92, 93, 228
Braudel, F. 74, 98
Braverman, H. 5, 18, 26, 39, 98, 110,
Brewer, J.D. 144
British productive system 247, 256, 258, 260, 261
Brown, C. 154, 158
Bryant, C.G. 66
Bryman, A. 165
bureaucracy 26, 93, 104, 495
Burrell, G. 3, 50, 90, 93

capitalist mode of production 39, 125, 132; relations of production, 35, 38
Carroll, S. J. 27, 31, 34, 74
Carter, P. 3
case study method 164–6, 186, 211, 215, 218
Casey, C. 59, 60, 61
Castells, M. 59
Castoriadis, C.
Castro, A. 221, 238, 262
causal independence 145
causal powers 28, 29, 30, 36, 39, 40, 41, 53, 55, 57, 58, 67, 68, 73, 74, 82, 208, 209, 210, 211, 212, 214, 217, 237
central conflation 73, 78
Chandler, A. 26, 31
Chia, R. 3, 46, 47, 49

Child, J. 102
choice 40, 49, 55, 106, 118, 162, 167,
    190, 194, 204, 217, 228
Chomsky, 5
Clark, P. 9, 24
class 26, 57, 59, 127; consciousness
    222; fractions 92; relations 6, 11, 12,
    35; structure 99, 237; struggle 221;
    under class 105; working class 101,
    228, 229, 230, 231
Clegg, S. 46
Clemson, B. 39
closed systems 12, 40, 118, 213
closure 28, 40, 86, 155
Cloward, R.A. 234
collective solidarity 91
Collier, A. 5, 52, 53, 68
Commons, J. 5
concept dependent 11, 12, 126, 215
concept determined 8, 12
constant conjunction 6, 12, 13, 110,
    111, 118, 144, 148, 158
constructivism 61, 207, 215, 216, 266
controlling 31, 37, 38, 103, 186, 199,
    201
convergence 119, 224, 246, 247, 250,
    260, 261, 262, 263
conversation 17, 48, 97, 150, 169, 171,
    172, 174, 195
Coombs, R. 225
Cooper, R. 3, 46, 50
Corbin, J. 183
Court, G. 233
Cowen, R. 184, 189
Cox, T. 82
Craib, I. 72, 147
Craig, C. 227, 230, 231, 232
Crane, D. 76
cultural system 76, 253
culture 17, 19, 61, 66, 67, 68, 70, 71,
    76, 77, 78, 82, 84, 86, 92, 99, 103,
    129, 153, 154, 168, 169, 172, 176,
    179, 188, 189, 190
Currie, D. 184
CVCP 189, 203
cybernetics 39

Daft, R. 31
David, P.A. 164
Deetz, S. 3
DeGross, J.I. 179, 180
Delbridge, R. 5
deregulation 235, 261

Dey, I. 183
diachronic analysis 239
DiMaggio, P.J. 103
discourses 4, 6, 7, 8, 10, 11, 12, 17, 21,
    48, 51, 52, 82, 167
discursive penetration 71, 73, 193, 195
disembedding 103, 104
dissent 22, 84, 97, 99, 101, 102
disturbance handling 37
divergence 126, 258, 259
Doeringer, P.B. 222, 223, 225
domain actual 13, 14, 27, 28, 30, 35,
    36, 38, 40, 111, 120, 164, 196, 197,
    207, 208, 210, 215, 111; empirical
    111; intransitive 113; real 111;
    transitive 113
Donaldson, L. 3
double hermeneutic 11
Douglas, J. 65
Douglas, M. 161
dualism, analytical 46, 48, 51, 61, 66,
    67, 68, 73, 74, 82, 84; Cartesian 67,
    68, 71, 72, 73, 77
Dunlop, J.T. 231
Durkheim, E. 5, 88, 90, 91

Easton, G. 11, 21, 205, 206
Edmondson, A. 195
Edwards, D. 222, 225
Edwards, R.C. 196
effectiveness 31, 34, 39, 40, 102, 116,
    146, 163, 207
efficiency 29, 39, 40, 102, 151, 235
Ehrenreich, B. 23
Eisenhardt, K.M. 165, 214
emancipatory potential, 23
embedding, 26, 103
emergent powers 30, 68, 83, 241
emergent/emergence 26, 32, 55, 71, 72,
    73, 74, 77, 109, 110, 127, 128, 239,
    257, 266
empirical techniques 4, 241
Engels, F. 120, 121, 122, 123
entrepreneurship 37
epistemic fallacy 15, 80, 266
epistemology 6, 10, 27, 53, 80, 144,
    207, 213, 216, 266; causal,
    positivist, realist
ethnographic research methods 19, 141
experiences 13, 28, 29, 31, 62, 111,
    119, 154, 179, 192, 208, 233
expert systems 105
explanation, 4, 13, 15, 17, 18, 29–42,

46, 53, 55, 72, 112–14, 118, 127, 134, 143, 152, 154, 157, 158, 164, 207, 209, 210, 212, 221, 236; deductive-nomological 23; inductive-probabilistic 23; realist, 55–8
explanatory pluralism 56
explanatory power 15, 46, 48, 49, 61, 134, 143, 214

Farr, J.L 181
Fayol, H. 26, 31
Ferguson, K.E. 57
fetishism 125
Feyerabend, P. 110
Fiske, D.W. 181
Fleetwood, S. 3, 9, 12
flexible firm 226
Fondas, N. 194
Fordist 104
formal subsumption of labour 128, 131, 132
Foucauldian 47, 48, 50, 51, 52, 93
frame breaking experiences 62
Freedman, M. 229, 230
Freeman, T. 98
Friedman, A.L. 18, 26, 40

Game, C. 184, 189
Gane, M. 50
Garland, D. 50
Garnsey, E. 102, 228
Geertz, C. 104
generative mechanisms 29
gender relations 6, 12, 13
Gergen, K. 3, 47
German Ideology 120, 267
Giddens, A. 11, 20, 30, 46, 47, 66, 67, 68, 70, 71, 72, 73, 74, 75, 87, 89, 90, 92, 93, 95, 97, 99, 101, 102, 103, 104, 108, 145, 164, 167, 168, 179, 181, 186, 188, 191, 192, 193, 194, 196, 199
Gillen, D.J. 27, 31, 34
Glaser, B.G. 183
Glover, I. 106
Goffman, E. 151, 156, 195, 196
Gordon, D.M. 222, 225
Granovetter, M. 5, 103, 107
Greenwood, R. 69, 87, 96
Gregory, K.L. 88, 249
Grey, C. 51
Grundrisse 120, 133, 137

Habermas, J. 89, 90, 92, 93, 106, 159
habitus 92, 228
Hales, C. 27, 34, 194
Hall, S. 176
Hallen, L. 206
Hampden-Turner, C. 82
Hannan, M. 98
Hanson, S. 110
Harré, R. 5
Harrington, D. 181
Hartman, H.I. 228
Hassard, J. 48,
Hatt, P.K. 210
Haughton, G. 234
Hays, S. 67, 76
Henwood, K. 183
Heraud, J-A. 225
Heritage, J. 48
Hiebert, D. 237
high-technology firms 20, 166, 169, 178, 179
Hinings, C.R. 69, 96
Hinrichs, K. 223, 227, 228, 230, 231, 232, 233, 235
Hodgson, G.M. 163
Hollander, E.P. 194
holocaust 89
Humphries, J. 229, 233
Hunt, S.D. 206, 218

Iacobacci, M. 239
idealism 4, 148
industrial networks 11, 21, 206, 215, 216, 217, 218
inequality/ies 223, 235, 236, 237
innovation 20, 21, 27, 33, 37, 44, 99, 101, 132, 181, 183, 184, 186, 187, 188, 189, 190, 191, 193, 195–9, 203, 224, 225
institutional theory 5, 47, 103, 104
institutionalisation 184, 188, 199, 201, 234, 238
integration 33, 68, 75, 83, 84, 91, 101, 105, 186, 188, 222, 241, 243, 246, 247, 248, 260, 261, 262, 263
inter-firm network 22
internationalisation 60, 247, 260
interpretivism 215
intransitive dimension 76, 77
intransitive object 112, 113

Jackson, N. 3
Jacoby, S. 239

Jermier, J. 50,
Johnson, G. 50
Johnson, T. 63, 155
Jones, E. 168, 226
Jones, M.R. 168
just-in-time 22, 188

Kahn, R.L. 194
Kalleberg, A.L. 222
Kaplan, R.E. 194
Katz, D. 194
Keat, R. 5,
Kellner, D. 51
Kelly, J. 38, 40
Kerr, C. 222
Knights, D. 18, 34, 46, 47, 50, 51, 97
knowledge-intensive firm 104
Koontz, H. 31
Kotter, J.P. 27, 34
Kuhn, T.S. 15, 110
Kumar, K. 61

labour markets, segmented, 11, 21, 242
labour power 38
labour process analysis 5, 18, 19, 35, 109
labour union structures 228, 230
Lakatos 110
language 82, 114, 115, 116, 121, 144, 154, 200, 208, 215
Lash, S. 104
Latour, B. 166, 178
Lau, A.W. 34
Law, J. 46, 48, 49
Lawson, N. 133, 165, 245
Lawson, T. 5, 113, 117
Layder, D. 5, 45, 47, 55, 56, 57, 58, 87, 165
Leach, S. 189
Legge, K. 8, 97, 189
Lenhardt, G. 235
Lever-Tracy, C. 237
Lewis, D. 161, 165
Liggett, H. 51, 64
Littler, C. 18, 26, 38, 40, 98
logics of action 188, 190, 196
Luckman, T. 70, 145, 215
Lupton, T. 39, 40

MacKenzie, D. 131
Maclure, M. 190
Madden, E.H. 28, 29
Mahoney, T.A. 31

Maier, F. 254
management 3, 4, 5, 8, 15, 16, 184, 187, 188, 189, 190, 201, 231, 248, 252, 259; classical school of 30, 31, 33, 35; historical approach 31, 32, 249
management functions 30, 31, 35, 37, 38, 40, 41; strategy 40
Manicas,T. 30, 75
Mann, K. 99
Mannheim, K. 5, 9
March, J.G. 162, 178, 180, 259
Marchington, M. 259
marginal groups 228, 231
markets 6, 11, 21, 26, 32, 39, 40, 60, 103, 104, 114, 220, 221, 222, 223, 224, 225, 226, 230, 232, 235, 236, 237, 245, 250
Marsden, D. 5, 220, 223
Marsh, C. 248, 249, 255
Marshall, A. 104, 163, 228, 229
Martin, J. 79, 82
Marx, K. 18, 26, 34, 38, 55, 66, 90, 91, 109, 119, 120, 121, 123, 124, 125, 134, 237
materialism 106, 109
matrix social, 103; structures 156
Maurice, M. 246
McDowell, L. 233
McIntosh, M. 229
McLennan, G. 54, 56
McNay, L. 50, 52
McRae, S. 50, 52
Meikle, S. 122
meso level 21
metatheory 16, 26, 27, 35, 36, 41
methological individualism 142–3; situationalism 142
methodology 3, 5, 45, 46, 47, 48, 51, 52, 127, 142, 144, 146, 164, 165, 182, 200, 205, 206, 218, 267
Michon, E. 220, 223, 240, 242
micro level 26, 35, 47, 49, 50, 51, 81; processes 49, 52
Middleton, D. 196
Miller, D. 31
Mills, A. 5
Mills, C. Wright 69, 76, 81
Mintzberg, H. 27, 31, 33, 34, 37
misbehaviour 101
Mitroff, I. 29
modernism 4, 205
modernity 88, 89, 99, 103, 104, 169
Morgan, G. 3, , 27,95, 165

Morishima, M. 104
Morrow, R.A. 47
Mouzelis, N. 51, 95
Murray, C. 99,
myths 103

narratives 49, 57, 181, 182, 183, 186,
    188, 189, 191, 194, 195, 196, 198
natural science 3, 118
Nelson, R.R. 161, 162
neo-Marxist 26, 34, 35, 38, 41
networks 56, 216; complex 111;
    industrial 11, 21, 205, 206, 209,
    215, 216–17; organisational 91;
    personal 209; social 209
Newman, A.R. 82
Newton, T. 51, 64
NHS 189, 193
non-reductive 54
Nord, W.R. 50, 64
normalised alienation 102
North, D.C. 162
nursing 150, 155, 159, 160
NVQs 254

objective facticity 137
objectivism 8; naïve 48
occupational closure 137; structuring 60
O'Donnell, C. 31
Offe, C. 228, 230, 231, 235
Offermann, L.R. 194
ontology 6, 8, 10, 12–17, 35, 45–8,
    51–58, 66–84, 96, 110, 120, 134,
    265; deep, flat, nested 54, 60, 178;
    dualist 17, 34, 46, 47, 68, 108, 142,
    222–6, 228, 233, 238; realist
    ontology 8, 27, 53, 58, 96, 112;
    positivist 6, 7, 13, 17, 24, 110, 111,
    112, 206, 207, 208, 213, 214, 266
open systems 40, 118, 144, 147, 213
O'Reilly, J. 249
organisational constitution 87, 88, 96,
    100, 102; flux 188; society 90, 105,
    107
organismic analogy
Orlikowski, W.J. 167, 178
Osborne, T. 50
Outhwaite, W. 28, 46, 55

Parker, M. 4, 259
Parsons, T. 86, 90, 91, 155
pattern maintenance 137
Patton, M.Q. 181

Peck, J. 11, 19, 21, 220, 237, 260
Penrose, E. 37, 104, 162
Perry, D.C. 51
Peters, T.J. 103, 188, 192
Pettigrew, A. 70
Pheysey, D.C. 82
philosophy of science 47, 53, 109, 110
Picchio, A. 229
Pike, J.E. 137
Piore, M.J. 104, 222, 223, 225, 233,
    250
Piven, E.F. 234
place of hierarchies 59
planning 31, 38, 123, 172, 183, 189,
    249
Poggi, G. 94
Polanyi, K. 5
Poole, E. 27
Popper, K.R. 77, 79, 80, 110
Porpora, D.V. 68, 72, 74
Porter, S. 19, 20, 52, 141, 153, 155
positivism 3–8, 12, 84, 110, 141, 144,
    206, 212, 215, 218
postmodernism 4–8, 12, 19, 61, 106,
    265
poststructuralism 46, 48
Powell, W.W. 47, 103
power 142, 143, 148, 149, 150, 153,
    154, 184, 200, 208, 216, 225, 230,
    233, 251
Pratten, S. 16, 18, 109
primitive accumulation 128
professionals/ism 97, 98, 106; ideology
    155; medical 155; sociology of 155

Quack, S. 254

racism 141, 146, 147, 148, 151–6
Ragin, C.C. 214
Ranson, S. 87, 96
rationalism 8, 25, 86
realism, contemporary 5, 9, 16, 19;
    critical 24, 53, 55–8, 61, 109, 110,
    113, 118–20, 127, 128, 133, 134,
    136,141, 142–6, 157, 164, 217,
    266, 267; empirical 164; 'naïve' 143,
    206–8; 'new' 19; transcendental, 69,
    73, 109, 110–13, 120, 134, 144,
    206
Reed, M. 16, 17, 20, 27, 45, 50, 60, 68,
    95
referential detachment 82
reflexivity 63, 73, 102–3

reification 14, 54, 55, 71, 72, 78, 143, 147
relations of production 30, 34, 38, 122, 123, 156
relativism 4, 5, 61; epistemic relativism 15, 70
representationalism 47
resource allocation 33, 184
retroduction 112, 165, 212
Riley, P. 69
Robbins, S. 31
Robinson, J. 238
Rodgers, G. and J. 243, 263
Rose, N. 50
Rosenau, P. 48
routines 11, 48, 97, 161, 163, 164, 166, 169, 176, 178, 191, 200
Rubery, J. 11, 19, 21, 221, 223, 224, 227, 235, 239, 245, 251
Ryan, T. 223, 243

Sabel C.F. 104, 250
Salaman, G. 38
Samuels, W.J. 161
Sauer, D. 235
Savage, M. 58
Sayer, A. 5, 9, 11, 12, 22, 28, 30, 47, 87, 119, 206, 207, 209, 212, 215, 216
Schumpeter, J.A. 49
Scott, J. 47, 99, 103
Seccareccia, M. 228
Secord, P.F. 28, 29
segmentation theory 220, 229, 237
Sengenberger, W. 229
Sewell, G. 51, 65, 93
sexism 81, 83, 84
short termism 98, 247, 251
Shotter, J. 196
Silverman, D. 48, 184
Simon, H.A. 31, 162, 178
Sizer, J. 189, 204
Smith C.4, 132
social construction, 145; socially constructed 8, 11, 12, 48, 61, 168, 207
social reproduction 59, 61, 102, 227, 228, 231, 233, 237, 243, 249, 254, 260
social structures 13, 14, 17, 23, 30, 45, 48, 51, 55, 59, 69, 73, 87, 90, 109, 114, 117, 121, 124, 127, 134, 142, 145, 156, 164, 178, 228, 232, 267

societal effect approach 247
societal structuration 87, 88, 90, 96, 105
socio-cultural interaction 180
Sorensen, A.B. 222
Sorge, A. 246
space of flows 59
Stanley, L. 79
status dilemma 153
Steedman, H. 252
Stewart, J. 194
Stewart, R. 27, 34
Storey, J. 38, 4, 184, 189, 204
strata 54, 66, 68, 70, 82, 84
stratified 13, 30, 46, 48, 50, 54, 58, 61, 67, 71, 75, 84, 112
Strauss, A.L. 149, 183
Streeck, W. 253
structuration theory 47, 66, 67, 68, 70, 75, 81, 84, 145, 165, 181, 186, 196
sui generis 52, 68, 74, 83, 143
surveillance 50, 51, 52, 60, 93
symbols 103, 161, 164
synchronic analysis 239
synergy 198
systems approach 30, 246, 269

Tanner, I. 43
Tarling, R. 227, 229, 235, 238
Taylor, F.W. 26, 44, 82, 104, 251
Taylorism 104
technology 20, 29, 40, 59, 99, 161, 166, 169, 174, 177, 178, 182, 184, 190, 210, 225, 244
Teece, D.J. 162, 163
tendential powers/liabilities 75
Tesch, R. 165
Teulings, A.W. 31, 44
Thompson, J.B. 4, 51
Thompson, P. 18, 26, 34, 39, 95, 102
Thurow, L.C. 223
T.M.S.A. 113, 116
Tolbert, P.S. 58, 62
trade unions 59, 117, 230, 253, 257, 259
transcendental realism 109, 110, 111, 134, 206
transfactual 13, 14, 77, 133
transformative capacity 46, 192
transitive object 113
Trigg, R. 82, 86
Tsoukas, H. 4, 9, 10, 12, 16, 28, 57, 65, 165, 206, 213

Turner, H.A. 27, 82
Turner, J. 155

umbrella management 187
under-society 105
unemployment 72, 222, 234, 257
Urry, J. 5, 55, 62, 95

valorisation 91
Van Maanen, J. 165, 169
Veblen, T. 5
verstehen 113
vicious circle 251, 256
Villa, P. 221, 227, 228, 238
virtuous circle 85, 249
Vurdubakis, T. 51, 64

Wagner, K. 252
Walker, R. 22
Wallerstein, I. 5
Walsham, G. 164, 178
Walter, N. 64
Waterman, R.H. 103, 188, 192
Watson, T.J. 39, 40, 183, 190, 192, 200
Weber, M. 4, 5, 9, 90, 91, 93
Weick, K.E. 68, 86, 108, 195, 204
Weisenthal, H. 230
welfare state 246
West, M.A. 43, 181, 195
Whitley, R. 31, 33, 34, 37, 39

Whittington, R. 57, 58, 65, 70, 95, 96,
   101, 188, 190
Wilkinson, B. 22, 25, 51, 65, 93, 107,
   221, 226, 228, 229, 230, 233, 234,
   238, 239
Wilkinson, F. 247
Williams, K. 249
Williamson, O.E. 26
Willis, P. 101, 108, 228
Willmott, H. 18, 34, 70, 95, 97, 137
Willmott, R. 16, 17, 20, 66
Wilson, D.T. 184, 189
Winter, S.G. 162
Wise, S. 79, 80
Witt, U. 179
Wittgenstein, L. 69
Wolfe, R.A. 181, 182, 186
Wolin, S. 50, 52
World One 77
World Three 77, 80
World Two 77, 76, 80, 81

Yin, R.K. 211
YT training 254

Zimmerman, D. 48, 65
Zuboff, S. 167, 177
Zukin, S. 59, 60
Zuscovitch, E, 225